D0842807

EURIPIDES
HELEN

EDITED WITH
INTRODUCTION AND COMMENTARY
BY
A. M. DALE

OXFORD
AT THE CLARENDON PRESS
1967

Oxford University Press, Ely House, London W.1

GLASGOW NEW YORK TORONTO MELBOURNE WELLINGTON
CAPE TOWN SALISBURY IBADAN NAIROBI LUSAKA ADDIS ABABA
BOMBAY CALCUTTA MADRAS KARACHI LAHORE DACCA
KUALA LUMPUR HONG KONG TOKYO

PRINTED IN GREAT BRITAIN

PREFACE

In preparing a commentary on the *Helen* I have tried first
and last to *interpret*. This may seem a statement of the
obvious, but is intended as an apology for many short-
comings. The book is not an 'edition', properly speaking,
since I accept the aim of the Press in reprinting Murray's
text and so, among other advantages, keeping the price
within undergraduate reach. It depends on no new examina-
tion of manuscripts—for careful correction of some points
in the apparatus criticus the new Teubner edition (1964) of
K. Alt may be consulted, and testimonia are easily accessible
in this or in Grégoire's edition in the Budé series. But the
most important task of any interpretation is to try to determine as best one can what Euripides wrote. This is inevitably
a wide-open question in a play which like the *Helen* has so
limited a manuscript transmission, and the commentary
therefore, which is aimed mainly at undergraduate level,
may seem disproportionately occupied with textual questions
and in places awkwardly out of relation to the given text
(though often a defence of it against other prevalent
versions). But it would after all be impossible to 'interpret'
a text in which one did not believe. I have wasted little time
over cruces that seem to me insoluble. For the sake of
clarity I have indicated (Appendix II) those lines of dialogue
where I should have actually ventured on revision if I had
been reconstituting the text; most of these are, naturally,
an eclectic gleaning from the labours of other scholars, to
whom I make acknowledgement in the commentary. A few
record my own suggestions or rejections. For the lyrics a
complete text by strophe and antistrophe is given with
metrical analysis in the course of the commentary.

These analyses are naturally not intended for beginners
in metric, nor did this seem the place for lengthy explana-
tions of the terms used. The relevant sections of the com-

mentary are reasonably self-contained, and all the essentials will, I hope, be found in my *Lyric Metres of Greek Drama* (C.U.P.), which should before long be available in a revised second edition; this contains in particular an expanded section on aeolo-choriambic metres.

My warm thanks are due to Professor G. Zuntz for making available to me, before its publication, the text of his invaluable *Inquiry into the Transmission of the Plays of Euripides*. I make no apology for having lingered in more detail, in Commentary and Appendix I, over the questions raised by that section of his book which deals with P.Oxy. 2336 and the new light it has shed on the text of the *Helen*, since his discussions, here and elsewhere, have made this a problem of particular interest to scholars. I am also grateful to Mr. W. S. Barrett for a stimulating discussion by correspondence of the Recognition Duo, and for sending me, with annotations, an unpublished paper (pre-P.Oxy. 2336) which illustrated how far an exact and sensitive analysis of our old texts can take us in a proper understanding of the spirit of this passage.

I am as ever deeply indebted to my husband for many hours of reading, discussion, and criticism, and also for indispensable help in many tedious tasks at the final stages. I should like also to make special acknowledgement to the infinite patience and vigilance of the staff of the Clarendon Press.

A. M. D.

London
May 1966

CONTENTS

ABBREVIATIONS   vi

INTRODUCTION

    I. Euripides and the figure of Helen   vii

    II. The Legend of the Phantom-Helen   xvii

    III. The Place of the *Helen* in the Sequence of Euripidean Tragedies   xxiv

    IV. The Text   xxix

TEXT   I

COMMENTARY   69

APPENDIXES

    I. Papyrus and Manuscript   170

    II. Suggestions for a Revised Text of the Dialogue   174

INDEXES   177

ABBREVIATIONS

LS	Liddell–Scott–Jones, *Greek–English Lexicon*, ed. 9.
Roscher *GRM*	W. H. Roscher, *Griechische u. römische Mythologie*.
Goodwin *MT*	W. W. Goodwin, *Syntax of Greek Moods and Tenses*.
Denn. *GP*	J. D. Denniston, *Greek Particles*, ed. 2.
Jackson	J. Jackson, *Marginalia Scaenica*, 1955.
Page *PMG*	Denys Page, *Poetae Melici Graeci*, 1962.
Wilam. *GV*	U. von Wilamowitz-Moellendorff, *Griechische Verskunst*
Wilam. *SS*	U. von Wilamowitz-Moellendorff, *Sappho und Simonides*.

METRICAL NOTATION

— ‿ ×   long, short, anceps

x̅ x̆   long anceps, short anceps (the latter rarely marked).

‿‿   resolved long

‿   brevis in longo at line-end

⸪   long contracted from double short

‖   period-close

For the symbols **d** and **s** used occasionally in the First Stasimon 1107 ff. see *CQ* N.S. 1, p. 21. Briefly, **d** = — ‿‿ —, **s** = — ‿ —, **ds** = — ‿‿ — ‿ —, **sd** = — ‿ — ‿‿ —, ∧ **dds** = ‿‿ — ‿‿ — ‿ —, **ddd** = — ‿‿ — ‿‿ — ‿‿ —. They are here simply as a supplementary notation for the convenience of readers accustomed to this way of defining vague terms like 'enoplian', 'aeolic hexasyllable'.

INTRODUCTION

I. *Euripides and the Figure of Helen*

WHAT are we to make of this play? Helen is one of the
supreme figures of Greek mythology, daughter of Zeus and
radiant exemplar of the power of Aphrodite, the living
symbol of all men's desires for beauty, married to men of
a little less than heroic stature, sinning and bringing destruction to a city and death to thousands yet herself curiously
unscathed and undimmed by it all. Neither Homer nor
any of his heroes sits in judgement on her, and we last see
her in the *Odyssey* restored to domestic tranquillity. Even
when, by a later generation of poets, she is execrated as
a traitor and adulteress, she is half-recognized as no ordinary
human sinner but a scourge used by the gods to work the
havoc they have planned among men. Later legend (Paus.
3. 19. 11), dreaming the ideally appropriate, unites her on
a kind of Blessed Isle to Achilles—the fairest to the bravest.

Tragedy, recognizing the impossible, did not dramatize
the central incidents of Helen's story, but took it up
obliquely. For Aeschylus, who assumes the straightforward
Homeric story, Helen was daemonic; the Chorus of the
Agamemnon, meditating on her destructive power, tell the
parable of the man who kept a lion-cub that was bright-
eyed and appealing, until one day its wild nature broke out.
One does not blame a lion-cub, nor even an 'Erinys, bride of
woe'. In Euripides she descends to human level, and behind
her move on occasion the puppet figures of the Judgement
of Paris, that naïve accretion of folk-tale which had attached itself in Cyclic epic to the figure of the shepherd-son
of Priam, and was available thenceforward for exculpation
or accusing rationalization. From *Andromache, Hecuba,
Electra, Iphigeneia in Tauris* to *Iphigeneia at Aulis*, where-
ever the subject touches the Trojan War, Helen is never
spoken of by actor or sung of by Chorus without a passing

curse of hatred and ill will, venomous or hopeless according
to mood. In *Troades* and *Orestes* she is a subordinate actor
in the play, in the former false, fluent, and self-righteous,
engaging with Hecuba in the debate which makes rhetori-
cally articulate all the ambivalence of her actions and moral
responsibility, in the latter a lightweight, almost a trivial
character whose deliverance and apotheosis make as it were
a casual mockery of the realities of human desperation
around her. And in between the Helen of *Troades* and the
Helen of *Orestes* comes the Helen of the play named after
her, a faithful innocent wife, victim of a diabolical plot of
the gods and the total misjudgement of men. The Judgement of Paris was a lamentable fact, and the origin of her
misfortunes. She has no vanity even—when she has to
feign mourning she cuts off the locks that in *Orestes* her
namesake will so artfully spare, and wishes without in-
sincerity she had a plainer face. She is *nice* to Menelaus,
careful to play down her superior cleverness and to build up
his heroic part in their coming escape. If we still feel her
eventual apotheosis, foretold by the Dioscuri, a shade in-
congruous it is because she has such perfect wifely charm
and tact.

One thing is quite clear: this is no 'rehabilitation' of the
Helen of Homer and tragedy. That task had been under-
taken (in prose argument) by Gorgias the Sicilian rhetor and
sophist, just to show that it could be done if you were clever
enough with words. But Euripides' heroine is quite simply
a different woman, with a different life-history. All the
hatred and the execration, like the actions which called
them forth, are there, current in the world about, but attached to the Phantom. When Euripides in later plays
reverted to the Trojan War or its consequences, all he had
to do was to re-embody the εἴδωλον, and the Helen of this
play became the disappearing phantom.

Is the whole of it then just a light-hearted interlude,
a romantic play where the sun shines and the sea is a
sparkling blue and the characters are bathed in a golden

brightness and their sufferings need not trouble us since we know all the time that they are only a foil to the happy ending? *Helen* has been seen as romance, or romantic comedy, or melodrama, or romance-coated anti-war manifesto. But none of these is a satisfactory description; they are either too loose and encumbered with modern associations or too narrow. For Euripides and his audience the *Helen* was a 'tragedy', and that concept is a hospitable one, embracing, for instance, within no great number of years this play, the *Oedipus Tyrannus*, the *Philoctetes*, and the *Bacchae*. All are composed and presented within certain established conventions, all are about figures taken from the national heritage of legend, moving in that world, and treated with fundamental seriousness. Within these limits the tragedy may be grave, terrible, exciting, witty, inventive; it may end happily (though only after troubling vicissitudes) or in catastrophe; the issues may vary greatly in profundity but there must *be* issues at stake, and something must emerge, however darkly, fitfully, or enigmatically, about the dealings of gods with men.

Helen, then, though not tragic in our sense, is a Greek tragedy. But within the source-matrix of inherited myth there are some stories sprung originally from folk-tales moulded on age-old story-patterns;[1] when these are adopted as the basis of tragedy they impose inescapably something of their own development and outcome, and the expectation of spectators or readers is geared accordingly. Whatever the brilliance, the diversity of a poet's individual adaptations of stories of this type, the audience know as well as he does that if the situation involves a recognition of two people, a male and a female, long lost to each other, of whom the latter is in some sort of durance or distress, then either the recognition will of itself bring about deliverance (as with Ion and Creusa, Hypsipyle and her sons), or a further stratagem will achieve rescue. The leading characters are

[1] Cf. especially R. Lattimore's excellent *Story Patterns in Greek Tragedy*, Athlone Press, 1964.

so represented that the audience is enlisted on their side;
and then success is assured, opponents overcome. If the
main object is escape, the planning and carrying out of the
scheme will absorb much of the interest of the drama; if it
is revenge and the overthrow of usurpers (as in the *Odyssey*,
the literary prototype of such stories), there may be at
times a grimmer note, but all will depend upon the por-
trayal of the victims—the killing of a cardboard tyrant or
wicked stepmother can hardly affect a 'happy ending'. It is
not quite safe to guess what the 'tone' was of such plays as
the *Cresphontes* or the *Antiope* or Sophocles' second *Tyro*,
even though we may suspect them of being no more 'tragic'
in the modern sense than the *Helen* or the *Iphigeneia in
Tauris*. On the other hand, no one could have guessed from
a summary of the incidents of the *Ion* what curious, bitter
cross-currents would trouble its romantic flow. The story
of Orestes' revenge can in terms of a structure of incidents
be made to sound rather like the *Cresphontes*, with the son
of the house growing to manhood in exile, returning and
finding by 'recognition' a female accomplice, and slaying
the evil-doers and usurpers; but the identity of one of the
victims transforms the story's nature. The position of the
Choephoroe in the grand design of the *Oresteia* trilogy makes
the recognition-and-stratagem category wholly irrelevant.
Euripides in his *Electra* turns aside to mock the naïvety of
his predecessor's contrivance for 'recognition', but annihi-
lates no less thoroughly than Aeschylus any possibility of
considering the outcome in terms of 'successful stratagem'.
It is Sophocles, strangely, who gives us a play[1] which from
summary description, and in its excitements, might seem to
qualify as a play of untragic, rewarded endeavour. Indeed
Orestes himself is shown in no other relation to Clytaemnestra than as her successful murderer, but that is because
the inwardness of the drama is concentrated in Electra, in
showing how she has become a woman passionate in loves

---

[1] His *Electra* was probably produced in 413 B.C., a year before the
Helen; see commentary on 1050 ff.

and hates, whose nature can only be fulfilled in reunion with Orestes and the long-awaited vengeance on her father's murderers.

Helen has no such tragic notes, and in the Prologue we are given a strong hint, in the promise of Hermes quoted in lines 57–59, that the ending will be happy. One would expect the audience, knowing the tranquil end of her story in Homer, and perhaps recalling the novelty a year or two before of the *Iphigeneia*, to settle down to enjoy vicissitudes and excitements rather than a purging of pity and fear, especially as the legend of an innocent Helen in Egypt was certainly known to some. The Prologue in fact brings Helen's fortunes to their lowest point; she describes her years of exile suffered under the world's hatred, with now the new threat of forced marriage; then Teucer brings her up to date in disasters of which she had been ignorant—above all, that Menelaus is missing, believed dead. She has indeed much to lament to the Chorus. Perhaps the Greek audience had a capacity greater than ours of immersing itself sympathetically in griefs eloquently expressed, so that it was less conscious of a distinction between pathos and tragedy. But Euripides does go further here than in any other extant play in distracting us as it were in the midst of gloom by nicely pointed ironies of situation, flashes of wit in the dialogue, even by a half-comic tone in the depiction of Menelaus' bewilderment. These, which for Greek taste would be out of place in a 'tragic' tragedy,[1] contribute much to the equilibrium of the play as a whole. Thus Helen enumerating her sorrows (255–305) can start with her birth from an egg; Menelaus has his delightful dialogue with the Portress and is worried about his clothes and the necessity of begging. But the comic aspect of Menelaus should not be pressed too far; he is no 'parody of a hero', but merely a hero in a predicament where no amount of courage or resource could possibly have availed him; so Euripides has

[1] The familiar instances of the Nurse in *Cho.* and the Guard in *Ant.* are quite different, involving only anonymous minor figures.

chosen to extract amusement instead of pathos from what is in effect a second Prologue (386–514). The variety is pleasing; more pathos would have been monotonous. In the Recognition and its after-lyric Menelaus is treated as seriously as Helen, and if in the planning of the Stratagem Helen's wits are quicker than his, it is common Euripidean form that it takes a woman to devise a clever μηχάνημα. There are one or two perilous moments in the sequel—in 1204–5 the manner of his emergence from hiding, and possibly Helen's speech in 1369 ff., if he comes out of the palace then rather than at 1390 (but the text is ambiguous).[1] But in general, and especially in the escape, his portrait is now given full heroic stature, and his ultimate translation to bliss (foretold at 1676) is made to sound better earned than in *Odyssey* 4. 561 ff.

The plotting and carrying out of the escape take up most of the second half of the play, and the elaboration of the details shows a theatre revelling in the excitements of the new fashion in plots. There is, however, a compensating factor here in the opposite sense; the Chorus, having had little to do since the parodos which it shared with Helen, now in the last 600 lines of the play sings three stasima, of which the first two are quite detached from the μηχάνημα in progress. The First Stasimon (1107 ff.) broods heavily on the sadness and waste of Helen's story, taking no account of the upward turn of her fortunes. In one stanza it laments the folly of war; and here one might expect the moral of this strange tale to be at least hinted. Ten years of war, the destruction of a great city, and heavy slaughter on both sides—and *all for a phantom*: a dour reflection for Athens in 412 B.C. But no; there is no word of the Phantom. It might be any ordinary war, taking the sword for arbiter 'when your quarrel, Helen, could have been settled by negotiation'. There is only one line in the play which is explicit of this irony: 707, where the Old Servant, hearing from Menelaus that the gods had cheated them with a νεφέλης ἄγαλμα asks

<hr />

[1] See commentary on 1369.

τί φῄς; / νεφέλης ἄρ᾽ ἄλλως εἴχομεν πόνους πέρι; But the point is not elaborated; the lesson the old man proceeds to draw from it is the apparent futility of all πόνοι, since Menelaus' efforts brought him nothing; it was only after he had given up trying that everything fell into his lap—so capricious (though ultimately justified) are the gods. Later, the Servant has a tirade, not against the cruelty of the gods or the folly of men, but against μαντική (why had not Calchas told them that they were dying for a phantom? Better to pray to the gods for blessings, not put your trust in mantic arts.). If this play was meant as anti-war propaganda the point is not very well driven home.

The Second Stasimon turns aside from the intrigue at its height to sing a dithyrambic interlude on the Great Mother, with scarcely a pretence of relevance to the events on stage.[1] Only the Third Stasimon looks forward to the happy end of the escaped exiles' voyage, and prays for the help of the Dioscuri who are presently to appear on the machine.

But the most serious note in the play is struck not by the Chorus but by Theonoe. Like her brother Theoclymenus she is essentially an invention of Euripides, though re-created from Eidothea, daughter of Proteus the Old Man of the Sea in *Odyssey* 4. Eidothea was an immortal like her father, but now that Proteus had faded from a god to a mortal king (though married to a Nereid) his daughter had to be mortal too, though gifted with divine knowledge inherited from Nereus; like the Homeric Proteus she knows the

---

[1] It is true that the last stanza is defective at the end and the beginning, where it appears to be saying that Helen had incurred the Mother's wrath, but there is no space for any significant point to be made. Various more or less far-fetched attempts have been made to devise some subtle connexion, e.g. that Helen, like Persephone, was carried off while picking flowers (so was Creusa!)—not that the flowers are mentioned in this ode; or that Euripides is composing this play as a solace of gaiety in the years of war disaster just as the Mother laughed with pleasure at the rumbling din of her new instruments even in the midst of her grief. Perhaps Euripides was conscious of such a thought, but is the audience supposed to have taken the point?

counsels of the gods and can foretell the future. She dominates all the central scene of the play, and Euripides prepares for this very carefully by introducing her near the beginning of Helen's Prologue speech, by making her reputation the cause of Teucer's arrival, and sending Helen and the Chorus off stage to consult her about Menelaus' present fate just as he arrives in person. Nor are we allowed to forget her at the end of the play, when the furious king is storming off to kill the sister who has traitorously joined with the abominable Greeks in making a mock of him; only the intervention of the Dioscuri calms him down.

The central scene intervenes drastically between Recognition and Stratagem, and one cannot help wondering whether the Greek audience felt a baffled impatience at the long hold-up in the action (this is a very long play). Or did they relish perhaps more than we do the eloquent forensic-sounding appeals of Helen and Menelaus in a kind of uncontested agon before this austere judge? One thing seems clear: it *mattered* to Euripides that this play should be seen to be more than a melodramatic piece of intrigue, rich in paradox and excitement but somewhat blunt morally. Before we settle down to the fooling of the stupid barbarian by sharper Greek wits (with an ample bonus of gifts tricked out of him) we are made to realize how wrong his cause is, not so much in terms of the will of the gods, who are still divided in counsel, but as a crime against justice and his father's good name. Theonoe examines both the Greeks, as it were, to make them declare their claims and their creed, and then declares her own, which makes her side with them against her brother. The decision comes at a crucial moment, on the day when the gods themselves are to hold a council under the presidency of Zeus, in which Hera and Aphrodite will argue out the quarrel which started with the Judgement of Paris; Hera now wishes the return of Menelaus to Sparta, so as to expose her rival's failure to make good her bribe, while Aphrodite would destroy him, to avoid exposure. Meanwhile Theonoe has to decide whether or not to denounce

Menelaus to her brother. It is her own decision, which she would have had to take anyway, and her knowledge of the conflicting desires of the goddesses is merely an added burden of responsibility to choose aright. The larger question of how to reconcile such mortal free will with the overriding power of the gods (or Zeus)—or for that matter with Theonoe's own knowledge of the future—is naturally left untouched. Euripides is writing a play, and for dramatic purposes Theonoe's mind must be still open, and only made up in the course of this scene. So her first impulse (892–3) is to think of her own safety, and Euripides takes the trouble to justify this in the last scene of the play, where Theoclymenus' first thought after learning the truth is to kill his sister. But her sense of justice prevails, and if on this occasion it means taking sides with Hera against Aphrodite that is appropriate too, since the Cyprian (may she be gracious!) has played no part in her life. The contrast between the frivolous divine motives and the seriousness of human is clear enough, but Theonoe is incapable of irreverence and the point is left without emphasis, like the whole discreditable origin of the Trojan War; this is not an angry play. And Theonoe is careful to advise the escaping pair (1024), whom she is leaving to devise their own plan, to 'begin with the gods', that is, to seek to propitiate them by prayer; Theonoe's 'decision' (τέλος 887) has merely given things a push when the even balance of the divine ἔρις had left them stuck; it cannot guarantee future success but merely promises that hope shall not be extinguished at the outset. Such prayer they duly make, Helen at 1093 ff., Menelaus at 1441 ff., not too subserviently but in the somewhat rallying tone with which Euripides' heroes and heroines in later tragedy admonish the gods when fortune seems at last to be going their way.

Taking one part with another, then, the *Helen* is an enjoyable variation on an old lost-and-found theme, exciting, witty, and sometimes half-comic, yet not devoid of moral issues, wryly critical of the gods of legend without raising

its voice louder than innuendo or breaking a discreet continuity of tone. The singularity of the situation leading to
Recognition in this version is that neither party has grown
from infancy to adulthood in the gap of years, so that each
is capable of recognizing the other at first sight. Menelaus,
like Teucer before him, does in fact so recognize Helen, but
rejects the evidence of his eyes because it is against common
sense—Helen's story of the Phantom is so fantastic that
he cannot take it seriously—until he sees how the Old
Servant, who so recently watched the Phantom disappear
and heard its words, falls into the same error in reverse and
greets the living Helen as the Phantom which had somehow
cheated him by pretending to vanish. This situation adds
a twist of paradox to the Recognition-theme, and the last
pang to Helen's despair when the husband she has waited so
long for sees her but cannot see the truth, and turns back to
the Phantom. But it is surely hardly justified to claim as
critics sometimes do that the *Helen* gains in profundity, or
qualifies as 'tragic' (in our sense), because it concerns the
interplay of illusion and reality. This is to allow oneself to
be mesmerized by abstract nouns. There is much play with
such antitheses as σῶμα / ὄνομα, and flashes of irony from
this source point the dialogue; but there is no metaphysical
or psychological depth here, nor would anything of the kind
be either conceivable or appropriate. The Menelaus who has
been living with the Phantom for the past seven years and
left it an hour ago[1] needs just a little more time than Helen,
a few more words of reassurance, before accepting whole-
heartedly the substitute the gods now offer him, but the
situation has as little to do with 'reality' as when in *Twelfth
Night* Olivia, having given her heart to a shadow, happily
accepts Sebastian in the place of Viola.

[1] The timing of the Phantom's disappearance, so dramatically apt,
was probably Euripides' own innovation; see below, p. xxiii, n. 1.

11. The Legend of the Phantom-Helen

The Byzantine scholar who wrote the Hypothesis to the *Helen* into the ms. P contrasts the Euripidean version of the story with that of Herodotus, which he attempts to bracket with Homer's in a confused and misleading statement: both of them, he says, brought Helen to Egypt with Menelaus after the sack of Troy, whereas Euripides claimed the real Helen was never in Troy, but only an image in her shape. It sounds as if he were unaware of any literary predecessor of Euripides in the legend of the Phantom that went to Troy.

Yet when Plato (*Rep.* 9. 586 c) speaks of the unreal pleasures, mere εἴδωλα of true pleasure, which men fight each other to possess, he illustrates these by the εἴδωλον of Helen 'which Stesichorus says men fought for at Troy, in ignorance of the true'. This then was a well-known story, needing only a brief allusion; Euripides himself had so used it (*El.* 1280–3) some years before the *Helen*[1] in the speech from the machine where the Dioscuri order the immediate departure from Argos of the three accomplices in murder, leaving their victims for others to bury, Aegisthus to the Argives, Clytaemnestra to the newly arrived Menelaus and Helen:

$$\Pi\rho\omega\tau\acute{\epsilon}\omega\varsigma\ \gamma\grave{\alpha}\rho\ \grave{\epsilon}\kappa\ \delta\acute{o}\mu\omega\nu$$
$$\mathring{\eta}\kappa\epsilon\iota\ \lambda\iota\pi o\hat{v}\sigma'\ A\H{\iota}\gamma\upsilon\pi\tau o\nu\ o\mathring{v}\delta'\ \mathring{\eta}\lambda\theta\epsilon\nu\ \Phi\rho\acute{v}\gamma\alpha\varsigma\cdot$$
$$Z\epsilon\grave{v}\varsigma\ \delta',\ \mathring{\omega}\varsigma\ \mathring{\epsilon}\rho\iota\varsigma\ \gamma\acute{\epsilon}\nu o\iota\tau o\ \kappa\alpha\grave{\iota}\ \phi\acute{o}\nu o\varsigma\ \beta\rho o\tau\hat{\omega}\nu,$$
$$\epsilon\H{\iota}\delta\omega\lambda o\nu\ `E\lambda\acute{\epsilon}\nu\eta\varsigma\ \grave{\epsilon}\xi\acute{\epsilon}\pi\epsilon\mu\psi'\ \grave{\epsilon}\varsigma\ "I\lambda\iota o\nu.$$

Having briefly admitted the guilt of Clytaemnestra (1244), the Dioscuri take the opportunity to exculpate their other sister, who thus becomes fit to perform her task reverently. Since Helen is with Menelaus at Nauplia and the sack of Troy is in the past (1279), he must have picked up Helen in Egypt on the way back (the Dioscuri need not explain in such detail). This much would be consistent with the version of Herodotus (2. 112 ff.), who, however, says nothing of an

---

[1] Not in 413 B.C.: Zuntz, *The Political Plays of Euripides*, 1955, pp. 66 ff.

εἴδωλον. Finding himself in a temple 'to the foreign Aphrodite' in the precinct of King Proteus at Memphis, he suspected that this was a memory of Tyndarid Helen who, the
story said, once lived under Proteus' guardianship; so he
asked the priests to tell him what they knew of Helen's
coming to Proteus. They spun him a circumstantial tale
(one would dearly like to know in what language and in
response to what leading questions), redounding greatly to
Egyptian credit, of how the eloping couple with their
treasure looted from Sparta were blown out of their course
and eventually brought to Memphis; Proteus in high moral
indignation detained Helen and the treasure, spared Paris'
life, and let him go alone to Troy. The rest was told to the
Egyptians by Menelaus when he arrived years later; he had
gone to Troy, he said, with a great Greek army and de-
manded back wife and treasure, but the Trojans had denied
having either, saying they were in Egypt with Proteus.
Believing this to be a lie, the Greeks had besieged and sacked
Troy but found no Helen, so now Menelaus came to Proteus
for her. Proteus gave him wife and treasure and hospitality,
which Menelaus requited ill by sacrificing two Egyptian
children to propitiate adverse winds, finally eluding Egyptian pursuit in the direction of Libya. That was all the
priests knew. The version commended itself to the rationalist
Herodotus, since the orthodox story (as in Homer) was hard
to believe; what people in their senses would have sacrificed
their best warriors one by one and their city in such a cause?
Homer chose the orthodox legend as more entertaining
matter for poetry, but his references to Helen in Egypt at
one time or another show him to have been aware of
this one also.

Herodotus makes no mention of Stesichorus. This is not
surprising, since undoubtedly the most memorable thing in
that story was the εἴδωλον, and it is not in Herodotus'
manner to argue against fantastications of that sort. Given
the historical reality of Paris, Helen, and Menelaus, which
Herodotus, like all Greeks, assumed, his version would

make a reasonably consistent account, cutting out miracles and magic, whatever one thinks of his rationale of Trojan behaviour. This latter is an exquisitely characteristic Herodotean comment, but the story as a whole he attributes to the Egyptian priests at Memphis. It is difficult to know just what to make of this, but certainly the circumstantial detail of the account of Paris' adventures in Egypt which led to his appearance before the king at Memphis strongly suggests a local tradition. If so, the Egyptians must have been aware of a current Greek version leaving Helen in Proteus' guardianship all through the Trojan War, and worked this over into the edifying story of Proteus' behaviour in contrast with the immorality of all the Greeks concerned. Was the version the famous one of Stesichorus? And if so, who suppressed the εἴδωλον, the priests or Herodotus?

Without the εἴδωλον the story is prosaic and rather ineffective, and it is difficult to see how it could have arisen (as a story) except as an attempted rationalization of an earlier supernatural version. In later antiquity there are traces of a version which ascribed to Proteus himself the manufacture of the εἴδωλον, which he gave to Paris: the Byzantine scholar Tzetzes, annotating the *Alexandra* of Lycophron, a preposterously obscure Hellenistic poem in iambic trimeters purporting to give the various prophecies uttered by Cassandra (Alexandra), states on l. 113: λέγουσιν ὅτι διερχομένῳ Ἀλεξάνδρῳ ὁ Πρωτεὺς Ἑλένην ἀφελόμενος εἴδωλον Ἑλένης αὐτῷ δέδωκεν, καὶ οὕτως ἔπλευσεν ἐς Τροίαν, ὡς φησὶ Στησίχορος· Τρῶες γὰρ οἱ τότ' ἦσαν Ἑλένης εἴδωλον ἔσχον. This might possibly be interpreted as a loose ambiguity of expression referring only the part about the εἴδωλον to Stesichorus, but this scholion appears to be supported by one on Aristides (a rhetor of the second-century neo-sophistic) *Orationes* 13. 131 : εἰς Στησίχορον αἰνίττεται· λέγει γὰρ ἐκεῖνος ὅτι ἐλθὼν ἐπὶ ταύτης τῆς νήσου τοῦ Φάρου ἀφηρέθη παρὰ τοῦ Πρωτέως τὴν Ἑλένην καὶ εἴδωλον αὐτῆς ἐδέξατο. (Another scholiast makes this into a painted

portrait—ἐν πίνακι τὸ εἴδωλον αὐτῆς γεγραμμένον—for the
bereaved lover to console himself with!) Here there is no
ambiguity, but Aristides himself, of course, makes no such
reference to Stesichorus, and the source could either be
simply Lycophron's own version (110–38), which looks like
a conflation (his own or another's) of Euripides and Herodotus, or possibly a misunderstanding of Stesichorus (v.
infr. p. xxii).[1] Not that there would be anything inappropriate in a Proteus with enough magic art to fashion an
εἴδωλον, but it is difficult to fit such a version into the older
tradition; it would be incompatible in the priests' story
with the moral indignation of Proteus' address to Paris,
and—the assertion of the two scholia notwithstanding—
impossible in Stesichorus.

For the one thing that is certain about Stesichorus' story
is that it was intended as a rehabilitation of Helen's character; it was a παλινῳδία, a recantation of the orthodox account of Helen's experiences which his earlier poetry had
described or implied. Whatever one makes of the legend of
the blindness which struck him and his recovery of sight
after the Palinode, no immortal could have regarded her
character as cleared by a version which had her eloping
with Paris and the treasure as far as Egypt and then being
detained by force from following him further.

The form which the Palinode took, and the offending
poetry which preceded it, are matters of unresolved con-
troversy which need not be discussed here. Some of this
has become irrelevant since the publication in 1963 of
a papyrus fragment (*P.Oxy.* 2506, fr. 26 i) of a commentary
on lyric poems quoting the Peripatetic Chamaeleon for a
statement that there were *two* palinodes of Stesichorus,
one beginning Δεῦρ' αὖτε, θεὰ φιλόμολπε and the other
Χρυσόπτερε παρθένε, the first finding fault with Homer for
sending Helen instead of her εἴδωλον to Troy, the second

---

[1] Virgil's commentator Servius also (on *Aen.* i. 651) knows 'regem
Proteum . . . eam subtraxisse et nescio quibus disciplinis phantasma in
similitudinem Helenae formatum Paridi dedisse'.

with Hesiod (reason unexplained). This comes as a complete surprise, since all ancient authorities speak of 'the Palinode'; the most famous of them, Plato in the *Phaedrus* (243 a, b), after quoting the lines that became proverbial:

οὐκ ἔστ᾽ ἔτυμος λόγος οὗτος·
οὐδ᾽ ἔβας ἐν νηυσὶν εὐσέλμοις[1]
οὐδ᾽ ἵκεο Πέργαμα Τροίας

adds καὶ ποιήσας δὴ πᾶσαν τὴν καλουμένην Παλινῳδίαν παραχρῆμα ἀνέβλεψεν. One may reasonably guess that this was the earlier, the grand Recantation, directed full-tilt against Homer and the tradition, and that Chamaeleon was rather proud of his acumen in elevating to the status of a second palinode another poem upholding the same view and objecting to a reference of Hesiod's on the old lines. It was in the first poem that Stesichorus announced with a flourish of trumpets his conversion to a new and truer inspiration and round this that the legends of his blindness and recovery collected. These are sometimes regarded as apocryphal later embroideries, or they *may* have started from no more than a metaphorically meant allusion of his own, but it is perfectly possible that he felt the launching of so revolutionary a notion required a special claim to revealed truth, and made it memorable in this form. The opening invocation to the Muse quoted by Chamaeleon has the same metre as the first line of Plato's quotation; so, though the metrical shape is quite uncertain, a legitimate guess might give a first stanza asking help to tell a true tale which may redeem him from blindness, while the second stanza then crashed in with its ringing challenge.[2]

The new Commentator puts an end to speculation on another point by continuing: αὐτὸς δὲ φησὶν ὁ Στησίχορος τὸ μὲν εἴδωλον ἐλθεῖν ἐς Τροίαν τὴν δ᾽ Ἑλένην παρὰ τῷ Πρωτεῖ καταμεῖναι. The commonest view hitherto was that Stesichorus

---

[1] Probably in the original, as Blomfield, εὐσσέλμοις.
[2] I agree whole-heartedly with those scholars who insist that in terms of style οὗτος must refer forward to the following words.

made the real Helen stay behind in Sparta, or at least
in Greece, while her phantom went in the benched ships
to Troy, this being presumably a version current in Sparta
where Helen was worshipped as a goddess. Plato's quotation
can easily be interpreted this way, and Dio Chrysostom
Orationes 11. 182 appears to support this when he says
that according to Stesichorus Helen never sailed anywhere
at all, though 'others' [Herodotus] claim she was abducted
by Paris as far as Egypt. Probably, as Wilamowitz suggested,[1] Dio was simply recalling the famous quotation.
Now, however, we know that Stesichorus before Herodotus
and Euripides used the refuge with Proteus. But this cannot mean that the version of Tzetzes and the scholiast on
Aristides (supr. p. xix; the one doubtless derives from the
other) is now triumphantly vindicated; by the time Helen
got to Egypt with Paris her reputation would be irretrievably gone, and she would merely be cleared of her later
marriage to Deiphobus. We do not know how Stesichorus
transported her to Proteus.[2] Nor do we know nearly enough
about his narrative habits to assume that he raised the
point at all. There is a strong probability that, like other
lyric poets, he often avoided anything like a straight narrative of events with all the connexions filled in, and rather
picked out salient points for decorative elaboration. Εἴδωλον
and Proteus are the two keys to his version: as the Commentator of *P.Oxy.* 2506 says, αὐτὸς δὲ φησὶν ὁ Στησίχορος τὸ μὲν
εἴδωλον ἐλθεῖν ἐς Τροίαν, τὴν δ᾽ Ἑλένην παρὰ Πρωτεῖ καταμεῖναι. καταμεῖναι means, not 'remained behind'—behind
Paris—but 'lodged', 'resided with', simply.[3] It would be
easy enough for prosaic commentators—or for Lycophron
either, for that matter—to fill this out, or confuse it, with
the Herodotean version.

[1] *Sappho und Simonides*, p. 241.

[2] As Wilamowitz (loc. cit.) points out, lines 2 and 3 of the Platonic
quotation can be taken closely together, so that the meaning is simply
'You never sailed to Troy', though the easier sense would imply something like air-portage with Hermes, as in Euripides.

[3] Cf. Eubulus 21 Kock.

Euripides, then, took from Stesichorus both the phantom-
Helen and the stay with the virtuous Proteus;[1] it was a
famous version, and though naturally it never displaced the
Homeric story it was well enough known for him to be able
to refer to it quite briefly in the exodos of the *Electra*—
together with the depopulation-motive of Zeus, whether this
was taken from Stesichorus or from the epic *Cypria*. It
appears in Helen's Prologue-speech as a piece of supplementary 'over-causation', since for this play Euripides
needed the Judgement of Paris as central cause.

There can be no serious doubt that, as all antiquity
believed, the εἴδωλον-story was the bold invention of Stesichorus, a volte-face in mid-career, possibly the outcome
of a visit to Sparta. One solitary voice, a scholiast para-
phrasing the *Alexandra* of Lycophron, confused the issue by
ascribing it to Hesiod: πρῶτος Ἡσίοδος περὶ τῆς Ἑλένης τὸ
εἴδωλον παρήγαγε· καὶ Ἡρόδοτος δὲ εἶπεν ὅτι ἡ ἀληθινὴ Ἑλένη
ἔμεινεν παρὰ Πρωτεῖ, τὸ δὲ εἴδωλον αὐτῆς συνέπλευσεν Ἀλεξάνδρῳ ἐπὶ τὴν Τροίαν. It is difficult to understand why this
obiter dictum should so often be taken as unarguable fact, in
view of the nonsense about Herodotus in the next sentence.
It is unsupported by any surviving word in Hesiod and inconsistent with the comment on the 'second Palinode' of
Stesichorus in the new papyrus. Marckscheffel, the editor of
Hesiod, was, in default of further evidence, quite justified in
treating 'Hesiod' as a mere blunder for 'Stesichorus'.

Servius on *Aeneid* ii. 592, referring to the 'phantasma in
similitudinem Helenae Paridi datum' records 'quod etiam
Homerum volunt tetigisse subtiliter, ubi Aeneas a Neptuno
opposita nube liberatur: ἀμφὶ δ' ἄρ' εἰδώλῳ Τρῶες καὶ δῖοι

---

[1] With, it seems, a significant modification in timing; Lycophron 822
puts the disappearance of the Phantom immediately after the capture
of Troy, and Menelaus' years of wandering are a long search for her
over the Mediterranean. This, which makes a more organic whole of
the story, probably comes from Stesichorus; Menelaus' seven years of
sailing (with the Phantom on board) in a continually frustrated effort
to reach Greece is an awkwardness which Euripides swallows for the
sake of his dramatic Recognition.

Ἀχαιοι' (E 451). *So* subtle an allusion is hardly in Homer's manner, but one wonders whether the line gave Stesichorus his idea.

III. *The Place of the* Helen *in the Sequence of Euripidean Tragedies*

The *Helen* is one of the mercifully fixed points in our chronology of Euripides. An intersection of Aristophanean scholia places it in the year 412: (1) it was the same year as the *Andromeda* (Σ *Thesm.* 1012); (2) the *Andromeda* was in the eighth year before the *Frogs* of 405 (Σ *Ran.* 53). Also (3) *Thesmophoriazusae* (Dionysia 411) 1060–1 refers to the performance of the *Andromeda* in 'last year's' competition (πέρυσιν), and at *Thesm.* 850 Mnesilochus proposes to act the part of τὴν καινὴν Ἑλένην (new-fangled as well as newly created) to induce Euripides–Menelaus to come and set him free.

The relative chronology of the *Helen* and other plays of this period, however, is not thus fixed by external evidence; in particular the question of the priority of *Helen* or *Iphigeneia in Tauris* has been endlessly argued, because of the close similarity of plot and sequence of incidents when reduced to formula.[1] Comparative analysis of structure and motifs has left honours fairly even, and judicial summing-up seems now content to pronounce the problem insoluble. This is to reckon without Zielinski's *Tragodoumenon II, De Trimetri Euripidei Evolutione* (1925). This brilliant work would have had more of the influence it deserved if its author had been ready to trust his own demonstrations more completely. Unfortunately, by taking the date 413 for the *Electra* as given,[2] he was forced to blur the ordering of his

---

[1] See Platnauer's commentary on *IT*, Introd. xv–xvi. A closer analysis could multiply the parallel details.

[2] V. supr. p. xvii n.

third chronological group of 'liberi stili' (415–409[1] B.C.) and
to introduce complicated extraneous reasons for reversing
some of the conclusions of his metrical analyses. These, as
he was the first to perceive, exhibit after the first deliberate
movement towards a freer, more resolved trimeter (in the
middle twenties) a steadily progressive infringement of
various 'laws'—prevailing observances—in the different
parts of the trimeter. So steady, in fact, is the progression
that it can only be explained as (in detail) half-conscious
and uncalculated, a willing habituation of the poet's ear to
various phenomena, so that they become each year a little
commoner. Not that every separate one of these infringe-
ments increases in a rigidly parallel order, but added up and
taken together with the relative order of the plays according
to total percentage of resolutions in each they give a re-
markably sensitive criterion for chronological placing, as
tested by the plays of known date and the space of years
between them. Thus Zielinski sums up his column for the
extant plays of *liberi stili* as follows: 'Longe primum locum
occupat *El.* (22 puncta), sequuntur *Tro.* (38), tum *IIF* (40),
IT (43), *Ion* (51), *Hel.* (56), *Phoen.* (58).' But he goes on:
'Num igitur hic ordo pro vero chronologico habendus est?
Minime: neque enim loco moveri possunt *El.* vel *Hel.* cer-
tissimis criteriis a. 413 et 412 indicatae.' On the contrary,
now we know that *Electra* may be back-dated some six
years as required by these figures, there is nothing against
identifying Zielinski's with the chronological order.

The great merit of Zielinski's work is that, unlike the
attempted refinements subsequently published (e.g. Ceadel
in *CQ* 35, 1941, 66), it starts, for its formulation of 'laws', not
from 'feet' ('tribrach' in the second foot, 'dactyl' in the
third, etc.), but from word-shapes in the trimeter. No one
could possibly suspect from later statistics that anything
mattered seriously for chronological placing or distinctions

---

[1] Or possibly 411 or 410 for *Phoen.*, in spite of *Σ* Ar. *Ran.* 53. But it
may be that extensive interpolation has slightly falsified our statistics
of this play. Its figures are fairly consistently closer to *Hel.* than to *Or.*

of authorship except mere frequency of resolution stated in terms of 'feet', and reduced to percentages, with careful subtraction of proper names. Yet Zielinski had shown again and again that the really crucial patterns mostly start in the middle of the 'foot' and cross the bar into the following one—naturally, since the words with which the dramatist operates are in overwhelming majority so distributed (in terms of the habits of Greek metric). The most sensitive, perhaps, of all criteria are the two shapes $\cup\cup-$ and $\cup\cup\cup-$. Euripides was the first tragedian to cultivate the use of the anapaestic word in the pre-caesural position ($\dot{\omega}s$ $\kappa\epsilon\hat{\iota}\nu os$ $\dot{a}\phi a\nu\dot{\eta}s$ $\overline{x}-\cup\widehat{\cup_2\cup}\,\overline{x}//$) instead of confining it to the opening of the line ($\delta\acute{\epsilon}\chi o\mu a\iota$, $\phi\acute{\iota}\lambda o\nu$ $\gamma\epsilon$ $\cup\cup\overline{\tau}\cup-\cup//$).[1] Thus, while in *Medea* pre-caesural $\widehat{\cup\cup}\,\overline{x}$ occurs only 3 times —twice in $\gamma o\nu\acute{a}\tau\omega\nu$ and once in $\Pi\epsilon\lambda\acute{\iota}o\nu$ (there is no reason to disregard proper names in this connexion, except for cases like '$E\lambda\acute{\epsilon}\nu\eta$ in her own play)—in *Iphigeneia in Tauris* there are 17 instances, the equivalent of 1 in 63 lines; in *Helen* (excluding '$E\lambda\acute{\epsilon}\nu\eta$, etc.) 24, or 1 in 52 lines; and in the last three plays (*liberrimi stili*), *Orestes* 1 in 38, *Bacchae* 1 in 35, *Iphigeneia at Aulis* (excluding the spurious end) 1 in 31. Contrast Sophocles with one in *Ajax*, one in *Antigone*, one in *Trachiniae*, two in *Oedipus Tyrannus*, none in *Electra*, four in *Philoctetes*, six in *Oedipus Coloneus* (the last two, in this as in all metrical aspects, are the only plays to betray some Euripidean influence). Aeschylus has only $o\hat{v}s$ $\pi\rho\acute{o}\sigma\theta\epsilon$ $Ma\rho a-\theta\hat{\omega}\nu$ (*Pers.* 475).

The paeonic $\cup\cup\cup-$ is even more significant. $\cup\cup-$ can only be fitted into two places in the trimeter, so that, since no tragedian wants too many initial licences of this form, to add it in pre-caesural position meant a real extension of range of vocabulary. But $\cup\cup\cup-$ is easily accommodated in the form $\widehat{\cup_3\cup}$ $\cup-$ or $\widehat{\cup_4\cup}$ $\cup-$ (post-penthemimeral or post-hephthemimeral position), and these are in fact the

---

[1] The numbers subscript indicate first long, second long, etc., of the trimeter. Long anceps is marked $\overline{x}$, resolution $\widehat{\cup\cup}$, caesura (where relevant) //.

commonest of the sparse resolutions admitted by Aeschylus (μάντις κεκενθὼς πολεμίας ὑπὸ χθονός) and Sophocles (ἔνθ᾽ ἐσπεσὼν ἔκειρε πολυκέρων φόνον). The effect is smooth because the resolution falls at the beginning of the word, a basic 'law' of iambic and trochaic metres (high style). To his innumerable examples of these two resolutions Euripides adds ⌣͡⌣₅ ⌣ – in his later plays, this being the only form of resolved fifth long which he admits. *Helen* contains eight of these, *Iphigeneia in Tauris* only two, ἀναφέρων (23) (if LP give the form correctly; in *Phoenissae* 1410 only V has ἀμφέρει, the other MSS. ἀναφέρει) and καὶ τὰ Πελοπιδῶν (985). But the most striking of his innovations is the paeonic word in pre-caesural position ⌣ ⌣͡⌣₂ –͟ ἐς γῆν ἐναλίαν, a deliberate roughening of texture much more noticeable than pre-caesural ⌣͡⌣ –͟ because it breaks the 'law' that in tragedy (except of course in the first long of a trimeter) resolution should be confined to the first two syllables of a word. This rhythm is frequent in comedy (there are 12 in the first 500 lines of *Acharnians*), but if Euripides was here discreetly edging the tragic trimeter towards comic freedom he still left the two styles, even in his latest plays, utterly distinct.

The use of this paeonic ⌣ ⌣͡⌣₂ –͟ is by itself an extraordinarily accurate criterion for dating. No play before 415 has one;[1] from then on we have *Troades* 2, *Hercules Furens* 3, *Iphigeneia in Tauris* 0, *Ion* 4 (one split, τίνα λόγον 931), *Helen* 5, *Phoenissae* 7, *Orestes* 16, *Bacchae* 19, *Iphigeneia at Aulis* 18 (of which 4 are in tetrameters before the diaeresis, as 1354 οἵ με τὸν γάμων ἀπεκάλουν, corresponding precisely to pre-caesural position in the trimeter). The only one out of step is *Iphigeneia in Tauris*, but it has two proceleusmatics in a similar rhythm, ⌣ ⌣͡⌣₂ ⌣ Ἀτρέως ἐλέγετο δή τις (545), and in a tetrameter ἐσόμεθα (1232). This is also a

---

[1] Unless *HF*, which is very close to *Tro.* in metrical statistics, is dated to 416, but the total count brings its number of 'points' slightly higher (40:38 on Zielinski's reckoning) and I would not hesitate myself to assign it to 414, assuming it to have been written nearer to *Tro.* than to *IT*.

late-appearing phenomenon, rarer than the form with long anceps, but more erratic in progression (one in *Helen* 976, nine in *Bacchae*, five in *Iphigeneia* at Aulis). The tetrameter-resolution should also weigh a little more heavily than in trimeters, so that for ⏑ ⏓⏓ ⏑ and ⏑ ⏓⏓ ⏓ together *Iphigeneia in Tauris* is only lagging slightly behind its averaged score in Zielinski's table, which takes no account of tetrameters.

It is qualitative distinctions such as these—there are others too, always giving the same result, but space forbids further analysis here, and I have selected these as the most frequently neglected phenomena—which cumulatively considered seem to me to make it impossible either to date *Iphigeneia in Tauris* down to 411 to follow *Helen* or to sit on the fence. Add the figures for trimeters with more than one resolution, 17 in *Iphigeneia in Tauris* or the equivalent of 1 in 63, 26 in *Helen* or 1 in 48, and we find *every* metrical test giving the same relative position for the two plays. However small the statistics in each case, it is the accumulation that counts, and the final distance between the two suggests 414 as the most likely date for *Iphigeneia in Tauris*. There is no need then to try to weigh the arguments from motif-analysis against each other, a procedure from which agreement will never be reached. Some points are raised in the commentary; see on 1388, 1451–1511, 1619, 1673.

The question of the relationship of *Helen* to *Ion* in the didascalic lists is an interesting one but incapable of exact answer. Statistics put *Ion* between *Iphigeneia in Tauris* and *Helen*, and rather nearer the latter. This is borne out by the striking and repeated echoes of elaborate metrical phrasing in the lyrics of the Recognition duos of the two plays (see the commentary on 642–5, 664, and 686–7), a parallelism difficult to imagine except between plays composed close together. But whether this means that *Ion* appeared in a 413 group or that it made a third with *Helen* and *Andromeda* in 412 is impossible to say. The process of trimeter-loosening went on apace regardless of year-ends!

iv. *The Text*

The *Helen* is one of the nine plays, forming an alphabetical group from E to K, which have reached us, complete but without scholia, only in a single medieval manuscript L, with its copy P.[1] L was much corrected by the hand which appears in our apparatus criticus as *l* and was securely identified by A. Turyn, *The Byzantine Tradition of Euripides*, 1957, as that of the well-known fourteenth-century Byzantine scholar Demetrius Triclinius. His corrections were heavily entered, with much erasure of the previous text, and it is fortunate for us that P was copied from L at a stage when only the first working-over had been completed. This first-aid is mostly ascribed to L^2 in our app. crit., not being earlier recognized as *l* because of its different-coloured ink. The later revision was more detailed, and included alterations in colon-division in the lyrics and marginal notes on metres. For Triclinius, almost uniquely among scholars of that period, was interested in metric and even (relatively) to some degree knowledgeable about it, though his little learning was certainly a dangerous thing for our textual tradition.

Triclinius's work seems to have been partly the competent correction of slips made by the copyists, partly his own conjectural emendation; and in a small number of cases (e.g. 74, 185, 1212, 1675) emendation of so much higher quality and so unobvious that we must suspect collation from a different source. What that source could have been is an unanswerable question, since we have no idea whence or in what form this wonderful cache of long-lost Euripidean plays came into the possession of Triclinius's scriptorium. Zuntz inclines to the view that they once belonged to Eustathius, archbishop of Thessalonica in the twelfth century and the outstanding

---

[1] This relationship of L and P *in the nine alphabetical plays* has been settled once for all by G. Zuntz's *Inquiry into the Transmission of the Plays of Euripides*, C.U.P. 1965. The following brief summary (on this page and the next) is based on the relevant part of his book.

scholar of his day; if so, they may at some stage have had authoritative variants recorded in the margin.

With the other 'alphabetical' plays, the *Helen* was copied from L by P, in a much clearer hand but with an additional crop of mistakes, unrevised by Triclinius. It enables us, as explained above, to recover some of the original L before Triclinius got to work on it in his later revisions. It also contains a Hypothesis to the play added by a different hand and possibly an original composition, referring with rather inaccurate brevity to the authority of Herodotus, and Homer before him, for an Egyptian visit of Helen, and stressing the difference in Euripides' version based on the Phantom; a short summary of the plot follows.

In addition to LP we have for the *Helen* a papyrus-fragment of the first century B.C., containing parts of ll. 630–74. This was edited in 1954 by C. H. Roberts as *P.Oxy.* 2336, and since then much the most important contribution to our understanding of the text and its significance has been made by G. Zuntz, op. cit. With some of his conclusions I have felt unable to agree, but now that he has put us all in his debt by demonstrating the problems that have to be faced in confronting our LP text with this papyrus, it can do no harm to state the case for a more reactionary attitude.

One other bonus available is the scene between the captive Mnesilochus–Helen and Euripides–Menelaus, her would-be rescuer, in *Thesmophoriazusae* 849–919, of unique interest for the study of Aristophanes' manner as a parodist but also a useful check on some bits of our text—it supplies a missing line of stichomythia, for instance, at 561, a copy-book illustration of the ease with which a line can drop out in the transmission of this kind of dialogue and of one simple reason for it (see commentary).

LP, like all other medieval manuscripts of Euripides, must be descended from the great edition made about 200 B.C. by Aristophanes of Byzantium for the library at Alexandria. The overwhelming dominance of this was first adequately stressed by Wilamowitz in his *Einleitung in die griechische Tragödie* (1889), but W. S. Barrett argues cogently in the Introduction to his edition of the *Hippolytus*, pp. 45 ff., against the view that the Alexandrian edition must have been the sole and exclusive source of the whole medieval tradition; it is unlikely that all ancient scholarship outside, or supplementary to, this work disappeared without a trace from textual history.

We can form some notion of how much the text of the 'alphabetical' plays has suffered from its limitation to one line of manuscript tradition and from the absence of scholia by comparing the L texts of the annotated plays with the versions arrived at with the help of other manuscripts. But all the surviving plays undoubtedly suffered much damage in the two centuries before Alexandrian scholarship began its work of rescue. The edict of Lycurgus (*c.* 330 B.C.) declaring an official text of the three tragedians, to which all performances must thenceforward conform, suggests a considerable scandal of unofficial liberties taken by actors, and it is likely that this was an attempt to check further deterioration rather than a retrospective cleaning-up of the newly established text. About a century later this official text was decoyed to the library at Alexandria and may be supposed to have subsequently formed the basis of Aristophanes' edition. In these circumstances Euripides' plays, the most frequently performed among old tragedies, must have offered the largest variety of texts in circulation; the wilder ones could easily be discarded, but inevitably much that was spurious must have filtered through. Difficult and even presumptuous as the task of overhaul must seem at this stage, modern editors cannot ignore the problem of interpolation set by our existing texts.

I have considered the possibility of interpolation with some care at the relevant places in the commentary on this play. No play is quite free from it, but its extent, and its causes, differ a good deal from one play to another. Ed. Fraenkel (*Sitzb. Bayer. Ak.* 1963) has argued a case for massive interpolation in *Phoenissae*, and *Iphigeneia at Aulis* has a spurious end and a contaminated beginning, but in most cases, fortunately, the damage is, on internal evidence, less serious. The plays with scholia help us out by occasional comment, especially the welcome precision of 'some versions omit this line [these lines]'; where they give merely an expression of opinion it is not more to be taken on trust than any modern scholar's—witness the havoc created by the scholiast who inferred on wholly mistaken grounds that *Orestes* 1366–8 had been interpolated by actors. But, at least where actors' interpolations are concerned, much of the damage was done before the ancient commentators got to work on the texts, and went unsuspected, or at least unmentioned. Left to their own judgement, modern editors have naturally differed a good deal in their application of square brackets. There was a time when excision became a fashionable mania, but in general our texts are probably over-conservative, and a great deal of ingenuity has been wasted in emending passages that should simply be removed. For there is no doubt that what may be termed the casual interpolation is most easily betrayed by its clumsiness. The style of Euripides' dialogue is characteristically clear, graceful, and pointed; his interpolators, even when they can manage the metre, achieve none of these qualities. It may of course be hard to decide, particularly in the 'alphabetical' plays, where corruption rather than interpolation is the cause of our difficulties; what should be decisive is the *combination* of clumsy expression or doubtful grammar or limping metre with expendability in sense, especially where the join-up after excision is neat or even restores a lost train of thought. (Cf. 297 ff., where the sense of 297 remains unclear until the meditations on suicide (298–302), borrowed for extra 'pathos' from the next ode, are removed and τὸ σῶμα is seen from the sequel to mean, naturally enough on Helen's lips, τὸ τοῦ σώματος κάλλος.)

Conversely, where no clumsiness or obscurity is in question we should scrutinize very carefully any impulse to be rid of an offending passage. Our ideas of taste, or logic, or relevance may not always coincide with the poet's. In 257-9, for instance, it is clearly dislike of what is felt to be a grotesque note that has led to excision; the objection to 'two unconnected senses of τέρας' (but the Greek word is the same) is only a secondary excuse, and the run-on, whether from 256 to 260 or from 255, is defective. And are we to credit an interpolator with the irresistible 'white chick-container'? In her thorough analysis of her predicament Helen starts at the very beginning. The speech is over-long—true, but removal of the intrusive 287-92 and 298-302 restores its proportions.

One kind of interpolation, however, is less easy to spot from these criteria. The sententious reflection was certainly more popular with the Athenian audience than with us, and in a speech that contains several of these we may feel suspicious that someone, actor or another, has been indulging his hearers or readers with an extra one or two. Such γνῶμαι are by their nature detachable from a context, so they can be lifted from one play to another, or added (through association of ideas) to existing ones on the principle that two are more impressive than one. The speeches of the Old Servant (711-57) illustrate a variety of problems here.

To the question who interpolated, and why, there is no satisfactory answer. Actors certainly are accountable for some of it, and in such matters as the expansion of a protagonist's part by extra declamatory touches it is easy to see why. They *may* also have added those lines intended to clear up grammar or meaning—and invariably obscuring it (see, for instance, on 324-6, 388-9, 416, 742, 764)—in the hope of getting points across to their audience more effectively. 'Associated parallels', lines apparently incorporated from elsewhere into the text because of some similarity of vocabulary or sentiment, are a much more doubtful case. The phenomenon is undeniable (in *Helen* infrequent, but see, for example, on 755-7, 780), but on the source and the process we are reduced to guessing. Perhaps they varied, some being oral in origin, others committed by pen on paper. Sometimes we seem to have a mere muddled conflation of two different versions, as here 121–2 looks like the wreck of a doublet (in reverse order) of 118–19. Where the process was set going by the loss of a line or lines it seems more natural to suppose an editor rather than an actor responsible: 86–88 are characteristic in their tags picked out for repetition from the surrounding context (cf. 324–6), and in their untidy break-up of stichomythia; 1512, perhaps hardly to be classed as an 'interpolation', is presumably a product of Byzantine scansion.

The editions and commentaries I have found most helpful are:

G. Hermann, 1837.

F. A. Paley, 1874.

H. van Herwerden, 1895.

N. Wecklein, Text 1898, Commentary 1907.

A. C. Pearson, 1903 (my debt to this scholar is ubiquitous, and frequently acknowledged).

G. Italie, 1949 (a brief Dutch commentary, full of good sense).

A. Y. Campbell, 1950 (for its occasional brilliant flashes).

ΕΛΕΝΗ

ΥΠΟΘΕΣΙΣ ΕΛΕΝΗΣ

Ἡρόδοτος ἱστορεῖ περὶ Ἑλένης καί φησιν ἐλθεῖν μὲν αὐτὴν εἰς
Αἴγυπτον, καὶ τοῦτο φάσκειν καὶ τὸν Ὅμηρον ποιοῦντα τὴν Ἑλένην
παρέχειν τῷ Τηλεμάχῳ ἐν Ὀδυσσείᾳ τὸ λαθικηδὲς φάρμακον τό οἱ
πόρε Πολυδάμνα Θόωνος παράκοιτις, οὐ μὴν δὲ οὕτως ὡς Εὐρι-
πίδης φησίν. οἱ μὲν γὰρ πλανωμένην φασὶν αὐτὴν μετὰ τοῦ Μενελάου 5
μετὰ τὴν τῆς Ἰλίου πόρθησιν καὶ εἰς Αἴγυπτον παραγενέσθαι κἀκεῖ-
θεν πεπορίσθαι τὰ φάρμακα· ὃ δὲ τὴν μὲν ἀληθῶς Ἑλένην φησὶ
μηδ' ὁπωσοῦν ἐλθεῖν εἰς Τροίαν, τὸ εἴδωλον δὲ αὐτῆς. κλέψας
γὰρ αὐτὴν ὁ Ἑρμῆς Ἥρας βουλῇ Πρωτεῖ τῷ βασιλεῖ τῆς Αἰγύπτου
φυλάττειν παρέδωκε· τούτου δὲ θανόντος ὁ υἱὸς αὐτοῦ Θεοκλύμενος 10
ἐπειρᾶτο γαμεῖν αὐτήν, ἡ δὲ ἱκέτις παρεκάθητο τῷ τοῦ Πρωτέως
μνήματι. ὅθεν αὐτῇ ἐπιφαίνεται Μενέλεως, τὰς μὲν ναῦς ἐν τῇ
θαλάσσῃ ἀπολέσας, ὀλίγους δέ τινας τῶν ἑταίρων ἐν ἄντρῳ καθειργμέ-
νους σώζων. εἰς λόγους δὲ ἐλθόντες καὶ μηχανορραφήσαντες ἀπα-
τῶσι μὲν τὸν Θεοκλύμενον, αὐτοὶ δὲ νηὶ ἐμβάντες ὡς δὴ τῷ Μενέλεῳ 15
θανόντι κατὰ θάλατταν θύσοντες, εἰς τὴν ἰδίαν διασώζονται.

Argumentum om. L, habet P ab alia manu postmodo additum
1 Cf. Hdt. ii. 113–119   3 Cf. δ 221–230 : cf. Χ 83 (λαθικηδέα)
4 οὐ μήν γε Kirchhoff

ΤΑ ΤΟΥ ΔΡΑΜΑΤΟΣ ΠΡΟΣΩΠΑ

ΕΛΕΝΗ   ΑΓΓΕΛΟΣ
ΤΕΥΚΡΟΣ   ΘΕΟΝΟΗ
ΧΟΡΟΣ   ΘΕΟΚΛΥΜΕΝΟΣ
ΜΕΝΕΛΕΩΣ   ΕΤΕΡΟΣ ΑΓΓΕΛΟΣ
ΓΡΑΥΣ   ΔΙΟΣΚΟΡΟΙ

Personarum indicem ex P descripsi : om. L

Acta anno A. C. 412 : cf. Schol. Ar. Thesm. 1012, 1040, Ran. 53.
Codices L P : Scholia nulla

ΕΛΕΝΗ

Νείλου μὲν αἵδε καλλιπάρθενοι ῥοαί,
ὃς ἀντὶ δίας ψακάδος Αἰγύπτου πέδον
λευκῆς τακείσης χιόνος ὑγραίνει γύας.

Πρωτεὺς δ᾽ ὅτ᾽ ἔζη τῆσδε γῆς τύραννος ἦν,
Φάρον μὲν οἰκῶν νῆσον, Αἰγύπτου δ᾽ ἄναξ,   5
ὃς τῶν κατ᾽ οἶδμα παρθένων μίαν γαμεῖ,
Ψαμάθην, ἐπειδὴ λέκτρ᾽ ἀφῆκεν Αἰακοῦ.
τίκτει δὲ τέκνα δισσὰ τοῖσδε δώμασι,
Θεοκλύμενον ἄρσεν᾽ [ὅτι δὴ θεοὺς σέβων
βίον διήνεγκ᾽] εὐγενῆ τε παρθένον   10
Εἰδώ, τὸ μητρὸς ἀγλάισμ᾽, ὅτ᾽ ἦν βρέφος·
ἐπεὶ δ᾽ ἐς ἥβην ἦλθεν ὡραίαν γάμων,
καλοῦσιν αὐτὴν Θεονόην· τὰ θεῖα γὰρ
τά τ᾽ ὄντα καὶ μέλλοντα πάντ᾽ ἠπίστατο,
προγόνου λαβοῦσα Νηρέως τιμὰς πάρα.   15

ἡμῖν δὲ γῆ μὲν πατρὶς οὐκ ἀνώνυμος
Σπάρτη, πατὴρ δὲ Τυνδάρεως· ἔστιν δὲ δὴ
λόγος τις ὡς Ζεὺς μητέρ᾽ ἔπτατ᾽ εἰς ἐμὴν
Λήδαν κύκνου μορφώματ᾽ ὄρνιθος λαβών,
ὃς δόλιον εὐνὴν ἐξέπραξ᾽ ὑπ᾽ αἰετοῦ   20

1–3 cf. scriptor. de incr. Nili I. p. 165, Schol. Apoll. Rhod. iv.
269   fortasse αἴδε (leg. οἴδε, cf. 89) καλλιπάρθενοι γύαι, et ὑγραίνει
ῥοαῖς   2 ψακάδος Ar. Thesm. 856, Aristides ii. p. 334 : ψεκάδος
L P   3 ὑγραίνει] ἀρδεύει Aristides   γύιας L vel L² (suprascripto
ut videtur κοινή) : γύην Schol. Apoll.   6 παρθένον P   7 Αἰακοῦ
Musgrave, cl. Hes. Theog. 1003 sq., Apollod. iii. 12. 6 : αἰόλου L P
8 δισσὰ τοῖσδε δώμασιν τέκνα Nauck   9 verba uncis inclusa eiecit
Nauck : (οὔτι δὴ...διήνεγκ᾽) Heel   11 Εἰδώ Matthiae : εἶδος L P
12 ὡραίων L P : corr. Reiske   15 λαβοῦσ* sequenti spatio vacuo
primitus L   16 ἡμῖν] ἐμοὶ Ar. Thesm. 859   17 ἔστι L : corr. L²P

1*

δίωγμα φεύγων, εἰ σαφὴς οὗτος λόγος·
Ἑλένη δ᾽ ἐκλήθην. ἃ δὲ πεπόνθαμεν κακὰ
λέγοιμ᾽ ἄν. ἦλθον τρεῖς θεαὶ κάλλους πέρι
Ἰδαῖον ἐς κευθμῶν᾽ Ἀλέξανδρον πάρα,
Ἥρα Κύπρις τε διογενής τε παρθένος,   25
μορφῆς θέλουσαι διαπεράνασθαι κρίσιν.
τοὐμὸν δὲ κάλλος, εἰ καλὸν τὸ δυστυχές,
Κύπρις προτείνασ᾽ ὡς Ἀλέξανδρος γαμεῖ,
νικᾷ. λιπὼν δὲ βούσταθμ᾽ Ἰδαῖος Πάρις
Σπάρτην ἀφίκεθ᾽ ὡς ἐμὸν σχήσων λέχος.   30
Ἥρα δὲ μεμφθεῖσ᾽ οὕνεκ᾽ οὐ νικᾷ θεάς,
ἐξηνέμωσε τἄμ᾽ Ἀλεξάνδρῳ λέχη,
δίδωσι δ᾽ οὐκ ἔμ᾽, ἀλλ᾽ ὁμοιώσασ᾽ ἐμοὶ
εἴδωλον ἔμπνουν οὐρανοῦ ξυνθεῖσ᾽ ἄπο,
Πριάμου τυράννου παιδί· καὶ δοκεῖ μ᾽ ἔχειν—   35
κενὴν δόκησιν, οὐκ ἔχων. τὰ δ᾽ αὖ Διὸς
βουλεύματ᾽ ἄλλα τοῖσδε συμβαίνει κακοῖς·
πόλεμον γὰρ εἰσήνεγκεν Ἑλλήνων χθονὶ
καὶ Φρυξὶ δυστήνοισιν, ὡς ὄχλου βροτῶν
πλήθους τε κουφίσειε μητέρα χθόνα   40
γνωτόν τε θείη τὸν κράτιστον Ἑλλάδος.
Φρυγῶν δ᾽ ἐς ἀλκὴν προυτέθην ἐγὼ μὲν οὔ,
τὸ δ᾽ ὄνομα τοὐμόν, ἆθλον Ἕλλησιν δορός.
λαβὼν δέ μ᾽ Ἑρμῆς ἐν πτυχαῖσιν αἰθέρος
νεφέλῃ καλύψας—οὐ γὰρ ἠμέλησέ μου   45
Ζεύς—τόνδ᾽ ἐς οἶκον Πρωτέως ἱδρύσατο,
πάντων προκρίνας σωφρονέστατον βροτῶν,
ἀκέραιον ὡς σώσαιμι Μενέλεῳ λέχος.
κἀγὼ μὲν ἐνθάδ᾽ εἴμ᾽, ὁ δ᾽ ἄθλιος πόσις
στράτευμ᾽ ἀθροίσας τὰς ἐμὰς ἀναρπαγὰς   50

26 θέλουσι primitus L   28 προτείνασ᾽ τ ex σ facto P   34 οὐρα-
νοῦ] cf. 584, Bac. 293, unde αἰθέρος Wecklein   ἄπο Reiske : ὕπο L P
35 τυράννῳ Hermann, cl. Alc. 1150   42 προυθέμην ut videtur L P :
corr. Musgrave   48 μενέλεω L P

θηρᾷ πορευθεὶς Ἰλίου πυργώματα.
ψυχαὶ δὲ πολλαὶ δι' ἔμ' ἐπὶ Σκαμανδρίοις
ῥοαῖσιν ἔθανον· ἡ δὲ πάντα τλᾶσ' ἐγὼ
κατάρατός εἰμι καὶ δοκῶ προδοῦσ' ἐμὸν
πόσιν συνάψαι πόλεμον Ἕλλησιν μέγαν.   55
τί δῆτ' ἔτι ζῶ; θεοῦ τόδ' εἰσήκουσ' ἔπος
Ἑρμοῦ, τὸ κλεινὸν ἔτι κατοικήσειν πέδον
Σπάρτης σὺν ἀνδρί, γνόντος ὡς ἐς Ἴλιον
οὐκ ἦλθον, ἵνα μὴ λέκτρ' ὑποστρώσω τινί.
ἕως μὲν οὖν φῶς ἡλίου τόδ' ἔβλεπεν   60
Πρωτεύς, ἄσυλος ἦ γάμων· ἐπεὶ δὲ γῆς
σκότῳ κέκρυπται, παῖς ὁ τοῦ τεθνηκότος
θηρᾷ γαμεῖν με. τὸν πάλαι δ' ἐγὼ πόσιν
τιμῶσα Πρωτέως μνῆμα προσπίτνω τόδε
ἱκέτις, ἵν' ἀνδρὶ τἀμὰ διασῴσῃ λέχη,   65
ὡς, εἰ καθ' Ἑλλάδ' ὄνομα δυσκλεὲς φέρω,
μή μοι τὸ σῶμά γ' ἐνθάδ' αἰσχύνην ὄφλῃ.

ΤΕΥΚΡΟΣ

τίς τῶνδ' ἐρυμνῶν δωμάτων ἔχει κράτος;
Πλούτου γὰρ οἶκος ἄξιος προσεικάσαι,
βασίλειά τ' ἀμφιβλήματ' εὔθριγκοί θ' ἕδραι.   70
ἔα·
ὦ θεοί, τίν' εἶδον ὄψιν; ἐχθίστην ὁρῶ
γυναικὸς εἰκὼ φόνιον, ἥ μ' ἀπώλεσεν
πάντας τ' Ἀχαιούς.   θεοί σ', ὅσον μίμημ' ἔχεις
Ἑλένης, ἀποπτύσειαν.   εἰ δὲ μὴ 'ν ξένῃ   75
γαίᾳ πόδ' εἶχον, τῷδ' ἂν εὐστόχῳ πτερῷ

51 ἡλίου P: corr. ipse   52 Σκαμανδρίαις Ar. Thesm. 864
56 τί οὖν ἔτι Ar. Thesm. 868 fortasse recte   57 κλεινόν μ' Hermann   58 γνόντι μ' p (et Badham)   59 λέκτρ'] λέχος Eustath.
Il. p. 30   60 ἔβλεπε L P: corr. l   61 ἦν L P   62 παῖς L :
πῶς P   63 ἐγὼ Dobree : ἐμὸν L P   64 προσπιτνῶ ut solent L P
67 μή τοι Kirchhoff   69 Πλούτῳ Nauck   72 ἐχθίστης Dingelstadt
74 sq. θεοῖς ὅσον μίσημ' ἔχεις ἑλένη σ' L P : corr. l   ἀποπτύσαιεν L P :
corr. Ludv. Dindorf   75 sq. μὴ ξένην γαίαν (sic) P¹ vel p   76
πόδ' Tan. Faber : ποτ' L P   πτερῷ Elmsley : πέτρω L P

ἀπόλαυσιν εἰκοῦς ἔθανες ἂν Διὸς κόρης.

Ελ. τί δ᾽, ὦ ταλαίπωρ᾽—ὅστις ὢν μ᾽ ἀπεστράφης
καὶ ταῖς ἐκείνης συμφοραῖς ἐμὲ στυγεῖς;

Τε. ἥμαρτον· ὀργῇ δ᾽ εἶξα μᾶλλον ἤ με χρῆν·   80
μισεῖ γὰρ Ἑλλὰς πᾶσα τὴν Διὸς κόρην.
σύγγνωθι δ᾽ ἡμῖν τοῖς λελεγμένοις, γύναι.

Ελ. τίς δ᾽ εἶ; πόθεν γῆς τῆσδ᾽ ἐπεστράφης πέδον;

Τε. εἷς τῶν Ἀχαιῶν, ὦ γύναι, τῶν ἀθλίων.

Ελ. οὐ τἆρα σ᾽ Ἑλένην εἰ στυγεῖς θαυμαστέον.   85
ἀτὰρ τίς εἶ πόθεν; τίνος δ᾽ αὐδᾶν σε χρή;

Τε. ὄνομα μὲν ἡμῖν Τεῦκρος, ὁ δὲ φύσας πατὴρ
Τελαμών, Σαλαμὶς δὲ πατρὶς ἡ θρέψασά με.

Ελ. τί δῆτα Νείλου τούσδ᾽ ἐπιστρέφῃ γύας;

Τε. φυγὰς πατρῴας ἐξελήλαμαι χθονός.   90

Ελ. τλήμων ἂν εἴης· τίς δέ σ᾽ ἐκβάλλει πάτρας;

Τε. Τελαμὼν ὁ φύσας.   τίν᾽ ἂν ἔχοις μᾶλλον φίλον;

Ελ. ἐκ τοῦ; τὸ γάρ τοι πρᾶγμα συμφορὰν ἔχει.

Τε. Αἴας μ᾽ ἀδελφὸς ὤλεσ᾽ ἐν Τροίᾳ θανών.

Ελ. πῶς; οὔ τί που σῷ φασγάνῳ βίον στερείς;   95

Τε. οἰκεῖον αὐτὸν ὤλεσ᾽ ἅλμ᾽ ἐπὶ ξίφος.

Ελ. μανέντ᾽; ἐπεὶ τίς σωφρονῶν τλαίη τάδ᾽ ἄν;

Τε. τὸν Πηλέως τιν᾽ οἶσθ᾽ Ἀχιλλέα γόνον;

Ελ. ναί·
μνηστήρ ποθ᾽ Ἑλένης ἦλθεν, ὡς ἀκούομεν.

Τε. θανὼν ὅδ᾽ ὅπλων ἔριν ἔθηκε συμμάχοις.   100

Ελ. καὶ δὴ τί τοῦτ᾽ Αἴαντι γίγνεται κακόν;

Τε. ἄλλου λαβόντος ὅπλ᾽ ἀπηλλάχθη βίου.

Ελ. σὺ τοῖς ἐκείνου δῆτα πήμασιν νοσεῖς;

77 ἀπόλαυσιν Reiske : ἀπώλυσ᾽. ἵν᾽ L P : ἀπώλεσ᾽ ἵν᾽ p   post
78 versum excidisse putabat Usener   79 ἐμὲ L²P : ἐμαῖς L
80 μ᾽ ἐχρῆν L P   85 οὔτ᾽ ἄρα L P : οὐκ ἄρα l   86 δ᾽ αὐδᾶν
Schneidewin : ἐξαυδᾶν L P : ἀτὰρ σὲ χρὴ 'ξαυδᾶν, τίς εἶ πόθεν τίνος ;
Dobree   89 τούσδ᾽ Elmsley : τάσδ᾽ L P   vv. 90–142 in P, 91–142 in
L paragraphi pro personarum notis praefixi   98 ναί hic L² P :
post γόνον habuisse videtur L   Ἀχιλλέα τιν᾽ οἶσθα, Πηλέως γόνον ;
Cobet   100 ὅδ᾽ Portus : δ᾽ L P   103 νοσοῖς L P : corr. p

Τε. ὁθούνεκ᾽ αὐτῷ γ᾽ οὐ ξυνωλόμην ὁμοῦ.

Ελ. ἦλθες γάρ, ὦ ξέν᾽, Ἰλίου κλεινὴν πόλιν; 105

Τε. καὶ ξύν γε πέρσας αὐτὸς ἀνταπωλόμην.

Ελ. ἤδη γὰρ ἧπται καὶ κατείργασται πυρί;

Τε. ὥστ᾽ οὐδ᾽ ἴχνος γε τειχέων εἶναι σαφές.

Ελ. ὦ τλῆμον Ἑλένη, διὰ σ᾽ ἀπόλλυνται Φρύγες.

Τε. καὶ πρός γ᾽ Ἀχαιοί· μεγάλα δ᾽ εἴργασται κακά. 110

Ελ. πόσον χρόνον γὰρ διαπεπόρθηται πόλις;

Τε. ἑπτὰ σχεδόν τι καρπίμους ἐτῶν κύκλους.

Ελ. χρόνον δ᾽ ἐμείνατ᾽ ἄλλον ἐν Τροίᾳ πόσον;

Τε. πολλὰς σελήνας, δέκα διελθούσας ἔτη.

Ελ. ἦ καὶ γυναῖκα Σπαρτιᾶτιν εἴλετε; 115

Τε. Μενέλαος αὐτὴν ἦγ᾽ ἐπισπάσας κόμης.

Ελ. εἶδες σὺ τὴν δύστηνον; ἢ κλύων λέγεις;

Τε. ὥσπερ γε σέ, οὐδὲν ἧσσον, ὀφθαλμοῖς ὁρῶ.

Ελ. σκοπεῖτε μὴ δόκησιν εἴχετ᾽ ἐκ θεῶν.

Τε. ἄλλου λόγου μέμνησο, μὴ κείνης ἔτι. 120

Ελ. οὕτω δοκεῖτε τὴν δόκησιν ἀσφαλῆ;

Τε. αὐτὸς γὰρ ὄσσοις εἰδόμην· καὶ νοῦς ὁρᾷ.

Ελ. ἤδη δ᾽ ἐν οἴκοις σὺν δάμαρτι Μενέλεως;

Τε. οὔκουν ἐν Ἄργει ⟨γ᾽⟩ οὐδ᾽ ἐπ᾽ Εὐρώτα ῥοαῖς.

Ελ. αἰαῖ· κακὸν τόδ᾽ εἶπας οἷς κακὸν λέγεις. 125

Τε. ὡς κεῖνος ἀφανὴς σὺν δάμαρτι κλῄζεται.

Ελ. οὐ πᾶσι πορθμὸς αὐτὸς Ἀργείοισιν ἦν;

Τε. ἦν, ἀλλὰ χειμὼν ἄλλοσ᾽ ἄλλον ὥρισεν.

Ελ. ποίοισιν ἐν νώτοισι ποντίας ἁλός;

Τε. μέσον περῶσι πέλαγος Αἰγαίου πόρου. 130

104 αὐτῷ γ᾽ *l p* : αὐτῶ L P, nisi forte αὐτῶ τ᾽ habuit L 105 ξέν᾽
l : ξεῖν᾽ P et sine dubio L Ἰλίου L² P : Ἴλιον L 109 ἀπώλλυνται L :
ἀπώλλυνται (sic) corr. in ἀπώλοντο P 112 καμπίμους Nauck 113 δ᾽
om. P 114 ἔτι P 115 σπαρτιάτην L P : corr. P² 118 ὥσπερ
σέ γ᾽ *l* 121 ᾽δοκεῖτε Badham 122 'Nam ipse vidi, et in visu
operatur intellectus': cf. fr. 909, 6 : εἶδον ἦν καὶ νοῦς ὁρᾷ Reiske
124 γ᾽ add. Musgrave 127 αὐτὸς L P 129 ἐνό τοισι P 130 πε-
ρῶντας Reiske

Ελ. κἀκ τοῦδε Μενέλαν οὔτις εἶδ' ἀφιγμένον;
Τε. οὐδείς· θανὼν δὲ κλήζεται καθ' Ἑλλάδα.
Ελ. ἀπωλόμεσθα· Θεστιὰς δ' ἔστιν κόρη;
Τε. Λήδαν ἔλεξας; οἴχεται θανοῦσα δή.
Ελ. οὔ πού νιν Ἑλένης αἰσχρὸν ὤλεσεν κλέος;   135
Τε. φασίν, βρόχῳ γ' ἅψασαν εὐγενῆ δέρην.
Ελ. οἱ Τυνδάρειοι δ' εἰσὶν ἢ οὐκ εἰσὶν κόροι;
Τε. τεθνᾶσι καὶ οὐ τεθνᾶσι· δύο δ' ἐστὸν λόγω.
Ελ. πότερος ὁ κρείσσων; ὦ τάλαιν' ἐγὼ κακῶν.
Τε. ἄστροις σφ' ὁμοιωθέντε φάσ' εἶναι θεώ.   140
Ελ. καλῶς ἔλεξας τοῦτο· θάτερον δὲ τί;
Τε. σφαγαῖς ἀδελφῆς οὕνεκ' ἐκπνεῦσαι βίον.
    ἅλις δὲ μύθων· οὐ διπλᾶ χρήζω στένειν.
    ὧν δ' οὕνεκ' ἦλθον τούσδε βασιλείους δόμους,
    τὴν θεσπιῳδὸν Θεονόην χρῄζων ἰδεῖν,   145
    σὺ προξένησον, ὡς τύχω μαντευμάτων
    ὅπῃ νεὼς στείλαιμ' ἂν οὔριον πτερὸν
    ἐς γῆν ἐναλίαν Κύπρον, οὗ μ' ἐθέσπισεν
    οἰκεῖν Ἀπόλλων, ὄνομα νησιωτικὸν
    Σαλαμῖνα θέμενον τῆς ἐκεῖ χάριν πάτρας.   150
Ελ. πλοῦς, ὦ ξέν', αὐτὸς σημανεῖ· σὺ δ' ἐκλιπὼν
    γῆν τήνδε φεῦγε πρίν σε παῖδα Πρωτέως
    ἰδεῖν, ὃς ἄρχει τῆσδε γῆς· ἄπεστι δὲ
    κυσὶν πεποιθὼς ἐν φοναῖς θηροκτόνοις·
    κτείνει γὰρ Ἕλλην' ὄντιν' ἂν λάβῃ ξένον.   155
    ὅτου δ' ἔκατι, μήτε σὺ ζήτει μαθεῖν
    ἐγώ τε σιγῶ· τί γὰρ ἂν ὠφελοῖμί σε;
Τε. καλῶς ἔλεξας, ὦ γύναι· θεοὶ δέ σοι
    ἐσθλῶν ἀμοιβὰς ἀντιδωρησαίατο.

---

131 Μενέλαν Paley : μενέλαον L P   κὰκ τοῦ Μενέλεων Radermacher
οἶδ' Musurus   135 οὔ που Seidler et, ut videtur, primitus L : οὔπω
nunc L : πού P : ἦ που suprascr. l   138 λόγω Schaefer : λόγοι L P
142 σφαγαῖς L P : φασὶν P²   144 βασιλικοὺς Wunder   146 συμ-
προξένησον L P : corr. Jacobs   τύχω ex ἴδω factum videtur in L
151 sc. ipsum fluit mare hinc usque Cyprum : cf. Bac. 406   157 ἐγὼ
δὲ P   158 Τε.] paragraphum L

Ἑλένῃ δ' ὅμοιον σῶμ' ἔχουσ' οὐ τὰς φρένας   160
ἔχεις ὁμοίας, ἀλλὰ διαφόρους πολύ.
κακῶς δ' ὄλοιτο μηδ' ἐπ' Εὐρώτα ῥοὰς
ἔλθοι· σὺ δ' εἴης εὐτυχὴς ἀεί, γύναι.

Ελ. ὤ, μεγάλων ἀχέων καταβαλλομένα μέγαν οἶκτον
ποῖον ἀμιλλαθῶ γόον; ἢ τίνα μοῦσαν ἐπέλθω   165
δάκρυσιν ἢ θρήνοις ἢ πένθεσιν; αἰαῖ.

πτεροφόροι νεάνιδες,   [στρ.
παρθένοι Χθονὸς κόραι
Σειρῆνες, εἴθ' ἐμοῖς γόοις
   μόλοιτ' ἔχουσαι Λίβυν   170
λωτὸν ἢ σύριγγας ἢ
φόρμιγγας, αἰλίνοις κακοῖς
τοῖς ἐμοῖσι σύνοχα δάκρυα·
πάθεσι πάθεα, μέλεσι μέλεα,
μουσεῖα θρηνήμα-
σι ξυνῳδὰ πέμψειε
   Φερσέφασσα   175
φόνια, χάριτας ἵν' ἐπὶ δάκρυσι
παρ' ἐμέθεν ὑπὸ μέλαθρα νύχια
παιᾶνα
νέκυσιν ὀλομένοις λάβῃ.

ΧΟΡΟΣ

κυανοειδὲς ἀμφ' ὕδωρ   [ἀντ.
ἔτυχον ἕλικά τ' ἀνὰ χλόαν   180
φοίνικας ἁλίου πέπλους
αὐγαῖσιν ἐν χρυσέαις

162 δ' del. Wilamowitz   164 ἑλ. P *l* : paragraphum L   ὤ L P
οἶκτον *l* (vel L²) : οἶκον L P   165 γόον] γόνον primitus P   166 αἰαῖ
hic scripsi: ἒ ἒ hic *l* : ἒ ἒ initio v. 167 L P   170 τὸν λίβυν *l*   171 αἵ
αἴνοις κακοῖς L P (in margine γρ. αἰλίνοις κακοῖς L¹) : ἢ φόρμιγγας del. *l*
et αἰλίνοις in textu scripsit   174 μουσεια τε *l*   174 sqq. μουσεῖα,
ut θρηνήμα- πέμψειε παιᾶνα, ditrochaeum valet, cf. ad 186   175 περ-
σέφασσα *p* rasura   176-178 φόνια φόνια et παιᾶνας *l* : unde φόνια
φόνι'. ἀχάριτας . . . . παιᾶνας νέκυσι μελομένους Lobeck   177 ἐμέθεν
Seidler : ἐμέθ' L P   181 ἁλίου *l* : ἁλίω L P   182 αὐγαῖσιν ἐν
ταῖς χρυσέαις *l* : ταῖς del. Hermann : χρυσέαισιν αὐγαῖς L P

ἀμφὶ δόνακος ἔρνεσιν
θάλπουσα· ⟨ποτνίας δ' ἐμᾶς,⟩
ἔνθεν οἰκτρὸν ἀνεβόασεν,
ὅμαδον ἔκλυον, ἄλυρον ἔλεγον,   185
ὅτι ποτ' ἔλακεν αἰάγμα-
σι στένουσα, Νύμφα τις
οἷα Ναῖς
ὄρεσι φυγάδα νόμον ἱεῖσα
γοερόν, ὑπὸ δὲ πέτρινα γύαλα
κλαγγαῖσι
Πανὸς ἀναβοᾷ γάμους.   190

Ελ.   ἰὼ ἰώ·   [στρ.
θήραμα βαρβάρου πλάτας,
Ἑλλανίδες κόραι,
ναύτας Ἀχαιῶν
τις ἔμολεν ἔμολε δάκρυα δάκρυσί μοι φέρων.   195
Ἰλίου κατασκαφαὶ
πυρὶ μέλουσι δαΐῳ
δι' ἐμὲ τὰν πολυκτόνον,
δι' ἐμὸν ὄνομα πολύπονον.
Λήδα δ' ἐν ἀγχόναις   200
θάνατον ἔλαβεν αἰσχύ-
νας ἐμᾶς ὑπ' ἀλγέων.
ὁ δ' ἐμὸς ἐν ἁλὶ πολυπλανὴς
πόσις ὀλόμενος οἴχεται,
Κάστορός τε συγγόνου τε   205

183 θάλπουσ' ἀμφὶ (ἀμφί τ' ἐν *l*) δόνακος ἔρνεσιν L P : traieci et hiatum ex. gr. supplevi   184 ἀνεβόασεν delevit Badham, cf. ad 171   185 ἔλεγον γρ. L : θρῆνον in textu L P (ἔλεγον in textu *l*)   186 ὅτι πόδ' *l* ὅτι ποτ' ἔλακεν ditrochaeum valet, cf. ad 174   188 νόμον Matthiae : γάμον *l* : γάμων L P   189 ante γύαλα habet μύαλα L : μύχαλα L¹ P, dittographia ut videtur, sed cf. fr. Niobae, Grenf. Pap. II. p. 14, Blass in Rh. M. LV 96 : μύχατα Canter   190 κλαγγαῖσιν (sic) Hermann : κλαγγὰς L : κλαγκὰς P : del. *l*   196 κατασκαφὰ πυρὶ μέλουσ' ἰδαίω L P : (κατασκαφὰν et μέλλουσαν *l*) : correxi   202 αἰσχύνας ἐμᾶς ὑπ' Muretus : αἰσχύνασ' ἡμᾶς ἐπ' L P

διδυμογενὲς ἄγαλμα πατρίδος
ἀφανὲς ἀφανὲς ἱππόκροτα λέ-
λοιπε δάπεδα γυμνάσιά τε
δονακόεντος Εὐρώ-   210
τα, νεανιᾶν πόνον.

Χο.   αἰαῖ αἰαῖ·   [ἀντ.
ὦ δαίμονος πολυστόνου
μοίρας τε σᾶς, γύναι,
αἰὼν δυσαίων
τις ἔλαχεν ἔλαχεν, ὅτε σ' ἐτέκετο ματρόθεν
χιονόχρως κύκνου πτερῷ   215
Ζεὺς πρέπων δι' αἰθέρος·
τί γὰρ ἄπεστί σοι κακῶν;
τίνα δὲ βίοτον οὐκ ἔτλας;
μάτηρ μὲν οἴχεται,
δίδυμά τε Διὸς οὐκ εὐ-   220
δαιμονεῖ τέκεα φίλα,
χθόνα δὲ πάτριον οὐχ ὁρᾷς,
διὰ δὲ πόλεας ἔρχεται
βάξις, ἅ σε βαρβάροισι,
πότνια, παραδίδωσι λέχεσιν,   225
ὁ δὲ σὸς ἐν ἁλὶ κύμασί τε λέ-
λοιπε βίοτον, οὐδέ ποτ' ἔτι
πάτρια μέλαθρα καὶ τὰν
Χαλκίοικον ὀλβιεῖς.

Ελ.   φεῦ φεῦ, τίς ἢ Φρυγῶν
ἢ τίς Ἑλλανίας ἀπὸ χθονὸς   230

207 ἱππόκρατα P   210 νεανίαν L P   211 αἰ αἰ αἰ αἰ ὦ l : αἰ αἰ
L P   214 τις] τίς σ' P et ut videtur primitus L   215, 216 in-
verso ordine collocat l, et inde editores   218 τί δ' ἀνὰ βίοτον Bruhn
βίοτον L² P (et l): βίον L   ἔτλης L P: corr. l   221 τέκεα l: τέκνα
L P   223 πόλεας L² P: πόλιας L   225 λέχεσι πότνια παραδίδωσι
L P: trai. Nauck, cl. 206   226 ἐν] ἐ primitus P   228 ὀλβιοῖς L P:
corr. P¹   229 personae notam om. L   ἢ Dindorf: ἦν L P

ἔτεμε τὰν δακρυόεσσαν
Ἰλίῳ πεύκαν;
ἔνθεν ὀλόμενον σκάφος
συναρμόσας ὁ Πριαμίδας
ἔπλευσε βαρβάρῳ πλάτᾳ
τὰν ἐμὰν ἐφ᾽ ἑστίαν,   235
ἐπὶ τὸ δυστυχέστατον
κάλλος, ὡς ἕλοι, γάμων
ἀμῶν· ἅ τε δόλιος
ἁ πολυκτόνος Κύπρις
Δαναΐδαις ἄγουσα θάνατον [Πριαμίδαις],
ὦ τάλαινα συμφορᾶς.   240
ἁ δὲ χρυσέοις θρόνοις
Διὸς ὑπαγκάλισμα σεμνὸν
Ἥρα τὸν ὠκύπουν
ἔπεμψε Μαιάδος γόνον·
ὅς με χλοερὰ δρεπομέναν
ἔσω πέπλων ῥόδεα πέταλα,
Χαλκίοικον ὡς [Ἀθάναν] μόλοιμ᾽,   245
ἀναρπάσας δι᾽ αἰθέρος
τάνδε γαῖαν εἰς ἄνολβον
ἔριν ἔριν τάλαιναν ἔθετο
Πριαμίδαισιν Ἑλλάδος·
τὸ δ᾽ ἐμὸν ὄνομα
παρὰ Σιμουντίοις ῥοαῖσι   250
μαψίδιον ἔχει φάτιν.

Χο. ἔχεις μὲν ἀλγείν᾽, οἶδα· σύμφορον δέ τοι

234 πλεῦσε P   236, 237 del. Dindorf, cl. 27 : fortasse ὁ Πριαμίδας (v. 234) post 237 (γάμων ἀμῶν) traiciendus   236 δυστυχὲς l   238
ἐμῶν LP : correxi ob metrum (γάμον ἐμὸν l)   ἅ τε Matthiae :
ἁ δὲ LP   ἁ πολύκτονος L : ἀπολύκτονος P   239 δαναΐδες P   πριαμίδαις LP : πριαμίδαις τε l : del. Nauck   240 paragraphum
praef. L   241 ἁ Dindorf : εἰ L : εἰ P : ἢ l   243 μεάδος P
245 πέτλα LP : corr. L² P¹   Ἀθάναν seclusi : verba Χαλκίοικον . . .
μ᾽λοιμ᾽ del. Dindorf   253 συμφέρον l   τοι Ludv. Dindorf : σοι
L P

ὡς ῥᾷστα τἀναγκαῖα τοῦ βίου φέρειν.

Ελ. φίλαι γυναῖκες, τίνι πότμῳ συνεζύγην;   255
ἆρ' ἡ τεκοῦσά μ' ἔτεκεν ἀνθρώποις τέρας;
[γυνὴ γὰρ οὔθ' Ἑλληνὶς οὔτε βάρβαρος
τεῦχος νεοσσῶν λευκὸν ἐκλοχεύεται,
ἐν ᾧ με Λήδαν φασὶν ἐκ Διὸς τεκεῖν.]
τέρας γὰρ ὁ βίος καὶ τὰ πράγματ' ἐστί μου,   260
τὰ μὲν δι' Ἥραν, τὰ δὲ τὸ κάλλος αἴτιον.
εἴθ' ἐξαλειφθεῖσ' ὡς ἄγαλμ' αὖθις πάλιν
αἴσχιον εἶδος ἔλαβον ἀντὶ τοῦ καλοῦ,
καὶ τὰς τύχας μὲν τὰς κακὰς ἃς νῦν ἔχω
Ἕλληνες ἐπελάθοντο, τὰς δὲ μὴ κακὰς   265
ἔσῳζον ὥσπερ τὰς κακὰς σῴζουσί μου.

ὅστις μὲν οὖν ἐς μίαν ἀποβλέπων τύχην
πρὸς θεῶν κακοῦται, βαρὺ μέν, οἰστέον δ' ὅμως·
ἡμεῖς δὲ πολλαῖς συμφοραῖς ἐγκείμεθα.
πρῶτον μὲν οὐκ οὖσ' ἄδικος, εἰμὶ δυσκλεής·   270
καὶ τοῦτο μεῖζον τῆς ἀληθείας κακόν,
ὅστις τὰ μὴ προσόντα κέκτηται κακά.
ἔπειτα πατρίδος θεοί μ' ἀφιδρύσαντο γῆς
ἐς βάρβαρ' ἤθη, καὶ φίλων τητωμένη
δούλη καθέστηκ' οὖσ' ἐλευθέρων ἄπο·   275
τὰ βαρβάρων γὰρ δοῦλα πάντα πλὴν ἑνός.
ἄγκυρα δ' ἥ μου τὰς τύχας ὦχει μόνη,
πόσιν ποθ' ἥξειν καί μ' ἀπαλλάξειν κακῶν—
οὗτος τέθνηκεν, οὗτος οὐκέτ' ἔστι δή.
μήτηρ δ' ὄλωλε, καὶ φονεὺς αὐτῆς ἐγώ,   280
ἀδίκως μέν, ἀλλὰ τἄδικον τοῦτ' ἔστ' ἐμόν·
ὁ δ' ἀγλάισμα δωμάτων ἐμοῦ τ' ἔφυ,

257-259 del. Wieland   260 καὶ τὰ lp : κάρτα L P   μου] μοι l
263 ἀντὶ τοῦ καλοῦ λαβεῖν L P : λάβω l et in marg. γρ. λάβω L² :
ἀντὶ τοῦ καλοῦ λαβὸν Porson : trai. Wilamowitz   264 et 265 κακὰς
apogr. Paris. : καλὰς L P   276 πλὴν L : πρὶν P   277 δ' ἤ
Scaliger : δή L P   ὦχει Musgrave : ὀχεῖ L P   279 ἐπεὶ τέθνηκεν
οὗτος Wilamowitz   281 τοῦτ'] τόδ' Elmsley   ἔστ' om. P
282 ἐμοῦ] ἐμόν Cobet

14   ΕΥΡΙΠΙΔΟΥ

θυγάτηρ ἄνανδρος πολιὰ παρθενεύεται·
τὼ τοῦ Διὸς δὲ λεγομένω Διοσκόρω
οὐκ ἐστόν. ἀλλὰ πάντ' ἔχουσα δυστυχῆ   285
τοῖς πράγμασιν τέθνηκα, τοῖς δ' ἔργοισιν οὔ.
τὸ δ' ἔσχατον τοῦτ', εἰ μόλοιμεν ἐς πάτραν,
κλῄθροις ἂν εἰργοίμεσθα—τὴν ὑπ' Ἰλίῳ
δοκοῦντες Ἑλένην Μενέλεω μ' ἐλθεῖν μέτα.
εἰ μὲν γὰρ ἔζη πόσις, ἀνεγνώσθημεν ἂν   290
ἐλθόντες, ἃ φανέρ' ἦν μόνοις, ἐς ξύμβολα.
νῦν δ' οὔτε τοῦτ' ἔστ' οὔτε μὴ σωθῇ ποτε.
τί δῆτ' ἔτι ζῶ; τίν' ὑπολείπομαι τύχην;
γάμους ἑλομένη τῶν κακῶν ὑπαλλαγάς,
μετ' ἀνδρὸς οἰκεῖν βαρβάρου πρὸς πλουσίαν   295
τράπεζαν ἵζουσ'; ἀλλ' ὅταν πόσις πικρὸς
ξυνῇ γυναικί, καὶ τὸ σῶμ' ἐστιν πικρόν.
θανεῖν κράτιστον· πῶς θάνοιμ' ἂν οὐ καλῶς;
[ἀσχήμονες μὲν ἀγχόναι μετάρσιοι,
κἂν τοῖσι δούλοις δυσπρεπὲς νομίζεται·   300
σφαγαὶ δ' ἔχουσιν εὐγενές τι καὶ καλόν,
σμικρὸν δ' ὁ καιρὸς σάρκ' ἀπαλλάξαι βίου.]
ἐς γὰρ τοσοῦτον ἤλθομεν βάθος κακῶν·
αἱ μὲν γὰρ ἄλλαι διὰ τὸ κάλλος εὐτυχεῖς
γυναῖκες, ἡμᾶς δ' αὐτὸ τοῦτ' ἀπώλεσεν.   305
Χο. Ἑλένη, τὸν ἐλθόνθ', ὅστις ἐστὶν ὁ ξένος,
μὴ πάντ' ἀληθῆ δοξάσῃς εἰρηκέναι.
Ελ. καὶ μὴν σαφῶς γ' ἔλεξ' ὀλωλέναι πόσιν.

283 πολιᾶ L P   284 Διὸς] πατρὸς Ribbeck   Διοσκόρω] δισσὼ κόρω
F. Gu. Schmidt   287 ἐς hic P   288 κλείθροις L P   288, 289 εἰργοιέν
με Badham : mavult δοκοῦσιν Wecklein, δοκοῦντος Scaliger   μ' ἐλθεῖν]
θανεῖν F. Gu. Schmidt : lacunam post 288 statuit Kayser : versus
fortasse sani   291 ἐς ξύμβολ' ἐλθόντες ἃ φανερὰ μόνοις ἂν ἦν L P
(ἐλθόνθ' ἃ φανερ' ἂν Porson : ἀμφανῆ Camper : tum μόνοιν Herwerden):
correxi   294 ἀπαλλαγάς ρ   297 τὸ σῶμ' sanum videtur :
τὸ δῶμ' Scaliger : τὸ σῶν Seidler   299–302 delevit Hartung
298 πῶς θάνοιμ' ἂν οὖν Stephanus : προθάνοιμ' ἂν οὐ L P   οὐ restituit Wilamowitz, cl. vv. 303–305   302 σμικρὸς Stephanus
σάρκ' Hermann : ἄρτ' L P   306 ἐλθόντ' L P   308 ἔλεξεν L P

ΕΛΕΝΗ 15

Χο. πόλλ' ἂν γένοιτο καὶ διὰ ψευδῶν ἔπη.
Ελ. καὶ τἄμπαλίν γε τῶνδ' ἀληθείᾳ σαφῆ. 310
Χο. ἐς ξυμφορὰν γὰρ ἀντὶ τἀγαθοῦ φέρῃ.
Ελ. φόβος γὰρ ἐς τὸ δεῖμα περιβαλών μ' ἄγει.
Χο. πῶς δ' εὐμενείας τοισίδ' ἐν δόμοις ἔχεις;
Ελ. πάντες φίλοι μοι πλὴν ὁ θηρεύων γάμους.
Χο. οἶσθ' οὖν ὃ δρᾶσον; μνήματος λιποῦσ' ἕδραν— 315
Ελ. ἐς ποῖον ἕρπεις μῦθον ἢ παραίνεσιν;
Χο. ἐλθοῦσ' ἐς οἴκους, ᾗ τὰ πάντ' ἐπίσταται,
τῆς ποντίας Νηρῇδος ἐκγόνου κόρης,
πυθοῦ πόσιν σὸν Θεονόης, εἴτ' ἔστ' ἔτι
εἴτ' ἐκλέλοιπε φέγγος· ἐκμαθοῦσα δ' εὖ 320
πρὸς τὰς τύχας τὸ χάρμα τοὺς γόους τ' ἔχε.
πρὶν δ' οὐδὲν ὀρθῶς εἰδέναι, τί σοι πλέον
λυπουμένῃ γένοιτ' ἄν; ἀλλ' ἐμοὶ πιθοῦ·
τάφον λιποῦσα τόνδε σύμμειξον κόρῃ·
ὅθενπερ εἴσῃ πάντα τἀληθῆ φράσαι 325
ἔχουσ' ἐν οἴκοις τοῖσδε, τί βλέπεις προσω;
θέλω δὲ κἀγὼ σοὶ συνεισελθεῖν δόμους
καὶ συμπυθέσθαι παρθένου θεσπίσματα·
γυναῖκα γὰρ δὴ συμπονεῖν γυναικὶ χρή.
Ελ. φίλαι, λόγους ἐδεξάμαν· 330
βᾶτε βᾶτε δ' ἐς δόμους,
ἀγῶνας ἐντὸς οἴκων
ὡς πύθησθε τοὺς ἐμούς.
Χο. θέλουσαν οὐ μόλις καλεῖς.
Ελ. ἰὼ μέλεος ἀμέρα. 335
τίν' ἄρα τάλαινα τίνα δακρυό-

309 ἔπη] σαφῆ Hermann   310 ἀληθείᾳ Kirchhoff: ἀληθείας
L P   ἀληθείας ἔπη Hermann: ἀλήθει' ἀσφαλής Wilamowitz   310–
317 paragraphi praefixi in P, 313–317 in L   312 φόβος L: φόνος P
περιλαβών p   313 τοισίδ' L P: τοῖσιν p (et Cobet): τοῖσί γ' l
324–326 delevit Goguel   325 φράσαι] μαθεῖν Badham   330 ἐδεξάμαν L²P: ἐδεξάμ** L   332 οἴκων L P: δόμων suprascr. l aut L²:
del. Badham   335, 340, 346, 348 paragraphos praef. L: personas
hic illic addidit l

εν+α λόγον ἀκούσομαι;

Χο.   μὴ πρόμαντις ἀλγέων
προλάμβαν᾽, ὦ φίλα, γόους.

Ελ.   τί μοι πόσις μέλεος ἔτλα;   340
πότερα δέρκεται φάος
τέθριππά θ᾽ ἁλίου κέλευθά τ᾽ ἀστέρων,
ἢ ᾽ν νέκυσι κατὰ χθονὸς
τὰν χρόνιον ἔχει τύχαν;   345

Χο.   ἐς τὸ φέρτερον τίθει
τὸ μέλλον, ὅ τι γενήσεται.

Ελ.   σὲ γὰρ ἐκάλεσα, σὲ δὲ κατόμοσα,
τὸν ὑδρόεντι δόνακι χλωρὸν
Εὐρώταν, θανόντος   350
εἰ βάξις ἔτυμος ἀνδρὸς
ἅδε μοι—τί τάδ᾽ ἀσύνετα;—
φόνιον αἰώρημα
διὰ δέρης ὀρέξομαι,
ἢ ξιφοκτόνον δίωγμα
λαιμορρύτου σφαγᾶς   355
αὐτοσίδαρον ἔσω πελάσω διὰ σαρκὸς ἅμιλλαν,
θῦμα τριζύγοις θεαῖσι
τῷ τε σήραγγας Ἰδαί-
ας ἐνίζοντι Πριαμί-
δᾳ ποτ᾽ ἀμφὶ βουστάθμους.

Χο.   ἄλλοσ᾽ ἀποτροπὰ κακῶν   360
γένοιτο, τὸ δὲ σὸν εὐτυχές.

342 τ᾽ ἀελίου L P : corr. Badham   343 fortasse ἄστρων ob
metrum, cf. 632 sqq.   κέλευθά L P: ἐς κέλευθά l   344 ἢ ᾽ν
Jacobs: ἢ L P   νέκυσι l: νέκυσιν L P   345 χρόνιον Orelli:
χθόνιον L P: cf. I. T. 481   348 σέ γ᾽ ἀνεκάλεσα Badham   κατώμοσα L P: corr. Elmsley   349 ὑδρόεντι Reiske: ὑδρόεντα L P
χλωρὸν Stephanus: χῶρον L P   352 verba τί τάδ᾽ ἀσύνετα Choro
vulgo tributa post correctorem apogr. Paris.   353 ὀρέξομαι P
355 δαῖγμὸν αἱμορύτου post Hartung Wecklein   λαιμορυτοῦ L P
σφαγὰς P   356 ἅμιλλα L P : corr. Musgrave   358 sq. σήραγγας
Ἰδαίας ἐνίζοντι Badham: σύραγγ᾽ ἀοιδαὶ σεβίζον L P: συρίγγων ἀοιδαῖς
σεβίζοντι Wilamowitz   πριαμίδα L P : πριαμίδας l

Ελ.   ἰὼ Τροία τάλαινα,
δι᾽ ἔργ᾽ ἄνεργ᾽ ὄλλυσαι
μέλεά τ᾽ ἔτλας· τὰ δ᾽ ἐμὰ δῶρα
Κύπριδος ἔτεκε πολὺ μὲν αἷμα,
πολὺ δὲ δάκρυον· ἄχεά τ᾽ ἄχεσι,   365
δάκρυα δάκρυσιν ἔλαβε, πάθεα. . . .
ματέρες τε παῖδας ὄλεσαν,
ἀπὸ δὲ παρθένοι κόμας
ἔθεντο σύγγονοι νεκρῶν Σκαμάνδριον
ἀμφὶ Φρύγιον οἶδμα.

βοὰν βοὰν δ᾽ Ἑλλὰς   370
κελάδησε κἀνοτότυξεν,
ἐπὶ δὲ κρατὶ χέρας ἔθηκεν,
ὄνυχι δ᾽ ἁπαλόχροα γένυν
δεῦσε φονίαισι πλαγαῖς.

ὦ μάκαρ Ἀρκαδίᾳ ποτὲ παρθένε Καλλιστοῖ, Διὸς   375
ἃ λεχέων ἐπέβας τετραβάμοσι γυίοις,
ὡς πολὺ ματρὸς ἐμᾶς ἔλαχες πλέον,
ἁ μορφᾷ θηρῶν λαχνογυίων—
ὄμματι δ᾽ ἁβρῷ σχῆμα λεαίνεις—
ἐξαλλάξασ᾽ ἄχθεα λύπης·   380
ἅν τέ ποτ᾽ Ἄρτεμις ἐξεχορεύσατο
χρυσοκέρατ᾽ ἔλαφον Μέροπος Τιτανίδα κούραν
καλλοσύνας ἕνεκεν· τὸ δ᾽ ἐμὸν δέμας
ὤλεσεν ὤλεσε πέργαμα Δαρδανίας
ὀλομένους τ᾽ Ἀχαιούς.   385

364 Κύπριδος Ludv. Dindorf: Κύπρις L P   366 varie tentati :
fortasse sani lacuna post πάθεα posita   367 ὤλεσαν L P   370,
371 ἑλλὰς αἲ ἐκελάδησ᾽ ἀνωτότυξεν Paley (κἀνωτότυξεν p)   374 ἔδευσε
L P   375 Καλλιστοῖ del. Nauck, Δίων pro Διὸς scribens   376 γυίοις
L P : corr. l   377 μῦρος L P   378 λάχνα γυίων L P : corr.
Reiske   379 sic nos : ' sed vultu delicato formam mitigas ' : ὄμματι
λάβρῳ σχῆμα λεαίνῃς L P : versum del. Dingelstadt   380 ἄχθεα
Hermann : ἄχεα L P   381 ἐξεκορεύσατο Verrall   382 χρυσόκερω
(voluit χρυσόκερων) l   384 ὤλεσεν ὤλεσεν L P

ΜΕΝΕΛΕΩΣ

ὦ τὰς τεθρίππους Οἰνομάῳ Πῖσαν κάτα
Πέλοψ ἁμίλλας ἐξαμιλληθείς ποτε,
εἴθ' ὤφελες τόθ', ἡνίκ' ἔρανον εἰς θεοὺς
πεισθεὶς ἐποίεις, ἐν θεοῖς λιπεῖν βίον,
πρὶν τὸν ἐμὸν 'Ατρέα πατέρα γεννῆσαί ποτε,   390
ὃς ἐξέφυσεν 'Αερόπης λέκτρων ἄπο
'Αγαμέμνον' ἐμέ τε Μενέλεων, κλεινὸν ζυγόν·
πλεῖστον γὰρ οἶμαι—καὶ τόδ' οὐ κόμπῳ λέγω—
στράτευμα κώπῃ διορίσαι Τροίαν ἔπι,
τύραννος οὐδὲν πρὸς βίαν στρατηλατῶν,   395
ἑκοῦσι δ' ἄρξας Ἑλλάδος νεανίαις.
καὶ τοὺς μὲν οὐκέτ' ὄντας ἀριθμῆσαι πάρα,
τοὺς δ' ἐκ θαλάσσης ἀσμένους πεφευγότας,
νεκρῶν φέροντας ὀνόματ' εἰς οἴκους πάλιν.
ἐγὼ δ' ἐπ' οἶδμα πόντιον γλαυκῆς ἁλὸς   400
τλήμων ἀλῶμαι χρόνον ὅσονπερ 'Ιλίου
πύργους ἔπερσα, κἀς πάτραν χρῄζων μολεῖν
οὐκ ἀξιοῦμαι τοῦδε πρὸς θεῶν τυχεῖν.
Λιβύης τ' ἐρήμους ἀξένους τ' ἐπιδρομὰς
πέπλευκα πάσας· χὤταν ἐγγὺς ὦ πάτρας,   405
πάλιν μ' ἀπωθεῖ πνεῦμα, κοὔποτ' οὔριον
ἐσῆλθε λαῖφος ὥστε μ' ἐς πάτραν μολεῖν.
καὶ νῦν τάλας ναυαγὸς ἀπολέσας φίλους
ἐξέπεσον ἐς γῆν τήνδε· ναῦς δὲ πρὸς πέτρας
πολλοὺς ἀριθμοὺς ἄγνυται ναυαγίων.   410
τρόπις δ' ἐλείφθη ποικίλων ἁρμοσμάτων,
ἐφ' ἧς ἐσώθην μόλις ἀνελπίστῳ τύχῃ
Ἑλένη τε, Τροίας ἣν ἀποσπάσας ἔχω.

388-9 suspecti   392 μενέλεω L P: corr. l   402 καὶ εἰς
L P   404 Λιβύης δ' Hermann   406 καὶ οὔποτ' L: κοὔποτ'
L² P   408 ἀπώλεσας P   411 ἐλήφθη L P: corr. Stephanus
412 ἧς apogr. Flor. (Laur. xxxi, 1): οἷς L P, sed in rasura scr. L
vel L²

ὄνομα δὲ χώρας ἥτις ἥδε καὶ λεὼς
οὐκ οἶδα· ὄχλον γὰρ ἐσπεσεῖν ᾐσχυνόμην   415
ὥσθ᾽ ἱστορῆσαι, τὰς ἐμὰς δυσχλαινίας
κρύπτων ὑπ᾽ αἰδοῦς τῆς τύχης.   ὅταν δ᾽ ἀνὴρ
πράξῃ κακῶς ὑψηλός, εἰς ἀηθίαν
πίπτει κακίω τοῦ πάλαι δυσδαίμονος.
χρεία δὲ τείρει μ᾽· οὔτε γὰρ σῖτος πάρα   420
οὔτ᾽ ἀμφὶ χρῶτ᾽ ἐσθῆτες· αὐτὰ δ᾽ εἰκάσαι
πάρεστι ναὸς ἐκβόλοις ἃ ἀμπίσχομαι.
πέπλους δὲ τοὺς πρὶν λαμπρά τ᾽ ἀμφιβλήματα
χλιδάς τε πόντος ἥρπασ᾽· ἐν δ᾽ ἄντρου μυχοῖς
κρύψας γυναῖκα τὴν κακῶν πάντων ἐμοὶ   425
ἄρξασαν ἥκω τούς τε περιλελειμμένους
φίλων φυλάσσειν τἄμ᾽ ἀναγκάσας λέχη.
μόνος δὲ νοστῶ, τοῖς ἐκεῖ ζητῶν φίλοις
τὰ πρόσφορ᾽ ἤν πως ἐξερευνήσας λάβω.
ἰδὼν δὲ δῶμα περιφερὲς θριγκοῖς τόδε   430
πύλας τε σεμνὰς ἀνδρὸς ὀλβίου τινός,
προσῆλθον· ἐλπὶς δ᾽ ἔκ γε πλουσίων δόμων
λαβεῖν τι ναύταις· ἐκ δὲ μὴ ἐχόντων βίον—
οὐδ᾽ εἰ θέλοιεν, ὠφελεῖν ἔχοιεν ἄν.
ὠή· τίς ἂν πυλωρὸς ἐκ δόμων μόλοι,   435
ὅστις διαγγείλειε τἄμ᾽ ἔσω κακά;

ΓΡΑΥΣ

τίς πρὸς πύλαισιν; οὐκ ἀπαλλάξῃ δόμων
καὶ μὴ πρὸς αὐλείοισιν ἑστηκὼς πύλαις
ὄχλον παρέξεις δεσπόταις; ἢ κατθανῇ
Ἕλλην πεφυκώς, οἷσιν οὐκ ἐπιστροφαί.   440

414 λεὼ Nauck   415 οἶδα L P   416 del. Dindorf   417 τῆς
τύχης Arnim : τὰς τύχας L P : maluit Nauck τῆς ἐμῆς v. 416 scribere
420 χρεία l : χεῖρα P et sine dubio L   σῖτος Musgrave : σῖτα L P :
σῖτον l   421 αὐτὸ Badham   422 ἃ ἀμπίσχομαι Herwerden :
ἀμπίσχομαι L P   426 τε Hermann : γε L P   430 ἰδὼ P : ἴδω p
432 γε Reiske : τε L P   433 οἱ δὲ μὴ ἔχοντες Wecklein   434
virgulam post ὠφελεῖν habent L P : ὠφελεῖν, ἔχοιμεν Paley   436 εἴσω
L P   438 θύραις Blaydes

2*

Με. ὦ γραῖα, ταῦτα, ταῦτ'· ἐπεὶ καλῶς λέγεις.

ἔξεστι, πείσομαι γάρ· ἀλλ' ἄνες λόγον.

Γρ. ἄπελθ'· ἐμοὶ γὰρ τοῦτο πρόσκειται, ξένε,

μηδένα πελάζειν τοισίδ' Ἑλλήνων δόμοις.

Με. ἆ· μὴ προσείλει χεῖρα μηδ' ὤθει βίᾳ.   445

Γρ. πείθῃ γὰρ οὐδὲν ὧν λέγω, σὺ δ' αἴτιος.

Με. ἄγγειλον εἴσω δεσπόταισι τοῖσι σοῖς. . . .

Γρ. πικρῶς ἄρ' οἶμαί γ' ἀγγελεῖν τοὺς σοὺς λόγους.

Με. ναυαγὸς ἥκω ξένος, ἀσύλητον γένος.

Γρ. οἶκον πρὸς ἄλλον νύν τιν' ἀντὶ τοῦδ' ἴθι.   450

Με. οὔκ, ἀλλ' ἔσω πάρειμι· καὶ σύ μοι πιθοῦ.

Γρ. ὀχληρὸς ἴσθ' ὤν· καὶ τάχ' ὠσθήσῃ βίᾳ.

Με. αἰαῖ· τὰ κλεινὰ ποῦ 'στί μοι στρατεύματα;

Γρ. οὐκοῦν ἐκεῖ που σεμνὸς ἦσθ', οὐκ ἐνθάδε.

Με. ὦ δαῖμον, ὡς ἀνάξι' ἠτιμώμεθα.   455

Γρ. τί βλέφαρα τέγγεις δάκρυσι; πρὸς τίν' οἰκτρὸς εἶ;

Με. πρὸς τὰς πάροιθεν συμφορὰς εὐδαίμονας.

Γρ. οὔκουν ἀπελθὼν δάκρυα σοῖς δώσεις φίλοις;

Με. τίς δ' ἥδε χώρα; τοῦ δὲ βασίλειοι δόμοι;

Γρ. Πρωτεὺς τάδ' οἰκεῖ δώματ', Αἴγυπτος δὲ γῆ.   460

Με. Αἴγυπτος; ὦ δύστηνος, οἶ πέπλευκ' ἄρα.

Γρ. τί δὴ τὸ Νείλου μεμπτόν ἐστί σοι γάνος;

Με. οὐ τοῦτ' ἐμέμφθην· τὰς ἐμὰς στένω τύχας.

Γρ. πολλοὶ κακῶς πράσσουσιν, οὐ σὺ δὴ μόνος.

Με. ἔστ' οὖν ἐν οἴκοις ὅντιν' ὀνομάζεις ἄναξ;   465

---

441 ἐπεὶ scripsi : ἔπη L P   κάλλως λέγειν ἔξεστι Herwerden
444 τοῖσι* P : τοῖσιν p   445 sq. post 452 trai. Schenkl
445 προσείλει L (et rescripsit l) P : γρ. πρόσαγε in marg. p : πρόσειε
Matthiae, cl. Her. 1218   446 σὺ δ' αἴτιος· πείθῃ γὰρ οὐδὲν ὧν λέγω
Dobree   447–483 paragraphi praef. in L : 447–476 in P   448
ἄρ' Hermann : ἂν L P : versus varie tentatus : ἂν ᾤμην Wecklein :
σοὺς ἀπαγγεῖλαι λόγους Nauck   450 νῦν L P   452 ἴσθ'] οἶσθ'
in ras. p   458 σώσεις Bruhn   460 Πρωτέως τάδ' ἐστὶ μέλαθρα Ar.
Thesm. 874 : Πρωτέως τάδ' ἐστὶ δώματ' Kirchhoff   461 οἶ πεπλώκαμεν
Ar. Thesm. 878, unde πέπλωκ' hic Paley; cf. 532   462 μεμπτόν P :
μεπτόν L   γάνος] γένος Musurus ex apogr. Paris.

Γρ. τόδ᾿ ἐστὶν αὐτοῦ μνῆμα, παῖς δ᾿ ἄρχει χθονός.

Με. ποῦ δῆτ᾿ ἂν εἴη; πότερον ἐκτὸς ἢ ᾿ν δόμοις;

Γρ. οὐκ ἔνδον· Ἕλλησιν δὲ πολεμιώτατος.

Με. τίν᾿ αἰτίαν σχὼν ἧς ἐπηυρόμην ἐγώ;

Γρ. Ἑλένη κατ᾿ οἴκους ἐστὶ τούσδ᾿ ἡ τοῦ Διός.   470

Με. πῶς φῄς; τίν᾿ εἶπας μῦθον; αὖθίς μοι φράσον.

Γρ. ἡ Τυνδαρὶς παῖς, ἣ κατὰ Σπάρτην ποτ᾿ ἦν.

Με. πόθεν μολοῦσα; τίνα τὸ πρᾶγμ᾿ ἔχει λόγον;

Γρ. Λακεδαίμονος γῆς δεῦρο νοστήσασ᾿ ἄπο.

Με. πότε; οὔ τί που λελήσμεθ᾿ ἐξ ἄντρων λέχος;   475

Γρ. πρὶν τοὺς Ἀχαιούς, ὦ ξέν᾿, ἐς Τροίαν μολεῖν.

ἀλλ᾿ ἕρπ᾿ ἀπ᾿ οἴκων· ἔστι γάρ τις ἐν δόμοις
τύχη, τύραννος ᾗ ταράσσεται δόμος.
καιρὸν γὰρ οὐδέν᾿ ἦλθες· ἢν δὲ δεσπότης
λάβῃ σε, θάνατος ξένιά σοι γενήσεται.   480
εὔνους γάρ εἰμ᾿ Ἕλλησιν, οὐχ ὅσον πικροὺς
λόγους ἔδωκα δεσπότην φοβουμένη.

Με. τί φῶ; τί λέξω; συμφορὰς γὰρ ἀθλίας
ἐκ τῶν πάροιθεν τὰς παρεστώσας κλύω,
εἰ τὴν μὲν αἱρεθεῖσαν ἐκ Τροίας ἄγων   485
ἥκω δάμαρτα καὶ κατ᾿ ἄντρα σῴζεται,
ὄνομα δὲ ταὐτὸν τῆς ἐμῆς ἔχουσά τις
δάμαρτος ἄλλη τοισίδ᾿ ἐνναίει δόμοις.
Διὸς δ᾿ ἔλεξε παῖδά νιν πεφυκέναι.
ἀλλ᾿ ἦ τις ἔστι Ζηνὸς ὄνομ᾿ ἔχων ἀνὴρ   490
Νείλου παρ᾿ ὄχθας; εἷς γὰρ ὅ γε κατ᾿ οὐρανόν.
Σπάρτη δὲ ποῦ γῆς ἐστι πλὴν ἵνα ῥοαὶ
τοῦ καλλιδόνακός εἰσιν Εὐρώτα μόνον;

466 μνῆμα] σῆμα Ar. Thesm. 886   474 γῆς p et Victorius :
τοῖς L P sed ἧς suprascr. L²   475 πότε L P   ἄντρω P   λέχος
Heath : λέχους L P   477 ἐν δόμοις] ἐμποδὼν Wecklein : ἐνθάδε
Herwerden ob v. sequentem   479 οὐδὲν L P : corr. Musgrave
484 τὰς L² P : τὼ L   488 δάμαρ δ᾿ ἔτ᾿ ἄλλη versu 487 deleto Vitelli
τοισίδ᾿] τοῖσιν p   491 ὅτε in ὅ γε mut. ut videtur L P   492
σπάρτης P   ἵνα Matthiae : ἵν᾿ αἱ L P

ἁπλοῦν δὲ Τυνδάρειον ὄνομα κλῄζεται.
Λακεδαίμονος δὲ γαῖα τίς ξυνώνυμος   495
Τροίας τε; ἐγὼ μὲν οὐκ ἔχω τί χρὴ λέγειν.
πολλοὶ γάρ, ὡς εἴξασιν, ἐν πολλῇ χθονὶ
ὀνόματα ταῦτ᾽ ἔχουσι καὶ πόλις πόλει
γυνὴ γυναικί τ᾽· οὐδὲν οὖν θαυμαστέον.
οὐδ᾽ αὖ τὸ δεινὸν προσπόλου φευξούμεθα·   500
ἀνὴρ γὰρ οὐδεὶς ὧδε βάρβαρος φρένας,
ὃς ὄνομ᾽ ἀκούσας τοὐμὸν οὐ δώσει βοράν.
κλεινὸν τὸ Τροίας πῦρ ἐγώ θ᾽ ὃς ἧψά νιν,
Μενέλαος, οὐκ ἄγνωστος ἐν πάσῃ χθονί.
δόμων ἄνακτα προσμενῶ· δισσὰς δέ μοι   505
ἔχει φυλάξεις· ἢν μὲν ὠμόφρων τις ᾖ,
κρύψας ἐμαυτὸν εἶμι πρὸς ναυάγια·
ἢν δ᾽ ἐνδιδῷ τι μαλθακόν, τὰ πρόσφορα
τῆς νῦν παρούσης συμφορᾶς αἰτήσομαι.
κακῶν μὲν ἡμῖν ἔσχατον τοῖς ἀθλίοις,   510
ἄλλους τυράννους αὐτὸν ὄντα βασιλέα
βίον προσαιτεῖν· ἀλλ᾽ ἀναγκαίως ἔχει.
λόγος γάρ ἐστιν οὐκ ἐμός, σοφὸν δ᾽ ἔπος,
δεινῆς ἀνάγκης οὐδὲν ἰσχύειν πλέον.

ΧΟΡΟΣ

   ἤκουσα τᾶς θεσπιῳδοῦ κόρας,   515
   ἃ χρῄζουσ᾽ ἐφάνη τυράννοις
   δόμοις, ὡς Μενέλαος οὔπω μελαμφαὲς οἴχεται
   δι᾽ ἔρεβος χθονὶ κρυφθείς,

494 διπλοῦν... κλῄζεται; Nauck   496 Τροίας τε L P   498 ταῦτ᾽
L P   504 seclusit Cobet   505–506 δισσὰς... ἔχει Musgrave:
ἔχει... δισσὰς L P   507 κρύψας Badham   509 ταῖς νῦν παρούσαις
συμφοραῖς Reiske: τῇ νῦν παρούσῃ συμφορᾷ σφ᾽ Hermann   510 κακὸν ἢ
μὲν Paley: δέ θ᾽ L P: δ᾽ ἔθ᾽ Hartung: δέ γ᾽ Lenting   τοῖς] τόδ᾽
Wilamowitz   513 σοφὸν L P: σοφῶν l   514 ἰσχύειν l vel L²:
ἰσχύει L P   516 χρήσασ᾽ Dindorf: ⟨ἄνασσ᾽⟩ ἃ χρῄζουσ᾽ Wilamowitz
ἐφάνη l, unde ἐφάνη ᾽ν Badham

ἀλλ' ἔτι κατ' οἶδμ' ἅλιον   520
τρυχόμενος οὔπω λιμένων
ψαύσειεν πατρίας γᾶς,
ἀλατείᾳ βιότου
ταλαίφρων, ἄφιλος φίλων,
παντοδαπᾶς †ἐπὶ γᾶς† πόδα   525
χριμπτόμενος εἰναλίῳ
κώπᾳ Τρῳάδος ἐκ γᾶς.

Ελ. ἥδ' αὖ τάφου τοῦδ' εἰς ἕδρας ἐγὼ πάλιν
στείχω, μαθοῦσα Θεονόης φίλους λόγους,
ἣ πάντ' ἀληθῶς οἶδε· φησὶ δ' ἐν φάει   530
πόσιν τὸν ἀμὸν ζῶντα φέγγος εἰσορᾶν,
πορθμοὺς δ' ἀλᾶσθαι μυρίους πεπλωκότα
ἐκεῖσε κἀκεῖσ' οὐδ' ἀγύμναστον πλάνοις,
ἥξειν ⟨δ'⟩ ὅταν δὴ πημάτων λάβῃ τέλος.
ἐν δ' οὐκ ἔλεξεν, εἰ μολὼν σωθήσεται.   535
ἐγὼ δ' ἀπέστην τοῦτ' ἐρωτῆσαι σαφῶς,
ἡσθεῖσ' ἐπεί νιν εἶπέ μοι σεσῳσμένον.
ἐγγὺς δέ νίν που τῆσδ' ἔφασκ' εἶναι χθονός,
ναναγὸν ἐκπεσόντα σὺν παύροις φίλοις.
ὤμοι, πόθ' ἥξεις; ὡς ποθεινὸς ἂν μόλοις.   540
    ἔα, τίς οὗτος; οὔ τί που κρυπτεύομαι
Πρωτέως ἀσέπτου παιδὸς ἐκ βουλευμάτων;
οὐχ ὡς δρομαία πῶλος ἢ Βάκχη θεοῦ
τάφῳ ξυνάψω κῶλον; ἄγριος δέ τις
μορφὴν ὅδ' ἐστίν, ὅς με θηρᾶται λαβεῖν.   545
Με. σὲ τὴν ὄρεγμα δεινὸν ἡμιλλημένην
    τύμβου 'πὶ κρηπῖδ' ἐμπύρους τ' ὀρθοστάτας,

525 sq. nondum emendati   526 ἐναλίῳ L P   532 πεπλευκότα
Matthiae, sed cf. ad 461   533 ἐκεῖσ'ἐκεῖσε L : ἐκεῖσ' ἐκεῖσ' P : corr.
Canter   534 δ' add. Wilamowitz   540 ὤμοι Dobree : ὥς μοι
L P   542 πρωτέως L² P : πρωτέος L   544 ἄγριός γέ τις
Kirchhoff

μεῖνον· τί φεύγεις; ὡς δέμας δείξασα σὸν
ἔκπληξιν ἡμῖν ἀφασίαν τε προστίθης

Ελ. ἀδικούμεθ', ὦ γυναῖκες· εἰργόμεσθα γὰρ   550
τάφου πρὸς ἀνδρὸς τοῦδε, καί μ' ἑλὼν θέλει
δοῦναι τυράννοις ὧν ἐφεύγομεν γάμους.

Με. οὐ κλῶπές ἐσμεν, οὐχ ὑπηρέται κακῶν.

Ελ. καὶ μὴν στολήν γ' ἄμορφον ἀμφὶ σῶμ' ἔχεις.

Με. στῆσον, φόβου μεθεῖσα, λαιψηρὸν πόδα.   555

Ελ. ἵστημ', ἐπεί γε τοῦδ' ἐφάπτομαι τόπου.

Με. τίς εἶ; τίν' ὄψιν σήν, γύναι, προσδέρκομαι;

Ελ. σὺ δ' εἶ τίς; αὐτὸς γὰρ σὲ κἄμ' ἔχει λόγος.

Με. οὐπώποτ' εἶδον προσφερέστερον δέμας.

Ελ. ὦ θεοί· θεὸς γὰρ καὶ τὸ γιγνώσκειν φίλους.   560

⟨Με. Ἑλληνὶς εἶ τις ἢ ἐπιχωρία γυνή;⟩

Ελ. Ἑλληνίς· ἀλλὰ καὶ τὸ σὸν θέλω μαθεῖν.

Με. Ἑλένῃ σ' ὁμοίαν δὴ μάλιστ' εἶδον, γύναι.

Ελ. ἐγὼ δὲ Μενέλεῳ γε σέ· οὐδ' ἔχω τί φῶ.

Με. ἔγνως γὰρ ὀρθῶς ἄνδρα δυστυχέστατον.   565

Ελ. ὦ χρόνιος ἐλθὼν σῆς δάμαρτος ἐς χέρας.

Με. ποίας δάμαρτος; μὴ θίγῃς ἐμῶν πέπλων.

Ελ. ἥν σοι δίδωσι Τυνδάρεως, ἐμὸς πατήρ.

Με. ὦ φωσφόρ' Ἑκάτη, πέμπε φάσματ' εὐμενῆ.

Ελ. οὐ νυκτίφαντον πρόπολον Ἐνοδίας μ' ὁρᾷς.   570

Με. οὐ μὴν γυναικῶν γ' εἷς δυοῖν ἔφυν πόσις.

Ελ. ποίων δὲ λέκτρων δεσπότης ἄλλων ἔφυς;

Με. ἦν ἄντρα κεύθει κἀκ Φρυγῶν κομίζομαι.

Ελ. οὐκ ἔστιν ἄλλη σή τις ἀντ' ἐμοῦ γυνή.

549 προστιθεὶς fere codd.   553-594 paragraphi praef. in L P
555 φόβον Valckenaer   556 τάφου Elmsley   557 ὦ θεοί, τίν' ὄψιν
εἰσορῶ ; τίς εἶ, γύναι; Ar. Thesm. 905   558 αὐτὸς L P   λόγος L
p Ar. Thesm. 906 : λόγου P   561 om. L P : restituit ex Ar. Thesm.
907 Markland   564 Μενέλεῳ Dindorf : μενελάῳ L P et codd. Ar.
Thesm. 910   σέ L P : σ' p   οὐδ' L : οὐκ P   565 γὰρ L P :
ἄρ' codd. Ar. Thesm. 911   566 ἐς hic L P   570-589 versuum
ordinem alii aliter mutaverunt ut 572 sq. post 581 sequerentur
570 πρόσπολον L P : corr. Canter   571 δυοῖν L : δυῖεν L² P

Με. οὔ που φρονῶ μὲν εὖ, τὸ δ' ὄμμα μου νοσεῖ;   575
Ελ. οὐ γάρ με λεύσσων σὴν δάμαρθ' ὁρᾶν δοκεῖς;
Με. τὸ σῶμ' ὅμοιον, τὸ δὲ σαφές μ' ἀποστερεῖ.
Ελ. σκέψαι· τί σοὔνδεῖ; τίς δὲ σοῦ σοφώτερος;
Με. ἔοικας· οὔτοι τοῦτό γ' ἐξαρνήσομαι.
Ελ. τίς οὖν διδάξει σ' ἄλλος ἢ τὰ σ' ὄμματα;   580
Με. ἐκεῖ νοσοῦμεν, ὅτι δάμαρτ' ἄλλην ἔχω.
Ελ. οὐκ ἦλθον ἐς γῆν Τρῳάδ', ἀλλ' εἴδωλον ἦν.
Με. καὶ τίς βλέποντα σώματ' ἐξεργάζεται;
Ελ. αἰθήρ, ὅθεν σὺ θεοπόνητ' ἔχεις λέχη.
Με. τίνος πλάσαντος θεῶν; ἄελπτα γὰρ λέγεις.   585
Ελ. Ἥρας, διάλλαγμ', ὡς Πάρις με μὴ λάβοι.
Με. πῶς οὖν ἂν ἐνθάδ' ἦσθά ⟨τ'⟩ ἐν Τροίᾳ θ' ἅμα;
Ελ. τοὔνομα γένοιτ' ἂν πολλαχοῦ, τὸ σῶμα δ' οὔ.
Με. μέθες με, λύπης ἅλις ἔχων ἐλήλυθα.
Ελ. λείψεις γὰρ ἡμᾶς, τὰ δὲ κέν' ἐξάξεις λέχη;   590
Με. καὶ χαῖρέ γ', Ἑλένῃ προσφερὴς ὁθούνεκ' εἶ.
Ελ. ἀπωλόμην· λαβοῦσά σ' οὐχ ἕξω πόσιν.
Με. τοὐκεῖ με μέγεθος τῶν πόνων πείθει, σὺ δ' οὔ.
Ελ. οἲ ἐγώ· τίς ἡμῶν ἐγένετ' ἀθλιωτέρα;
οἱ φίλτατοι λείπουσί μ' οὐδ' ἀφίξομαι   595
Ἕλληνας οὐδὲ πατρίδα τὴν ἐμήν ποτε.

ΑΓΓΕΛΟΣ

Μενέλαε, μαστευων σε κιγχάνω μόλις
πᾶσαν πλανηθεὶς τήνδε βάρβαρον χθόνα,
πεμφθεὶς ἑταίρων τῶν λελειμμένων ὕπο.

575 οὔπου L P : ἦ που lp   578 σοὔνδεῖ Seidler : σου δεῖ L P
δὲ Fix : ἔστι L P : τὰ σ' οὐδείς ἐστι Elmsley   τί σοι δεῖ πίστεως
σαφεστέρας ; Badham   580 τὰ σ' p rasura post σ' facta : τὰ σὰ γ'
L (sic)   581 ἐκεῖνο σοῦ μὲν L P : corr. Scaliger   585 ἄελπτα L :
εὔελπτα P   586 Ἥρας Scaliger : ἥρα L P   λάβοι] λάβῃ primitus P
587 ἂν] ἅμ' anonymus   ἦσθά τ' Barnes : ἦσθ' L P : ἦσθας Nauck :
cf. Menand. Discept. 156, Her. 10   589 λύπης Elmsley : λύπας L P
592 ἀπολόμην P   σ' L² P : σε L   595 λείπουσί μ' Musgrave :
λείπουσιν L P   597 κιχάνω L P : corr. Matthiae

Με. τί δ᾽ ἔστιν; οὔ που βαρβάρων συλᾶσθ᾽ ὕπο;　　　600

Αγ. θαῦμ᾽ ἔστ᾽, ἔλασσον τοὔνομ᾽ ἢ τὸ πρᾶγμ᾽ ἔχον.

Με. λέγ᾽· ὡς φέρεις τι τῇδε τῇ σπουδῇ νέον.

Αγ. λέγω πόνους σε μυρίους τλῆναι μάτην.

Με. παλαιὰ θρηνεῖς πήματ᾽· ἀγγέλλεις δὲ τί;

Αγ. βέβηκεν ἄλοχος σὴ πρὸς αἰθέρος πτυχὰς　　　605
　　ἀρθεῖσ᾽ ἄφαντος· οὐρανῷ δὲ κρύπτεται
　　λιποῦσα σεμνὸν ἄντρον οὗ σφ᾽ ἐσῴζομεν,
　　τοσόνδε λέξασ᾽· Ὦ ταλαίπωροι Φρύγες
　　πάντες τ᾽ Ἀχαιοί, δι᾽ ἔμ᾽ ἐπὶ Σκαμανδρίοις
　　ἀκταῖσιν Ἥρας μηχαναῖς ἐθνῄσκετε,　　　610
　　δοκοῦντες Ἑλένην οὐκ ἔχοντ᾽ ἔχειν Πάριν.
　　ἐγὼ δ᾽, ἐπειδὴ χρόνον ἔμειν᾽ ὅσον με χρῆν,
　　τὸ μόρσιμον σώσασα, πατέρ᾽ ἐς οὐρανὸν
　　ἄπειμι· φήμας δ᾽ ἡ τάλαινα Τυνδαρὶς
　　ἄλλως κακὰς ἤκουσεν οὐδὲν αἰτία.　　　615
　　　　ὦ χαῖρε, Λήδας θύγατερ, ἐνθάδ᾽ ἦσθ᾽ ἄρα;
　　ἐγὼ δέ σ᾽ ἄστρων ὡς βεβηκυῖαν μυχοὺς
　　ἤγγελλον εἰδὼς οὐδὲν ὡς ὑπόπτερον
　　δέμας φοροίης.　οὐκ ἐῶ σε κερτομεῖν
　　ἡμᾶς τόδ᾽ αὖθις, ὡς ἅδην ἐν Ἰλίῳ　　　620
　　πόνους παρεῖχες σῷ πόσει καὶ συμμάχοις.

Με. τοῦτ᾽ ἔστ᾽ ἐκεῖνο· ξυμβεβᾶσιν οἱ λόγοι
　　οἱ τῆσδ᾽ ἀληθεῖς. ὦ ποθεινὸς ἡμέρα,
　　ἥ σ᾽ εἰς ἐμὰς ἔδωκεν ὠλένας λαβεῖν.

Ελ. ὦ φίλτατ᾽ ἀνδρῶν Μενέλεως, ὁ μὲν χρόνος　　　625
　　παλαιός, ἡ δὲ τέρψις ἀρτίως πάρα.
　　　　ἔλαβον ἀσμένα πόσιν ἐμόν, φίλαι,

600 οὔπου L P : ἢ που l　　601 θαῦμ᾽ ἔστ᾽ Scaliger : θαυμά ᾽στ L :
θαυμάστ᾽ P　　ἔχον p : ἔχων L P　　602-605 paragraphi praef. in L P
602 φέρῃς P　　605 πτύχας L P　　607 λιποῦσ᾽ ἐρεμνὸν Schneidewin
612 μ᾽ ἐχρῆν L P　　617 βεβηκυίης l ut videtur　　621 σῷ
Milton : ᾧ L P　　623 τοῖς τῆσδ᾽ ἀληθῶς Herwerden　　624 ἥ σ᾽
Canter : ὡς L P

περί τ' ἐπέτασα χέρα
φίλιον ἐν μακρᾷ φλογὶ φαεσφόρῳ.

Με. κἀγὼ σέ· πολλοὺς δ' ἐν μέσῳ λόγους ἔχων   630
οὐκ οἶδ' ὁποίου πρῶτον ἄρξωμαι τὰ νῦν.

Ελ. γέγηθα, κρατὶ δ' ὀρθίους ἐθείρας
ἀνεπτέρωκα καὶ δάκρυ σταλάσσω,
περὶ δὲ γυῖα χέρας ἔβαλον, ἡδονάν,
ὦ πόσις, ὡς λάβω.   635

Με. ὦ φιλτάτη πρόσοψις, οὐκ ἐμέμφθην·
ἔχω τὰ τῆς Διός τε λέκτρα Λήδας θ',
ἂν ὑπὸ λαμπάδων κόροι λεύκιπποι
ξυννομαίμονες ὤλβισαν ὤλβισαν   640
τὸ πρόσθεν, ἐκ δόμων δὲ νοσφίσας σ' ἐμοῦ
πρὸς ἄλλαν ἐλαύνει
θεὸς συμφορὰν τάσδε κρείσσω.
τὸ κακὸν δ' ἀγαθὸν σέ τε κἀμὲ συνάγαγε, πόσιν
χρόνιον, ἀλλ' ὅμως ὀναίμαν τύχας.   645

Χο. ὄναιο δῆτα.   ταὐτὰ δὴ ξυνεύχυμαι·
δυοῖν γὰρ ὄντοιν οὐχ ὁ μὲν τλήμων, ὁ δ' οὔ.

Ελ. φίλαι φίλαι, τὰ πάρος οὐκέτι
στένομεν οὐδ' ἀλγῶ.
πόσιν ἐμὸν ἔχομεν [ἔχομεν,] ὃν [ἔμενον]

628 περί τ' ἐπέτασα Hermann : περιπετάσασα L P   χέρα L¹ vel L², sed α super rasuram scripto   630–683 paragraphi pro personarum notis in L, excepto 656 Ελ.   631 ἄρξομαι L P : corr. Hermann   633 δάκρυ] δάρυ P   634 χεῖρας L P   635 ὡς λάβω ὦ πόσις L P, trai. Elmsley   636 verba ὦ φιλτάτη πρόσοψις Helenae continuant L P : corr. Reisig   637 τῆς Schaefer : τοῦ L P   Διός τε Reisig : διὸς L P   λήδας τε L P : τὰ τῆς Λήδας Διός τε λέκτρα Wilamowitz, ne in catalectico elideretur   641 δὲ νοσφίσας Elmsley : δ' ἐνόσφισαν θεοί L P, cf. v. sequentem   σ' ἐμοῦ Portus : σ' ὁμοῦ L P   642 ἄλλαν Elmsley : ἄλλαν δ' L P   644 Helenae tribuit Hermann   συνάγαγε πόσιν L P : συνάγαγεν, ὦ πόσι Dindorf 646 Χο. Wilamowitz : Με. Tyrwhitt : Helenae tribuunt L P   ταὐτὰ (sic) ut videtur L : ταῦτα P   647 δυοῖν lp (vel L² P²) : δυεῖν L P 648 Ελ. notam erasam in L om. P   650 aut uncis inclusa dele aut ἐμὸν cum Seidlero duplica : χρόνον post Τροίας addebat Blass ex Bacch. Introd. Mus. p. 25 ἔνατος δὲ δόχμιος . . . οἷον ἔμμεν ἐκ Τροίας χρόνον

ἔμενον ἐκ Τροίας πολυετῆ μολεῖν.　　651

Με. ἔχεις, ἐγώ τε σέ· ἡλίους δὲ μυρίους
μόλις διελθὼν ᾐσθόμην τὰ τῆς θεοῦ.
ἐμὰ δὲ χαρμονὰ δάκρυα· πλέον ἔχει
χάριτος ἢ λύπας.　　655

Ελ. τί φῶ; τίς ἂν τάδ' ἤλπισεν βροτῶν ποτε;
ἀδόκητον ἔχω σε πρὸς στέρνοις.

Με. κἀγὼ σὲ τὴν δοκοῦσαν Ἰδαίαν πόλιν
μολεῖν Ἰλίου τε μελέους πύργους.
πρὸς θεῶν, δόμων πῶς τῶν ἐμῶν ἀπεστάλης;　　660

Ελ. ἒ ἔ· πικρὰς ἐς ἀρχὰς βαίνεις,
ἒ ἔ· πικρὰν δ' ἐρευνᾷς φάτιν.

Με. λέγ'· ὡς ἀκουστὰ πάντα δῶρα δαιμόνων.

Ελ. ἀπέπτυσα μὲν λόγον, οἷον οἷον ἐσοίσομαι.

Με. ὅμως δὲ λέξον· ἡδύ τοι μόχθων κλύειν.　　665

Ελ. οὐκ ἐπὶ βαρβάρου λέκτρα νεανία
πετομένας κώπας,
πετομένου δ' ἔρωτος ἀδίκων γάμων . .

Με. τίς ⟨γάρ⟩ σε δαίμων ἢ πότμος συλᾷ πάτρας;

Ελ. ὁ Διὸς ὁ Διός, ὦ πόσι, παῖς μ' . . .　　670
ἐπέλασεν Νείλῳ.

Με. θαυμαστά· τοῦ πέμψαντος; ὦ δεινοὶ λόγοι.

Ελ. κατεδάκρυσα καὶ βλέφαρον ὑγραίνω
δάκρυσιν· ἁ Διός μ' ἄλοχος ὤλεσεν.

Με. Ἥρα; τί νῷν χρῄζουσα προσθεῖναι κακόν;　　675

Ελ. ὤμοι ἐμῶν δεινῶν, λουτρῶν καὶ κρηνῶν,
ἵνα θεαὶ μορφὰν

652 ἔχεις μ' Jacobs　　δὲ] δὴ l　　654 δάκρυα χαρμονὰ L P (χαρμονᾶν l) : trai. Elmsley (χαρμονᾶν legens)　　656 τί φῶ om. P ἤλπισεν L : ἤλπισε L² P　　661 πικρὰς ἐς ἀρχὰς γρ. L : πικρὰν ἐς ἀρχὰν L P in textu　　665 τοι l : τι L P　　666 βαρβάρου λέκτρα post L. Dindorfium Kluge : λέκτρου βαρβάρου L P　　667 πετομένας lp : πετωμένας L P　　669 γάρ om. L P : add. Barnes　　670 παῖς μ'] με παῖς Ἑρμᾶς vel με παῖς Μαίας τ' Hermann　　671 ἐπέλασε L 673 φλέφαρον L : corr. L²　　675 Με. Ἥρα L P (paragraphum L) : Ἥρα. Μεν. l　　τί νῷν Hermann : τίνων L P　　676 ὤμοι Ἰδαίων Wilamowitz

ἐφαίδρυναν, ἔνθεν ἔμολεν κρίσις.

Με. τὰ δ' ἐς κρίσιν σοι τῶνδ' ἔθηχ' Ἥρα κακῶν . . .;

Ελ. Πάριν ὡς ἀφέλοιτο . . . Με. πῶς; αὔδα. 680

Ελ. Κύπρις ᾧ μ' ἐπένευσεν . . . Με. ὦ τλᾶμον.

Ελ. τλάμων, τλάμων· ὧδ' ἐπέλασ' Αἰγύπτῳ·

Με. εἶτ' ἀντέδωκ' εἴδωλον, ὡς σέθεν κλύω.

Ελ. τὰ δὲ ⟨σὰ⟩ κατὰ μέλαθρα πάθεα πάθεα, μᾶ-
τερ, οἲ 'γώ. Με. τί φής; 685

Ελ. οὐκ ἔστι μάτηρ· ἀγχόνιον δὲ βρόχον
δι' ἐμὰν κατεδήσατο δύσγαμος αἰσχύναν.

Με. ὤμοι· θυγατρὸς δ' Ἑρμιόνης ἔστιν βίος;

Ελ. ἄγαμος ἄτεκνος, ὦ πόσι, καταστένει
γάμον ἄγαμον ⟨ἐμόν⟩. 690

Με. ὦ πᾶν κατ' ἄκρας δῶμ' ἐμὸν πέρσας Πάρις,
τάδε καὶ σὲ διώλεσε μυριάδας τε
χαλκεόπλων Δαναῶν.

Ελ. ἐμὲ δὲ πατρίδος ἄπο κακόποτμον ἀραίαν
ἔβαλε θεὸς ἀπό ⟨τε⟩ πόλεος ἀπό τε σέθεν, 695
ὅτε μέλαθρα λέχεά τ' ἔλιπον—οὐ λιποῦσ'
ἐπ' αἰσχροῖς γάμοις.

Χο. εἰ καὶ τὰ λοιπὰ τῆς τύχης εὐδαίμονος
τύχοιτε, πρὸς τὰ πρόσθεν ἀρκέσειεν ἄν.

Αγ. Μενέλαε, κἀμοὶ πρόσδοτον τῆς ἡδονῆς, 700

678 ἔμολε L P   679 τάδ' L P   si lectio sana fractus est
sermo : supple αἰτίαν : τήνδ' et κακά Wilamowitz   680–681 Πάριν . . .
Κύπρις Reiske : κύπριν . . . πάριν L P : κύπρις . . . πάριν apogr.
Par. fortasse recte   681 ἐπένευσ' l   τλῆμον L P : corr. Musurus
682 τλάμονα τλαμόνως Kirchhoff   684 σὰ add. Hermann   685
Με. P : paragraphum L   687 ἐμὰν Duport : ἐμὲ L P : ἐμὲ et αἰσχύνᾳ
Hermann   688 ἔστιν l : ἔστι L P   689 ἄτεκνος semel l : bis L P
πόσι Musurus : πόσις L P   690 ἐμόν Hermann : αἰσχύνα L P
(αἰσχύναν l) ex 687   694 Helenae notam om. L P: hic add. l,
v. 692 male praef. P¹ vel p   695 ἔβαλλε L P : corr. apogr. Flor.
(Laur. xxxi, 1)   τε πόλεος Matthiae : πόλεος L P   696 ὅτε
Dobree : ὅτι L P   700 πρόσδοτον Cobet : πρόσδοτε L P : προσ-
δοτέα Elmsley

ἦν μανθάνω μὲν καὐτός, οὐ σαφῶς δ' ἔχω.

Με. ἀλλ', ὦ γεραιέ, καὶ σὺ κοινώνει λόγων.

Αγ. οὐχ ἥδε μόχθων τῶν ἐν Ἰλίῳ βραβεύς;

Με. οὐχ ἥδε, πρὸς θεῶν δ' ἦμεν ἠπατημένοι,
νεφέλης ἄγαλμ' ἔχοντες ἐν χεροῖν [λυγρόν].   705

Αγ.   τί φής;
νεφέλης ἄρ' ἄλλως εἴχομεν πόνους πέρι;

Με. Ἥρας τάδ' ἔργα καὶ θεῶν τρισσῶν ἔρις.

Αγ. ἡ δ' οὖσ' ἀληθῶς ἐστιν ἥδε σὴ δάμαρ;

Με. αὕτη· λόγοις [δ'] ἐμοῖσι πίστευσον τάδε.   710

Αγ. ὦ θύγατερ, ὁ θεὸς ὡς ἔφυ τι ποικίλον
καὶ δυστέκμαρτον. εὖ δέ πως πάντα στρέφει
ἐκεῖσε κἀκεῖσ' ἀναφέρων· ὁ μὲν πονεῖ,
ὁ δ' οὐ πονήσας αὖθις ὄλλυται κακῶς,
βέβαιον οὐδὲν τῆς ἀεὶ τύχης ἔχων.   715
σὺ γὰρ πόσις τε σὸς πόνων μετέσχετε,
σὺ μὲν λόγοισιν, ὁ δὲ δορὸς προθυμίᾳ.
σπεύδων δ' ὅτ' ἔσπευδ' οὐδὲν εἶχε· νῦν δ' ἔχει
αὐτόματα πράξας τἀγάθ' εὐτυχέστατα.
οὐκ ἄρα γέροντα πατέρα καὶ Διοσκόρω   720
ᾔσχυνας, οὐδ' ἔδρασας οἷα κλῄζεται.
νῦν ἀνανεοῦμαι τὸν σὸν ὑμέναιον πάλιν
καὶ λαμπάδων μεμνήμεθ' ἃς τετραόροις
ἵπποις τροχάζων παρέφερον· σὺ δ' ἐν δίφροις
ξὺν τῷδε νύμφη δῶμ' ἔλειπες ὄλβιον.   725
κακὸς γὰρ ὅστις μὴ σέβει τὰ δεσποτῶν
καὶ ξυγγέγηθε καὶ συνωδίνει κακοῖς.

701 μὲν καὶ αὐτὸς L : δὲ καὶ αὐτὸς P   704–711 paragraphi
praefixi in L : 704 Nuntio, 705 Menelao tribuit P   705 λυγρόν
seclusit Badham   706 ante τί φής deest paragraphus in L : τί φής
del. Matthiae   710 δ' seclusit Herwerden   711 σκέψαι γὰρ
ὁ θεὸς ὃς ἔχει τι ποικίλον Stob. Ecl. i. 7. 6   712 πως πάντα
στρέφει Herwerden : πως ἀναστρέφει L P : πάντ' ἀναστρέφει Schenkl
713 χ⟨ὢ⟩ μὲν Wilamowitz   717 δορὸς τρικυμίᾳ Bruhn   725 σὺν
L P   ἔλιπες L P

ἐγὼ μὲν εἴην, κεἰ πέφυχ' ὅμως λάτρις,
ἐν τοῖσι γενναίοισιν ἠριθμημένος
δούλοισι, τοὔνομ' οὐκ ἔχων ἐλεύθερον,   730
τὸν νοῦν δέ· κρεῖσσον γὰρ τόδ' ἢ δυοῖν κακοῖν
ἕν' ὄντα χρῆσθαι, τὰς φρένας τ' ἔχειν κακὰς
ἄλλων τ' ἀκούειν δοῦλον ὄντα τῶν πέλας.

Με. ἄγ', ὦ γεραιέ, πολλὰ μὲν παρ' ἀσπίδα
μοχθήματ' ἐξέπλησας ἐκπονῶν ἐμοί,   735
καὶ νῦν μετασχὼν τῆς ἐμῆς εὐπραξίας
ἄγγειλον ἐλθὼν τοῖς λελειμμένοις φίλοις
τάδ' ὡς ἔχονθ' ηὕρηκας οἵ τ' ἐσμὲν τύχης,
μένειν τ' ἐπ' ἀκταῖς τούς τ' ἐμοὺς καραδοκεῖν
ἀγῶνας οἳ μένουσί μ', ὡς ἐλπίζομεν,   740
κεἰ τήνδε πως δυναίμεθ' ἐκκλέψαι χθονός,
φρουρεῖν ὅπως ἂν εἰς ἓν ἐλθόντες τύχης
ἐκ βαρβάρων σωθῶμεν, ἢν δυνώμεθα.

Αγ. ἔσται τάδ', ὦναξ. ἀλλά τοι τὰ μάντεων
ἐσεῖδον ὡς φαῦλ' ἐστὶ καὶ ψευδῶν πλέα.   745
οὐδ' ἦν ἄρ' ὑγιὲς οὐδὲν ἐμπύρου φλογὸς
οὐδὲ πτερωτῶν φθέγματ'· εὔηθες δέ τοι
τὸ καὶ δοκεῖν ὄρνιθας ὠφελεῖν βροτούς.
Κάλχας γὰρ οὐκ εἶπ' οὐδ' ἐσήμηνε στρατῷ
νεφέλης ὑπερθνῄσκοντας εἰσορῶν φίλους   750
οὐδ' Ἕλενος, ἀλλὰ πόλις ἀνηρπάσθη μάτην.
εἴποις ἄν· Οὕνεχ' ὁ θεὸς οὐκ ἠβούλετο;
τί δῆτα μαντευόμεθα; τοῖς θεοῖσι χρὴ
θύοντας αἰτεῖν ἀγαθά, μαντείας δ' ἐᾶν·

728 κεἰ Musgrave : καὶ L P: εἰ Stob. fl. 62. 2   731 δυοῖν l :
δυεῖν L P   732 ἕν' l : ἓν L P   734 ἄγ'] ἀλλ' p   735 ἐκ
πόνων ἐμῶν L P : corr. Barnes   738 ἔχονθ' Stephanus : ἔχων L P
εὕρηκας L P   οἵ] οὗ Tyrwhitt   740 μένουσί μ' ὡς Musgrave :
μένουσιν οὓς L : μέλλουσιν οὓς P   741 κεἰ τήνδε πως Ludw. Dindorf :
καὶ τήνδε πῶς L P   ἐκκλέψαι p : ἐκπλέξαι L P   745 ἐσεῖδον hic
L P   747 οὐδὲ Kirchhoff : οὔτε L P   751 οὐδ' Ἕλενος Porson :
οὐδέν γε L : οὐδέν γ' P   752 εἴποι P   v. del. Cobet   753
μαντευόμεσθα L P

βίου γὰρ ἄλλως δέλεαρ ηὑρέθη τόδε,   755
κοὐδεὶς ἐπλούτησ' ἐμπύροισιν ἀργὸς ὤν·
γνώμη δ' ἀρίστη μάντις ἥ τ' εὐβουλία.

Χο. ἐς ταὐτὸ κἀμοὶ δόξα μαντειῶν πέρι
χωρεῖ γέροντι· τοὺς θεοὺς ἔχων τις ἂν
φίλους ἀρίστην μαντικὴν ἔχοι δόμοις.   760

Ελ. εἶέν· τὰ μὲν δὴ δεῦρ' ἀεὶ καλῶς ἔχει.
ὅπως δ' ἐσώθης, ὦ τάλας, Τροίας ἄπο,
κέρδος μὲν οὐδὲν εἰδέναι, πόθος δέ τις
τὰ τῶν φίλων φίλοισιν αἰσθέσθαι κακά.

Με. ἢ πόλλ' ἀνήρου μ' ἑνὶ λόγῳ μιᾷ θ' ὁδῷ.   765
τί σοι λέγοιμ' ἂν τὰς ἐν Αἰγαίῳ φθορὰς
τὰ Ναυπλίου τ' Εὐβοϊκὰ πυρπολήματα
Κρήτην τε Λιβύης θ' ἃς ἐπεστράφην πόλεις,
σκοπιάς τε Περσέως; οὐ γὰρ ἐμπλήσαιμί σ' ⟨ἂν⟩
μύθων, λέγων τ' ἄν σοι κάκ' ἀλγοίην ἔτι,   770
πάσχων τ' ἔκαμνον· δὶς δὲ λυπηθεῖμεν ἄν.

Ελ. κάλλιον εἶπας ἤ σ' ἀνηρόμην ἐγώ.
ἐν δ' εἰπὲ πάντα παραλιπών, πόσον χρόνον
πόντου 'πὶ νώτοις ἅλιον ἐφθείρου πλάνον;

Με. ἐν ναυσὶν ὢν πρὸς τοῖσιν ἐν Τροίᾳ δέκα   775
ἔτεσι διῆλθον ἑπτὰ περιδρομὰς ἐτῶν.

Ελ. φεῦ φεῦ· μακρόν γ' ἔλεξας, ὦ τάλας, χρόνον
σωθεὶς δ' ἐκεῖθεν ἐνθάδ' ἦλθες ἐς σφαγάς.

Με. πῶς φής; τί λέξεις; ὥς μ' ἀπώλεσας, γύναι.

Ελ. φεῦγ' ὡς τάχιστα τῆσδ' ἀπαλλαχθεὶς χθονός.   780

755 εὑρέθη LP   758 μαντειῶν Wilamowitz : μάντεων LP
759 γέρον τί LP : corr. l   760 ἔχει L et suprascr. P : ἔχοι P et
suprascr. L   765 ἑνὶ λόγῳ Pierson : ἐν ὀλίγῳ LP   767 εὐβοϊκὰ LP
768 Κρήτης Kirchhoff   Λιβύης Reiske : λιβύην LP   769 σ' ἂν
Dindorf : σε LP   οὐ γὰρ ἂν παυσαίμεθα Herwerden   770 λέγων
τ' ἂν Lp : λέγοντα P   771 πάσχον P : corr. p   ἔκαμνον l :
ἔκαμον LP   775 ἐν ναυσὶν ὢν Apelt : ἐνιαύσιον LP : ἐνιαυσίους
Boissonade, cf. ἐτῶν ἐνιαντούς   776 διῆλθον P : διῆλθον δ' L
780 = Phoen. 972 : delevit Valckenaer

θανῇ πρὸς ἀνδρὸς οὗ τάδ' ἐστὶ δώματα.

Με. τί χρῆμα δράσας ἄξιον τῆς συμφορᾶς;

Ελ. ἥκεις ἄελπτος ἐμποδὼν ἐμοῖς γάμοις.

Με. ἦ γὰρ γαμεῖν τις τἄμ' ἐβουλήθη λέχη;

Ελ. ὕβριν θ' ὑβρίζειν εἰς ἔμ', ἣν ἔτλην ἐγώ.   785

Με. ἰδίᾳ σθένων τις ἢ τυραννεύων χθονός;

Ελ. ὃς γῆς ἀνάσσει τῆσδε Πρωτέως γόνος.

Με. τόδ' ἔστ' ἐκεῖν' αἴνιγμ' ὃ προσπόλου κλύω.

Ελ. ποίοις ἐπιστὰς βαρβάροις πυλώμασιν;

Με. τοῖσδ', ἔνθεν ὥσπερ πτωχὸς ἐξηλαυνόμην.   790

Ελ. οὔ που προσῄτεις βίοτον; ὦ τάλαιν' ἐγώ.

Με. τοὔργον μὲν ἦν τοῦτ', ὄνομα δ' οὐκ εἶχεν τόδε.

Ελ. πάντ' οἶσθ' ἄρ', ὡς ἔοικας, ἀμφ' ἐμῶν γάμων.

Με. οἶδ'· εἰ δὲ λέκτρα διέφυγες τάδ' οὐκ ἔχω.

Ελ. ἄθικτον εὐνὴν ἴσθι σοι σεσωσμένην.   795

Με. τίς τοῦδε πειθώ; φίλα γάρ, εἰ σαφῆ λέγεις.

Ελ. ὁρᾷς τάφου τοῦδ' ἀθλίους ἕδρας ἐμάς;

Με. ὁρῶ, τάλαινα, στιβάδας, ὧν τί σοὶ μέτα;

Ελ. ἐνταῦθα λέκτρων ἱκετεύομεν φυγάς.

Με. βωμοῦ σπανίζουσ' ἢ νόμοισι βαρβάροις;   800

Ελ. ἐρρύεθ' ἡμᾶς τοῦτ' ἴσον ναοῖς θεῶν.

Με. οὐδ' ἄρα πρὸς οἴκους ναυστολεῖν ⟨σ'⟩ ἔξεστί μοι;

Ελ. ξίφος μένει σε μᾶλλον ἢ τοὐμὸν λέχος.

Με. οὕτως ἂν εἴην ἀθλιώτατος βροτῶν.

Ελ. μή νυν καταιδοῦ, φεῦγε δ' ἐκ τῆσδε χθονός.   805

Με. λιπών σε; Τροίαν ἐξέπερσα σὴν χάριν.

Ελ. κρεῖσσον γὰρ ἤ σε τἄμ' ἀποκτεῖναι λέχη.

782–842 paragraphi praefixi in L P   783 ἐμποδὼν Badham :
ἐμποδών τ' L P   785 εἰς ἐμὴν εὐνὴν ἔτλη F. Gu. Schmidt   786 σθένων Musurus : θένων L P   787 προτέως P : corr. p   788
αἴνιγμ᾽ Canter : αἴαγμ᾽ L P   790 τοῖσδ᾽ Scaliger : τοῖς L P
791 ἤπου l p   792 ὄνομ᾽ οὐκ P : corr. p   εἶχεν Wecklein : εἶχον
L P   798 ταλαίνας p   800 βωμὸν P : corr. p   802 σ᾽
add. Musgrave   803 μένει σε Musgrave : μὲν εἶσι L P   805 νῦν
L P

Με. ἄνανδρά γ᾽ εἶπας Ἰλίου τ᾽ οὐκ ἄξια.

Ελ. οὐκ ἂν κτάνοις τύραννον, ὃ σπεύδεις ἴσως.

Με. οὕτω σιδήρῳ τρωτὸν οὐκ ἔχει δέμας;   810

Ελ. εἴσῃ.   τὸ τολμᾶν δ᾽ ἀδύνατ᾽ ἀνδρὸς οὐ σοφοῦ.

Με. σιγῇ παράσχω δῆτ᾽ ἐμὰς δῆσαι χέρας;

Ελ. ἐς ἄπορον ἥκεις· δεῖ δὲ μηχανῆς τινος.

Με. δρῶντας γὰρ ἢ μὴ δρῶντας ἥδιον θανεῖν.

Ελ. μί᾽ ἔστιν ἐλπίς, ᾗ μόνῃ σωθεῖμεν ἄν.   815

Με. ὠνητὸς ἢ τολμητὸς ἢ λόγων ὕπο;

Ελ. εἰ μὴ τύραννός ⟨σ᾽⟩ ἐκπύθοιτ᾽ ἀφιγμένον.

Με. ἐρεῖ δὲ τίς μ᾽; οὐ γνώσεταί γ᾽ ὅς εἰμ᾽ ἐγώ.

Ελ. ἔστ᾽ ἔνδον αὐτῷ ξύμμαχος θεοῖς ἴση.

Με. φήμη τις οἴκων ἐν μυχοῖς ἱδρυμένη;   820

Ελ. οὔκ, ἀλλ᾽ ἀδελφή· Θεονόην καλοῦσί νιν.

Με. χρηστήριον μὲν τοὔνομ᾽· ὅ τι δὲ δρᾷ φράσον.

Ελ. πάντ᾽ οἶδ᾽, ἐρεῖ τε συγγόνῳ παρόντα σε.

Με. θνῄσκοιμεν ἄν· λαθεῖν γὰρ οὐχ οἷόν τέ μοι.

Ελ. ἴσως ἂν ἀναπείσαιμεν ἱκετεύοντέ νιν—   825

Με. τί χρῆμα δρᾶσαι; τίν᾽ ὑπάγεις μ᾽ ἐς ἐλπίδα;

Ελ. παρόντα γαίᾳ μὴ φράσαι σε συγγόνῳ.

Με. πείσαντε δ᾽ ἐκ γῆς διορίσαιμεν ἂν πόδα;

Ελ. κοινῇ γ᾽ ἐκείνῃ ῥᾳδίως, λάθρᾳ δ᾽ ἂν οὔ.

Με. σὸν ἔργον, ὡς γυναικὶ πρόσφορον γυνή.   830

Ελ. ὡς οὐκ ἄχρωστα γόνατ᾽ ἐμῶν ἕξει χερῶν.

Με. φέρ᾽, ἢν δὲ δὴ νῶν μὴ ἀποδέξηται λόγους;

Ελ. θανῇ· γαμοῦμαι δ᾽ ἡ τάλαιν᾽ ἐγὼ βίᾳ.

Με. προδότις ἂν εἴης· τὴν βίαν σκήψασ᾽ ἔχεις.

808 ἄνανδρά γ᾽ Cobet : ἄνανδρ᾽ ἄρ᾽ L P   809 κτάνῃς L P   ὃ Seidler : ὃν
L P   811 ἀδύνατ᾽ p et Stob. fl. 54. 50 : ἀδύνατον L P   816 ὕπο] ἄπο Wilamowitz, cf. Andr. 321, Cycl. 358   817 σ᾽ add. Schaefer   818 οὐ γνώσεταί
γ᾽ ὃς L² P (me iudice : aliis hoc l, οὐ γνώσεται ὃς P habere videtur) : οὐ
γνώσετ᾽ ὃς L : ἢ γνώσεταί γ᾽ ὃς p : lectio incerta   825 ἴσως Kirchhoff : εἴ πως L P   827 παρόντα l : τὸ παρόντα P et sine dubio L
829 γ᾽ Reiske : τ᾽ L P   λάθρᾳ δ᾽ ἂν οὐ Ludv. Dindorf : λάθρα δ᾽ ὁμοῦ
L P : γρ. οὐδαμοῦ suprascr. l   830 γυνή ex Plut. Mor. p. 51 E Brodeau : γύναι L P   834 προδότης L P : corr. l   τὴν Scaliger : τὴν δὲ L P

Ελ. ἀλλ' ἁγνὸν ὅρκον σὸν κάρα κατώμοσα . . .   835
Με. τί φῄς; θανεῖσθαι; κοὔποτ' ἀλλάξεις λέχη;
Ελ. ταὐτῷ ξίφει γε· κείσομαι δὲ σοῦ πέλας.
Με. ἐπὶ τοῖσδε τοίνυν δεξιᾶς ἐμῆς θίγε.
Ελ. ψαύω, θανόντος σοῦ τόδ' ἐκλείψειν φάος.
Με. κἀγὼ στερηθεὶς σοῦ τελευτήσειν βίον.   840
Ελ. πῶς οὖν θανούμεθ' ὥστε καὶ δόξαν λαβεῖν;
Με. τύμβου 'πὶ νώτῳ σὲ κτανὼν ἐμὲ κτενῶ.
    πρῶτον δ' ἀγῶνα μέγαν ἀγωνιούμεθα
    λέκτρων ὑπὲρ σῶν. ὁ δὲ θέλων ἴτω πέλας·
    τὸ Τρωικὸν γὰρ οὐ καταισχυνῶ κλέος   845
    οὐδ' Ἑλλάδ' ἐλθὼν λήψομαι πολὺν ψόγον,
    ὅστις Θέτιν μὲν ἐστέρησ' Ἀχιλλέως,
    Τελαμωνίου δ' Αἴαντος εἰσεῖδον σφαγάς,
    τὸν Νηλέως τ' ἄπαιδα· διὰ δὲ τὴν ἐμὴν
    οὐκ ἀξιώσω κατθανεῖν δάμαρτ' ἐγώ;   850
    μάλιστά γε· εἰ γάρ εἰσιν οἱ θεοὶ σοφοί,
    εὔψυχον ἄνδρα πολεμίων θανόνθ' ὕπο
    κούφῃ καταμπίσχουσιν ἐν τύμβῳ χθονί,
    κακοὺς δ' ἐφ' ἕρμα στερεὸν ἐκβάλλουσι γῆς.
Χο. ὦ θεοί, γενέσθω δή ποτ' εὐτυχὲς γένος   855
    τὸ Ταντάλειον καὶ μεταστήτω κακῶν.
Ελ. οἳ ἐγὼ τάλαινα· τῆς τύχης γὰρ ὧδ' ἔχω.
    Μενέλαε, διαπεπράγμεθ'· ἐκβαίνει δόμων
    ἡ θεσπιῳδὸς Θεονόη· κτυπεῖ δόμος
    κλήθρων λυθέντων. φεῦγ'· ἀτὰρ τί φευκτέον;   860
    ἀποῦσα γάρ σε καὶ παροῦσ' ἀφιγμένον

---

836 ἀλλάξεις L P : ειν suprascriptum in L   838 τοῖσδε L :
τῆσδε P   τοίνυν Canter : τοῖς νῦν L : τῆς νῦν P   840 τελευτήσειν Musgrave : τελευτήσω L P   841 λάβῃ P : corr. p
842 νώτοις Herwerden   κτενῶ post Heathium Matthiae : κτανεῖ
L P   845 κλέος Scaliger : λέχος L P   849 Νηλέως τ' ἄπαιδα
Lenting : θησέως τε παῖδα L P   851 γε L   852 εὔψυχον l :
ἔμψυχον L P   854 ἐκβαλλοῦσι L P : accentum corr. l p   855 Χο.
notam om. L

3*

δεῦρ' οἶδεν· ὦ δύστηνος, ὡς ἀπωλόμην.
Τροίας δὲ σωθεὶς κἀπὸ βαρβάρου χθονὸς
ἐς βάρβαρ' ἐλθὼν φάσγαν' αὖθις ἐμπεσῇ.

ΘΕΟΝΟΗ

ἡγοῦ σύ μοι φέρουσα λαμπτήρων σέλας   865
θεῖόν τε, σεμνοῦ θεσμὸν αἰθέρος, μυχῶν,
ὡς πνεῦμα καθαρὸν οὐρανοῦ δεξώμεθα·
σὺ δ' αὖ κέλευθον εἴ τις ἔβλαψεν ποδὶ
στείβων ἀνοσίῳ, δὸς καθαρσίῳ φλογί,
κροῦσον δὲ πεύκην, ἵνα διεξέλθω, πυρός.   870
νόμον δὲ τὸν ἐμὸν θεοῖσιν ἀποδοῦσαι πάλιν
ἐφέστιον φλόγ' ἐς δόμους κομίζετε.
    Ἑλένη, τί τἀμὰ—πῶς ἔχει—θεσπίσματα;
ἥκει πόσις σοι Μενέλεως ὅδ' ἐμφανής,
νεῶν στερηθεὶς τοῦ τε σοῦ μιμήματος.   875
    ὦ τλῆμον, οἵους διαφυγὼν ἦλθες πόνους,
οὐδ' οἶσθα νόστον οἴκαδ' εἴτ' αὐτοῦ μενεῖς·
ἔρις γὰρ ἐν θεοῖς σύλλογός τε σοῦ πέρι
ἔσται πάρεδρος Ζηνὶ τῷδ' ἐν ἤματι.
    Ἥρα μέν, ἥ σοι δυσμενὴς πάροιθεν ἦν,   880
νῦν ἐστιν εὔνους κἀς πάτραν σῶσαι θέλει
ξὺν τῇδ', ἵν' Ἑλλὰς τοὺς Ἀλεξάνδρου γάμους,
δώρημα Κύπριδος, ψευδονυμφεύτους μάθῃ·
Κύπρις δὲ νόστον σὸν διαφθεῖραι θέλει,
ὡς μὴ 'ξελεγχθῇ μηδὲ πριαμένη φανῇ   885

862 οἶδεν L : ἦλθεν P   864 φάσγαν' αὖθις L : βάρβαρ' αὖθις P
866 θείου p   τε scripsi : δὲ L P : lectio incerta   εἰς σεμνοῦ l   θείου
δὲ σεμνὸν θεσμὸν αἰθέρος μυχούς Wecklein : σεμνοῦ pro σέμνυνε accipit
Wilamowitz : θεῖον σύμβολον αἰθέρος διὰ τὸ ταχὺ ἐξάπτον dicit L² scholion scribens   867 δεξαίμεθα L P : corr. Schaefer   870 πυρός]
πάρος Reiske   871 πόνον δὲ νόμιμον Kirchhoff   875 μιμήματος Stephanus : τιμήματος L P   878 θεοῖς Barnes : θεοῖσι
L² P : θεοῖς τε ut videtur L   881 κεῖς L P   883 ψευδονυμφεύτους L P : corr. l   885 μὴ 'ξελέγχθῃ Ludv. Dindorf : μήτ'
ἐλεγχθῇ L P

τὸ κάλλος, Ἑλένης οὕνεκ᾽, ἀνονήτοις γάμοις.
τέλος δ᾽ ἐφ᾽ ἡμῖν, εἴθ᾽, ἃ βούλεται Κύπρις,
λέξασ᾽ ἀδελφῷ σ᾽ ἐνθάδ᾽ ὄντα διολέσω,
εἴτ᾽ αὖ μεθ᾽ Ἥρας στᾶσα σὸν σώσω βίον,
κρύψασ᾽ ὁμαίμον᾽, ὅς με προστάσσει τάδε   890
εἰπεῖν, ὅταν γῆν τήνδε νοστήσας τύχῃς. . . .
    τίς εἶσ᾽ ἀδελφῷ τόνδε σημανῶν ἐμῷ
παρόνθ᾽, ὅπως ἂν τοὐμὸν ἀσφαλῶς ἔχῃ;
Ελ. ὦ παρθέν᾽, ἱκέτις ἀμφὶ σὸν πίτνω γόνυ
καὶ προσκαθίζω θᾶκον οὐκ εὐδαίμονα   895
ὑπέρ τ᾽ ἐμαυτῆς τοῦδέ θ᾽, ὃν μόλις ποτὲ
λαβοῦσ᾽ ἐπ᾽ ἀκμῆς εἰμι κατθανόντ᾽ ἰδεῖν·
μή μου κατείπῃς σῷ κασιγνήτῳ πόσιν
τόνδ᾽ εἰς ἐμὰς ἥκοντα φιλτάτας χέρας,
σῶσον δέ, λίσσομαί σε· συγγόνῳ δὲ σῷ   900
τὴν εὐσέβειαν μὴ προδῷς τὴν σήν ποτε,
χάριτας πονηρὰς κἀδίκους ὠνουμένη.
μισεῖ γὰρ ὁ θεὸς τὴν βίαν, τὰ κτητὰ δὲ
κτᾶσθαι κελεύει πάντας οὐκ ἐς ἁρπαγάς.
[ἐατέος δ᾽ ὁ πλοῦτος ἄδικός τις ὤν.]   905
κοινὸς γάρ ἐστιν οὐρανὸς πᾶσιν βροτοῖς
καὶ γαῖ᾽, ἐν ᾗ χρὴ δώματ᾽ ἀναπληρουμένους
τἀλλότρια μὴ σχεῖν μηδ᾽ ἀφαιρεῖσθαι βίᾳ.
ἡμᾶς δὲ μακαρίως μέν, ἀθλίως δ᾽ ἐμοί,
Ἑρμῆς ἔδωκε πατρὶ σῷ σῴζειν πόσει   910
τῷδ᾽ ὃς πάρεστι κἀπολάζυσθαι θέλει.
πῶς οὖν θανὼν ἂν ἀπολάβοι; κεῖνος δὲ πῶς

---

886 ἀνονήτοις Pierson (non fruendis, cf. λ 324): ὠνητοῖς L P: οὐκ
ἄρ᾽ ὠνητοῖς Herwerden   888 σ᾽ Reiske: γ᾽ P: in L γ᾽ aut add.
L² aut rescr. l   890 ὁμαίμον᾽ L (fuit puto ὁμαίμονα)   892 ση-
μανῶν Scaliger: σημανῶ γ᾽ L P   893 παρόντ᾽ L (eraso α) et P
896 τοῦδέ τ᾽ L P   898 μή μοι Seidler   899 φίλτατον Cobet
902 καὶ ἀδίκους L   903 βίας P: corr. p   905 damnavit
Hermann: 903-908 del. Dindorf   908 σχεῖν Headlam: ἔχειν L P
909 μακαρίως] καιρίως Badham

τὰ ζῶντα τοῖς θανοῦσιν ἀποδοίη ποτ' ἄν;
ἤδη τὰ τοῦ θεοῦ καὶ τὰ τοῦ πατρὸς σκόπει·
πότερον ὁ δαίμων χὠ θανὼν τὰ τῶν πέλας   915
βούλοιντ' ἂν ἢ οὐ βούλοιντ' ἂν ἀποδοῦναι πάλιν;
δοκῶ μέν.　οὔκουν χρή σε συγγόνῳ πλέον
νέμειν ματαίῳ μᾶλλον ἢ χρηστῷ πατρί.
εἰ δ' οὖσα μάντις καὶ τὰ θεῖ' ἡγουμένη
τὸ μὲν δίκαιον τοῦ πατρὸς διαφθερεῖς,   920
τῷ δ' οὐ δικαίῳ συγγόνῳ σώσεις δίκην,
αἰσχρὸν τὰ μέν σε θεῖα πάντ' ἐξειδέναι,
τά τ' ὄντα καὶ μέλλοντα, τὰ δὲ δίκαια μή.
τήν τ' ἀθλίαν ἔμ', οἷσιν ἔγκειμαι κακοῖς,
ῥῦσαι, πάρεργον δοῦσα τοῦτο τῆς τύχης·   925
Ἑλένην γὰρ οὐδεὶς ὅστις οὐ στυγεῖ βροτῶν·
ἢ κλήζομαι καθ' Ἑλλάδ' ὡς προδοῦσ' ἐμὸν
πόσιν Φρυγῶν ᾤκησα πολυχρύσους δόμους.
ἢν δ' Ἑλλάδ' ἔλθω κἀπιβῶ Σπάρτης ⟨πάλιν⟩,
κλύοντες εἰσιδόντες ὡς τέχναις θεῶν   930
ὤλοντ', ἐγὼ δὲ προδότις οὐκ ἄρ' ἦ φίλων,
πάλιν μ' ἀνάξουσ' ἐς τὸ σῶφρον αὖθις αὖ,
ἐδνώσομαί τε θυγατέρ', ἣν οὐδεὶς γαμεῖ,
τὴν δ' ἐνθάδ' ἐκλιποῦσ' ἀλητείαν πικρὰν
ὄντων ἐν οἴκοις χρημάτων ὀνήσομαι.   935
κεἰ μὲν θανὼν ὅδ' ἐν πυρᾷ κατεσφάγη,
πρόσω σφ' ἀπόντα δακρύοις ἂν ἠγάπων·

913 ἀποδοίη ποτ' ἂν Porson : ἂν ἀποδοίη ποτέ L P　　914 ἤ δὴ L P :
ἤ δὴ l : corr. Barnes　　915 καὶ ὁ L　　916 ἢ οὐ Canter : ἢ L P
921 σώσεις Bruhn : δώσεις L P (δώσεις χάριν Reiske)　　923 μέλλοντα, τὰ δὲ δίκαια μή W. G. Clark : μή, τὰ δὲ δίκαια μὴ εἰδέναι L P
post 923 lacunam indicavit Hermann : sed sensus est ' Iustitiam cole
erga deos et mortuos—et quidem, dum id facis, me serva'　　924 ἐμέ
L　　929 πάλιν om. L P : add. apogr. Paris.　　931 προδότης P
ἦν L P : οὐκ ἤμην τέκνον (voluit τέκνων) citat Choerob. can. ii. p. 882,
9　　932 αὖ Canter : ἂν L P　　933 ἐδνώσομαί Hermann (et voluit
puto Musurus) : ἐδώσομαί L P : ἐκδώσομαί p　　935 ὀνήσομαι Musurus :
ὠνήσομαι L P　　936 κατεστάλη Reiske

νῦν δ' ὄντα καὶ σωθέντ' ἀφαιρεθήσομαι;
μὴ δῆτα, παρθέν', ἀλλά σ' ἱκετεύω τόδε·
δὸς τὴν χάριν μοι τήνδε καὶ μιμοῦ τρόπους 940
πατρὸς δικαίου· παισὶ γὰρ κλέος τόδε
κάλλιστον, ὅστις ἐκ πατρὸς χρηστοῦ γεγὼς
ἐς ταὐτὸν ἦλθε τοῖς τεκοῦσι τοὺς τρόπους.
Χο. οἰκτρὸν μὲν οἱ παρόντες ἐν μέσῳ λόγοι,
οἰκτρὰ δὲ καὶ σύ. τοὺς δὲ Μενέλεω ποθῶ 945
λόγους ἀκοῦσαι τίνας ἐρεῖ ψυχῆς πέρι.
Με. ἐγὼ σὸν οὔτ' ἂν προσπεσεῖν τλαίην γόνυ
οὔτ' ἂν δακρῦσαι βλέφαρα· τὴν Τροίαν γὰρ ἂν
δειλοὶ γενόμενοι πλεῖστον αἰσχύνοιμεν ἄν.
καίτοι λέγουσιν ὡς πρὸς ἀνδρὸς εὐγενοῦς 950
ἐν ξυμφοραῖσι δάκρυ' ἀπ' ὀφθαλμῶν βαλεῖν.
ἀλλ' οὐχὶ τοῦτο τὸ καλόν, εἰ καλὸν τόδε,
αἱρήσομαι 'γὼ πρόσθε τῆς εὐψυχίας.
ἀλλ', εἰ μὲν ἄνδρα σοι δοκεῖ σῶσαι ξένον
ζητοῦντά γ' ὀρθῶς ἀπολαβεῖν δάμαρτ' ἐμήν, 955
ἀπόδος τε καὶ πρὸς σῶσον· εἰ δὲ μὴ δοκεῖ,
ἐγὼ μὲν οὐ νῦν πρῶτον ἀλλὰ πολλάκις
ἄθλιος ἂν εἴην, σὺ δὲ γυνὴ κακὴ φανῇ.
ἃ δ' ἄξι' ἡμῶν καὶ δίκαι' ἡγούμεθα
καὶ σῆς μάλιστα καρδίας ἀνθάψεται, 960
λέξω τάδ' ἀμφὶ μνῆμα σοῦ πατρὸς πόθῳ·
Ὦ γέρον, ὃς οἰκεῖς τόνδε λάινον τάφον,
ἀπόδος, ἀπαιτῶ τὴν ἐμὴν δάμαρτά σε,
ἣν Ζεὺς ἔπεμψε δεῦρό σοι σῴζειν ἐμοί.
οἶδ' οὕνεκ' ἡμῖν οὔποτ' ἀποδώσεις θανών· 965

941 παισὶ Stob. fl. 89. 2: παιδὶ L P 943 τῶν τρόπων Reiske 944-
946 Theonoae tribuunt L P: Choro Ludv. Dindorf 944 οἰκ-
τροὶ p 945 τοὺς Hermann: τοῦ L P 953 'γὼ Porson: τὸ L P
εὐψυχίας Tyrwhitt: εὐδαιμονίας L P (glossema fortasse corruptae l.
εὐτυχίας): εὐανδρίας p 957 Cf. Med. 446: iniuria suspectus
961 τάδ'] τόδ' Tyrwhitt πόθῳ] πεσών Badham 962 ὃς L² P:
ὣς L λᾶον P: corr. p 965 ἀποδώσεις Stephanus: ἀπολέσεις
L P: ὀφλήσεις Nauck αὐτὸς οὔποτ' ἀποδώσεις Kirchhoff

ἀλλ᾽ ἥδε πατέρα νέρθεν ἀνακαλούμενον
οὐκ ἀξιώσει τὸν πρὶν εὐκλεέστατον
κακῶς ἀκοῦσαι· κυρία γάρ ἐστι νῦν.
ὦ νέρτερ᾽ Ἅιδη, καὶ σὲ σύμμαχον καλῶ,
ὃς πόλλ᾽ ἐδέξω τῆσδ᾽ ἕκατι σώματα   970
πεσόντα τὠμῷ φασγάνῳ, μισθὸν δ᾽ ἔχεις·
ἢ νῦν ἐκείνους ἀπόδος ἐμψύχους πάλιν,
ἢ τήνδε πατρὸς εὐσεβοῦς ἀνάγκασον
κρείσσω φανεῖσαν τἀμά γ᾽ ἀποδοῦναι λέχη.
εἰ δ᾽ ἐμὲ γυναῖκα τὴν ἐμὴν συλήσετε,   975
ἅ σοι παρέλιπεν ἥδε τῶν λόγων, φράσω.
ὅρκοις κεκλήμεθ᾽, ὡς μάθῃς, ὦ παρθένε,
πρῶτον μὲν ἐλθεῖν διὰ μάχης σῷ συγγόνῳ·
κἀκεῖνον ἢ ᾽μὲ δεῖ θανεῖν· ἁπλοῦς λόγος.
ἢν δ᾽ ἐς μὲν ἀλκὴν μὴ πόδ᾽ ἀντιθῇ ποδί,   980
λιμῷ δὲ θηρᾷ τύμβον ἱκετεύοντε νώ,
κτανεῖν δέδοκται τήνδε μοι κἄπειτ᾽ ἐμὸν
πρὸς ἧπαρ ὦσαι δίστομον ξίφος τόδε
τύμβου ᾽πὶ νώτοις τοῦδ᾽, ἵν᾽ αἵματος ῥοαὶ
τάφου καταστάζωσι· κεισόμεσθα δὲ   985
νεκρὼ δύ᾽ ἑξῆς τῷδ᾽ ἐπὶ ξεστῷ τάφῳ,
ἀθάνατον ἄλγος σοί, ψόγος δὲ σῷ πατρί.
οὐ γὰρ γαμεῖ τήνδ᾽ οὔτε σύγγονος σέθεν
οὔτ᾽ ἄλλος οὐδείς· ἀλλ᾽ ἐγώ σφ᾽ ἀπάξομαι,
εἰ μὴ πρὸς οἴκους δυνάμεθ᾽, ἀλλὰ πρὸς νεκρούς.   990
τί ταῦτα; δακρύοις ἐς τὸ θῆλυ τρεπόμενος
ἐλεινὸς ἦν ἂν μᾶλλον ἢ δραστήριος.

---

973 seq. ἢ τήνδ᾽ ἀνάγκασόν γε εὐσεβοῦς πατρὸς κρείσσω φανεῖσαν τἄμ᾽
ἀποδοῦναι λέχη L P : traieci : μὴ εὐσεβοῦς πατρὸς ἥσσω Hermann :
tum τἄμ᾽ ἐμοὶ δοῦναι Pflugk   977 κεκλήμεθ᾽ ut videtur primitus L :
κεκλήμεθ᾽ L² P   980 ἐς hic L P   πόδ᾽ Brodeau : πότ᾽ L P
981 λιμὸν P   θηρᾷ Canter : θηρᾶν L P   982 τήνδ᾽ ἐμοὶ L P
984 τοῦδε L   985 καταστάζωσι L² P² : καταστάζουσι L P   ante
991 Theonoae ante 992 Menelai nota in P, et δακρύεις pro δακρύοις p
991 τερπόμενος P : corr. p   992 ἐλεεινὸς L P

κτεῖν᾽, εἰ δοκεῖ σοι· δυσκλεᾶς γὰρ οὐ κτενεῖς·
μᾶλλόν γε μέντοι τοῖς ἐμοῖς πείθου λόγοις,
ἵν᾽ ᾖς δικαία καὶ δάμαρτ᾽ ἐγὼ λάβω.   995

Χο. ἐν σοὶ βραβεύειν, ὦ νεᾶνι, τοὺς λόγους·
οὕτω δὲ κρῖνον, ὡς ἅπασιν ἁνδάνῃς.

Θέ. ἐγὼ πέφυκά τ᾽ εὐσεβεῖν καὶ βούλομαι,
φιλῶ τ᾽ ἐμαυτήν, καὶ κλέος τοὐμοῦ πατρὸς
οὐκ ἂν μιάναιμ᾽, οὐδὲ συγγόνῳ χάριν   1000
δοίην ἂν ἐξ ἧς δυσκλεὴς φανήσομαι.
ἔνεστι δ᾽ ἱερὸν τῆς δίκης ἐμοὶ μέγα
ἐν τῇ φύσει· καὶ τοῦτο Νηρέως πάρα
ἔχουσα σῴζειν, Μενέλεως, πειράσομαι.
Ἥρᾳ δ᾽, ἐπείπερ βούλεταί σ᾽ εὐεργετεῖν,   1005
ἐς ταὐτὸν οἴσω ψῆφον· ἡ Χάρις δ᾽ ἐμοὶ
ἵλεως μὲν εἴη, ξυμβέβηκε δ᾽ οὐδαμοῦ·
πειράσομαι δὲ παρθένος μένειν ἀεί.
ἃ δ᾽ ἀμφὶ τύμβῳ τῷδ᾽ ὀνειδίζεις πατρί,
ἡμῖν ὅδ᾽ αὐτὸς μῦθος. ἀδικοίημεν ἄν,   1010
εἰ μὴ ἀποδώσω· καὶ γὰρ ἂν κεῖνος βλέπων
ἀπέδωκεν ἂν σοὶ τήνδ᾽ ἔχειν, ταύτῃ δὲ σέ.
καὶ γὰρ τίσις τῶνδ᾽ ἐστὶ τοῖς τε νερτέροις
καὶ τοῖς ἄνωθεν πᾶσιν ἀνθρώποις· ὁ νοῦς
τῶν κατθανόντων ζῇ μὲν οὔ, γνώμην δ᾽ ἔχει   1015
ἀθάνατον εἰς ἀθάνατον αἰθέρ᾽ ἐμπεσών.
ὡς οὖν παραινῶ μὴ μακράν, σιγήσομαι
ἅ μου καθικετεύσατ᾽, οὐδὲ μωρίᾳ
ξύμβουλος ἔσομαι τῇ κασιγνήτου ποτέ.
εὐεργετῶ γὰρ κεῖνον οὐ δοκοῦσ᾽ ὅμως,   1020

993 δυσκλεᾶς Wilamowitz: δυσκλεῶς L P : δυσκλεᾶ Barnes   994
πιθοῦ Dindorf   997 κρῖνον L P² : κρίνειν P   1001 φανήσεται
Badham   1002 ἱρὸν P   1004 σῴζειν Μενέλεων Brodeau
1005 Ἥρα L P   1006 ἡ Κύπρις Canter perperam   δέ μοι vulgo
1007 συμβέβηκε L P : ξυμβέβηκα Herwerden   1010 αὐτὸς L P
ἀδικοίην νιν ἂν Porson   1012 τήνδ᾽ Reiske : τήν γ᾽ L P   1013 τίσεις
P : corr. p   1017 περαίνω Stephanus   1019 τῇ Dobree :
τοῦ L P

ἐκ δυσσεβείας ὅσιον εἰ τίθημί νιν.
αὐτοὶ μὲν οὖν ὁδόν τιν' ἐξευρίσκετε,
ἐγὼ δ' ἀποστᾶσ' ἐκποδὼν σιγήσομαι.
ἐκ τῶν θεῶν δ' ἄρχεσθε χἰκετεύετε
τὴν μέν σ' ἐᾶσαι πατρίδα νοστῆσαι Κύπριν,   1025
Ἥρας δὲ τὴν ἔννοιαν ἐν ταὐτῷ μένειν
ἣν ἐς σὲ καὶ σὸν πόσιν ἔχει σωτηρίας.
σὺ δ', ὦ θανών μοι πάτερ, ὅσον γ' ἐγὼ σθένω,
οὔποτε κεκλήσῃ δυσσεβὴς ἀντ' εὐσεβοῦς.
Χο. οὐδείς ποτ' εὐτύχησεν ἔκδικος γεγώς,   1030
ἐν τῷ δικαίῳ δ' ἐλπίδες σωτηρίας.
Ελ. Μενέλαε, πρὸς μὲν παρθένου σεσώσμεθα·
τοὐνθένδε δὴ σὲ τοὺς λόγους φέροντα χρὴ
κοινὴν ξυνάπτειν μηχανὴν σωτηρίας.
Με. ἄκουε δή νυν· χρόνιος εἶ κατὰ στέγας   1035
καὶ συντέθραψαι προσπόλοισι βασιλέως.
Ελ. τί τοῦτ' ἔλεξας; ἐσφέρεις γὰρ ἐλπίδας
ὡς δή τι δράσων χρηστὸν ἐς κοινόν γε νῷν.
Με. πείσειας ἄν τιν' οἵτινες τετραζύγων
ὄχων ἀνάσσουσ', ὥστε νῷν δοῦναι δίφρους;   1040
Ελ. πείσαιμ' ⟨ἄν⟩· ἀλλὰ τίνα φυγὴν φευξούμεθα
πεδίων ἄπειροι βαρβάρου τ' ὄντες χθονός;
Με. ἀδύνατον εἶπας. φέρε, τί δ', εἰ κρυφθεὶς δόμοις
κτάνοιμ' ἄνακτα τῷδε διστόμῳ ξίφει;
Ελ. οὐκ ἄν σ' ἀνάσχοιτ' οὐδὲ σιγήσειεν ἂν   1045
μέλλοντ' ἀδελφὴ σύγγονον κατακτενεῖν.
Με. ἀλλ' οὐδὲ μὴν ναῦς ἔστιν ᾗ σωθεῖμεν ἂν
φεύγοντες· ἣν γὰρ εἴχομεν θάλασσ' ἔχει.

1021 ἐκ δυσσεβείας . . . νιν Brodeau : ἐξ εὐσεβείας . . . νῦν L P
1022 ὁδόν τιν' ἐξευρίσκετε Nauck : τὴν ἔξοδόν γ' εὑρίσκετε L P : εὑρίσκετ'
ἔξοδόν τινα Hermann   1024 καὶ ἰκετεύετε L   1026 εὔνοιαν ut vid.
P : corr. ρ   1033 προσφέροντα χρὴ λόγους Vitelli   1035 δὴ νῦν
L P   1041 ἂν add. Canter   1042 ὄντος P   1043 notam
Menelai post ἀδύνατον εἶπας habent L P, ante versum trai. Matthiae
1045 ἄν σ' Portus : ἂν L P   1046 κατακτανεῖν L P : corr. Dindorf

Ελ. ἄκουσον, ἤν τι καὶ γυνὴ λέξῃ σοφόν.

βούλῃ λέγεσθαι, μὴ θανών, λόγῳ θανεῖν;　　　1050

Με. κακὸς μὲν ὄρνις· εἰ δὲ κερδανῶ, λέγειν
ἕτοιμός εἰμι μὴ θανὼν λόγῳ θανεῖν.

Ελ. καὶ μὴν γυναικείοις σ' ἂν οἰκτισαίμεθα
κουραῖσι καὶ θρήνοισι πρὸς τὸν ἀνόσιον.

Με. σωτηρίας δὲ τοῦτ' ἔχει τί νῷν ἄκος;　　　1055
παλαιότης γὰρ τῷ λόγῳ γ' ἔνεστί τις.

Ελ. ὡς δὴ θανόντα σ' ἐνάλιον κενῷ τάφῳ
θάψαι τύραννον τῆσδε γῆς αἰτήσομαι.

Με. καὶ δὴ παρεῖκεν· εἶτα πῶς ἄνευ νεὼς
σωθησόμεσθα κενοταφοῦντ' ἐμὸν δέμας;　　　1060

Ελ. δοῦναι κελεύσω πορθμίδ', ᾗ καθήσομαι
κόσμον τάφῳ σῷ πελαγίους ἐς ἀγκάλας.

Με. ὡς εὖ τόδ' εἶπας πλὴν ἕν· εἰ χέρσῳ ταφὰς
θεῖναι κελεύσει σ', οὐδὲν ἡ σκῆψις φέρει.

Ελ. ἀλλ' οὐ νομίζειν φήσομεν καθ' Ἑλλάδα　　　1065
χέρσῳ καλύπτειν τοὺς θανόντας ἐναλίους.

Με. τοῦτ' αὖ κατορθοῖς· εἶτ' ἐγὼ συμπλεύσομαι
καὶ συγκαθήσω κόσμον ἐν ταὐτῷ σκάφει.

Ελ. σὲ καὶ παρεῖναι δεῖ μάλιστα τούς τε σοὺς
πλωτῆρας οἵπερ ἔφυγον ἐκ ναυαγίας.　　　1070

Με. καὶ μὴν ἐάνπερ ναῦν ἐπ' ἀγκύρας λάβω,
ἀνὴρ παρ' ἄνδρα στήσεται ξιφηφόρος.

Ελ. σὲ χρὴ βραβεύειν πάντα· πόμπιμοι μόνον

1049-1085 paragraphos pro personarum notis praef. L　1049 καὶ
om. P　1050 θανών, τεθνηκέναι Cobet, sed cf. sequentia　1051 κερδανῶ,
λέγε· Seidler: leniter inridens, ni fallor, iterat vir quae illa nimis
timide dixit　1053 γυναικείους P　σ' ἂν Hermann: ἂν L P　1056
Menelao continuat P: Helenae tribuit *l* potius quam L, idem paragraphum ante 1057 videtur delevisse　ἀπαιόλη γὰρ Hermann
1059 παρεῖκεν Musurus: παρῆκεν L P　1060 supra κενοταφοῦντ' scr. δνικῶς in L　1061 καθήσομεν Heath　1062 πελαγίους
Fritzsche, cl. 1436: πελαγίας L P　ἐς hic L P　1064 κελεύσει
Ludv. Dindorf: κελεύει L P　σ' L² P: σε L: ἐς Markland　1067
τοῦτ' αὖ L² P: ταῦτ' οὖν ut videtur L　1069 καὶ] γὰρ Dobree　1073
πόμποιμι P

λαίφει πνοαὶ γένοιντο καὶ νεὼς δρόμος.

Με. ἔσται· πόνους γὰρ δαίμονες παύσουσί μου.　　1075
ἀτὰρ θανόντα τοῦ μ' ἐρεῖς πεπυσμένη;

Ελ. σοῦ· καὶ μόνος γε φάσκε διαφυγεῖν μόρον
'Ατρέως πλέων σὺν παιδὶ καὶ θανόνθ' ὁρᾶν.

Με. καὶ μὴν τάδ' ἀμφίβληστρα σώματος ῥάκη
ξυμμαρτυρήσει ναυτικῶν ἐρειπίων.　　1080

Ελ. ἐς καιρὸν ἦλθε, τότε δ' ἄκαιρ' ἀπώλλυτο·
τὸ δ' ἄθλιον κεῖν' εὐτυχὲς τάχ' ἂν πέσοι.

Με. πότερα δ' ἐς οἴκους σοὶ συνεισελθεῖν με χρὴ
ἢ πρὸς τάφῳ τῷδ' ἥσυχοι καθώμεθα;

Ελ. αὐτοῦ μέν'· ἢν γὰρ καί τι πλημμελές σε δρᾷ,　　1085
τάφος σ' ὅδ' ἂν ῥύσαιτο φάσγανόν τε σόν.
ἐγὼ δ' ἐς οἴκους βᾶσα βοστρύχους τεμῶ
πέπλων τε λευκῶν μέλανας ἀνταλλάξομαι
παρῇδί τ' ὄνυχα φόνιον ἐμβαλῶ χροός.
μέγας γὰρ ἀγών, καὶ βλέπω δύο ῥοπάς·　　1090
ἢ γὰρ θανεῖν δεῖ μ', ἢν ἁλῶ τεχνωμένη,
ἢ πατρίδα τ' ἐλθεῖν καὶ σὸν ἐκσῷσαι δέμας.
ὦ πότνι' ἢ Δίοισιν ἐν λέκτροις πίτνεις
"Ηρα, δύ' οἰκτρὼ φῶτ' ἀνάψυξον πόνων,
αἰτούμεθ' ὀρθὰς ὠλένας πρὸς οὐρανὸν　　1095
ῥίπτονθ', ἵν' οἰκεῖς ἀστέρων ποικίλματα.
σύ θ', ἣ 'πὶ τὠμῷ κάλλος ἐκτήσω γάμῳ,
κόρη Διώνης Κύπρι, μή μ' ἐξεργάσῃ.
ἅλις δὲ λύμης ἥν μ' ἐλυμήνω πάρος
τοὔνομα παρασχοῦσ', οὐ τὸ σῶμ', ἐν βαρβάροις.　　1100
θανεῖν δ' ἔασόν μ', εἰ κατακτεῖναι θέλεις,
ἐν γῇ πατρῴᾳ.　　τί ποτ' ἄπληστος εἶ κακῶν,

1080 συμμάρτυρές σοι A. C. Pearson　1082 εὐτυχῶς Blaydes　1083 δ'
in ras. in L: fuit fortasse πότερον　χρὴ P: χρήν suprascripto ἢ L
1085 πλημελὲς L: πλη*μελὲς eraso σ vel γ P　1089 παρηΐδι
L P　χερός Jacobs　1090 ἀγὼν L P　δύω L P: fortasse
δυοῖν　1091 δεῖ om. P　1095 ὀργὰς P: corr. p　1096 ῥι-
πτοῦνθ' L (corr. Elmsley): ῥιπτοῦσ' P　1097 γάμῳ] κακῷ Nauck
1098 κούρη L P　1099 μ' om. P

ἔρωτας ἀπάτας δόλιά τ' ἐξευρήματα
ἀσκοῦσα φίλτρα θ' αἱματηρὰ δωμάτων;
εἰ δ' ἦσθα μετρία, τἄλλα γ' ἡδίστη θεῶν   1105
πέφυκας ἀνθρώποισιν· οὐκ ἄλλως λέγω.

Χο.   σὲ τὰν ἐναύλοις ὑπὸ δενδροκόμοις   [στρ. α'
μουσεῖα καὶ θάκους ἐνί-
ζουσαν ἀναβοάσω,
σὲ τὰν ἀοιδοτάταν ὄρνιθα μελῳδὸν
ἀηδόνα δακρυόεσσαν,   1110
ἔλθ' ὦ διὰ ξουθᾶν
γενύων ἐλελιζομένα
θρήνων ἐμοὶ ξυνεργός,
Ἑλένας μελέας πόνους
τὸν Ἰλιάδων τ' ἀει-
δούσᾳ δακρυόεντα πόνον   1115
Ἀχαιῶν ὑπὸ λόγχαις·
ὅτ' ἔδραμε ῥόθια πεδία βαρβάρῳ πλάτᾳ
ὅτ' ἔμολεν ἔμολε, μέλεα Πριαμίδαις ἄγων
Λακεδαίμονος ἄπο λέχεα
σέθεν, ὦ Ἑλένα, Πάρις αἰνόγαμος   1120
πομπαῖσιν Ἀφροδίτας.

πολλοὶ δ' Ἀχαιῶν δορὶ καὶ πετρίναις   [ἀντ. α'
ῥιπαῖσιν ἐκπνεύσαντες Ἅι-
δαν μέλεον ἔχουσιν,

1104 φίλτα L P : corr. L² P²   1107 ἐναύλοις Scaliger : ἐναυλείοις
L P   1108 μουσία P : corr. p   θάκους] θάμνους Herwerden, sed
cf. Ar. Ran. 1319   1110 δακρυόεσαν P   1111 ἔλθ' ὦ Musgrave :
ἔλθε L P   1112 θρήνων ἐμοὶ Wilamowitz : θρήνοις ἐμῶν L P (ἐμοῖς l)
1113 πόνους suspectum : cf. 1115   1114 ἀείδουσα L P : corr. Lach-
mann   πόνον] πότμον Badham: cf. 1130   1117, 1118 (γ) ὃς ἔδραμε
ῥόθια μέλεα | πριαμίδαις ἄγων | (α) ὃς ἔμολεν ἔμολε πεδία | (β) βαρβάρῳ
πλάτα L P sed litteras transpositionem significantes praescripsit l:
οθια in rasura est in P : ὅτ' pro ὃς Lenting: cetera corr. O. Schultze :
ὃς ἔδραμε ῥόθια Μάλεα β. π. ὃς ἔμολεν ἔμολε πεδία, Π. ἀ. Wilamowitz
1120 ὦ Ἑλένα Seidler : ὡς εἷλε L P   ἐνόγαμος P : corr. p   1121 πομ-
πᾶσιν P : corr. p   1122 δορὶ] ἐν δορὶ l ob metrum

ταλαινᾶν ἀλόχων κείραντες ἔθειραν·
ἄνυμφα δὲ μέλαθρα κεῖται·   1125
πολλοὺς δὲ πυρσεύσας
φλογερὸν σέλας ἀμφιρύταν
Εὔβοιαν εἷλ' Ἀχαιῶν
μονόκωπος ἀνήρ, πέτραις
Καφηρίσιν ἐμβαλὼν
Αἰγαίαις τ' ἐνάλοις δόλιον   1130
ἀκταῖς ἀστέρα λάμψας.
ἀλίμενα δ' ὄρεα Μάλεα χειμάτων πνοᾷ,
ὅτ' ἔσυτο πατρίδος ἀποπρό, βαρβάρου στολᾶς
γέρας, οὐ γέρας ἀλλ' ἔριν,
Δαναῶν νεφέλαν ἐπὶ ναυσὶν ἄγων,   1135
εἴδωλον ἱερὸν Ἥρας.

ὅ τι θεὸς ἢ μὴ θεὸς ἢ τὸ μέσον,   [στρ. β'
τίς φησ' ἐρευνήσας βροτῶν
μακρότατον πέρας εὑρεῖν
ὃς τὰ θεῶν ἐσορᾷ   1140
δεῦρο καὶ αὖθις ἐκεῖσε
καὶ πάλιν ἀντιλόγοις
πηδῶντ' ἀνελπίστοις τύχαις;
σὺ Διὸς ἔφυς, ὦ Ἑλένα, θυγάτηρ·
πτανὸς γὰρ ἐν κόλποις σε Λή-   1145

1124 ταλαινᾶν Wilamowitz, ἀοιδοτάταν v. 1109 choriambum fa-
ciens : τάλαιναν L P : τάλαιναν τῶν l : τάλαιναν ὧν Matthiae, sed ὃς de
eo quod plurium est vix Attice dicitur   1125 μέλαθρα δὲ Dindorf
1126 πολλοὺς L P : πολλὰ l   ἀμφὶ ῥυτὰν L P : ἀμφιρύταν Matthiae :
tum ptcp. quale est περιπλέων pro Ἀχαιῶν desiderat Wilamowitz
1127 εἷλ' l : εἷλες P et ut videtur L   1129 Καφηρίσιν Heath :
καφηρίαις L P   1130 ἐναλίοις ἀκταῖς δόλιον L P : corr. Hermann
1131 ἀστέρ' ἀνάψας Verrall   1132, 1133 Μάλεα Hermann, cf.
γ 287: μέλεα L P   ὅτ' ἔσυτο Musgrave: ὅτε σὺ τὸ L P: ὅδ'
ἔσυτο Wilamowitz   χειμάτων Heath : χαυμάτων L P   βαρβάρου
στολᾶς post μέλεα (1132) χαυμάτων πνοᾷ post ἀποπρὸ (1133) L P : transposui   1134 γέρας οὐ γέρας Badham : τέρας οὐ τέρας L P   1135 νεφέλαν L P : νεφέλας l : Μενέλας Wilamowitz   1138 τί φησ L P : corr.
Bamberger: τίς φύσιν et v. sequenti ηὗρεν Hermann : βροτῶν; et
ηὗρεν Wilamowitz   1141 δεῦρο Dobree : δεινὰ L P

δας ἐτέκνωσε πατήρ.
κᾆτ᾽ ἰαχήθης καθ᾽ Ἑλλανίαν
προδότις ἄπιστος ἄδικος ἄθεος· οὐδ᾽ ἔχω
τί τὸ σαφὲς ἔτι ποτ᾽ ἐν βροτοῖς·
τὸ τῶν θεῶν ⟨δ᾽⟩ ἔπος ἀλαθὲς ηὗρον.   1150

ἄφρονες ὅσοι τὰς ἀρετὰς πολέμῳ   [ἀντ. β΄
λόγχαισί τ᾽ ἀλκαίου δορὸς
κτᾶσθε, πόνους ἀμαθῶς θνατῶν καταπαυόμενοι·
εἰ γὰρ ἅμιλλα κρινεῖ νιν   1155
αἵματος, οὔποτ᾽ ἔρις
λείψει κατ᾽ ἀνθρώπων πόλεις·
ᾇ Πριαμίδος γᾶς ἔλαχον θαλάμους,
ἐξὸν διορθῶσαι λόγοις
σὰν ἔριν, ὦ Ἑλένα.   1160
νῦν δ᾽ οἳ μὲν Ἅιδᾳ μέλονται κάτω,
τείχεα δὲ φλογερός, ὥστε Διός, ἐπέσυτο φλόξ,
ἐπὶ δὲ πάθεα πάθεσι φέρεις
†ἀθλίοις συμφοραῖς αἰλίνοις.†

ΘΕΟΚΛΥΜΕΝΟΣ

ὦ χαῖρε, πατρὸς μνῆμ᾽· ἐπ᾽ ἐξόδοισι γὰρ   1165
ἔθαψα, Πρωτεῦ, σ᾽ ἕνεκ᾽ ἐμῆς προσρήσεως·

1147 κᾆτ᾽ ἰαχήθης Hermann : καὶ ἰαχὴ σὴ L p: καὶ ἰαχὴ σὺ P   fortasse
καθ᾽ Ἑλλάδ᾽ αἶαν : cf. 1161   1148 ἀδίκως προδότης (προδότις L² P²)
ἄπιστος ἄδικος L P : ἀδίκως in ἄδικος mutavit, ἄδικος (post ἄπιστος)
delevit l : corr. Hermann   1149 sq. locus difficilis : ἔτι Musgrave :
ὅτι L P   δ᾽ om. L P : add. Barnes, cf. El. 399 sq. : ὅτι ποτ᾽ ἐν βροτοῖς
ἀμφὶ θεῶν Kirchhoff   τῶν delevit l   1151 ἄφονες P : corr. p
1152 sq. κτᾶσθε δορός τ᾽ ἀλκαίου λόγχαισι καταπαυόμενοι πόνους θνατῶν
ἀπαθῶς L P, nullo metro: transposui, cf. vv. 1138 sq.   1153 ἀμαθῶς
Musgrave : ἀπαθῶς L P, quod si sanum, οὐ (Wecklein) vel μὴ καταπαυόμενοι legendum   1155 εἰ] ἤ P   κρινεῖ Heath : κρίνει L P
1158 ᾇ] αἱ L P   ἔλαχον Pflugk : ἔλιπον L P   1161 fortasse κάτω
μέλονται : cf. 1147   1162 aut φλογερός aut φλόξ corruptum : φόνιος
Herwerden : φλογμὸς apogr. Paris.   ἐπέσσυτο L P : corr. l   1164
ἀθλίοις L P : tum notam τι λείπει L² : notam del. et ἐν ἀθλίοις scr. l
αἰλίνοις L² P : ἰλίνοις primitus L : γρ. ἰλίοις suprascr. l : ἐλεινοῖς Nauck :
possis ἄεθλα (vel ἆθλα) δὲ ξύμφορ᾽ αἰλίνοισιν   1166 ἔθραψα P : corr. p

ἀεὶ δέ σ᾽ ἐξιών τε κἀσιὼν δόμους
Θεοκλύμενος παῖς ὅδε προσεννέπει, πάτερ.
ὑμεῖς μὲν οὖν κύνας τε καὶ θηρῶν βρόχους,
δμῶες, κομίζετ᾽ ἐς δόμους τυραννικούς·   1170
ἐγὼ δ᾽ ἐμαυτὸν πόλλ᾽ ἐλοιδόρησα δή·
οὐ γάρ τι θανάτῳ τοὺς κακοὺς κολάζομεν;
καὶ νῦν πέπυσμαι φανερὸν Ἑλλήνων τινὰ
ἐς γῆν ἀφῖχθαι καὶ λεληθέναι σκοπούς,
ἤτοι κατόπτην ἢ κλοπαῖς θηρώμενον   1175
Ἑλένην· θανεῖται δ᾽, ἤν γε δὴ ληφθῇ μόνον.
ἔα·
ἀλλ᾽, ὡς ἔοικε, πάντα διαπεπραγμένα
ηὕρηκα· τύμβου γὰρ κενὰς λιποῦσ᾽ ἕδρας
ἡ Τυνδαρὶς παῖς ἐκπεπόρθμευται χθονός.
ὠή, χαλᾶτε κλῇθρα· λύεθ᾽ ἱππικὰ   1180
φάτνης, ὀπαδοί, κἀκκομίζεθ᾽ ἅρματα,
ὡς ἂν πόνου γ᾽ ἕκατι μὴ λάθῃ με γῆς
τῆσδ᾽ ἐκκομισθεῖσ᾽ ἄλοχος, ἧς ἐφίεμαι.—
ἐπίσχετ᾽· εἰσορῶ γὰρ οὓς διώκομεν
παρόντας ἐν δόμοισι κοὐ πεφευγότας.   1185
αὕτη, τί πέπλους μέλανας ἐξήψω χροὸς
λευκῶν ἀμείψασ᾽ ἔκ τε κρατὸς εὐγενοῦς
κόμας σίδηρον ἐμβαλοῦσ᾽ ἀπέθρισας
χλωροῖς τε τέγγεις δάκρυσι σὴν παρηίδα
κλαίουσα; πότερον ἐννύχοις πεπεισμένη   1190
στένεις ὀνείροις, ἢ φάτιν τιν᾽ οἴκοθεν
κλύουσα λύπῃ σὰς διέφθαρσαι φρένας;
Ελ. ὦ δέσποτ᾽—ἤδη γὰρ τόδ᾽ ὀνομάζω σ᾽ ἔπος—
ὄλωλα· φροῦδα τἀμὰ κοὐδέν εἰμ᾽ ἔτι.
Θε. ἐν τῷ δὲ κεῖσαι συμφορᾶς; τίς ἡ τύχη;   1195

1167 κεῖσιὼν L P   1168 προσεννέπω Lenting   1172 interrogative
scripsimus   1178 εὕρηκα L P   1179 ἐκπεπόρθευται P   1180 sq.
ἱππικὰ φάτνης Cron : ἱππικὰς φάτνας L P   1182 ἂν] οὐ Barthold
1183 ἐκκομισθεὶς L P   1186 χροὸς L : χθονὸς P   1192 φρένας]
fortasse γένυς   1194 εἴμ᾽ L P

Ελ. Μενέλαος—οἴμοι, πῶς φράσω;—τέθνηκέ μοι.

Θε. οὐδέν τι χαίρω σοῖς λόγοις, τὰ δ᾽ εὐτυχῶ.

πῶς ⟨δ᾽⟩ οἶσθα; μῶν σοι Θεονόη λέγει τάδε;

Ελ. κείνη τε φησὶν ὅ τε παρὼν ὅτ᾽ ὤλλυτο.

Θε. ἥκει γὰρ ὅστις καὶ τάδ᾽ ἀγγέλλει σαφῆ;   1200

Ελ. ἥκει· μόλοι γὰρ οἷ σφ᾽ ἐγὼ χρῄζω μολεῖν.

Θε. τίς ἐστι; ποῦ 'στιν; ἵνα σαφέστερον μάθω.

Ελ. ὅδ᾽ ὃς κάθηται τῷδ᾽ ὑποπτήξας τάφῳ.

Θε. Ἄπολλον, ὡς ἐσθῆτι δυσμόρφῳ πρέπει.

Ελ. οἴμοι, δοκῶ μὲν κἀμὸν ὧδ᾽ ἔχειν πόσιν.   1205

Θε. ποδαπὸς δ᾽ ὅδ᾽ ἀνὴρ καὶ πόθεν κατέσχε γῆν;

Ελ. Ἕλλην, Ἀχαιῶν εἷς ἐμῷ σύμπλους πόσει.

Θε. θανάτῳ δὲ ποίῳ φησὶ Μενέλεων θανεῖν;

Ελ. οἰκτρόταθ᾽, ὑγροῖσιν ἐν κλυδωνίοις ἁλός.

Θε. ποῦ βαρβάροισι πελάγεσιν ναυσθλούμενον;   1210

Ελ. Λιβύης ἀλιμένοις ἐκπεσόντα πρὸς πέτραις.

Θε. καὶ πῶς ὅδ᾽ οὐκ ὄλωλε κοινωνῶν πλάτης;

Ελ. ἐσθλῶν κακίους ἐνίοτ᾽ εὐτυχέστεροι.

Θε. λιπὼν δὲ ναὸς ποῦ πάρεστιν ἔκβολα;

Ελ. ὅπου κακῶς ὄλοιτο, Μενέλεως δὲ μή.   1215

Θε. ὄλωλ᾽ ἐκεῖνος. ἦλθε δ᾽ ἐν ποίῳ σκάφει;

Ελ. ναῦταί σφ᾽ ἀνεῖλοντ᾽ ἐντυχόντες, ὡς λέγει.

Θε. ποῦ δὴ τὸ πεμφθὲν ἀντὶ σοῦ Τροίᾳ κακόν;

Ελ. νεφέλης λέγεις ἄγαλμα; ἐς αἰθέρ᾽ οἴχεται.

Θε. ὦ Πρίαμε καὶ γῆ Τρῳάς, ⟨ὡς⟩ ἔρρεις μάτην.   1220

Ελ. κἀγὼ μετέσχον Πριαμίδαις δυσπραξίας.

Θε. πόσιν δ᾽ ἄθαπτον ἔλιπεν ἢ κρύπτει χθονί;

1197 τάδ᾽ L P   τάδ᾽ εὐτυχῶν Wilamowitz   1198 δ᾽ add. Hermann
1201-1278 paragraphi pro personarum notis in P: item in L praeter
1251, 1252   1201 μόλει P: corr. p   οἷ σφ᾽ Lenting: ὡς L P
1206 ἀνὴρ L P   1209 οἰκτρόταθ᾽ ὑγροῖσιν ἐν Hermann: οἰκτρότατον
ὑγροῖσι L P: οἰκτρόταταν ὑγροῖς ἐν et supra θάνατον δὲ ποῖον Scaliger
1212 κοινωνῶν πλάτης l (vel L²): κοινωνῶν πλάταις (sic) P: κοινῶν
πλάταις L   1213 ἐσθλῶ P: corr. p   1217 ἀνείλοντ᾽ Cobet: ἀνεῖλον L P
1218 δὴ Scaliger: δὲ L P   1219 ἄγαλμα L P   1220 ὡς add. Scaliger

Ελ. ἄθαπτον· οἲ ἐγὼ τῶν ἐμῶν τλήμων κακῶν.

Θε. τῶνδ᾽ οὕνεκ᾽ ἔταμες βοστρύχους ξανθῆς κόμης·

Ελ. φίλος γάρ ἐστιν, ὅς ποτ᾽ ἐστίν, ἐνθάδ᾽ ὤν.　1225

Θε. ὀρθῶς μὲν ἥδε συμφορὰ δακρύεται. . . .

Ελ. ἐν εὐμαρεῖ γοῦν σὴν κασιγνήτην λαθεῖν.

Θε. οὐ δῆτα.　πῶς οὖν; τόνδ᾽ ἔτ᾽ οἰκήσεις τάφον;

Ελ. τί κερτομεῖς με, τὸν θανόντα δ᾽ οὐκ ἐᾷς;

Θε. πιστὴ γὰρ εἶ σὺ σῷ πόσει φεύγουσά με.　1230

Ελ. ἀλλ᾽ οὐκέτ᾽· ἤδη δ᾽ ἄρχε τῶν ἐμῶν γάμων.

Θε. χρόνια μὲν ἦλθεν, ἀλλ᾽ ὅμως αἰνῶ τάδε.

Ελ. οἶσθ᾽ οὖν ὃ δρᾶσον; τῶν πάρος λαθώμεθα.

Θε. ἐπὶ τῷ; χάρις γὰρ ἀντὶ χάριτος ἐλθέτω.

Ελ. σπονδὰς τέμωμεν καὶ διαλλάχθητί μοι.　1235

Θε. μεθίημι νεῖκος τὸ σόν, ἴτω δ᾽ ὑπόπτερον.

Ελ. πρός νύν σε γονάτων τῶνδ᾽, ἐπείπερ εἶ φίλος—

Θε. τί χρῆμα θηρῶσ᾽ ἱκέτις ὠρέχθης ἐμοῦ;

Ελ. τὸν κατθανόντα πόσιν ἐμὸν θάψαι θέλω.

Θε. τί δ᾽; ἔστ᾽ ἀπόντων τύμβος; ἢ θάψεις σκιάν;　1240

Ελ. Ἕλλησίν ἐστι νόμος, ὃς ἂν πόντῳ θάνῃ—

Θε. τί δρᾶν; σοφοί τοι Πελοπίδαι τὰ τοιάδε.

Ελ. κενοῖσι θάπτειν ἐν πέπλων ὑφάσμασιν.

Θε. κτέριζ᾽· ἀνίστη τύμβον οὗ χρῄζεις χθονός.

Ελ. οὐχ ὧδε ναύτας ὀλομένους τυμβεύομεν.　1245

Θε. πῶς δαί; λέλειμμαι τῶν ἐν Ἕλλησιν νόμων.

Ελ. ἐς πόντον ὅσα χρὴ νέκυσιν ἐξορμίζομεν.

Θε. τί σοι παράσχω δῆτα τῷ τεθνηκότι;

Ελ. ὅδ᾽ οἶδ᾽, ἐγὼ δ᾽ ἄπειρος, εὐτυχοῦσα πρίν.

1223 οἲ ἐγὼ L P : οἲ 'γὼ l　1225 ἐστί, καὶ θανών Herwerden :
possis traicere ἔστιν γὰρ ἔστιν, ὥς ποτ᾽ ἐνθάδ᾽ ὤν, φίλος　1227 λαθεῖν
Jacobs : θανεῖν L P　1230 εἶ σὺ Elmsley : ἔσσι L P　γὰρ οὖσα σῷ
πόσει φεύγεις ἐμέ Paley　1232 ἦλθεν Musgrave : ἦλθες (sed χρόνια) L P
1233 λαθώμεθα Schaefer : λαθοίμεθα L P　1236 μεθῆκα Cobet
1237 πρὸς νῦν L P　1243 πέπλων Scaliger : πέπλοις L P　1246 sq.
om. P　1246 πῶς δαί L : cf. Med. 1012 (339), Ion 275, El. 244,
1116, I. A. 1444, 1448　1247 ἐξορίζομεν Ellis　1249 ὅδ᾽
Hartung : οὐκ L P

ΕΛΕΝΗ 51

Θε. ὦ ξένε, λόγων μὲν κληδόν᾽ ἤνεγκας φίλην.   1250
Με. οὔκουν ἐμαυτῷ γ᾽ οὐδὲ τῷ τεθνηκότι.
Θε. πῶς τοὺς θανόντας θάπτετ᾽ ἐν πόντῳ νεκρούς;
Με. ὡς ἂν παρούσης οὐσίας ἕκαστος ᾖ.
Θε. πλούτου λέγ᾽ οὕνεχ᾽ ὅ τι θέλεις ταύτης χάριν.
Με. προσφάζεται μὲν αἷμα πρῶτα νερτέροις.   1255
Θε. τίνος; σύ μοι σήμαινε, πείσομαι δ᾽ ἐγώ.
Με. αὐτὸς σὺ γίγνωσκ᾽· ἀρκέσει γὰρ ἂν διδῷς.
Θε. ἐν βαρβάροις μὲν ἵππον ἢ ταῦρον νόμος.
Με. διδούς γε μὲν δὴ δυσγενὲς μηδὲν δίδου.
Θε. οὐ τῶνδ᾽ ἐν ἀγέλαις ὀλβίαις σπανίζομεν.   1260
Με. καὶ στρωτὰ φέρεται λέκτρα σώματος κενά.
Θε. ἔσται· τί δ᾽ ἄλλο προσφέρειν νομίζεται;
Με. χαλκήλαθ᾽ ὅπλα· καὶ γὰρ ἦν φίλος δορί.
Θε. ἄξια τάδ᾽ ἔσται Πελοπιδῶν ἃ δώσομεν.
Με. καὶ τἄλλ᾽ ὅσα χθὼν καλὰ φέρει βλαστήματα.   1265
Θε. πῶς οὖν; ἐς οἶδμα τίνι τρόπῳ καθίετε;
Με. ναῦν δεῖ παρεῖναι κἀρετμῶν ἐπιστάτας.
Θε. πόσον δ᾽ ἀπείργει μῆκος ἐκ γαίας δόρυ;
Με. ὥστ᾽ ἐξορᾶσθαι ῥόθια χερσόθεν μόλις.
Θε. τί δή; τόδ᾽ Ἑλλὰς νόμιμον ἐκ τίνος σέβει;   1270
Με. ὡς μὴ πάλιν γῇ λύματ᾽ ἐκβάλῃ κλύδων.
Θε. Φοίνισσα κώπη ταχύπορος γενήσεται.
Με. καλῶς ἂν εἴη Μενέλεῳ τε πρὸς χάριν.
Θε. οὔκουν σὺ χωρὶς τῆσδε δρῶν ἀρκεῖς τάδε;
Με. μητρὸς τόδ᾽ ἔργον ἢ γυναικὸς ἢ τέκνων.   1275
Θε. ταύτης ὁ μόχθος, ὡς λέγεις, θάπτειν πόσιν.

1251 Menelai, 1252 Theoclymeni notas praef. L, non ut solet
paragraphos: cf. ad 1201   1255 προσφάζεται P   1257 ἀρκέσει...
διδῷς Barnes: ἀρκέσειε... δίδως L P: ἀρκέσεις... διδῶς p   1258 ἵππων ἢ ταύρων P: corr. p   1259 γε μέντοι Nauck   1260 οὐχ ὧδ᾽
Bruhn   1261 φέρεται Canter: φέρετε L P   1263 χαλκήλατα L P
1267 ναῦν Canter: νῦν L P   δεῖ L: δὴ P   καὶ ἐρετμῶν L: καὶ ᾽ρετμῶν
L² P   1268 πόσον L: πόσιν P   ἀπείργεις Wecklein   1272
ταχυπόρος L P   1273 τε Reiske: γε L P   1276 μόχος P: corr. p

4*

Με. ἐν εὐσεβεῖ γοῦν νόμιμα μὴ κλέπτειν νεκρῶν.

Θε. ἴτω· πρὸς ἡμῶν ἄλοχον εὐσεβῆ τρέφειν.

ἐλθὼν δ' ἐς οἴκους ἐξελοῦ κόσμον νεκρῷ·
καὶ σὲ οὐ κεναῖσι χερσὶ γῆς ἀποστελῶ,   1280
δράσαντα τῇδε πρὸς χάριν· φήμας δ' ἐμοὶ
ἐσθλὰς ἐνεγκὼν ἀντὶ τῆς ἀχλαινίας
ἐσθῆτα λήψῃ σῖτά θ', ὥστε σ' ἐς πάτραν
ἐλθεῖν, ἐπεὶ νῦν γ' ἀθλίως ἔχονθ' ὁρῶ.

σὺ δ', ὦ τάλαινα, μὴ 'πὶ τοῖς ἀνηνύτοις   1285
τρύχουσα σαυτήν . . . Μενέλεως δ' ἔχει πότμον,
κοὐκ ἂν δύναιτο ζῆν ὁ κατθανὼν πόσις.

Με. σὸν ἔργον, ὦ νεᾶνι· τὸν παρόντα μὲν
στέργειν πόσιν χρή, τὸν δὲ μηκέτ' ὄντ' ἐᾶν·
ἄριστα γάρ σοι ταῦτα πρὸς τὸ τυγχάνον.   1290
ἢν δ' Ἑλλάδ' ἔλθω καὶ τύχω σωτηρίας,
παύσω ψόγου σε τοῦ πρίν, ἢν γυνὴ γένῃ   1293
οἵαν γενέσθαι χρή σε σῷ ξυνευνέτῃ.   1292

Ελ. ἔσται τάδ'· οὐδὲ μέμψεται πόσις ποτὲ
ἡμῖν· σὺ δ' αὐτὸς ἐγγὺς ὢν εἴσῃ τάδε.   1295
ἀλλ', ὦ τάλας, εἴσελθε καὶ λουτρῶν τύχε
ἐσθῆτά τ' ἐξάλλαξον. οὐκ ἐς ἀμβολὰς
εὐεργετήσω σ'· εὐμενέστερον γὰρ ἂν
τῷ φιλτάτῳ μοι Μενέλεῳ τὰ πρόσφορα
δρῴης ἄν, ἡμῶν τυγχάνων οἵων σε χρή.   1300

Χο.   Ὀρεία ποτὲ δρομάδι κώ-   [στρ. α
              λῳ μάτηρ θεῶν ἐσύθη ἀν'
              ὑλάεντα νάπη

1278 ἴτω] γρ. ἤτω in margine L² vel l: merus error   1279 ἐξελοῦ
Badham : ἐξελῶ L P   1282 post ἐνεγκών habet γ' L : οὐγ P : delet
Hermann   τῆς] τῆσδ' Hartung   1283 θ']τ' L P   1286 τρύχου
σεαυτήν, quasi a τρυχόω, Scaliger : lacunam indicavit Matthiae
δ' fortasse delendum   1287 πόσις] πάλιν Reiske   1292,
1293 transposuit Canter   1293 ψόγον P   1297 ἐς hic L P
1300 χρή Matthiae : χρῆν L P   1303 videtur ἀνά et prodelisionem
et elisionem pati, cf. antistr. : ἀν' ὑλᾶντα Dindorf

ποτάμιόν τε χεῦμ' ὑδάτων
βαρύβρομόν τε κῦμ' ἅλιον   1305
πόθῳ τᾶς ἀποιχομένας
ἀρρήτου κούρας.

κρόταλα δὲ βρόμια διαπρύσιον
ἰέντα κέλαδον ἀνεβόα,
θηρῶν ὅτε ζυγίους   1310
ζευξάσᾳ θεᾷ σατίνας
τὰν ἁρπασθεῖσαν κυκλίων
χορῶν ἔξω παρθενίων
μετὰ κούραν, ἀελλόποδες,
ἃ μὲν τόξοις Ἄρτεμις, ἃ δ'   1315
ἔγχει Γοργῶπις πάνοπλος,
⟨συνείποντο. Ζεὺς δ' ἑδράνων⟩
αὐγάζων ἐξ οὐρανίων
ἄλλαν μοῖραν ἔκραινε.

δρομαῖον δ' ὅτε πολυπλάνη-   [ἀντ. α'
τον μάτηρ ἔπαυσε πόνον,   1320
μαστεύουσα †πόνους†
θυγατρὸς ἁρπαγὰς δολίους,
χιονοθρέμμονάς γ' ἐπέρασ'
Ἰδαιᾶν Νυμφᾶν σκοπιάς·
ῥίπτει δ' ἐν πένθει   1325
πέτρινα κατὰ δρία πολυνιφέα·

1307 κούρας L² P : κόρας L, et υ deletum in P   1310 sq. θηρῶντο
τε ζυγίους ζεύξασαι θεαὶ σατίνας post Badhamum Wecklein   1311 ζευξάσᾳ θεᾷ Hermann : ζεύξασα θεὰ L P   σατίνας Musgrave : σατίναν L P
1314 μετὰ κουρᾶν δ' L P : δ' delevit Pflugk : μεταθῦσαν Wilamowitz
1316 Γοργῶπις Heath : γοργὼ L P : καὶ γοργοῖ Seidler   post 1316
lacunam indicavit Hermann (post 1317 Dindorf) : eius monitu ex. gr.
supplevi   1317 αὐγάζων Hermann : αὐλάζων δ' P : αὐλάζων δ' vel
αὐγάζων δ' difficili discrimine L   1319 sq. δρομαίων . . . πολυπλανήτων
. . . πόνων L P : correxi : (ἐπαύσατ' ἀλῶν F. Gu. Schmidt : πόδα πλανή-
των Herwerden)   1321 ματεύουσα Hermann   πόνυυς corruptum :
ἀπόνους (demens) Verrall   1323 χιονιθρέμονάς P : corr. p   γ' L P :
δ' l p : fortasse χιονοθρέμμον' ἄγ' ἐπέρασ' . . . σκοπιάν, cf. Tro. 1069
1324 ἰδαίαν L P, fortasse recte   1326 δρίους ut videtur P : δρύα p

βροτοῖσι δ' ἄχλοα πεδία γᾶς
οὐ καρπίζουσ' ἀρότοις
λαῶν [δὲ] φθείρει γενεάν·
ποίμναις δ' οὐχ ἵει θαλερὰς　　　　1330
βοσκὰς εὐφύλλων ἑλίκων,
πόλεων δ' ἀπέλειπε βίος·
οὐδ' ἦσαν θεῶν θυσίαι,
βωμοῖς δ' ἄφλεκτοι πέλανοι·
πηγὰς δ' ἀμπαύει δροσερὰς　　　　1335
λευκῶν ἐκβάλλειν ὑδάτων
πένθει παιδὸς ἀλάστωρ.

ἐπεὶ δ' ἔπαυσ' εἰλαπίνας　　　[στρ. β'
θεοῖς βροτείῳ τε γένει,
Ζεὺς μειλίσσων στυγίους
Ματρὸς ὀργὰς ἐνέπει·　　　　　1340
Βᾶτε, σεμναὶ Χάριτες,
ἴτε, τᾷ περὶ παρθένῳ
Δηοῖ θυμωσαμένᾳ
λύπαν ἐξαλλάξατ' ἀλαλᾷ,
Μοῦσαί θ' ὕμνοισι χορῶν.　　　　1345
χαλκοῦ δ' αὐδὰν χθονίαν
τύπανά τ' ἔλαβε βυρσοτενῆ
καλλίστα τότε πρῶτα μακά-
ρων Κύπρις· γέλασέν τε θεὰ

1329 λαῶν Barnes: λαῶν δὲ L P　　　γενεάν Seidler: γένναν L P
1330 ποίμναις Canter: ποίμνας L P　　　1332 πολέων l　　　ἀπέλειπε
l: ἀπέλιπε L P: fortasse ἐξέλειπε, cf. 1314　　　1334 et 1335 δ' post
Hartungum scripsi: τ' L P　　　1337 ἀλάστωρ] ἀλάστῳ Ludv. Dindorf:
sed cf. Nicoch. incert. 4 (Mein.) de Sphinge　versui περισσόν suprascr.
l, cum iam in stropha versus periisset: itaque omittebant veteres edd.
1339 μειλίσσω P　　　1340 ἐννέπει L P　　　1342 τᾷ Musgrave: τὰν
L P　　　1343 Δηοῖ Canter: δηίω L P, δηι in ras. P　　　1344 v. 1360
non respondet: ἐξαλλάξατ' ἀλᾶν Bothe, sed sanum videtur ἀλαλᾷ:
ἀλλάξαιτ' Fritzsche　　　1345 χορῶν Matthiae: χορόν L P　　　1347
τύμπανα L P: corr. Heath　　　τ' ἔλαβε Hermann: τε λάβετε L P
βυρσοτενῆ Canter: πυρσογενῆ L P　　　1348 κάλλιστα L P: cf. 1364
1349 γέλασε L P　　　τε] δὲ Wecklein

δέξατό τ᾽ ἐς χέρας   1350
βαρύβρομον αὐλὸν
τερφθεῖσ᾽ ἀλαλαγμῷ.

ὧν οὐ θέμις ⟨σ᾽⟩ οὔθ᾽ ὁσία   [ἀντ. β᾽
᾽πύρωσας ἐν ⟨θεῶν⟩ θαλάμοις,
μῆνιν δ᾽ ἔσχες μεγάλας   1355
ματρός, ὦ παῖ, θυσίας
οὐ σεβίζουσα θεᾶς.
μέγα τοι δύναται νεβρῶν
παμποίκιλοι στολίδες
κισσοῦ τε στεφθεῖσα χλόα   1360
νάρθηκας εἰς ἱερούς,
ῥόμβου θ᾽ εἱλισσομένα
κύκλιος ἔνοσις αἰθερία,
βακχεύουσά τ᾽ ἔθειρα Βρομί-
ῳ καὶ παννυχίδες θεᾶς.   1365
†εὖ δέ νιν ἅμασιν
ὑπέρβαλε σελάνα†
μορφᾷ μόνον ηὔχεις.

Ελ. τὰ μὲν κατ᾽ οἴκους εὐτυχοῦμεν, ὦ φίλαι·
ἡ γὰρ συνεκκλέπτουσα Πρωτέως κόρη   1370
πόσιν παρόντα τὸν ἐμὸν ἱστορουμένη
οὐκ εἶπ᾽ ἀδελφῷ· κατθανόντα δ᾽ ἐν χθονὶ
οὔ φησιν αὐγὰς εἰσορᾶν ἐμὴν χάριν.

.   .   .   .

κάλλιστα δῆτ᾽ ἀνήρπασ᾽ ἐν τύχῃ πόσις·

1350 χέρα Hermann   1353 σ᾽ post multos addidi   1354 θεῶν ex.
gr. addidi   ἐπύρωσας L P   1355 ἔσχες Hermann: ἔχεις L P   1357 θεᾶς
Heath: θεοῖς L P   1358 δύναται Musgrave: δύνανται L P   1360 κισσοῦ Musgrave: κισσῶ L P   1361 εἰς] ἐς L P   1362 ῥόμβου Heath:
ῥόμβῳ L P   ἑλισσομένα L P   1363 κύκλιος Scaliger: κυκλίοις
L P   1366 sq. locus conclamatus   1366 εὖ γε P   1372 ἐν
χθονὶ suspectum   ante 1374 lacunam indicavit Hermann, ex. gr.
ἔπειτα τεύχη τῶν ἔσω φρουρουμένων: δὴ τάδ᾽ ἥρπασ᾽ sine lacuna Fix
1374 ἀνήρπασεν ἐν L P

ἃ γαρ καθήσειν ὅπλ' ἔμελλεν εἰς ἅλα,   1375
ταῦτ' ἐμβαλὼν πόρπακι γενναίαν χέρα
αὐτὸς κομίζει δόρυ τε δεξιᾷ λαβών,
ὡς τῷ θανόντι χάριτα δὴ συνεκπονῶν.
προύργου δ' ἐς ἀλκὴν σῶμ' ὅπλοις ἠσκήσατο,
ὡς βαρβάρων τρόπαια μυρίων χερὶ   1380
θήσων, ὅταν κωπῆρες ἐσβῶμεν σκάφος,
πέπλους δ' ἀμείψασ' ἀντὶ ναυφθόρου στολῆς
ἐγώ νιν ἐξήσκησα, καὶ λουτροῖς χρόα
ἔδωκα, χρόνια νίπτρα ποταμίας δρόσου.
ἀλλ', ἐκπερᾷ γὰρ δωμάτων ὁ τοὺς ἐμοὺς   1385
γάμους ἑτοίμους ἐν χεροῖν ἔχειν δοκῶν,
σιγητέον μοι· καὶ σὲ προσποιούμεθα
εὔνουν κρατεῖν τε στόματος, ἢν δυνώμεθα
σωθέντες αὐτοὶ καὶ σὲ συνσῶσαί ποτε.

Θε. χωρεῖτ' ἐφεξῆς, ὡς ἔταξεν ὁ ξένος,   1390
δμῶες, φέροντες ἐνάλια κτερίσματα.
Ἑλένη, σὺ δ', ἤν σοι μὴ κακῶς δόξω λέγειν,
πείθου, μέν' αὐτοῦ· ταὐτὰ γὰρ παροῦσά τε
πράξεις τὸν ἄνδρα τὸν σὸν ἤν τε μη παρῇς.
δέδοικα γάρ σε μή τις ἐμπεσὼν πόθος   1395
πείσῃ μεθεῖναι σῶμ' ἐς οἶδμα πόντιον
τοῦ πρόσθεν ἀνδρὸς χάρισιν ἐκπεπληγμένην·
ἄγαν γὰρ αὐτὸν οὐ παρόνθ' ὅμως στένεις.

Ελ. ὦ καινὸς ἡμῖν πόσις, ἀναγκαίως ἔχει
τὰ πρῶτα λέκτρα νυμφικάς θ' ὁμιλίας   1400
τιμᾶν· ἐγὼ δὲ διὰ τὸ μὲν στέργειν πόσιν

1376 πόρπακι Victorius : ὅρπακι L : ὄρπακι P   1378 δῆθεν ἐκπονῶν
χάριν Herwerden   1381 στήσων anonymus   εἰσβῶμεν ** σκάφος P : εἰσβῶμεν εἰς σκάφος L   1382 sq. ἀμείψας . . . ἀγώ L P :
corr. Pierson   1387 sq. fortasse προσποιούμεθ' εὖ | νοεῖν : cf.
Xen. Cyr. i. 18   κρατῆσαι στόματος Heimsoeth   1393 πιθοῦ
Dindorf   μὲν P : corr. p   1394 πράξῃς P : corr. p   1397 ἐκ-
πεπληγμένου P   1398 παροῦσ' Vitelli   1399 καινὸς Beck :
κλεινὸς L P

καὶ ξυνθάνοιμ' ἄν· ἀλλὰ τίς κείνῳ χάρις
ξὺν κατθανόντι κατθανεῖν; ἔα δέ με
αὐτὴν μολοῦσαν ἐντάφια δοῦναι νεκρῷ.
θεοὶ δὲ σοί τε δοῖεν οἷ' ἐγὼ θέλω,   1405
καὶ τῷ ξένῳ τῷδ', ὅτι συνεκπονεῖ τάδε.
ἕξεις δέ μ' οἵαν χρή σ' ἔχειν ἐν δώμασι
γυναῖκ', ἐπειδὴ Μενέλεων εὐεργετεῖς
κᾆμ'· ἔρχεται γὰρ δή τιν' ἐς τύχην τάδε.
ὅστις δὲ δώσει ναῦν ἐν ᾗ τάδ' ἄξομεν,   1410
πρόσταξον, ὡς ἂν τὴν χάριν πλήρη λάβω.
Θε. χώρει σὺ καὶ ναῦν τοῖσδε πεντηκόντορον
Σιδωνίαν δὸς κἀρετμῶν ἐπιστάτας.
Ελ. οὔκουν ὅδ' ἄρξει ναὸς ὃς κοσμεῖ τάφον;
Θε. μάλιστ'· ἀκούειν τοῦδε χρὴ ναύτας ἐμούς.   1415
Ελ. αὖθις κέλευσον, ἵνα σαφῶς μάθωσί σου.
Θε. αὖθις κελεύω καὶ τρίτον γ', εἴ σοι φίλον.
Ελ. ὄναιο· κἀγὼ τῶν ἐμῶν βουλευμάτων.
Θε. μή νυν ἄγαν σὸν δάκρυσιν ἐκτήξῃς χρόα.
Ελ. ἥδ' ἡμέρα σοι τὴν ἐμὴν δείξει χάριν.   1420
Θε. τὰ τῶν θανόντων οὐδέν, ἀλλ' ἄλλως πόνος.
Ελ. ἔστιν τι κἀκεῖ κἀνθάδ' ὧν ἐγὼ λέγω.
Θε. οὐδὲν κακίω Μενέλεώ μ' ἕξεις πόσιν.
Ελ. οὐδὲν σὺ μεμπτός· τῆς τύχης με δεῖ μόνον.
Θε. ἐν σοὶ τόδ', ἢν σὴν εἰς ἔμ' εὔνοιαν διδῷς.   1425
Ελ. οὐ νῦν διδαξόμεσθα τοὺς φίλους φιλεῖν.
Θε. βούλῃ ξυνεργῶν αὐτὸς ἐκπέμψω στόλον;
Ελ. ἥκιστα· μὴ δούλευε σοῖς δούλοις, ἄναξ.

1403 ξυγκατθανόντι L P   κατθανεῖν μ' Lenting   1406 τῷδ'
L² P : δ' L   1407 χρή σ' Matthiae : χρῆν L P   1413 καὶ 'ρετμῶν
L² P : καὶ ἐρετμῶν L   1415 χρὴ Reiske : χρῆν L P   1416-1429 paragraphos pro personarum notis praef. L P   1417 γ' l : om. L P
1419 ἐκτήξεις P : corr. p   1421 ἄλως P : ἅλως p   1422, 1423 in-
verso ordine habet L sed numeris appictis rectum ordinem restituit
1422 ἔστιν l : ἔστι L P   κἀκεῖ τὰ ἐνθάδ', ὡς Herwerden
1424 om. P   με δεῖ Musgrave : μέλει L

Θε. ἀλλ᾽ εἶα· τοὺς μὲν Πελοπιδῶν ἐῶ νόμους·
   καθαρὰ γὰρ ἡμῖν δώματ᾽· οὐ γὰρ ἐνθάδε   1430
   ψυχὴν ἀφῆκε Μενέλεως· ἴτω δέ τις
   φράσων ὑπάρχοις τοῖς ἐμοῖς φέρειν γάμων
   ἀγάλματ᾽ οἴκους εἰς ἐμούς· πᾶσαν δὲ χρὴ
   γαῖαν βοᾶσθαι μακαρίαις ὑμνῳδίαις
   ὑμέναιον Ἑλένης κἀμόν, ὡς ζηλωτὸς ᾖ.   1435
   σὺ δ᾽, ὦ ξέν᾽, ἐλθών, πελαγίους ἐς ἀγκάλας
   τῷ τῆσδε πρίν ποτ᾽ ὄντι δοὺς πόσει τάδε,
   πάλιν πρὸς οἴκους σπεῦδ᾽ ἐμὴν δάμαρτ᾽ ἔχων,
   ὡς τοὺς γάμους τοὺς τῆσδε συνδαίσας ἐμοὶ
   στέλλῃ πρὸς οἴκους ἢ μένων εὐδαιμονῇς.   1440
Με. ὦ Ζεῦ, πατήρ τε καὶ σοφὸς κλήζῃ θεός,
   βλέψον πρὸς ἡμᾶς καὶ μετάστησον κακῶν.
   ἕλκουσι δ᾽ ἡμῖν πρὸς λέπας τὰς συμφορὰς
   σπουδῇ σύναψαι· κἂν ἄκρᾳ θίγῃς χερί,
   ἥξομεν ἵν᾽ ἐλθεῖν βουλόμεσθα τῆς τύχης.   1445
   ἅλις δὲ μόχθων οὓς ἐμοχθοῦμεν πάρος.
   κέκλησθέ μοι, θεοί, πολλά, χρῆσθ᾽ ὁμοῦ κλύειν
   καὶ λύπρ᾽· ὀφείλω δ᾽ οὐκ ἀεὶ πράσσειν κακῶς,
   ὀρθῷ δὲ βῆναι ποδί· μίαν δέ μοι χάριν
   δόντες τὸ λοιπὸν εὐτυχῆ με θήσετε.   1450

Χο.   Φοίνισσα Σιδωνιὰς ὦ   [στρ. α′
             ταχεῖα κώπα ῥοθίοισι, μᾶτηρ
             εἰρεσίας φίλα,
             χοραγὲ τῶν καλλιχόρων
                 δελφίνων, ὅταν αὔραις   1455
             πέλαγος ἀνήνεμον ᾖ,

1433 χρὴ Matthiae : χρῆν L P   1435 ᾖ] ᾧ Wecklein   1441 τε]
γὰρ Kirchhoff   1443 λέπας Musgrave : λύπας L P   1447 χρῆστ·
ἐμοῦ L P: corr. Nauck   1448 λυπρά· L : λυπρά γ᾽ L² P   1452 ῥοθίοισι
Canter : ῥόθοισι L P   μάτηρ Matthiae : μήτηρ L P : Νηρέως Badham   1453 εἰρεσίας Fritzsche : εἰρεσία l : ἐρεσία L P   1456 ἀνή·
νεμον scripsi : νήνεμον L P

γλαυκὰ δὲ Πόντου θυγάτηρ
Γαλάνεια τάδ᾽ εἴπῃ·
Κατὰ μὲν ἱστία πετάσατ᾽ αὔ-
ραις λιπόντες εἰναλίαις,   1460
λάβετε δ᾽ εἰλατίνας πλάτας,
ὦ ναῦται, ναῦται,
πέμποντες εὐλιμένους
Περσείων οἴκων Ἑλέναν ἐπ᾽ ἀκτάς.

ἦ που κόρας ἂν ποταμοῦ   [ἀντ. α΄
παρ᾽ οἶδμα Λευκιππίδας ἢ πρὸ ναοῦ   1466
Παλλάδος ἂν λάβοις
χρόνῳ ξυνελθοῦσα χοροῖς
ἢ κώμοις Ὑακίνθου
νύχιον ἐς εὐφροσύναν,   1470
ὃν ἐξαμιλλησάμενος
τροχῷ τέρμονα δίσκου
ἔκανε Φοῖβος, τᾷ Λακαί-
νᾳ γᾷ βούθυτον ἀμέραν·
ὁ Διὸς δ᾽ εἶπε σέβειν γόνος·   1475
μόσχον θ᾽, ἂν οἴκοις
⟨ἔλειπες, Ἑρμιόναν,⟩
ἇς οὔπω πεῦκαι πρὸ γάμων ἔλαμψαν.

δι᾽ ἀέρος εἴθε ποτανοὶ   [στρ. β΄
γενοίμεσθ᾽ ᾇ Λιβύας

1459 sq. λείποντες Seidler   εἰναλίαις Seidler : ἐναλίαις L P
λιπόντες ἐναύλια Kirchhoff: possis etiam αὐλοῖς ᾄδοντες εἰναλίοις, cf.
Tro. 126 simm.   1461 εἰλαπίνας P   πλάτας om. P   1462 ἰὼ ante
alterum ναῦται add. l : cf. 1476   1466 προνάου L P : corr. Canter
1470 ἐς L P : εἰς l   εὐφροσύναν Matthiae : εὐφρόναν L P   1472
τέρμονα Matthiae : τέρμονι L P   1473 τᾷ] τᾷ δὲ Wilamowitz : ὅθεν
Hermann : puncta mutavi   1474 ἡμέραν L P   1475 δ᾽ seclusit
Musgrave   1476 ἂν λίποιτ᾽ οἴκοις L P : λίποιτ᾽ delevi : cf. 1462 : post
h. v. lacunam indicavit Heath : ex. gr. explevi ⟨ἂν λείπεις οἴκοισιν
Wilamowitz⟩   1477 πρὸ Canter : πρὸς L P   1478 εἴθε Barnes : εἰ
L P   1479 γενοίμεσθ᾽ ᾇ Musgrave : γενοίμεθα L P   Λιβύας
scripsi : λίβυες L P

οἰωνοὶ στοχάδες   1480
ὄμβρον λιποῦσαι χειμέριον
νίσονται πρεσβυτάτᾳ
σύριγγι πειθόμεναι
ποιμένος, ὃς ἄβροχα πεδία καρποφόρα τε γᾶς   1485
ἐπιπετόμενος ἰαχεῖ.
Ὦ πταναὶ δολιχαύχενες,
σύννομοι νεφέων δρόμου,
βᾶτε Πλειάδας ὑπὸ μέσας
Ὠρίωνά τ' ἐννύχιον·   1490
καρύξατ' ἀγγελίαν,
Εὐρώταν ἐφεζόμεναι,
Μενέλεως ὅτι Δαρδάνου
πόλιν ἑλὼν δόμον ἥξει.

μόλοιτέ ποθ' ἵππιον οἶμον   [ἀντ. β'
δι' αἰθέρος ἱέμενοι   1496
παῖδες Τυνδαρίδαι,
λαμπρῶν ἄστρων ὑπ' ἀέλλαισιν·
οἳ ναίετ' οὐράνιοι,
σωτῆρες τᾶς Ἑλένας,   1500
γλαυκὸν ἔπιτ' οἶδμα κυανόχροά τε κυμάτων
ῥόθια πολιὰ θαλάσσας,
ναύταις εὐαεῖς ἀνέμων

1480 στοχάδες L² (vel L¹) P : στολάδες primitus L : de synaphea
fracta cf. antistr. 1497   1482 νίσονται (sic) L P   πρεσβυτάτου Paley
1484 cf. 1501   1487 ὦ πταναὶ Canter (ὦ ποταναὶ Stephanus) :
ὁπόταν αἱ L P   1489 βᾶσαι Herwerden   Πλειάδας Stephanus :
πελειάδες L P   1490 Ὀαρίωνα Nauck   1492 Εὐρώταν Victorius :
εὐρώπαν L P   1493 Μενέλαος L P : corr. Matthiae   1495 linea
circumscripsit et περισσόν add. l   οἶμον scripsi et metri causa et usus
Euripidei : οἶμα L : οἶδμα L² P : γρ. ἄρμα in margine l   1497
τυνδαρίδες L P, corr. l   1498 ἀέλαισιν P : corr. p   1500 σωτῆρε Musgrave   1501 ἔπιτ' οἶδμα Wilamowitz : ἐπ' οἶδμ'
ἅλιον (glossema ad γλαυκὸν) L P : quo servato possis ἄβροχά θ' ὃς
v. 1484

πέμποντες Διόθεν πνοάς· 1505
δύσκλειαν δ' ἀπὸ συγγόνου
βάλετε βαρβάρων λεχέων,
ἃν Ἰδαίων ἐρίδων
ποιναθεῖσ' ἐκτήσατο, γᾶν
οὐκ ἐλθοῦσά ⟨ποτ'⟩ Ἰλίου 1510
Φοιβείους ἐπὶ πύργους.

Αγ. †ἄναξ, τὰ κάκιστ' ἐν δόμοις εὑρήκαμεν·†
ὡς καίν' ἀκούσῃ πήματ' ἐξ ἐμοῦ τάχα.

Θε. τί δ' ἔστιν;   Αγ. ἄλλῃς ἐκπόνει μνηστεύματα
γυναικός· Ἑλένη γὰρ βέβηκ' ἔξω χθονός. 1515

Θε. πτεροῖσιν ἀρθεῖσ' ἢ πεδοστιβεῖ ποδί;

Αγ. Μενέλαος αὐτὴν ἐκπεπόρθμευται χθονός,
ὃς αὐτὸς αὑτὸν ἦλθεν ἀγγέλλων θανεῖν.

Θε. ὦ δεινὰ λέξας· τίς δέ νιν ναυκληρία
ἐκ τῆσδ' ἀπῆρε χθονός; ἄπιστα γὰρ λέγεις. 1520

Αγ. ἣν γε ξένῳ δίδως σύ· τούς τε σοὺς ἔχων
ναύτας βέβηκεν, ὡς ἂν ἐν βραχεῖ μάθῃς.

Θε. πῶς; εἰδέναι πρόθυμος· οὐ γὰρ ἐλπίδων
ἔσω βέβηκα μίαν ὑπερδραμεῖν χέρα
τοσούσδε ναύτας, ὧν ἀπεστάλης μέτα. 1525

Αγ. ἐπεὶ λιποῦσα τούσδε βασιλείους δόμους
ἡ τοῦ Διὸς παῖς πρὸς θάλασσαν ἐστάλη
σοφώταθ' ἁβρὸν πόδα τιθεῖσ' ἀνέστενε
πόσιν πέλας παρόντα κοὐ τεθνηκότα.

1509 πονηθεῖσ' L: πονηθήσ' P: corr. Scaliger Hermann   γᾶν
Musgrave: τὰν L P   1510 ἐλθοῦσά ποτ' Bothe (περ Fix): ἐλθοῦσαν
ἐς L P: ἐς del. l   1511 φοιβίους P   1512 corruptus: fortasse totus ad lacunam explendam fictus   1514 ante ἄλλης
et vv. 1516, 1517, 1526 paragraphos pro personarum notis praef.
L   1517 ἐκπεπόρθευται P: corr. p   1520 ἀπῆρεν L: corr. L²
1521 γε] τῷ Wilamowitz   τε] δὲ Kirchhoff   ἔχων] ἑλὼν Schenkl
1524 εἴσω L P   fortasse βέβηκε   1528 σοφώτατ' L: corr. L²
1529 καὶ οὐ L

ὡς δ' ἤλθομεν σῶν περίβολον νεωρίων,   1530
Σιδωνίαν ναῦν πρωτόπλουν καθείλκομεν
ζυγῶν τε πεντήκοντα κἀρετμῶν μέτρα
ἔχουσαν. ἔργου δ' ἔργον ἐξημείβετο·
ὃ μὲν γὰρ ἱστόν, ὃ δὲ πλάτην καθίσατο
ταρσόν τε χειρί, λευκά θ' ἱστί' εἰς ἓν ἦν,   1535
πηδάλιά τε ζεύγλαισι παρακαθίετο.

κἂν τῷδε μόχθῳ, τοῦτ' ἄρα σκοπούμενοι,
Ἕλληνες ἄνδρες Μενέλεῳ ξυνέμποροι
προσῆλθον ἀκταῖς ναυφθόροις ἠσθημένοι
πέπλοισιν, εὐειδεῖς μέν, αὐχμηροὶ δ' ὁρᾶν.   1540
ἰδὼν δέ νιν παρόντας Ἀτρέως γόνος
προσεῖπε δόλιον οἶκτον ἐς μέσον φέρων·
Ὦ τλήμονες, πῶς ἐκ τίνος νεώς ποτε
Ἀχαιῖδος θραύσαντες ἥκετε σκάφος;
ἆρ' Ἀτρέως παῖδ' ὀλόμενον συνθάπτετε,   1545
ὃν Τυνδαρὶς παῖς ἥδ' ἀπόντα κενοταφεῖ;
οἱ δ' ἐκβαλόντες δάκρυα ποιητῷ τρόπῳ
ἐς ναῦν ἐχώρουν Μενέλεῳ ποντίσματα
φέροντες. ἡμῖν δ' ἦν μὲν ἥδ' ὑποψία
λόγος τ' ἐν ἀλλήλοισι, τῶν ἐπεσβατῶν   1550
ὡς πλῆθος εἴη· διεσιωπῶμεν δ' ὅμως
τοὺς σοὺς λόγους σῴζοντες· ἄρχειν γὰρ νεὼς
ξένον κελεύσας πάντα συνέχεας τάδε.

καὶ τἄλλα μὲν δὴ ῥᾳδίως ἔσω νεὼς
ἐθέμεθα κουφίζοντα· ταύρειος δὲ ποὺς   1555
οὐκ ἤθελ' ὀρθὸς σανίδα προσβῆναι κάτα,

1530 περιβόλων P : corr. p   1532 καὶ ἐρετμῶν L   μέτρα l p :
μέτα L P   1534 καθίστατο Barnes   1535 τε χειρὶ] τ' ἐνεῖρε
Badham : fortasse τ' ἐνῆρη   ἱστί' L² P : ἱστία L   εἰς ἓν ἦν] εἰσένει
olim Herwerden : lectio totius v. dubia   1537 μόχθου Kirchhoff :
cf. Ion 1196, Phoen. 1396   1538 συνέμποροι P   1539 ἀκτὰς
Heiland   ἠσκημένοι Blomfield   1540 εὐηδεῖς P : corr. p   1545 ὀλού-
μενον L P : corr. Stephanus   συνθάψετε Badham   1546 ἀπόντα
Brodeau : ἄκοντα L P   1550 τ' Ludv. Dindorf : δ' L P   1554 τἄλλα
Canter : ταῦτα L P   εἴσω L P   1555 ἐθέμεσθα L P   1556 ὀρθῶς P

ἀλλ' ἐξεβρυχατ' ὄμμ' ἀναστρέφων κύκλῳ
κυρτῶν τε νῶτα κἀς κέρας παρεμβλέπων
μὴ θιγγάνειν ἀπεῖργεν. ὁ δ' Ἑλένης πόσις
ἐκάλεσεν· Ὦ πέρσαντες Ἰλίου πόλιν,   1560
οὐκ εἶ' ἀναρπάσαντες Ἑλλήνων νόμῳ
νεανίαις ὤμοισι ταύρειον δέμας
ἐς πρῷραν ἐμβαλεῖτε, φάσγανόν θ' ἅμα
πρόχειρον ὥσει σφάγια τῷ τεθνηκότι ;
   οἱ δ' ἐς κέλευσμ' ἐλθόντες ἐξανήρπασαν   1565
ταῦρον φέροντές τ' εἰσέθεντο σέλματα.
μονάμπυκον δὲ Μενέλεως ψήχων δέρην
μέτωπά τ' ἐξέπεισεν ἐσβῆναι δόρυ.
   τέλος δ', ἐπειδὴ ναῦς τὰ πάντ' ἐδέξατο,
πλήσασα κλιμακτῆρας εὐσφύρου ποδὸς   1570
Ἑλένη καθέζετ' ἐν μέσοις ἐδωλίοις,
ὅ τ' οὐκέτ' ὢν λόγοισι Μενέλεως πέλας·
ἄλλοι δὲ τοίχους δεξιοὺς λαιούς τ' ἴσοι
ἀνὴρ παρ' ἄνδρ' ἔζωνθ', ὑφ' εἵμασι ξίφη
λαθραῖ' ἔχοντες, ῥόθιά τ' ἐξεπίμπλατο   1575
βοῆς κελευστοῦ φθέγμαθ' ὡς ἠκούσαμεν.
   ἐπεὶ δὲ γαίας ἦμεν οὔτ' ἄγαν πρόσω
οὔτ' ἐγγύς, οὕτως ἦρετ' οἰάκων φύλαξ·
Ἔτ', ὦ ξέν', ἐς τὸ πρόσθεν—ἢ καλῶς ἔχει—
πλεύσωμεν; ἀρχαὶ γὰρ νεὼς μέλουσι σοί.   1580
ὁ δ' εἶφ'· Ἅλις μοι. δεξιᾷ δ' ἑλὼν ξίφος
ἐς πρῷραν εἷρπε κἀπὶ ταυρείῳ σφαγῇ

1558 κεὶς L P   1560 ἐκέλευσεν Cobet   1561 οὐκ εἶ'] οὔκουν
suprascr. L² 1564 (φάσγανόν...ὠθεῖ) Bothe 1565 post ἐξανήρπασαν
deletum πόλιν in L   1566 τ' Musgrave: δ' L P   1567 μονάμπυκος
Schenkl : sed vide Ox. Pap. VIII. 1087   1567 sq. delevit W. G.
Clark   1570 κλιμαντῆρας L P : corr. Hervagiana altera   1571
ἐδωλίων primitus L   1574 ἔζοντο L : ἔζοντ' P   εἵμασιν L P :
ν delevit l   1575 λαθραῖ' l : λάθρ* L (fuit λάθρα) : λάθρ' L² P ut
videtur   ῥόθια Pierson : ὄρθρια L : ὄρθια P   1576 κελευστοῦ
Pierson : κελεύθου L P   1580 σοι Elmsley : μοι L P   1581 εἶπεν
L P   ἑλὼν] ἔχων Cobet, cl. 1564

σταθεὶς νεκρῶν μὲν οὐδενὸς μνήμην ἔχων,
τέμνων δὲ λαιμὸν ηὔχετ'· Ὦ ναίων ἅλα
πόντιε Πόσειδον Νηρέως θ' ἀγναὶ κόραι,　　　　1585
σώσατέ μ' ἐπ' ἀκτὰς Ναυπλίας δάμαρτά τε
ἄσυλον ἐκ γῆς. αἵματος δ' ἀπορροαὶ
ἐς οἶδμ' ἐσηκόντιζον οὔριοι ξένῳ.
καί τις τόδ' εἶπε· Δόλιος ἡ ναυκληρία.
πάλιν πλέωμεν· δεξιὰν κέλευε σύ,　　　　　　1590
σὺ δὲ στρέφ' οἴακ'. ἐκ δὲ ταυρείου φόνου
Ἀτρέως σταθεὶς παῖς ἀνεβόησε συμμάχους·
Τί μέλλετ', ὦ γῆς Ἑλλάδος λωτίσματα,
σφάζειν φονεύειν βαρβάρους νεώς τ' ἄπο
ῥίπτειν ἐς οἶδμα; ναυβάταις δὲ τοῖσι σοῖς　　　1595
βοᾷ κελευστὴς τὴν ἐναντίαν ὄπα·
Οὐκ εἶ' ὁ μέν τις λοῖσθον ἀρεῖται δόρυ,
ὁ δὲ ζύγ' ἄξας, ὁ δ' ἀφελὼν σκαλμοῦ πλάτην
καθαιματώσει κρᾶτα πολεμίων ξένων;
ὀρθοὶ δ' ἀνῇξαν πάντες, οἳ μὲν ἐν χεροῖν　　　1600
κορμοὺς ἔχοντες ναυτικούς, οἳ δὲ ξίφη·
φόνῳ δὲ ναῦς ἐρρεῖτο. παρακέλευσμα δ' ἦν
πρύμνηθεν Ἑλένης· Ποῦ τὸ Τρωικὸν κλέος;
δείξατε πρὸς ἄνδρας βαρβάρους· σπουδῆς δ' ὕπο
ἔπιπτον, οἳ δ' ὠρθοῦντο, τοὺς δὲ κειμένους　　　1605
νεκροὺς ἂν εἶδες. Μενέλεως δ' ἔχων ὅπλα,
ὅποι νοσοῖεν ξύμμαχοι κατασκοπῶν,
ταύτῃ προσῆγε χειρὶ δεξιᾷ ξίφος,

1583 ἔχων] fortasse ἔχει　　　1584 λαιμὸν Stephanus : δαίμον' L P
1586 Ναυπλίους Wecklein　　　1587 ἐκ γῆς suspectum : nisi sensus est
'cum Terra eam incolumem praestiterit'　　　1588 ἐς hic L P　　οὔριοι
Elmsley : οὔρια L P　　　1590 ·δεξιὰν Baynes : ἀξίαν· L P : super
ἀ να scripsit l : ἀντίαν· Badham　　　1592 συμμάχοις Nauck
1595 ναυβάταις p : ναυάταις L P　　　1596 ἐναντίαν l : ἐναντίον L P
1597 οὐκ εἶ'] γρ. οὔκουν L²　　λοῖσθον suspectum : fortasse θᾶσσον
ἀρεῖται Elmsley : αἰρεῖται P : αἱρεῖται L　　　1598 πλάταν P　　1604 δείξατε L : δείξαντες P : κλέος δείξετε Hartung　　　1607 νοσεῖεν P
1608 δεξιᾷ] fortasse δεξιὸν

ὥστ᾽ ἐκκολυμβᾶν ναός· ἠρήμωσε δὲ
σῶν ναυβατῶν ἐρετμά. ἐπ᾽ οἰάκων δὲ βὰς   1610
ἄνακτ᾽ ἐς Ἑλλάδ᾽ εἶπεν εὐθύνειν δόρυ.
οἱ δ᾽ ἱστὸν ἦρον, οὔριαι δ᾽ ἦκον πνοαί.
  βεβᾶσι δ᾽ ἐκ γῆς. διαφυγὼν δ᾽ ἐγὼ φόνον
καθῆκ᾽ ἐμαυτὸν εἰς ἅλ᾽ ἄγκυραν πάρα·
ἤδη δὲ κάμνονθ᾽ ὁρμιατόνων μέ τις   1615
ἀνείλετ᾽, ἐς δὲ γαῖαν ἐξέβησέ σοι
τάδ᾽ ἀγγελοῦντα. σώφρονος δ᾽ ἀπιστίας
οὐκ ἔστιν οὐδὲν χρησιμώτερον βροτοῖς.
Χο. οὐκ ἄν ποτ᾽ ηὔχουν οὔτε σ᾽ οὔθ᾽ ἡμᾶς λαθεῖν
  Μενέλαον, ὦναξ, ὡς ἐλάνθανεν παρών.   1620
Θε. ὦ γυναικείαις τέχναισιν αἱρεθεὶς ἐγὼ τάλας·
ἐκπεφεύγασιν γάμοι με. κεἰ μὲν ἦν ἁλώσιμος
ναῦς διώγμασιν, πονήσας εἷλον ἂν τάχα ξένους·
νῦν δὲ τὴν προδοῦσαν ἡμᾶς τεισόμεσθα σύγγονον,
ἥτις ἐν δόμοις ὁρῶσα Μενέλεων οὐκ εἶπέ μοι.   1625
τοιγὰρ οὔποτ᾽ ἄλλον ἄνδρα ψεύσεται μαντεύμασιν.

ΘΕΡΑΠΩΝ

  οὗτος ὤ, ποῖ σὸν πόδ᾽ αἴρεις, δέσποτ᾽, ἐς ποῖον φόνον;
Θε. οἷπερ ἡ δίκη κελεύει με· ἀλλ᾽ ἀφίστασ᾽ ἐκποδών.
Θερ. οὐκ ἀφήσομαι πέπλων σῶν· μεγάλα ⟨γὰρ⟩ σπεύδεις
  κακά.
Θε. ἀλλὰ δεσποτῶν κρατήσεις δοῦλος ὤν;   Θερ. φρονῶ
  γὰρ εὖ.   1630

1610 ἐρετμὰ L P   1611 ἄνακτ᾽ Emper : ἄναξ L P   εἰς
L P   1612 ἐστί· ἦρον Emper   οὔριοι Elmsley   1615 κάμνοντ᾽
L² P : κάμνοντα L   ὁρμιατόνων L P, sed in ras. scripsit α P² : γρ.
ὁρμιὰν τίνων μέ τις l   1618 χρησιμώτερον L : σωφρονέστερον P
1621 γυναικείοις Hermann   1627 ΘΕΡΑΠΩΝ] Χο. L P : 1629–1639
paragraphos habent pro personarum notis : has partes mulieris non
esse sed viri arguit v. 1630, cf. ad Hipp. 1102 sq. : igitur vel
Nuntio vel potius post Clarkium Θεράποντι Theonoae tribuendae, qui
regi in regiam inrumpenti obvius fiat   ὦ ποῖ L (nescio an in rasura) :
ὅποι P   1629 γὰρ om. L P : add. l

Θε. οὐκ ἔμοιγ᾽, εἰ μή μ᾽ ἐάσεις—   Θερ. οὐ μὲν οὖν σ᾽
  ἐάσομεν.

Θε. σύγγονον κτανεῖν κακίστην—   Θερ. εὐσεβεστάτην
  μὲν οὖν.

Θε. ἤ με προύδωκεν—   Θερ. καλήν γε προδοσίαν, δίκαια
  δρᾶν.

Θε. τἀμὰ λέκτρ᾽ ἄλλῳ διδοῦσα.   Θερ. τοῖς γε κυριωτέροις.

Θε. κύριος δὲ τῶν ἐμῶν τίς;   Θερ. ὃς ἔλαβεν πατρὸς
  πάρα.   1635

Θε. ἀλλ᾽ ἔδωκεν ἡ τύχη μοι.   Θερ. τὸ δὲ χρεὼν ἀφείλετο.

Θε. οὐ σὲ τἀμὰ χρὴ δικάζειν.   Θερ. ἤν γε βελτίω λέγω.

Θε. ἀρχόμεσθ᾽ ἄρ᾽, οὐ κρατοῦμεν.   Θερ. ὅσια δρᾶν, τὰ
  δ᾽ ἔκδικ᾽ οὔ.

Θε. κατθανεῖν ἐρᾶν ἔοικας.   Θερ. κτεῖνε· σύγγονον δὲ σὴν
  οὐ κτενεῖς ἡμῶν ἑκόντων, ἀλλ᾽ ἔμε· ⟨ὡς⟩ πρὸ δεσποτῶν
  τοῖσι γενναίοισι δούλοις εὐκλεέστατον θανεῖν.   1641

ΔΙΟΣΚΟΡΟΙ

  ἐπίσχες ὀργὰς αἷσιν οὐκ ὀρθῶς φέρῃ,
  Θεοκλύμενε, γαίας τῆσδ᾽ ἄναξ· δισσοὶ δέ σε
  Διόσκοροι καλοῦμεν, οὓς Λήδα ποτὲ
  ἔτικτεν Ἑλένην θ᾽, ἣ πέφευγε σοὺς δόμους·   1645
  οὐ γὰρ πεπρωμένοισιν ὀργίζῃ γάμοις,
  οὐδ᾽ ἡ θεᾶς Νηρῇδος ἔκγονος κόρη
  ἀδικεῖ σ᾽ ἀδελφὴ Θεονόη, τὰ τῶν θεῶν
  τιμῶσα πατρός τ᾽ ἐνδίκους ἐπιστολάς.

    ἐς μὲν γὰρ αἰεὶ τὸν παρόντα νῦν χρόνον   1650
  κείνην κατοικεῖν σοῖσιν ἐν δόμοις ἐχρῆν·

1633 προύδωκε L P   1635 ἔλαβε L P   1638 ἀρχόμεθ᾽ L P :
corr. l   τὰ δ᾽ ἔκδικ᾽ οὔ Porson : τάνδ᾽ ἐκδικῶ L P   1639 κτεῖναι P
1640 paragraphus praefixa et deleta in L : 1640 et 1641 paragraphos
praef. P   ἔμ᾽· ὡς Porson : ἐμὲ L P   1641 γενναίοις L P : corr. l
1643 γαίας Nauck : γῆς L P : τῆσδε γῆς Mekler   1647 ἔκγονος
Matthiae : ἐκγόνη L P : εὐγενὴς Nauck   1650 ἐς] εἰς Stephanus : εἰ
L P   ἀεὶ L P

ἐπεὶ δὲ Τροίας ἐξανεστάθη βάθρα,
καὶ τοῖς θεοῖς παρέσχε τοὔνομ', οὐκέτι·
ἐν τοῖσι δ' αὐτῆς δεῖ νιν ἐζεῦχθαι γάμοις
ἐλθεῖν τ' ἐς οἴκους καὶ συνοικῆσαι πόσει.   1655
ἀλλ' ἴσχε μὲν σῆς συγγόνου μέλαν ξίφος,
νόμιζε δ' αὐτὴν σωφρόνως πράσσειν τάδε.
πάλαι δ' ἀδελφὴν κἂν πρὶν ἐξεσώσαμεν,
ἐπείπερ ἡμᾶς Ζεὺς ἐποίησεν θεούς·
ἀλλ' ἥσσον' ἦμεν τοῦ πεπρωμένου θ' ἅμα   1660
καὶ τῶν θεῶν, οἷς ταῦτ' ἔδοξεν ὧδ' ἔχειν.
σοὶ μὲν τάδ' αὐδῶ, συγγόνῳ δ' ἐμῇ λέγω·
πλεῖ ξὺν πόσει σῷ· πνεῦμα δ' ἕξετ' οὔριον·
σωτῆρε δ' ἡμεῖς σὼ κασιγνήτω διπλῶ
πόντον παριππεύοντε πέμψομεν πάτραν.   1665
ὅταν δὲ κάμψῃς καὶ τελευτήσῃς βίον,
θεὸς κεκλήσῃ καὶ Διοσκόρων μέτα
σπονδῶν μεθέξεις ξένιά τ' ἀνθρώπων πάρα
ἕξεις μεθ' ἡμῶν· Ζεὺς γὰρ ὧδε βούλεται.
οὗ δ' ὥρισέν σοι πρῶτα Μαιάδος τόκος,   1670
Σπάρτης ἀπάρας, τὸν κατ' οὐρανὸν δρόμον,
κλέψας δέμας σὸν μὴ Πάρις γήμειέ σε,
—φρουρὸν παρ' Ἀκτὴν τεταμένην νῆσον λέγω—
Ἑλένη τὸ λοιπὸν ἐν βροτοῖς κεκλήσεται,
ἐπεὶ κλοπαίαν σ' ἐκ δόμων ἐδέξατο.   1675

1654 τοῖσι δ' Bothe : τοῖσιν L P, quo servato del. v. 1653
Nauck   αὐτῆς Nauck : αὐτοῖς L P   1655 τ' Hermann : δ' L P
συνηκῆσαι P   1656 ἴσχε l : ἔσχε L P   1657 πράττειν L P
1658 κἂν πρὶν Heath : καὶ πρὶν L teste Vitellio, nam καὶ suprascr.
L¹ : πρίν γ' ut videtur P : ἂν Ἑλένην καὶ πρὶν Badham   1659 del.
Nauck   1660 ἥσσον' Pierson : ἥσσονες L P   1663 πλεῖ
Cobet : πλεῖν L P   σὺν P   1664 δ' L : θ' P   1666 κάμψεις
. . . τελευτήσεις P : corr. p   1667 sq. verba ξένιά . . . ἡμῶν
delebat Herwerden   1670 ὥρισέν σε Madvig (σε apogr. Paris.)
1671 τὸν P et suprascr. L¹ vel L² : τῶν L   δρόμον Wilamowitz : δόμων
L P : δρόμων Paley   1673 φρουρὸν Hermann : φρουροῦ L P
τεταμένην νῆσον Reiske : τεταγμένη μνῆσον L P : γρ. νῆσον L¹ in
marg. : μνῆσοι p   1675 κλοπαίαν σ' Herwerden : κλοπὰς L P :
κλοπὰς σὰς l

5*

καὶ τῷ πλανήτῃ Μενέλεῳ θεῶν πάρα
μακάρων κατοικεῖν νῆσόν ἐστι μόρσιμον·
τοὺς εὐγενεῖς γὰρ οὐ στυγοῦσι δαίμονες,
τῶν δ' ἀναριθμήτων μᾶλλόν εἰσιν οἱ πόνοι.

Θε. ὦ παῖδε Λήδας καὶ Διός, τὰ μὲν πάρος   1680
νείκη μεθήσω σφῷν κασιγνήτης πέρι·
ἐγὼ δ' ἀδελφὴν οὐκέτ' ἂν κτάνοιμ' ἐμήν.
κείνη δ' ἴτω πρὸς οἶκον, εἰ θεοῖς δοκεῖ.
ἴστον δ' ἀρίστης σωφρονεστάτης θ' ἅμα
γεγῶτ' ἀδελφῆς ὁμογενοῦς ἀφ' αἵματος.   1685
καὶ χαίρεθ' Ἑλένης οὕνεκ' εὐγενεστάτης
γνώμης, ὃ πολλαῖς ἐν γυναιξὶν οὐκ ἔνι.

Χο.   πολλαὶ μορφαὶ τῶν δαιμονίων,
πολλὰ δ' ἀέλπτως κραίνουσι θεοί·
καὶ τὰ δοκηθέντ' οὐκ ἐτελέσθη,   1690
τῶν δ' ἀδοκήτων πόρον ηὗρε θεός.
τοιόνδ' ἀπέβη τόδε πρᾶγμα.

1679 v. multum sollicitatus   1685 ἀδελφοῦ ut vid. P : corr. p
ὁμογενοῦς Canter : μονογενοῦς L P   1686 καὶ om. P   1687
γνώμην Wilamowitz   1691 εὗρεν P Subscr. **** εὐριπίδου ἑλένη
(erasum videtur τέλος) L : τέλος εὐριπίδου ἑλένης P

COMMENTARY

THE Prologue is of the type Eur. uses most: an explanatory monologue addressed to the audience, followed by a scene in dialogue. The σκηνή represents a palace-front with central double-doors, and somewhere on the stage is the Tomb of Proteus, where Helen has to spend much of her time sitting or standing. This, with its 'base and uprights' (547), needs a little more than the ordinary stele on a raised mound and step, but cannot be a free-standing affair or (in spite of 1165) in front of the door, where it would impede movement and visibility. The situation recalls the opening of the *Andromache*, where the heroine has taken refuge at a shrine of Thetis which is δόμων πάροικον, and it is reasonable to suppose a regular stage-property which could be set up against the back wall to one side or the other of the central door, with step or steps where Helen can sit and pilasters beside which Menelaus could be half-concealed (507, 1203). If this were on the audience's left, the king would pass it on his return from hunting, and Helen would be well placed to confront those of her interlocutors who arrive from the sea. Helen probably speaks most of her monologue standing centre-stage and moves over to sit at the tomb about l. 63. The αἵδε of the first line *may* imply a painted panel set in the wall to the right of the σκηνή.

1. καλλιπάρθενοι ῥοαί: probably 'fair virgin streams' as Hermann takes it, the Nile receiving its flow only from the melting snows, not (it was thought) from the mingling of tributaries. There is no close parallel: καλλιπαρθένου δέρης *IA* 1574 is literal; *Bacch.* 520 εὐπάρθενε Δίρκα is a straightforward personification; A. *Pers.* 613 παρθένου πηγῆς is pure spring-water for libations. Others take it as 'the stream of Nile with its fair nymphs', and Pearson as 'streams of Nile's fair daughters', with reference to the 'hundred mouths' (*Bacch.* 406) of the Delta, each with its presiding nymph. Perhaps Eur. did not think very closely about it.

3. Anaxagoras' view of this disputed phenomenon, to which Eur. defiantly returns in the prologue of *Archelaus*, fr. 228N². Hdt. 2. 22 thought differently.

There is an embarrassment of objects for ὑγραίνει here, which Hartung would resolve by reading πέδου in 2. But the double gen. is not very attractive, and πέδον is defended by the parody in Ar. *Thesm.* 855–7, which then repeats the dilemma by continuing λευκῆς νοτίζει μελανοσυρμαῖον λεών. Curious as the coincidence is, it is hardly to be reckoned a defence of this inexplicable double object; perhaps γύας and πέδον were just variants written one above the other in 2, and 3 ended in some word like Heiland's δρόσῳ.

5. The detail seems to be added simply to come into line with *Od.* 4. 355. But in Homer Proteus is the Old Man of the Sea, though in Hdt. he has become a king. Here his prophetic powers are given to his daughter Theonoe and inherited from her mother's father Nereus.

7. More adjustment to tradition, cf. Hes. *Theog.* 1003–5.

9–10. The interpolation is unmetrical, and senseless without, e.g., καλούμενον. Presumably it was intended to balance 13–14, though the etymology does not work very well, nor is the description suitable to the age or the conduct of the new king.

Θεοκλύμενον: this character of Eur.'s invention doubtless owes his name to the seer in the *Odyssey*; there is a kind of prophetic aura about the family of Proteus, though only Theonoe has the mystical powers of the Homeric γέρων ἅλιος νημερτής. The name, in Homer ∪ – ∪ ∪ –, is unhandy in the trimeter; there is more than one way of scanning it, and of its three instances two are complicated by textual uncertainties. H. D. Broadhead points out to me that one would expect ∪ ᴖ̆ ∪ – on the analogy of Περικλύμενος *Phoen.* 1157, but only 1168 fits that (it could also, with less probability, take the Homeric form). 9, on this text, requires – ᴖ̆ ∪ with synizesis, and 1643 would follow suit if with Nauck we emend to γαίας—but I confess to a perhaps irrational preference for γῆς τῆσδε in that quite unemphatic phrase (*Hipp.* 973 and *Or.* 1644 are of very different effect, and τῆσδε γῆς gives a weak caesura-rhythm). Since nothing will reduce the three instances to a single form, one might as well take ∪ – ∪ ᴖ̆ (the form doubtless intended in 9 also by the interpolator!) in 1643, and note that it was of no importance for a tragedian to reduce the same name to a single scansion throughout (cf. Νεοπτόλεμος).

16 ff. Helen at length introduces herself—as the Tyndarid, 'though there is of course a story that . . .'. This hint of scepticism returns in 259, though elsewhere in the play—by the Dioscuri, for instance—the parentage of Zeus is taken for granted. Doubt of the swan-story is more strongly expressed in *IA* 793–800, but here from Helen's own lips the effect of ambivalence is curious and a little upsetting. The same sort of ambiguity of parentage appears more starkly in *HF*.

20–21. ὑπ᾽ αἰετοῦ δίωγμα φεύγων: usually explained as retention of its verbal construction in the noun δίωγμα. Or perhaps φεύγων δίωγμα = 'put to flight', 'made to flee'. **σαφής**: 'true' (as often).

22. δ᾽: resumes from πατὴρ δὲ *T*.

23 ff. The Judgement of Paris, as the beginning of all the troubles, is accepted as literal truth in this play, with no hint of scepticism or rationalizing interpretation. It is the starting-point of the εἴδωλον-legend on which the play is based.

28. προτείνασ᾽: 'offering as a lure.' The construction is a mixture of προτείνασα τὸ κάλλος and προτείνασα ὡς γαμεῖ τὸ κάλλος.

32. ἐξηνέμωσε: 'turned to thin air', an appropriate word since the 'breathing image' was made of οὐρανοῦ, the air of heaven, = αἰθήρ 584.

33. δίδωσι: for an abiding gift the present tense is regular, cf. 568, 1521.   δοκεῖ 35 is probably 'fancies' [still]; Helen knows nothing of his death.

36. κενὴν δόκησιν: with this punctuation accus. in apposition to the sentence, like ἀπόλαυσιν 77, or τέρψιν Alc. 353. But here it is easier to take it as internal object to δοκεῖ, 'idly fancies' he possesses me.

36–41. 'Again the plans of Zeus in their turn (ἄλλα = "besides", "separately") work in with these afflictions.' The oldest known source for Zeus' desire to relieve Mother Earth of surplus human population by means of the Trojan War is the Cypria, fr. 1, quoted in a scholion on Il. 1. 5. The glorification of Achilles (τὸν κράτιστον Ἑλλάδος) is a third motive, either deduced from the Iliad or taken from some other epic source. How Helen came to know of this unedifying conjunction of separate divine wills is not explained; perhaps Hermes told her on their flight. The Dioscuri (El. 1282-3) and Apollo (Or. 1639-42), as gods from the machine, are more naturally informative, though less specific.

42–43. Φρυγῶν ἐς ἀλκὴν = the Trojan War, simply; ἀλκή has become a generalized word for 'fight', whether individual or collective. ἐγὼ . . . ὄνομα: Helen's most characteristic antithesis for the confusion wrought by the εἴδωλον.

44. πτυχαῖσιν: easier to understand when of mountains. Eur. likes it in this periphrasis, perhaps for the suggestion of vast stretches behind the clouds.

50. ἀναρπαγὰς: went to Troy to hunt down 'my ravishing', me his ravished wife, abstract for concrete as in 1675 κλοπὰς σάς. The ἀπ. λεγ. seems to be coined from ἀναρπάζω.

56. τί δῆτ' (cf. 293) = the τί οὖν of Ar.'s parody Thesm. 868. The answer follows in asyndeton.

57–59. κλεινόν ⟨μ'⟩ Hermann, whom most edd. follow. γνόντος for γνόντος αὐτοῦ gen. abs., although the noun of reference, ἀνδρί, is available in the dative, is defended by Pearson (app., with good examples) and Page on Med. 910. The new point emerges more clearly than with, e.g., the old conjecture γνόντι μ'.   ὑποστρώσω: subj. not opt. is usually explained with Goodwin, MT 318, as giving the agent's motive at the time of the action—only Helen's motives were not then in question. I should prefer to take it not with οὐκ ἦλθον but with εἰσήκουσ' ἔπος Ἑρμοῦ, implying 'he said it so that I should think chastity worth while'. She still thinks so, therefore subj.

63. ἐγὼ: the emphatic ἐμόν of LP is quite superfluous after τὸν πάλαι. H. D. Broadhead suggests δέ μου, certainly an easier corruption.

65. The inelegant change from ἵνα to ὡς in a double final clause leads some edd. to delete the line with Schenkl; but the active protection (διασώσῃ) of Proteus at his tomb does seem to require emphasis, since this is to be Helen's constant posture for so long.

69. γὰρ explains Teucer's wonder at the imposing scale of the palace (represented, of course, by the ordinary σκηνή), 'its royal circuit and corniced mass'. Of the many ways in which this line has been taken, with or without emendation, Hermann's is perhaps simplest: Πλούτου sc. οἴκῳ, 'a house worthy to compare with Plutus' own'. But Eur. may have been moved by reminiscence of *Od.* 4. 74 Ζηνός που τοιήδε γ' Ὀλυμπίου ἔνδοθεν αὐλή to put the comparison the other, less obvious, way round: 'Plutus' house makes a worthy comparison.' Here Teucer's inquiries are diverted by the sight of Helen, and it is not till 144 that we learn he knows it to belong to the King of Egypt and is seeking the Princess Theonoe.

72. ἐχθίστης is perhaps an improvement.

74. ὅσον in a kind of subordinated exclamatory construction: 'so like are you to H.' Cf. *Hipp.* 879, with Barrett's note.

76. τῷδ' . . . πτερῷ: Teucer the Archer carries his bow and arrows.

77. ἀπόλαυσιν: appositional accus. For the corruption and its attempted correction v. infr. on 1660.

78. Murray's punctuation is right: this is anacoluthon, and no lacuna or emendation is necessary. Instead of ὅστις εἶ, ὅστις ὤν has been assimilated to the following construction, and καί is the ordinary copula, not, as Pearson and others take it, 'indeed'. None of the examples cited (εἰ καὶ, ποῦ καὶ, etc.) is remotely parallel to this position between two clauses.

79. ἐκείνης συμφοραῖς = her misfortunes simply, not those she caused.

82. ἡμῖν τοῖς: double dative, for the more usual τινι τι.

83–88. This clumsy and repetitious exchange, breaking up the stichomythia just getting under way, must be drastically cut. The betraying line is 86: ἀτὰρ τίς εἶ; πόθεν; τίνος; ἐξαυδᾶν σε χρή. Name—country—father (the classic triple question): then a fill-up, 'you must speak out', not evasively like 84. Repetition, metrical solecisms and all, it cries aloud interpolator; and emendation (a dozen to choose from, none tempting) is a waste of time. Even Jackson (p. 181) fails through equating ἐξαυδᾶν with αὐδᾶν and (ἐξ)ονομάζω, though the example he gives, *Hipp.* 590, is clearly nothing of the kind. Of deleters, Badham would remove 85–88, which would leave Teucer unnamed throughout the scene; Page (*Actors' Interpolations,* 79), 84–86, with suspicions further extended. Both of these cut out 85, a pointed line—Helen throughout this scene brings the talk round to her own name at every opportunity—and elegantly expressed, with its σε proleptic of Ἑλ. εἰ στυγεῖς: 85 and 86 were never written by the same hand. 87–88, intended as a smart reply to the three questions, and anticipating the words of 92, must follow 86 into

oblivion; presumably Teucer's real reply to 83, a single line completing his statement begun in 84, fell out of the text and started all
the trouble; then the interpolator, not realizing the provisional
nature of 84, with Helen's swift intervention, began all over again.
If someone should object that this could be conversational realism,
the answer is 'Not in Euripidean stichomythia'.

Putting a dash then after 84, with 85 as an interposed comment,
I would mark a lacuna of one line [something like Σαλαμῖνα δ' ἥκω
πατρίδ' ἐμὴν Τεῦκρος λιπών. Or, perhaps better, with Herwerden,
εἰς ὢν at the beginning of 84, and then, e.g., Σαλαμῖνα Τεῦκρος
πατρίδ' ἐμὴν ἥκω λιπών.] Line 92, clearly the first mention of Telamon,
completes his statement of identity.

91. τλήμων ἂν εἴης: 'how wretched for you!' The potential optative
in these short sentences has an exclamatory force which has not
been adequately recognized. Cf. 824 θνήσκοιμεν ἄν (N.B. not θάνοιμεν
ἄν): 'that's the end of me!'; 834 προδότις ἂν εἴης· τὴν βίαν σκήψασ'
ἔχεις: 'False woman! that "force" is just an excuse'; see also Or.
735, 764. The negative is more familiar: Phoen. 926 οὐ σιωπήσαιμεν ἄν:
'I will not keep it quiet!'; IA 310 οὐκ ἂν μεθείμην: 'I will not let go' (cf.
Ar. Ran. 830). There is also the impatient question: IA 843 τί δῆτ' ἂν
εἴη; 'What can it mean?'; Ar. Thesm. 847 τί δῆτ' ἂν εἴη τοὐμποδών;
'What can be holding him up?' and πῶς ἄν in abrupt, ironical dis-
belief: Ion 543 πῶς ἂν οὖν εἴην σός; Andr. 1165 πῶς ἂν οὖν εἴη σοφός;
'And then people call him wise!'

92. μᾶλλον φίλον = more of an intimate than a father is (there is an
awkward absence of simple English equivalents for the concept of
φίλος as one 'near and dear'). Pearson compares A. Cho. 219 μὴ μάστευ'
ἐμοῦ μᾶλλον φίλον. Teucer's meaning is 'the last person you would
expect'.

93. 'herein lies some calamity.'

95. οὔ τί που: of something you hope is not true, cf. 135 οὔ που (better
than ἦ που, which Tricl. regularly substitutes, cf. 575, 600).   βίον:
βίου (Burges) is so easy a correction (cf. 282, 866) that it seems better
to bring this into line with Eur.'s regular gen. with this verb.

96. οἰκεῖον: not simply with ξίφος but with ἅλμα-ἐπὶ-ξίφος, his own act
and his own weapon. ἐπὶ construed with the verbal notion in ἅλμα
is less ordinary than in English.

98. τὸν Π. τιν': 'you have heard of one Achilles, the son of P.?' The
combination is quite natural, though the order in Greek is a little
more wrapped up.

99. This detail, inconsistent with prevailing versions of the legend,
brings Helen into the picture. The name and fame of all the heroes
and great deeds of Troy must be supposed (when Eur. is being careful, cf. 41!) unknown to her in her Egyptian isolation, except for such
as she could have known in her young days in Greece.

100. ὅδ': a certain emendation. Such a use of the pronoun, where the person is not on the stage or to be indicated by a gesture toward the σκηνή, is rare but has a close parallel *Or.* 1189 τήνδε, where again the person has been explicitly summoned into the speakers' thoughts by the formula 'you know . . .?'

104. γ' in assent; καὶ . . . γε 106 and 110, 'yes, and . . .', 108 οὐδ' . . . γε 'yes, not even . . .'.

105. γάρ: 'does that mean you went to Troy?' Cf. 107.

109. ἀπόλλυνται: one of the verbs in which the present can be used as a perfect in sense, Goodwin, *MT* 27.

111. γὰρ: in a request for supplementary information, Denn. *GP.* 83.

112. καρπίμους: i.e. seven revolving years have borne their harvest. Nauck's καμπίμους is unnecessary, cf. *El.* 1152 with Denniston's note.

119. σκοπεῖτε: the plural makes no sense. σκοπεῖ δὲ A. Y. Campbell: 'you're sure it wasn't something the gods made all of you imagine?'

121-2. καὶ νοῦς ὁρᾷ is supposed to be an allusion to the famous line of Epicharmus νοῦς ὁρῇ καὶ νοῦς ἀκούει, τἄλλα κωφὰ καὶ τυφλά. But the suddenness of the quotation, its allusiveness and brevity in the middle of plain dialogue, and the obscurity of the point here (? 'I saw with my eyes, and seeing involves the use of the mind') make it improbable to the point of absurdity. εἰδόμην is common in late prose, but in Eur. is rare, and confined to lyric; hence such emendations as εἶδον, εἰ καὶ νῦν σ' ὁρῶ. But their only effect is to emphasize the redundancy of the whole couplet after 118-19. In any case Teucer has peremptorily requested her to drop the hated subject, and Helen's manners would not have allowed her to maunder on with the same question once more, nor would Teucer have repeated his answer so patiently. 120 closes the point irretrievably, and 121-2 should (as by W. Ribbeck) be deleted.

125. An obscure line. Pearson accepts the redundancy of expression, comparing *Ion* 1561 δίδωσι δ' οἷς ἔδωκεν, and translates, 'Sad news for whom the sad news touches', i.e. (privately) for me, who am more affected than you know. This is probably better than to make a deliberate ambiguity of οἷς κακὸν λέγεις as (1) for those whose misfortune you are describing, (2) for those whom you are abusing. The audience would have to work very hard for an unrewarding point. Helen is passing off her unguarded αἰαῖ, which might have surprised Teucer: such *sad* news for those concerned.

126. ὡς: 'know that . . .' in emphatic further confirmation, cf. infr. 831, *Andr.* 255.

128. ἄλλον: sc. πορθμόν, given dat. περῶσι 130.

131. The MSS. have Μενέλαον. Μενέλας, etc., is elsewhere only lyric, Μενέλεων as a trisyllable only at the beginning of the line (in Ar. *Thesm.* 901 it is Bentley's emendation); the latter seems more likely.

133. ἀπωλόμεσθα must be spoken aside, like half 139 below, and most of 475. The device is not common in tragedy; the most striking instance is Hekabe in *Hec.* 736–51, introduced with much more circumstance. Thestios, Leda's father, was king of Aetolia.

134. δή: probably not temporal (= ἤδη) but for emotional emphasis, Denn. *GP* 214 (8).

135. οὖ που: v. ad 95.

136. γ': after φασίν 'adding detail to assent already expressed' (Denn.). The suicide of Leda seems to be Eur.'s own invention.

138. Eur.'s favourite kind of riddle, cf. Ar. *Ach.* 396. It seems better to write κοὐ as Triclinius rather than *scriptio plena* καὶ οὐ.

139. κρείσσων: 'truer.'

140. ἄστροις: apparently a familiar post-Homeric legend, cf. *Tro.* 1001. The Chorus in 1498 already know of it, with pardonable lack of logic.

142. A version not found elsewhere—naturally, since it is invented *ad hoc* by Eur., as an unfounded rumour to add to Helen's load of misery.

143. οὐ διπλᾶ χρῄζω στένειν: by first suffering and then recounting troubles; enough of a commonplace by now to be thus elliptically expressed. Cf. *Hec.* 518, and infr. 770–1.

144–50. Teucer's long wanderings and quest were well enough known to make this explanation of his coming seem natural to the audience, and Theonoe is credited with international fame to make his motive more precise. He hopes the friendly unknown woman will act as his πρόξενος (146), the intermediary usual for an oracle-seeker. Helen, belatedly aware of his urgent danger, hurries him away.

151. To Teucer's request for prophetic guidance on how to steer a favourable course to Cyprus, Helen replies, 'The voyage will show you how, without help.' There is no need to apply to *Bacch.* 406 for the sense (the audience might have been at a loss if so); Teucer wants to know *where in* Cyprus to make for rather than where Cyprus is, and Helen implies, 'you will find the city where your ship comes ashore'—Apollo will see to the fulfilment of his oracle.

156. ὅτου δ' ἔκατι: the king's reason, as we can guess from Helen's monologue and as he clearly implies in 1173–6, is the fear of someones spying on and even carrying off Helen.

162–3. The effect of the bad omen is carefully undone. κακῶς δ': Wilamowitz is probably right in throwing out the particle, which is often fussily added in our MSS.

The Parodos proper does not begin till 179, but the whole lyric takes the form of a κομμός, a lyric interchange between stage and orchestra, and Helen sings the first stanza before the Chorus arrives —it arrives in fact because it hears her plaintive notes (antist.). After a second strophe and antistrophe, Helen 229–51 sings a long epode. As prelude to the whole, Helen chants three dactylic lines, two hexameters and a pentameter (Murray's conversion of ἒ ἒ into αἰαῖ makes clearer the continuity of the last line; ἒ ἓ can either be extra metrum or take whatever metrical quantity the context requires).

164. καταβαλλομένα: lit. 'laying the foundations of', hence 'beginning', cf. Callim. fr. 392 Pf. γάμον καταβάλλομ᾽ ἀείδειν, in fact very little different from the more technical ἀναβάλλομαι, 'strike up'.

165. ἁμιλλαθῶ: cf. Hec. 271, as it were 'enter as my contribution to the contest'; the word comes from the notion of outdoing rival performances on a public occasion, but here means little more than 'contribute', 'utter'. **μοῦσαν:** I supply the words (γόον); where shall I go for musical inspiration? and the answer is: The Sirens with their musical instruments could give it; if Persephone would send them I could make her the gift of a paean for the acceptance of the dead in her chambers of night. (For in her mood of despair, she thinks all she cares for must be among the shades.)

For the Sirens, bird-women connected in popular religion with souls and the underworld, see Roscher, *GRM*, with the Louvre amphora F486, or B.M. B651. As gentle, sorrowing companions of the dead they appear on the white lekythos Hampe–Simon 38. Were they perhaps a motif painted on the tomb of Proteus?

167–252. Like many of the songs in *Hel.* this is an operatic aria whose words must not be expected to bear too close a scrutiny of their meaning. This aggravates the problems of a sketchily transmitted text with defective responsion. Metre often gives a firmer lead than verbal expression; the whole of the lyric down to 374 is in a peculiarly Euripidean style of iambo-trochaic (mostly trochaic, but easily passing from the one to the other in a continuous flow). There is much resolution, not always in strict responsion, and some syncopation (*always* in responsion), usually of palimbacchiac type −·−∪ but occasionally double −·−·; anceps is mostly short. The smooth, light movement might suggest the conventional Greek description (as in Aristotle) of trochaic as a 'running' or dancing rhythm; perhaps it is the smoothness of one rocking herself with grief. The cola are dimeters with occasional trimeters, and no aberrations such as odd 'feet' or double-short or 'irrational long' can be tolerated.

167–78 = 179–90.

πτεροφόροι νεάνιδες, κυανοειδὲς ἀμφ᾽ ὕδωρ	∪∪ ∪ − ∪ − ∪ −	lek.
παρθένοι Χθονὸς κόραι ἔτυχον ἕλικά τ᾽ ἀνὰ χλόαν	∞ ∪ ∞ ∪ ∞ ∪ −	lek.
Σειρῆνες, εἴθ᾽ ἐμοῖς γόοις φοίνικας ἁλίου πέπλους	x − ∪ − ∪ − ∪ −	i. dim.
170 μόλοιτ᾽ ἔχουσαι Λίβυν 182 αὐγαῖσιν ἐν χρυσέαις	∪ − ∪ −·− ∪ −	sync. i. dim.

λωτὸν ἢ σύριγγας ἢ   – ◡ ⌣⌣ ◡ – ◡ –   tr. dim. cat.
ἀμφὶ δόνακος ἔρνεσιν

172 φόρμιγγας, αἰλίνοισι   –˙– ◡ – ◡ – ◡̲   sync. tr. dim.
183 θάλπουσα· ⟨τᾶς Λακαίνας δ',⟩
   τοῖς ἐμοῖσι σύνοχα δάκρυα,   – ◡ – ◡ ◡̑◡ ◡ ◡̲̑◡ ◡   tr. dim.
   ἔνθεν οἰκτρὸν ἀνεβόασεν,
   πάθεσι πάθεα, μέλεσι μέλεα·   ◡̑◡ ◡ ◡̑◡ ◡ ◡̑◡ ◡ ◡̑◡ ◡ tr. dim.
   ὅμαδον ἔκλυον, ἄλυρον ἔλεγον,
175 - - - - - - - - θρηνήμασι ξυνῳδὰ   ◡̑◡ ◡ ◡̑◡ ◡ – ˙ – ◡ – ◡ – ◡
186 ὅτι ποτ' ἔλακεν αἰάγμασι στένουσα,   sync. tr. trim.
   πέμψειε Φερσέφασσα   – ˙ – ◡ – ◡ – ◡   sync. tr. dim.
   Νύμφα τις οἷα Ναῖς
   φόνια, χάριτας ἵν' ἐπὶ δάκρυσι   ◡̑◡ ◡ ◡̑◡ ◡ ◡̑◡ ◡ ◡̲̑◡ ◡ tr. dim.
   ὄρεσι φυγάδα νόμον ἱεῖσα
   παρ' ἐμέθεν ὑπὸ μέλαθρα νύχια   ◡̑◡ ◡ ◡̑◡ ◡ ◡̑◡ ◡ ◡̑◡ ◡ tr. dim.
   γοερόν, ὑπὸ δὲ πέτρινα γύαλα
178 παιᾶνα νέκυσιν ὀλομένοις λάβῃ.   – ˙ – ◡ ◡̲̑◡ ◡ ◡̑◡ ◡ – ◡ –
190 κλαγγαῖσι Πανὸς ἀναβοᾷ γάμους.   sync. tr. trim. cat.

An alternative version of the last lines which has found much
favour, is:

177 φόνια φόνι' ἀχάριτας ἵν' ἐπὶ   ◡̑◡ ◡ ◡̑◡ ◡ ◡̑◡ ◡ ◡̲̑◡ ◡ tr. dim.
188 ὄρεσι φυγάδα νόμον ἱεῖσα
   δάκρυσι παρ' ἐμέθεν ὑπὸ μέλαθρα   ◡̑◡ ◡ ◡̑◡ ◡ ◡̑◡ ◡ ◡
   γοερόν, ὑπὸ δὲ πέτρινα μύχαλα   +tr. dim.
   νύχια παιᾶνας   ◡̑◡ ◡ – ˙ – ˙ – ˙   sync. tr. dim.
   γύαλα κλαγγαῖσιν
179 νέκυσι μελομένους λάβῃ.   ◡̲◡̲ ◡ ◡̑◡ ◡ – ◡ –   lek.
190 Πανὸς ἀναβοᾷ γάμους.

All turns on the acceptability of Triclinius's modifications φόνια φόνια
and παιᾶνας. He is apt, especially in lyric, to introduce his own conjectures metri gratia, but he clearly sometimes had access to other
evidence besides L, the traditional value of which is often hard to
assess. Here the total result of his work on strophe and antistrophe
is neither coherent nor intelligible, and some of it therefore may
come from collation. If so, it is easier to account for the dropping
of one φόνια than for the insertion of an extra one, and in ant.
μύχαλα seems to be a genuine word, presumably much the same as
μύχατα 'inmost', which some would prefer here. πέτρινα μύχαλα
γύαλα might seem excessive in any other style, and μύχαλα or μύαλα
may be simply a dittographia as Murray suggests. Metrically
the double syncopated metron in the penultimate place matches
the next pair of stanzas; on the other hand it loses much of the

neat coincidence of phrasing and cola. In such inconclusive cases preferences are likely to be personal; I greatly prefer the earlier version.

167–78. 'Feathered maidens, virgin daughters of Earth, would that you might come bearing Libyan flute or pipes or lyres to accompany my lament, with tears to match my cries of grief, sorrow answering sorrow, strain answering strain; O that Persephone would send me [your music, songs] to chime with my lament, songs of blood, so that down in her chambers of night she may receive from me as thank-offering a paean accompanied by tears for the dead and gone.'

172. The lyre is cleared away from many texts, from Triclinius's downwards, in an effort to accommodate to the antistrophe. If the deletion of ἢ φόρμιγγας solved the awkward problem of responsion here one might acquiesce, even though the lyre is on vases the normal instrument of the Sirens; but no one could think λωτὸν ἢ σύριγγας αἰλίνοις in responsion to θάλπουσ' ἀμφὶ δόνακος ἔρνεσιν very satisfactory (presumably − ∪ − − − ∪ − ∪ − = · − · − ∪ ∾ ∪ − ∪ −). There is no adequate evidence for any licence of irregular responsion in syncopated cola. Murray's transposition of θάλπουσα in ant. to a position corresponding to φόρμιγγας is a much better solution; then, since a feminine subject in some form is needed in the following sentence in ant., the rest of the line after θάλπουσα is available. Murray's supplement assumes φόρ-, θάλ- to be long anceps ⊼ − ∪ − ∪ − ∪ −; preferring a different supplement, I have taken it as starting a palimbacchiac and deleted κακοῖς with Hartung and others, since αἴλινον is more often substantival than adjectival.

174. Punctuation can connect this line with the preceding, sc. σύνοχα, or with the following, sc. ξυνῳδά.

175–7. μουσεῖα is always local: 'halls of song', lit. or met., and the ambiguous translation 'chorus' or 'concerts' is illegitimate, even with the magic word 'metonymy'. This line is not good evidence by itself for an extension of the meaning to 'songs' or 'choirs', since the word is also out of responsion, and Triclinius's insertion of τε to get an extra syllable is useless. Persephone can send music ξυνῳδὰ and φόνια only through her intermediaries the Sirens, and no alternative conjectured on these lines is acceptable. The only suggestion worth recording is Fix's μοῦσ' ἱεῖσα, with Φερσεφάσσᾳ (Hermann), reversing the direction of the traffic: χάριτας in that case must be taken, as Pearson, with νέκυσιν, 'an offering welcome to the dead', cf. A. Cho. 320–1 with Σ.

178. παιᾶνα: applicable to θρηνήματα only by a kind of oxymoron, cf. Alc. 424. νέκυσιν ὀλομένοις: the same tautology appears in Phoen. 1295. Lobeck, who takes the second version of 177–9 quoted above, prefers ἀχάριτας παιᾶνας νέκυσι μελομένους, cf. IT 183 and Phoen. 1303.

179–90. The Parodos recalls the 'washing-scene' of *Hipp.* 121–30. 'By the deep dark pool I chanced, and on the young curling grass, to be brightening in the sun's gold rays my purple robes, near the young bulrushes.' Triclinius and Hermann having disposed neatly of the unmetrical 182, the next problem is to fit in a subject for ἀνεβόασεν and ἔλακεν. (1) Those who got rid of ἢ φόρμιγγας 171 now have to delete the blameless ἀνεβόασεν 'as a gloss', move up the next three metra and make a lacuna before αἰάγμασι corresponding to the problematic μουσεῖα or μουσεῖα τε. (Grégoire's ἁ Λάκαιν' ἐν is sensible but his stanzas do not correspond.) ἔρνεσιν in 183 then ends brevis in longo—there is another at 230—and ἔνθεν means 'from there', my washing-place. (2) Murray, by transposing θάλπουσα and adding a gen. construed with ὅμαδον and ἔλεγον, makes ἔνθεν 'from where' she raised her pitiful cry. This, unlike (1), makes responsion possible. ποτνίας, however, suggested perhaps by δεσποίνας *Hipp.* 130, seems the wrong word for Helen; there is nowhere any suggestion that the Chorus were Helen's servants. (πότνια voc., of course, as in 225, has no such implication.) τᾶς Λακαίνας δ' needs αἰλίνοισι in str.; with αἰλίνοις one might have τᾶς φίλας δ'.

185. ἄλυρον ἔλεγον: 'a song of grief not meet for the lyre' need not be taken as an argument against φόρμιγγας in str.; it has become a conventional description.

190. For Pan and the Nymphs, cf. P. Maas, *Epid. Hymn.*, p. 130.

191–210 ‒ 211–228.

191	ἰὼ ἰώ·		
211	αἰαῖ αἰαῖ·		
	θήραμα βαρβάρου πλάτας,	$\overline{\times} - \cup - \cup - \cup -$	i. dim.
	ὦ δαίμονος πολυστόνου		
	Ἑλλανίδες κόραι,	$- \cdot - \cup - \cup - \|$	sync. tr. dim.
	μοίρας τε σᾶς, γύναι,		
194	ναύτας Ἀχαιῶν τις	$- \cdot - \cup - \cdot - \cup$	sync. tr. dim.
213	αἰὼν δυσαίων τις		
	ἔμολεν ἔμολε δάκρυα δάκρυσί μοι φέρων.		tr. trim. cat.
	ἔλαχεν ἔλαχεν, ὅτε σ' ἐτέκετο ματρόθεν		
	Ἰλίου κατασκαφαὶ	$\sigma\sigma \cup - \cup - \cup -$	lek.
	χιονόχρως κύκνου πτερῷ		
197	πυρί μέλουσι δαΐῳ	$\widehat{\cup\cup} \cup - \cup - \cup -$	lek.
216	Ζεὺς πρέπων δι' αἰθέρος·		
	δι' ἐμὲ τὰν πολύκτονον,	$\widehat{\cup\cup} - \cup - \cup -$	lek.
	τί γὰρ ἄπεστί σοι κακῶν;		
	δι' ἐμὸν ὄνομα πολύπονον.	$\widehat{\cup\cup} \cup \widehat{\cup\cup} \cup \widehat{\cup\cup} \cup -$	lek.
	τίνα δὲ βίοτον οὐκ ἔτλας;		

Λήδα δ' ἐν ἀγχόναις	—.— ∪ — ∪ —	sync. tr. dim.
μάτηρ μὲν οἴχεται,		
201 θάνατον ἔλαβεν αἰσχύ-	⌣⌣ ∪ ⌣⌣ ∪ —.—.	sync. tr. dim.
220 δίδυμά τε Διὸς οὐκ εὐ-		
-νας ἐμᾶς ὑπ' ἀλγέων.	— ∪ — ∪ — ∪ —	+lek.
-δαιμονεῖ τέκεα φίλα,		
ὁ δ' ἐμὸς ἐν ἁλὶ πολυπλανὴς	⌣⌣ ∪ ⌣⌣ ∪ ⌣̲⌣̲ ∪ —	lek.
χθόνα δὲ πάτριον οὐχ ὁρᾷς,		
πόσις ὀλόμενος οἴχεται,	⌣⌣ ∪ ⌣⌣ ∪ — ∪ —	lek.
διὰ δὲ πόλιας ἔρχεται		
205 Κάστορός τε συγγόνου τε	— ∪ — ∪ — ∪ — ∪	tr. dim.
224 βάξις, ἅ σε βαρβάροισι		
διδυμογενὲς ἄγαλμα πατρίδος	⌣⌣ ∪ ⌣⌣ ∪ ⊽⊽ ∪ ⌣̲⌣̲ ∪	tr. dim.
λέχεσι, πότνια, παραδίδωσιν		
ἄφανες ἄφανες ἱππόκροτα λέλοιπε δάπεδα		tr. trim.
ὁ δὲ σὸς ἐν ἁλὶ κύμασί τε λέλοιπε βίοτον		
γυμνάσιά τε δονακόεντος	— ∪ ⌣⌣ ∪ ⌣⌣ ∪ ⊽⊽ ∪	tr. dim.
οὐδέ ποτ' ἔτι πάτρια μέλαθρα		
210 Εὐρώτα, νεανιᾶν πόνον.	—.—.— ∪ — ∪ — ∪ —	
228 καὶ τὰν Χαλκίοικον ὀλβιεῖς.		sync. tr. trim. cat.

The trochaic metre continues, with only the first line iambic. The first clear pause of the ode comes after the second line (hiatus ant.). There is some very close responsion of words and resolution, as a glance will show, but as this cannot be carried through quite consistently it is doubtful whether we should help it out by transposition, as Nauck at 225 (v. app. crit.); certainly not by transposing 215 and 216, a conjecture of Triclinius for misguided metrical ends (v. Zuntz, p. 42).

191–228. Helen summarizes Teucer's information, and the Chorus then repeats it back to her with sympathy.

192. θήραμα: 'catch', abstract for concrete = those hunted down and taken captive. This serves as the introduction to the audience which the Chorus has failed to give of itself.

196–7. Murray's **κατασκαφαὶ** is simpler and better than Triclinius's acc. and participle κατασκαφὰν μέλ(λ)ουσαν, which whatever its origin introduces a mid-verse long anceps, which would be unique in this pair. **μέλουσι,** lit. 'are the business of', is an odd, affected word here, since the dative is usually personal (but cf. *IT* 645). It *is* a word Eur. affects, more often in the middle, cf. 1161. Pearson compares Ar. *Lys.* 1306 τᾷ σίων χόροι μέλοντι. The present tense in effect means 'Troy is a smoking ruin'; the fires of Troy are almost timeless.

199 as it were corrects 198.

205–11. 'their country's twin glory, Castor and his brother, is vanished, vanished, leaving the plains that rang beneath their horses' hoofs and reedy Eurotas' wrestling-grounds, the exercise of youth' (= scene of youthful exercise; the phrase cannot possibly mean leaving Sparta's youth to mourn for them, as the Budé translation takes it).

211–12. Cf. φεῦ τῆς ἀνοίας S. *El.* 920. In tragedy an introductory exclamation, as ὦ here, is usually necessary to carry this gen., v. *Alc.* 832 with my note.

214. ἔλαχεν: σε is to be supplied back from the following clause. This inversion—the lot gets you, rather than you the lot—recalls the old Homeric notion of original forces in the universe (κήρ *Il.* 23. 79) that seize upon the unformed soul at birth.

216. πρέπων δι' αἰθέρος: the flash of white as the swan descends through the upper air.

221. οὐκ εὐδαιμονεῖ: If this is sound, the Chorus must be deducing that wherever they are the D. no longer enjoy the εὐδαιμονία, the untroubled bliss, which the favourite sons of Zeus might expect. But Herwerden's οὐκ ἐν γᾷ μένει (ἄφανες 208, no longer in Sparta) is ingenious, and perhaps right.   τέκεα (prob. a dissyllable, cf. *Hipp.* 126): Triclinius for the unmetrical τέκνα.

223. πόλιας: Ionic as *Andr.* 484; πόλεας is unparalleled. (Zuntz, p. 44.)

226. ὁ δὲ σὸς ἐν ἁλί: an echo of ὁ δ' ἐμὸς ἐν ἁλί 203 but without πόσις, which has to be supplied out of βαρβάροις λέχεσιν above.

227–8: 'never again will you make glad your father's halls and the Bronze-Housed Goddess.' The Spartan Athena was regularly given this epithet from her famous bronze-plated temple.

229–52. Epode.

φεῦ φεῦ.		
τίς ἢ Φρυγῶν ἢ τίς Ἑλ-	∪−∪− −∪−	sync. i. dim.
-λανίας ἀπὸ χθονὸς	−∪−∪−∪ ⌣ ‖	+lek.
ἔτεμε τὰν δακρυόεσ-	≈∪−≈∪−	sync. i. dim.
-σαν Ἰλίῳ πεύκαν;	∪−∪− −·−·	
		+sync. i. dim.
ἔνθεν ὀλόμενον σκάφος	−∪≈∪−∪− •	lek.
συναρμόσας ὁ Πριαμίδας ⟨τ'⟩	∪−∪−∪≈∪−	i. dim.
ἔπλευσε βαρβάρῳ πλάτᾳ	∪−∪−∪−∪−	i. dim.
235 τὰν ἐμὰν ἐφ' ἑστίαν	−∪−∪−∪−	lek.
ἐπὶ τὸ δυστυχέστατον	≈∪−∪−∪−	lek.
κάλλος, ὡς ἕλοι γαμῶν,	−∪−∪−∪−	lek.
238 ἅ τε δόλιος, ἁ πολυκτόνος Κύπρις	−∪≈∪−∪−∪−∪−	
		tr. trim. cat.
Δαναΐδαις ἄγουσα θάνατον.	≈∪−∪−∪≈∪	tr. dim.
ὦ τάλαινα συμφορᾶς.	−∪−∪−∪−	lek.
ἁ δὲ χρυσέοις θρόνοις	−∪−∪−∪−	lek.
Διὸς ὑπαγκάλισμα σεμνὸν	≈∪−∪−∪−∪	tr. dim.

242 Ἥρα τὸν ὠκύπουν ἔ-   —.—◡—◡—◡   tr. dim.
     -πεμψε Μαιάδος γόνον·   —◡—◡—◡ ‿ ‖   +lek.
     ὅς με χλοερὰ δρεπομέναν ἔσω —◡ ⌒◡ ⌒◡—◡—◡—
     πέπλων   tr. trim. cat.
245 ῥόδεα πέταλα, Χαλκίοικον   ⌒◡ ⌒◡—◡—◡   tr. dim.
     ὡς Ἀθάναν μόλοιμ᾽, ἀν-   —◡—.—◡—◡   sync. tr. dim.
     -αρπάσας δι᾽ αἰθέρος   —◡—◡—◡—   +lek.
     τάνδε γαῖαν εἰς ἄνολβον   —◡—◡—◡—◡   tr. dim.
     ἔριν ἔριν τάλαιναν ἔθετο   ⌒◡—◡—◡ ⌒◡   tr. dim.
250 Πριαμίδαισιν Ἑλλάδος.   ⌒◡—◡—◡—   lek.
     τὸ δ᾽ ἐμὸν ὄνομα παρὰ Σιμουντίοις ⌒◡ ⌒◡ ⌒◡—◡—◡—◡
     ῥοαῖσι   tr. trim.
     μαψίδιον ἔχει φάτιν.   —◡ ⌒◡—◡—   lek.

Period-end is audible twice (brevis in longo). All down to 237 could be taken as iambic, since the lekythion is an ambiguous colon; all beyond that is trochaic. This colometry 244–5 keeps each resolution at the beginning of a word, with much advantage in smoothness.

230. A Greek hand cutting down the pine for Paris' ship seems an unlikely thought; this is an extreme instance of 'polar expression' for 'Who, of all men, was it . . .?' Cf. *Med.* 3–4.

233 ff. Since the only construction available for Cypris 238 is as a fellow traveller with Paris, the τ᾽ here might prepare the hearer for it. Even so the hyperbaton, with zeugma, is considerable; the meaning is, in effect, συνέπλευσε δὲ καὶ ἡ Κύπρις. It would be easier if we cut out the unmetrical 236–7, ἐπὶ τὸ δυστυχέστατον | κάλλος ὡς ἕλοι γάμων ἐμῶν, which Dindorf believed to be scrambled together out of 27–28 and 30. Triclinius dealt with this by the conjecture γάμον ἐμόν, which with a metrical harshness unparalleled in this parodos produces a resolution across the two words | ◡ ⌣◡ ◡. Zuntz, *CQ* 5, 1955, 68–69, incorporates this in more acceptable form: ἐπὶ τὸ δυστυχές τ᾽ ἐμὸν | κάλλος, ὡς ἕλοι γάμον. I feel, however, that the τε linking two different senses of ἐπί, ἐφ᾽ ἑστίαν and ἐπὶ τὸ κάλλος, rather adds to the awkwardness of the whole. Murray puts ἀμῶν into the next line, but the gen. makes an awkward construction anyway. If the lines are to be kept I should prefer the version given here: τὸ δυσ. κάλ. that [promised] ill-fated beauty (no need for ἐμὸν after ἐμὰν ἑστίαν), that he might win it in the bed of love.

241. Homer's χρυσόθρονος Ἥρη.

242. 'august bedfellow of Zeus': ὑπ. poetic abstract for concrete, used also for babe-in-arms, *Tro.* 757.

243. Hermes' mother is Μαιάς, -άδος, or Μαῖα, Μαίας.

244. δρεπομέναν ἔσω πέπλων = ἐς πέπλους: the usual occupation of the abducted, like Persephone, Creusa (*Ion* 888), Europa.

245 etc. μόλοιμ᾽: i.e. meaning to visit the temple. Weak enough to make Dindorf delete the line. If Ἀθάναν were cut out, the article τὰν Χαλκίοικον would be necessary.

247. Probably ἀναρπάσας carries through to ἄνολβον, with ἔθετο governing ἔριν, rather than 'set me down here *to be* a source of strife'.

251. μαψίδιον: empty talk because it is about her empty name without herself.

252 ff. The Chorus administers a conventional exhortation to patience. Lyric lament is, here as often, followed by a rhetorical demonstration of the speaker's peculiar and unexampled misery.

255. συνεζύγην: one's fate, πότμος, δαίμων (*Andr.* 98) is one's uneasy yokefellow.

256 ff. Are these words from Helen—a 'white vessel for chicks' and the rest—tastelessly grotesque? Even so, that would not in itself justify deletion; since the lines are technically irreproachable, we should have to demonstrate that they spoil the train of thought, which emerges better without them. The argument that γὰρ 257 awkwardly anticipates γὰρ 260 because someone is contriving to interpolate an irrelevant explanation of τέρας is hardly fair. Teratogenesis is indeed a somewhat different issue from the general 'prodigiousness' of Helen's life and misfortunes, but, after all, the word is the same, and she could easily pass from the one sense to the other. 260 ['And indeed it seems as if it (256) must be so,] *for* [not only was I born a τέρας but] my life in general and my fortunes are thus extraordinary.' Both γὰρ 257 and γὰρ 260 have the same reference, cf. 477/479, Denn. *GP* 64. And it is difficult to see how the phrasing of 256 with its emphasis on τεκεῖν could avoid the association of ideas expressed in 257-9. Nor is the repetition of τέρας in 260 immediately after the end of 256 very attractive. Denniston in fact (*GP* 581) is undoubtedly right in saying that if 257-9 are rejected 256 had better go too; 255/260 is a neater join. But then where does the idea of τέρας come from? In this applied sense it is a far from familiar concept in tragic diction, or in poetry at all. I cannot share Denniston's misgivings about ἆρα 256. It is the rhetorical appeal to look at the evidence and judge how good the proof is, as in *Alc.* 341.

257-9 then must be left as a half-parenthetical *literal* explanation of τέρας 256, followed by the wider and more general application of the idea. And the grotesque element is something we have to take into account as a given aspect of this play (see Introd., pp. xi, xxxiii).

This is the earliest literary reference we have to the egg as laid by Leda (see Roscher, *GRM*).

262 ff. ἄγαλμα: here 'painting', not as more usually a figure in the round, since ἐξαλείφω must mean obliterate, not wipe clean. 'Oh if only I could be expunged like a painted picture and start again with a plainer appearance in place of this beauty, and then the Greeks could have forgotten the ill fate which now is mine and remembered what was not ill as well as they now remember what is ill.' The translation fits better the MS. reading ἀντὶ τοῦ καλοῦ λαβεῖν, an infinitive which in two passages of the *Odyssey*, 7. 311 and 24. 380, and nowhere else, is used with αἲ γὰρ to express a wish for the present time ('O to be . . .'). This is slender support for the construction with εἴθε here, and if we find it insufficient Porson's ᵕλαβον is easy though not very elegant. For the prodelision at the end of the line compare *Auge* fr. 266N² εἰ δ' ἐγὼ ᵕτεκον, but there the clause is very short and there is no choice of position; here one wonders why not as Wilamowitz–Murray—only then the corruption would have been inexplicable. (λάβω is a desperate attempt to construe with ὥς = ἵνα.)

With ἔλαβον, wherever placed, Helen's wish is neither clear nor logical: if she *had been* ordinary instead of beautiful none of this would have happened and the Greeks would not have needed to forget it. Yet the underlying thought is quite natural: it is this accursed beauty which makes her notorious and execrated; the plainer are more fairly judged. The language (αὖθις πάλιν) suggests rather a wish to make a fresh start, now in mid-career, as an ordinary woman. Either Eur. did here use the rare Homeric construction, with ὥς for καὶ in 264—'that so the Greeks might . . .', continuing with past indicatives because of the inherent impossibility of such a wish; or the illogicality must be accepted (so Porson) as a piece of naturalism.

267–8. 'When a man sets his hopes on one thing and is cheated of that by the gods, it is hard, but must be borne.' For ὅστις = εἴ τις or the infin. with τὸ (267, 272), see Platnauer on *IT* 606.

The absence of normal caesura in 267 is softened by the proclitic ἐς, which is better than no word-end at all, and also by the resolution in ἐς μίαν ⨯ ⌣⌣ which slides smoothly into the next word, unlike ⨯ – |. The loose technique could only belong to Eur.'s latest period.

269 ff. This is the orator's style, accumulating proofs that one is *peculiarly* hard hit. They are numbered off helpfully: 270 πρῶτον μὲν, 273 ἔπειτα, 277 ἄγκυρα δ' (Menelaus), 280—there should be no new paragraph—μήτηρ δ' (Leda), 282 ὁ δ' (Hermione), 284 τὼ τοῦ Διὸς δὲ (Dioscuri), 285 summing up: 'All this, and still I do not die.'

276. ἑνός: Helen had no appeal in Egypt from Theoclymenus' wishes, and this dependence on arbitrary royal whim was what shocked a Greek most.

277–9. The 'sole anchor' at which her fortunes rode was 'the hope that my husband . . .'. There would be nothing against the anacolouthon here, with its substitution of '*he*' (πόσις) as subject; but the repetition in οὗτος τέθνηκεν, οὗτος οὐκέτ' ἔστι δή is rather feeble, and εἴπερ (Hermann; ἐπεί, εἴ που, ἀφ' οὗ al.) τέθνηκεν οὗτος, οὐκέτ' ἔστι δή leaves ἄγκυρα as subject.

281. Variously rendered: (1) unjustly indeed, but such injustice is my portion; (2) oui, sa mort est un crime, et ce crime est le mien.

It must surely be intended as an epigram: 'the guilt is, though guiltlessly, mine.'

282–3. Grégoire assumes a lacuna in the stichomythia after 136, giving news of Hermione, but as Helen did not mention her in the lyric she is probably making the deduction here, just to complete the recital. ἐμοῦ: if, as seems probable, the genitives are possessive, Cobet's ἐμόν should be read.   πολιά neut. plur. adverbial, as it were 'is greyingly a virgin'.

284. One would like to think Eur. wrote πατρὸs, with Ribbeck.

285–6. The contrast of πράγματα and ἔργα is not between fortunes and deeds, since τέθνηκα cannot be used for ὄλωλα, and she cannot need to say again that she is not to blame for any of this.   ἔργοισιν plur. = ἔργῳ, as S. OC 782; though she οὕτω κακῶς πράσσει that she is as good as dead (cf. Hec. 431), she is in fact alive.

287–92. The last two lines had an air of finality, but now we find an addition: 'last and worst of all', in apposition to the following sentence. And what is this fate worse than death? 'If I reached home I should find the gates barred against me', because she could not establish her identity. If Menelaus had been there she could have persuaded him by tokens of proof known only to the two of them, 'but now this cannot be and he can never return safe home'.

Lost identity as the ἔσχατον κακόν? I suspect the idea of being a post-Kafka nightmare rather than a natural rhetorical climax in Greek literature. And Helen has just seen the effect of her appearance on Teucer; one would suppose she would fear a traitor's death by stoning rather than being refused admission to Sparta. But if we take this as simply the rhetorician's tiresome trick of concentrating on one aspect of τὸ εἰκός to the temporary exclusion of all others, how can the text be translated? 'Thinking me to be Trojan Helen returning with Menelaus' (who might be coming along presently)? Then why keep her out? 'Thinking that if I were Trojan Helen I should be returning with Menelaus'? But that would need ἄν. Emendations are numerous, e.g. (1) Zuntz, l.c., δίχα for μέτα, 'thinking me to be the Trojan Helen returning without Menelaus'. But the trouble she is anticipating is of not being able to prove herself Helen at all. (2) Grégoire, μ' ἔρρειν for μ' ἐλθεῖν; but they could not simultaneously think she was Trojan Helen and that she had perished with Menelaus. (3) F. W. Schmidt, θανεῖν for μ' ἐλθεῖν: 'thinking Trojan Helen had perished with Menelaus.' Sense at last, but drastic; how would the corruption have arisen?

For the construction, δοκοῦντες 'probably makes the harshest anacolouthon in Eur.'—Zuntz, who would nevertheless accept it. Only one cannot imagine why Eur. did not write Ἑλένην δοκούντων, thus avoiding the confusion of a nom. part. which at first appears to refer to the subject of εἰργ.—'seeming', especially with ἐλθόντες

just below, which *could* be a similar masculine for a woman who is
speaking of herself in the plural (cf. *Alc.* 383) though it could also
mean herself and Menelaus—the ambiguity is total. Further, a
minor worry, ὑπ' Ἰλίῳ has everywhere else in Eur. its proper
meaning of the plains of Troy, where the fighting and the Greeks
were. Next, line 291 has to be completely rewritten (though in
terms of longs and shorts it *would* scan!—cf. on 9) and in all its
various transformations it is difficult to construe—is it ἐλθόντες 'when
I had come', and ἀνεγ. ἂν ἐς ξύμβολα, 'I (we) could have put my (our)
recognition to the test of tokens', or ἐλθόντες ἐς ξύμβολα 'coming to
tokens' = having recourse to them? Either is dubious Greek, and
ἀναγ. in this sense is a ἅπ. λεγ. in tragedy. Does 292 return to
Menelaus' fate, or should one read σωθῶ with Orelli?

If we find this accumulation of troubles too much, and (with
Goguel) reject 287–92 as a typically clumsy interpolation, 286 joins up
smoothly with 293 (no new paragraph): what then have I to live for?

293. ὑπολείπομαι τύχην: pass. with retained object, what fate am I
left?

297. τὸ σῶμ': if we try to derive this from what precedes—a life of
plenty with a barbarian husband—the sentiment is certainly obscure
enough to have given rise to a number of desperate conjectures:
τὸ δῶμ', τὸ πῶμ', τὸ βρῶμ', κἀξίωμ', τὸ σῶν, even τὸ ζῆν was taken up,
according to whether the life or the plenty was taken up.
Of these only τὸ δῶμ' is worth considering because of the frequent
confusion of δ and σ in these MSS; the sentiment, however, is flat
and lumpish. But the point is explained in what follows—that is,
in 303 ἐς γὰρ τοσοῦτον. That 299–302 should be seriously defended is
surprising; apart from their silliness and their awkward Greek, the
sentiment of 300 is shockingly out of place when she has just heard of
the manner of her mother's death, nor is it any defence that a lyric
review of methods of suicide occurs 352 ff. A reasoned exposition
in iambics following a lyric lament is one thing; a lyric rehash of
sentiments already expounded in iambics to the same audience is
another. Besides, the situation at 352 is different. Here, after recounting her griefs, she wonders what she has left to live for; there,
she has agreed to appeal to Theonoe's second sight but hardly dares
to use this last resource—if the prophetess takes away the last re-
maining doubt of Menelaus' death, she warns them that she will kill
herself. *That* is the climax. But the interpolator who put together
299–302 must also have been responsible for the lead-in 298 (reading
οὖν) which is the question he solemnly sets himself to answer. For
298, however emended, is betrayed by its stupidity: with οὖν it cannot possibly be taken as a wish (Pearson); one can say *in extremis*
πῶς ἂν ὀλοίμαν; 'O that I could die!'—but *not* with the addition of οὖν
and καλῶς, in a rhetorical analysis. And with οὐ—'how would it

not be well for me to die?'—not only is the negative in a very awkward position, after the verb and separated from πῶς, but also the
line causes a limping peroration, almost a *non sequitur*, with 303-5.
The reference to her beauty at the end must be led up to, and the
lead-in is 297, in which σῶμα now acquires a meaning; it is Helen's
own lovely person that would become hateful to her, '*for* . . .'.

304. μὲν γάρ: the two lines define τοσοῦτον, instead of a ὥστε clause.

306-29. But is it all true? say the Chorus; let us at least go and ask
Theonoe if your husband is really dead. (This will leave the stage
empty for Menelaus' arrival.)

308-10. As they stand, with Kirchhoff's not altogether satisfactory
ἀληθείᾳ σαφῆ 310, these lines appear to mean:

He was quite explicit about my husband's death anyway.
Many communications might be lyingly made.
And the opposite kind are explicit because true.

It is not a very sparkling exchange, and would be tightened up considerably by Hermann's transposition of σαφῆ to 309, with ἀληθείας
ἔπη 310: 'There could well be such a thing as an explicit lie.'—'Yes,
and its opposite kind of truth', i.e. an inexplicit truth. The brachy-
logy of the last line certainly demands a little goodwill for its
interpretation, and it is not the position Helen started from in 308—
though Teucer had not in fact been so very explicit; he had said (132)
θανὼν κλῄζεται καθ' Ἑλλάδα. Many emendations have been proposed,
but none very attractive.

311. φέρῃ: like a chariot veering off the straight course to one side or
the other.

312. φόβος: the emotion; **τὸ δεῖμα**: the thing dreaded.

313. εὐμενείας: gen. of 'field of reference', with ἔχειν and an adverb
such as πῶς, ὡς, εὖ. 'How do you stand for sympathy in the palace?'

315: cf. 1233; the common Euripidean idiom, v. Platnauer on *IT* 759.

316. ἕρπεις: a word much affected by tragedians. Helen is inclined
to be horrified at so dangerous a course.

317-29. This is a long speech for a Chorus, and certainly three lines
longer than it was meant to be. 324-6 are impossible to construe and
wholly superfluous. The interpolator seems to have been misled by
ἀλλ' ἐμοὶ πιθοῦ (the word πιθοῦ often, e.g. *Hec.* 842, sums up an appeal
already made: '*please* do this'), and felt impelled to start all over
again, with ideas collected from the immediate context.

321. πρὸς: in accordance with, cf. *Hipp.* 701.

330-74.

	φίλαι, λόγους ἐδεξάμαν·	∪ − ∪ − ∪ − ∪ −	i. dim.
	βᾶτε βᾶτε δ' ἐς δόμους	− ∪ − ∪ − ∪ −	lek.
333	ἀγῶνας ἐντὸς ὡς πύθησθε τοὺς	∪ − ∪ − ∪ − ∪ −	i. trim.
	ἐμούς.		

— θέλουσαν οὔ με δὶς καλεῖς.	◡ – ◡ – ◡ – ◡ –	i. dim.
— ἰὼ, μέλεος ἁμέρα.	◡ –·◠◡ ◡ – ◡ –	sync. i. dim.
336 τιν' ἄρα τάλαινα τίνα λόγον	◡ ◠◡ – ◡ ◠◡ –	i. dim.
δακρυόεντ' ἀκούσομαι;	◠◡ – ◡ – ◡ –	lek.
— μὴ πρόμαντις ἀλγέων	– ◡ – ◡ – ◡ –	lek.
προλάμβαν', ὦ φίλα, γόους.	◡ – ◡ – ◡ – ◡	i. dim.
— τί μοι πόσις μέλεος ἔτλα;	◡ – ◡ – ◡ ◠◡ –	i. dim.
πότερα δέρκεται φάος	◠◡ – ◡ – ◡ –	lek.
342 τέθριππά θ' ἁλίου κέλευθά τ'	i. trim.	
ἀστέρων,		
ἢ 'ν νέκυσι κατὰ χθονὸς	– ◡ ◠◡ – ◡ –	lek.
τὰν χρόνιον ἔχει τύχαν;	– ◡ ◠◡ – ◡ –	lek.
— ἐς τὸ φέρτερον τίθει	– ◡ – ◡ – ◡ –	lek.
τὸ μέλλον, ὅ τι γενήσεται.	◡ – ◡ ◠◡ – ◡ –	i. dim.
348 — σὲ γὰρ ἐκάλεσα, σέ τε κατόμοσα	◠◡ – ◡ ◠◡ ◠◡ ◡	tr. dim.
τὸν ὑδρόεντι δόνακι χλωρὸν	◠◡ – ◡ ◠◡ – ◡	tr. dim.
Εὐρώταν, θανόντος	–·–·◡ – ◡	sync. tr. dim.
εἰ βάξις ἔτυμος ἀνδρὸς ἅδε μοι	–·– ◡ ◠◡ – ◡ – ◡ –	
		sync. tr. trim. cat.
352 — τί τάδ' ἀσύνετα;	◠◡ ◡ ◠◡ ◡	
— φοινίοισι	– ◡ – ◡	tr. dim.
μέλεον αἰωρήμα-	◠◡ –·–·◡	sync. tr. dim.
-σιν δέρην ἐνέξομαι,	– ◡ – ◡ – ◡ – ‖	+ lek.
ἢ ξιφοκτόνον δίωγμα	– ◡ – ◡ – ◡ – ◡	tr. dim.
λαιμορρύτου σφαγᾶς	–·– ◡ – ◡ –	sync. tr. dim. cat.
356 αὐτοσίδαρον ἔσω πελάσω διὰ		
σαρκὸς ἄμιλλαν,		dact. hexam.
θῦμα τριζύγοις θεαῖσι	– ◡ – ◡ – ◡ – ◡	tr. dim.
τῷ τε σύριγγος αὐ-	– ◡ – ◡ – ◡ –·	sync. tr. dim.
-δᾷ σεβίζοντι Πριαμί-	– ◡ –·– ◡ ◠◡ – ◡	sync. tr. dim.
359 -δᾳ ποτ' ἀμφὶ βουστάθμους.	– ◡ – ◡ – ◡ –	lek.
— ἄλλοσ' ἀποτροπὰ κακῶν	– ◡ ◠◡ – ◡ –	lek.
γένοιτο, τὸ δὲ σὸν εὐτυχές.	◡ – ◡ ◠◡ ◡ – ◡ –	i. dim.
362 — ἰὼ τάλαινα Τροία,	◡ – ◡ – ◡ – –	i. dim. cat.
δι' ἔργ' ἄνεργ' ὄλλυσαι μέλεά τ'	◡ – ◡ – – ◡ – ◡ ◠◡ –	
ἔτλας·		sync. i. trim.
τὰ δ' ἐμὰ δῶρα Κύπριδος ἔτεκε	◠◡ – ◡ ◠◡ ◡ ◠◡ ◡	tr. dim.
πολὺ μὲν αἷμα, πολὺ δὲ δάκρυον,	◠◡ – ◡ ◠◡ ◡ ◠◡ ◡	tr. dim.
365 ἄχεά τ' ἄχεσι, πάθεα πάθεσι·	◠◡ ◠◡ ◡ ◠◡ ◡ ◠◡ ◡	tr. dim.
ματέρες τε παῖδας ὄλεσαν,	– ◡ – ◡ – ◠◡ ◡	tr. dim.
ἀπὸ δὲ παρθένοι κόμας	◠◡ – ◡ – ◡ –	lek.
(ἔ)θεντο σύγγονοι νεκρῶν	(◡) – ◡ – ◡ – ◡	
		i. dim. or lek.
ἀμφὶ Φρύγιον οἶδμα.	– ◡ ◠◡ ◡ – ◡ ‖	ithyph.
370 βοὰν βοὰν δὲ κελάδησ'	◡ – ◡ – ◠◡ ◡ –	sync. i. dim.

ἀνοτότυξέ θ᾽ Ἑλλάς   ⏗⏗ ∪ – ∪ – ⏗ ‖   ithyph.
ἐπὶ δὲ κρατὶ χέρας ἔθηκεν   ⏗⏗ ∪ – ∪ ⏗⏗ ∪ – ∪   tr. dim.
ὄνυχι δ᾽ ἁπαλόχροα γένυν   ⏗⏗ ∪ ⏗⏗ ∪ ⏗⏗ ∪ –   lek.
374   ἔδευσεν φοινίαισι πλαγαῖς.   ∪ – – – ∪ – ∪ – –   sync. i. trim.

This κομμός or lyric dialogue continues in iambo-trochaic, which breaks out at one passionate moment (356) into a striking hexameter (anticipating 375 ff.). Helen's solo 361–74 has some new modifications, dropping the palimbacchiac syncopation and introducing ithyphallics (with period-close) and an iambic clausula picking up in syncopated form from the trimeter 363.

330. ἐδεξάμαν: the common aor. of a decision just now taken, 'I accept', cf. 348 'I swear'.

332. [οἴκων]: the δόμων noted (as a variant?) by Triclinius doubtless shows the earlier stage of this superfluous addition. The same metrical pattern, dim., lek., trim., recurs 340–2.   ἀγῶνας: learn [the truth about] my trials.

334. οὐ μόλις: (1) non parum, i.e. 'willing and eager, Hermann, approved by Fraenkel on A. Ag. 1082; (2) haud aegre, 'easily', Page–Denniston ad loc. Either way the phrase is curiously off-colour, and unlike the Aeschylean examples. It is tempting to read Elmsley's οὔ με δὶς καλεῖς (as A. Pers. 173), adopted by A. Y. Campbell and palaeographically easy. καλεῖς is then future.

335 ff. Helen is so afraid of what she will hear that she cannot bring herself to enter for 50 lines.

336. The metre limps suspiciously. As printed by edd., it gives a dubious resolution before a syncopated long syllable δακρυό-εντα ... ∪ ⏗⏗ /– ∪ ..., which destroys iambo-trochaic continuity. The only alternative is to divide the cola τίν᾽ ἄρα τάλαι-να τίνα δακρυ-/όεντα λόγον κτλ. ∪ ⏗⏗ ∪ – · ⏗⏗ ∪ ⏗⏗ / ∪ – ∪ ⏗⏗, with resolution across two words. Either is harshly against the grain of these smooth iambo-trochaics, and Hermann's simple transposition is a great improvement.

338–9 and 346–7: the same moral as 311.

345. χθόνιον after χθονὸς seems weakly redundant, though χρόνιον τύχαν of long time spent among the dead is not so ready a cliché in a pre-Christian era.

348. γάρ: not sc. 'Hear my words] for . . .' as some take it, for which a preceding vocative would be necessary. Helen carries on unheeding from her former words. Is my husband alive or dead? for I swear that if he is dead I will kill myself.

352. ἀσύνετα: 'not sensible' in the sense of 'not to be understood'. Is this a parenthesis of Helen's or an interjection of the Chorus, as conjectured by the correcting hand in a late copy? If Helen's, τάδε would seem to refer to ἅδε βάξις—what do these obscure tidings signify?

This would be an echo of her attitude at 310 rather than at 308, when she was irrationally certain. The words are more natural coming from the Chorus, anxious for what she is leading up to: 'I don't understand you; what are you saying?' and she continues, 'I will hang or stab myself'. The interruption comes more easily at the beginning of a colon, and even then must have needed some deft timing in performance.

353 is a locus conclamatus, where we can only make guesses. The metre is blameless, the words untranslatable. διὰ δέρης cannot mean that the rope will cut into her neck, nor that it will pass by way of her neck, nor can ὀρέξομαι be anything to do with 'stretching [a noose] tight for myself' on the analogy of stretching out the hand; the recurrence of 'stretching' here is an accident of modern idiom. Jackson, p. 55, thinks διὰ δέρης implies a lacuna in which the classic third alternative for suicides, poison, was put forward; cf. *Or.* 41 οὔτε σῖτα διὰ δέρης ἐδέξατο, he hasn't eaten anything. But ὀρέξομαι is by no means as appropriate with διὰ δέρης as δέξομαι ['yearn after poison through the throat'?], and indeed I suspect that it is just an adscript of the *Orestes* passage which has bedevilled our text. On the whole, 'neck' connects more easily with 'noose' than with poison; moreover, to be held up by the addition of a third alternative would be a little tiresome. If one decides on rewriting, A. Y. Campbell's version, quoted here *exempli gratia*, gives the sort of sense one wants.

354–6. In so highly poeticized a piece of diction the foreigner's sense of what is possible in Greek is unreliable, and it is better to accept the text without tinkering. Lit. (or nearly so!) 'I shall drive within me a sword in murderous pursuit of throat-streaming slaughter, a swift thrust of cold steel through the flesh'. αὐτ. ἄμιλλαν appears to be in apposition to the 'internal' acc. δίωγμα πελάσω. The manner of the suicide is appropriate to the sacrificial victim (θῦμα 357) she feels herself to be.

358–9. LP σύραγγ' ἀοιδαὶ σεβίζον are a nonsensical group of words, and the line of restoration will depend on the treatment of the first: a corruption of σύριγγ' or σήραγγ'? The syrinx is clearly appropriate to Paris (cf. *IA* 576); σῆραγξ is a tragic word (S. fr. 549), but both there and in *Phaedo* 110 appears to be a cave hollowed out by the sea, and there is no evidence to show whether it could be extended to 'cave' in general. A cave is not part of one's normal picture of Paris on Ida, unless taken as a synonym for νάπος or κευθμών—'hollow cleft' smooths it over unduly; but certainly σύραγγ' is an easier corruption from σήραγγ' than from σύριγγ'. ἀοιδαὶ might conceal Ida in some form, or with the syrinx might be 'song'. The 'song of the pipes' (see Wilamowitz in app. crit.) is a doubtful metaphor for musical instruments (but cf. Timotheus 238); 'song *to* the pipes', however, a singing and playing in alternate phrases, is hard to get out of the Greek. σεβίζον can hardly conceal anything else than a dat. part., but it is difficult to see what meaning is intended by those (Hermann, Bothe, Pearson, Grégoire) who make σεβίζοντι govern σύριγγα or συρίγγων ἀοιδὰν ('cultivate', i.e. 'practise on'?). Badham's suggestion, adopted by Wecklein and Murray, is ingenious, but ἐνίζοντι with the plur. σήραγγας is an unpictorial and inappropriate phrase for 'sitting in a cave', and the word cannot be used for 'dwell in', 'haunt', other than metaphorically. Perhaps with σῆραγξ one might try τῷ τε σήραγγ' ἀν' 'Ιδαίαν σεβίζοντι, or, with σύριγξ, τῷ τε σύριγγος αὐδᾷ σεβίζοντι. In either case the object to be supplied with σεβίζοντι must be 'them', the team of three goddesses. I incline to the second because it would accord with Helen's vision, a scene of sacrifice complete with its accompanying musician.

360. A formula to deflect such ill-omened words.

362–85. A lament for her beauty and the death and sorrow it has caused both Troy and Greece. Perhaps the Chorus should have got themselves into the palace by 374, leaving Helen to sing her dactylic coda by the door before she too withdraws.

362. The line as it stands seems metrically unsatisfactory. Τροία would be indefensible, and the rhythm ∪ – · – – ∪ – ∪ does not occur in dramatic lyric and in any case would bring anceps iuxta anceps with the next colon. Hermann's transposition restores the rhythm.

363. ἔργ' ἄνεργ': as 'deeds of ill-doing' the formula would be ordinary; but perhaps it should here be taken as 'deeds never committed', as Pearson suggests.

364. ἐμὰ δῶρα Κύπριδος: a combination of subjective and objective.

365–6. The repetitions are intolerable, and the 'cumulative' construction, as in 195, so loose that the passage is here left with rough-and-ready first aid.

368. [Σκαμάνδριον] with final brevis in longo is unwanted with Φρύγιον, another local adjective of the same form. ἀπὸ . . . ἔθεντο tmesis. Perhaps we should read θέντο to match ὄλεσαν, where LP ὤλεσαν shows the common tendency to fill in the augment.

371 is as it stands hopelessly unmetrical. The worst thing to do with it is to read κελάδησεν with the idea of making a paroemiac (of impossible form, by its word-division). Alii alia; this is my suggestion, with the ithyphallic repeating from above.

373. γένυν as El. 1214 (v. Denniston's note).

374. The final clausula marks a variation from the earlier ones, which were all lekythia. I slightly prefer the ordinary sync. trim. to dim. with opening ⏓ ∪͜∪ ∪ – as given in the Oxford text.

375–85.

ὦ μάκαρ Ἀρκαδίᾳ ποτὲ παρθένε	4 dact. – ∪ ∪
Καλλιστοῖ, Διὸς ἃ λεχέων ἐπέ-	
-βας τετραβάμοσι γυίοις,	7 dact. – –

ὡς πολὺ ματρὸς ἐμᾶς ἔλαχες πλέον,　　　　4 dact. ‒ ∪ ∪

ἁ μορφᾷ θηρῶν λαχνογυίων　　　　　　　　4 dact. ‒ ‒

ὄμματι λαβρῷ σχῆμα λεαίνης　　　　　　　4 dact. ‒ ‒

380　ἐξαλλάξασ᾽ ἄχθεα λύπης·　　　　　　　　　4 dact. ‒ ‒

ἄν τέ ποτ᾽ Ἄρτεμις ἐξεχορεύσατο　　　　　4 dact. ‒ ∪ ∪

χρυσοκέρατ᾽ ἔλαφον Μέροπος Τιτανίδα κούραν　hexam.

καλλοσύνας ἕνεκεν· τὸ δ᾽ ἐμὸν δέμας　　　　4 dact. ‒ ∪ ∪

ὤλεσεν ὤλεσε πέργαμα Δαρδανίας　　　　　5 dact. cat.

ὀλομένους τ᾽ Ἀχαίους.　　　　　　　　　　ithyph.

375–85. A complex stanza. By a deliberate paradox, two fair women whose sufferings from divine resentment might be thought the extreme possible are apostrophized as 'blessed': 'O fortunate Callisto who . . . , and [381 sc. μάκαρ] she too whom Artemis . . . because of her beauty.' Callisto is compared with Leda, who like her had an unnatural mating with Zeus, but ended in suicide and shame, whereas Callisto, changed into a bear, 'lifted from her the burden of grief' (380). The second, daughter of Titan-born Merops (nothing else is known of the legend), was for her beauty's sake chased by Artemis out of her attendant band in the shape of a golden hind (and therefore also forgot her griefs), while Helen's beauty brought down not her alone but Troy and the Greeks who died there.

376. τετραβάμοσι γυίοις: in performance it would be impossible to indicate that this was to be a 'dat. of cause with μάκαρ', and it could only convey 'ascended Zeus' bed with four paws'. Then Zeus, one would suppose, must have had four paws too, and this would make a better parallel with Leda; in the ordinary version the transformation came later as a punishment. But perhaps the line is only meant to convey vaguely 'Zeus-beloved and four-footed' as a summary of her destiny; the dithyrambic style eludes our analysis. More worrying is the confusion of animals. Callisto should be changed into a bear, not a lioness, and the adjective λαχνογυίων (a certain restoration) inescapably implies bear here, not the smooth feline. Murray's apostrophe to the bear with the 'gentle look' that mitigates her fierceness is a touch of pathetic realism not wanted here. Since the construction is also not very obvious (σχῆμα in apposition to ἁ and ὄμματι sociative or descriptive, 'with fierce expression'?), much the easiest solution is to cut out 379. But (1) the reason for its intrusion is obscure; (2) the metre, with two lines, 379–80, hovering towards anapaestic rhythm in the middle of a dactylic passage, is Euripidean (cf. *Phoen.* 1575–6, *Or.* 1006–8); (3) S. *Inachus*, P.Oxy. 2369 fr. 1, col. ii. 14, appears once more to offer us a γυνὴ λέαινα where Io has just been transformed into a cow. It seems just possible that λέαινα can be used of a 'beast-woman' in a generalized sense. 'You who in your guise of one of the shaggy-limbed creatures of the wild, a fierce-eyed beast-shape, put off your burden of sorrow.'

In all these strange legends of metamorphosis, particularly those
of Io, Callisto, Leda, and all the animal amours of Zeus, any hint of
too close or too visual an approach slides perilously towards bathos
or the grotesque. Open burlesque, as in comedy, is quite easy to
take, but a blend of sophistication, acceptance, and artistic seriousness leaves us somewhat baffled: witness now our difficulties over the
fragments of the *Inachus* of Sophocles, where we find ourselves uncertain of the prevailing tone, and even whether the play must be
satyric or not. How was the subject treated by Sophocles in the
Tereus? One note that often recurs in this later Greek thinking,
with a sort of puzzled tenderness, is the uncertain hope that the
sharpness of human suffering is somehow mitigated and made
tolerable by the change to the animal or vegetable or astronomical
world, even if the πάθος is thereby in a sense perpetuated and eter-
nally renewed. (Cf. A. *Ag.* 1146–8.) Certainly Eur. intends no burlesque here.

386. On to the empty scene, from the sea-coast to the spectator's right,
comes Menelaus, giving the necessary information *sans façons* direct
to the audience, as in a prologue. He does not open, however, in the
very baldest prologue-style; the genealogy is touched up by apostrophe and indirect allusion. 'O Pelops, who once with Oenomaus
raced the famous (τὰς) chariot-race' in Elis, and thus came to found
the dynasty in Greece.

388–90: would that you had died before you ever got so far, the obvious chance being when he was served up by his father Tantalos
to the gods at a feast, to test their omniscience. But the text is, to
say the least, uncertain. The phrase **ἔρανον ἐποίεις**, for the unfortunate boy who was the main dish, is odd, still more so with **εἰς
θεοὺς** instead of θεοῖς, and **πεισθείς** would imply a version otherwise
unknown to us: did he consent to the experiment, or was he 'persuaded to make a banquet' in a more innocuous sense, as he supposed,
by a diabolical father? **ἐν θεοῖς** after **εἰς θεοὺς** could only be defended
as a deliberate echo: ... 'left his life there inside them.' πατὴρ
ἐποίει σ᾽ οϊ προθεὶς σ᾽ ἐποίει Τάνταλος, or the like, fall down on the
habits of these genealogies: once a start is made at Pelops there can
be no going back a step to Tantalos. As for the general probability
of Menelaus' reference to the episode, it is not relevant that a year
or two earlier, *IT* 387–8 Iphigeneia had said ἐγὼ μὲν οὖν | τὰ Ταντάλου
θεοῖσιν ἑστιάματα | ἄπιστα κρίνω, παιδὸς ἡσθῆναι βορᾷ, unmistakably
Eur.'s own conviction though an appropriate part of Iphigeneia's
argument in the context. There is no reason why Menelaus should
not believe the story. The difficulty lies in the tone and phrasing,
possible in comedy but not here unless he is being deliberately droll,
and nothing else in the context suggests that; and also in the unnatural recited order of events: Pelops could still have died in the

chariot-race 'before begetting Atreus'. Nauck's excision of the two half-lines, giving εἴθ' ὤφελες τότ' εὐθέως λιπεῖν βίον, is to be recommended; if the interpolator read τότ' ἐν θεοῖς, it would be enough to make him dislocate the context in an effort to explain.

390: probably dissyllabic Ἀτρέα – ⏑⏑.

393. γὰρ: explaining not κλεινὸν but why he wishes he had never been born. It carries through in effect to 407, a miserable sequel to so much glory.

394. διορίσαι: trans., 'took over' in ships.

395. τύραννος: inside the neg. statement, 'no despot leading troops by force'.

397. ἀριθμῆσαι: 'count up', 'call the roll of'. The roll can be called of some because they are dead, and of others because they returned home after being given up for dead (νεκρῶν φέρ. ὀν. This phrase could alternatively mean 'with a list of their drowned comrades'). Some died at Troy or at sea; others ran into storms and were despaired of but returned eventually; only I wander on and on . . . .

401. χρόνον ὅσονπερ: 'ever since', normally only with continuing actions or states, not with past events as ἔπερσα here: as if τὸν πάντα χρόνον ἐξ οὗ.

404. δέ and τε are constantly mixed, and the δ' (Hermann) seems essential here after the οὐκ ἀξιοῦμαι clause. **ἐπιδρομὰς:** 'approaches.'

406. οὔριον: sc. πνεῦμα.

410. ἀριθμοὺς: except for the keel, quantitative rather than usefully qualitative pieces of wrecked ship, cf. Dodds's note on *Bacch.* 209.

411. ἐλείφθη (a certain emendation): of the skilfully jointed whole which had been the ship only the keel remained intact. Not, as Pearson, gen. of separation 'parted from': such a construction is found only of human beings, with a pathetic overtone, 'forsaken of', as *El.* 1310 σοῦ δὲ λειπόμενος.

412. This was the classic shipwreck escape, but somewhat simplified from *Od.* 12. 420–5. It is more effective for a solitary survivor than for a tandem, and we presently find others of the crew also 426, the wreck being close inshore.

413. ἀποσπάσας ἔχω: 'whom I dragged out of Troy and have with me'; the degree of difference between this idiom and the plain aor. varies considerably with the context.

414. λεὼς: sc. ὅστις. The construction is indirect interrog., the sentence as a whole being an illogical but perfectly intelligible mixture of ὄνομα δὲ χώρας οὐκ οἶδα and ἥτις ἡ χώρα ἥδε οὐκ οἶδα. Nauck takes ἥτις as rel. 'whatever it is', and so emends to gen. λεώ.

416–17. τὰς ἐμὰς . . . [τὰς τύχας] LP: (1) This can only be construed by deleting the comma after ἱστορῆσαι, 'and so get questions asked about my shabby clothes'; then κρύπτων τὰς τύχας together. This is the normal use of ὥστε but leaves an awkward lack of subject to

LINES 390–433 95

ἱστορῆσαι and an unexpected plural δυσχλαινίας. (2) leg. τῆς τύχης,
dependent on ὑπ' αἰδοῦς, ἱστορῆσαι sc. ὄνομα: 'I was ashamed to go
up to people and so make inquiries', with ὥστε almost = ἵνα. Still
δυσχ. plur. (3) leg. τῆς ἐμῆς δυσχ., *either* dependent on τὰς τύχας, 'concealing in shame the misfortunes which had produced this shabbiness', *or* double gen. with ὑπ' αἰδοῦς, 'concealing my misfortunes in
shame at my shabbiness'. Still ὥστε = ἵνα. There is not much to
choose on balance between these three. But the main objection to
all is the premature reference to δυσχλαινίας, which is brought in as
a new and important aspect of the situation 421. 416 should therefore be deleted with Dindorf, as the kind of interpolation intended
to make a point clearer and instead of that introducing an element
of muddle. The thought in 418, πράξῃ κακῶς, goes on simply from
τὰς τύχας (to be retained from LP), his misfortunes, not his shabbiness.

418–19. εἰς ἀηθίαν (for the usual form ἀήθειαν) κτλ. must mean 'into
an unfamiliar state which is worse than *that of* [abbreviated com-
parison] a man long used to trouble', i.e. into a state which because
of its unfamiliarity is worse . . . . Although doubly elliptical it is not
difficult to understand at a first hearing.

422. LP have ἐκβόλοις ἀμπίσχομαι. If this conceals ἐκβόλοις ἀμπίσχομαι
there is a dubious crasis and a dubious sense (in this position of the
word) of αὐτά = τοῦτο, unemphatic 'this' or 'it': 'you can infer it
[the fact that I have no clothes] from the bits of wreckage I am
wearing.' Also, ἃ would normally become οἷς by attraction. Reiske's
ἔκβολ' οἷς is preferable, with εἰκάσαι = judge from the look of a thing
that it is . . . : '. . . no clothes for my back; you can guess from the
look of them that these are just (αὐτὰ) cast-ups from the wreck that
I am wearing.'   ναὸς ἔκβολα: one would like to know just what
the audience saw Menelaus wearing. Aristophanes at least (*Thesm.*
935 ἀνὴρ ἱστιόρραφος) took it as cobbled-up bits of sail, but the costume
of his Eur.-Men. was doubtless much more striking, and we do not
know how far a tragic actor could go in this respect. The emphasis
on Menelaus' odd appearance (554, 1204) may have been needed to
keep the matter sufficiently before the audience's attention.

425–6. κρύψας only with γυναῖκα: before coming here I hid her and
made them keep guard.

428. νοστῶ: simply 'come', as 474.

430. περιφερὲς θριγκοῖς: cf. 70, 'with its walls surmounted by coping
all round'—no roughly made house but a piece of solid, finished
stone-work.

433. The anacolouthon is not attractive. It would be better to delete
the comma after θέλοιεν, and with ἔχοιεν ἄν sc. λαβεῖν and subject
ναῦται, taking ναύταις 432 with ἐλπὶς, hope for [shipwrecked] sailors
like us, not 'hope to get for my crew'. 'From a rich house sailors

can hope to get something, but from those who have not enough to support life they could not get anything even if there were willingness to help.' If the change of subject from θέλοιεν to ἔχοιεν is not obvious enough from the sense, one could with Paley read ἔχοιμεν.

435. τίς ἂν μόλοι: A request to someone unspecified of the servant class, from among those present, may conveniently be put in interrog. form with τίς, cf. 892 τίς εἶσι; 'will one of you go?', or in the optative *Bacch.* 1257 τίς ἂν καλέσειεν; 'would one of you call . . .?' Here it is combined with a knock on the door and the query whether there is someone available: 'is there some porter who would come and take a message for me . . .?' When the further request is defined as here by a ὅστις clause, or by ἵνα or ὅπως, the verb of this is optative too by a kind of attraction.

437. Portress rather than porter, to make the dialogue more amusing, and to underline Menelaus' plight, bandying words helplessly with an old woman. It is also more plausible that she should refrain from reporting him to the master.

437-8. The common idiom in tragedy by which οὐ + fut. interrog. is used for a sharp command: 'you'd better . . .' (threateningly). A prohibition of this kind needs οὐ μή, while command followed by prohibition, the pos. and neg. aspects of the same desired line of conduct (go away and stop bothering us), has first a single οὐ, then καὶ μὴ or μηδὲ in the following clause.

438. αὔλειοι or ἔρκειοι πύλαι, originally outer gates leading into the courtyard, then just 'outer door' in general. Proteus' palace 1180 ff. is conceived as a heroic-age house, with an αὐλή through which a chariot can drive.

439. δεσπόταις: the 'servant's plural'.

440. How does she know him to be a Greek? οἷσιν plur. after a generic sing. antecedent: editors compare *Or.* 920 αὐτουργός, οἵπερ καὶ μόνοι σῴζουσι γῆν.

441-2. ὦ γραῖα, ταῦτα ταῦτ' ἔπη καλῶς λέγεις.

ἔξεστι, πείσομαι γάρ. ἀλλ' ἄνες λόγον.

Murray's attempt to give sense to ταῦτα ταῦτ'—there, there!— is amusing but unsupported by Greek usage. ταῦτα πάντ' ἔπη (Stephanus) is accepted by Pearson and others, surprisingly, since the line sounds like a schoolboy's exercise and the sense is manifestly not what Menelaus means; moreover, ἔξεστι by itself in the next line is meaningless. To call it a 'formula of acquiescence' explains nothing; Pearson quotes *Hec.* 238, where it confirms εἰ δ' ἔστι 234, and *Bacch.* 844, where it is Dionysus' permission for Pentheus' proposal 843. In every case where it occurs in isolation it is an invitation to proceed, in response to some request or statement of intention. Herwerden's ταὐτὰ ταῦτ' ἔπη κάλλως λέγειν ἔξεστι, is neat, and gives a possible sense: 'those same words can be spoken in a different tone,

for I shall be amenable; only, not so cross, please.' Startled by the
outburst, Menelaus has noticed the abusive tone rather than the
content, and returns a soft answer. ἄνες λόγον ἴ suspect, since it
ought to mean not 'mitioribus verbis utere' (Matthiae) but 'verba
remitte', and ἀνίημι needs an object that admits of degrees of inten-
sity. χόλον (Heimsoeth) is a reasonable guess.

445. προσείλει χεῖρα: εἱλέω, an epic and later prose form, might be
used here for ἵλλω, but the meaning is obscure. (Paley's 'don't
squeeze my arm in the door' is not right, and in any case should be
your arm.) It can mean 'round up towards' a confined space, or, in
the simple verb, 'send circling round' a limited area, like Soph.'s
ploughs *Ant.* 340, but that is still a long way from 'laying hands on'
me (*p* records an unmetrical variant πρόσαγε). Perhaps it could
mean 'close up your hand', clench your fist. Matthiae suggests
πρόσειε χ. as a gesture discouraging nearer approach, as *HF* 1218,
but that goes badly with μηδ' ὤθει βίᾳ.

446: 'your fault for not taking notice . . .'; for the anticipatory γάρ-
clause Wecklein compares *IT* 646.

447. ἄγγειλον εἴσω = εἰσαγγέλλειν, go in and announce [me], not
necessarily with aposiopesis.

448. LP cannot be accepted here, since ἄν with the fut. is hardly defensible in Eur., and γ' has no meaning where it stands. πικρούς has
won much favour, but should mean 'your message would be unwelcome to them', cf. *El.* 418; but surely it is the consequences of
trying to deliver it that would be unpleasant, to the sender or the
intermediary; πικρῶς as Andr. 1002. πικρῶς ἂν οἶμαι σούς γ' ἐσαγγέλλειν
λόγους would give the right emphasis.

449. As a stranger and a castaway Menelaus would have a religious
claim to protection in a civilized community.

454. οὐκοῦν ἐκεῖ που: 'somewhere, evidently, you were a great figure;
here you aren't.' The retort has the devastating completeness of the
best stichomythia.

455-8. The four lines must be taken together. The plur. ἤτιμ. 'you
and I' is addressed to his δαίμων, the inescapable personal destiny
which accompanies each man like his own shadow. The Old Woman,
impatient rather than pitying or curious, asks to whom (πρὸς τίν',
not to be emended) he is addressing his complaint. His reply, 'Only
to my former fortunes, which were so happy', switches to the more
impersonal, plural, sense of δαίμων, but her retort brings it back to
the personal, 'then go and present *them* (your intimate connexions)
with the tears'. Menelaus can only change the subject.

460. 'X lives in this house' for 'This is X's house' would normally
be a distinction without a difference, but here X is dead, and there
seems no particular point in misleading Menelaus, though Premer-
stein thinks Ar. *Thesm.* 874-8 is ridiculing Eur. for doing just that.

Even Kirchhoff's adaptation from Ar. (v. app. crit.) is inconsistent with 5 in the prologue, not that that would matter much. Possibly the Old Woman makes a gesture towards the tomb, Proteus being for her still the Master.

461. The Ionic πεπλώκαμεν of *Thesm.* 878 defends πεπλωκότα 532, but does not oblige us to introduce it here; Ar. simply transfers the affectation to the finite form.

462–3. τὸ Νείλου γάνος: a type of periphrasis of which Eur. is fond, for water or wine. ἐμέμφθην: pres. sense, 'I have no complaint'.

464: 'the familiar consolation' edd., but the point is that it is not meant as a consolation here.

465. ὄντιν' ὀνομάζεις ἄναξ: King what's-his-name. Menelaus has never heard of him.

467. See on 91. 'Then where *is* he?'

469. ἐπηυρόμην: 'I get the benefit', ironical.

470–2. ἡ τοῦ Διός . . . ἡ Τυνδαρὶς παῖς: no ambiguity; her official title is merely additional confirmation of identity.

475. οὔ τί που cf. 95. The rest is an aside.   λέχος: the usual retained acc. with a verb which in the act. has two.

477–8. ἔστι . . . τύχη: 'for things have taken a turn [the wooing of Helen by the king] within there . . . .'   δόμοις . . . δόμος: as the plur. and the sing. have rather different meanings one probably need not emend the first to ἔνδοθεν as Broadhead suggests. γάρ 477 and γὰρ 479 have the same reference, cf. 257/260.

479. καιρὸν οὐδέν': adverbial acc., cf. S. *Aj.* 34 καιρὸν δ' ἐφήκεις, Ar. *Ach.* 23 ἀωρίαν ἥκοντες.

481–2. οὐχ ὅσον: 'for all the bitterness of my words'; lit. 'to an extent not to be measured by . . .'. Exit γραῦς, shutting the door against Menelaus.

484. ἐκ: in succession to: the new thing 'takes over from' the last. ἀθλίας predic. after κλύω.

485. εἰ: if, as seems to be the case . . . , like εἴπερ.

487–8. τῆς ἐμῆς δάμαρτος does not strictly go with ταὐτὸν (which would need a dat.) but with ὄνομα, and is then reinforced by ταὐτὸν— my wife's name, exactly the same. Pearson compares *HF* 31. The idiom is the line's defence against Vitelli (app. crit.). 489 must continue in the εἰ construction from 485, with only a comma after δόμοις. It would not be so awful to find another woman called Helen, but a Helen said to be daughter of Zeus—*that* was alarming indeed.

492. ἵνα ῥοαί: Matthiae's emendation for αἱ ῥοαὶ is necessary if the following gen. is not to be out of order; the lengthening of short vowel before initial ῥ (cf. 1090), which tragedy retained from Homer, disappeared later.

497. The personal construction of parenthetic ὡς ἔοικ(α), etc., is confined to poetry, cf. 793.

Menelaus' endeavour to analyse his bewildering predicament has often been found unsatisfactory, and lines have been excised or transposed to make it more logical, but all remedies introduce fresh difficulties. The main point to grasp is that a Greek hero must not be expected to calculate the odds against a string of coincidences as opposed to one, or two. For him, Helen, Zeus, Sparta, Tyndareos, Troy *add up* to five curious points; they do not multiply. Thus even after 496 he can go on to say, Well, the world's a big place, so all this is not really surprising. γάρ 497 is all right, cf. Denn. *GP* 581: [I suppose I must accept it], for . . . . From this relatively optimistic conclusion he goes on valiantly (500) οὐδ' αὖ . . . : nor am I to be frightened off . . . . The impression of some degree of naïvety and incapacity for hard reasoning is not out of place in Menelaus, like his later failure to devise a plan of escape. The audience would enjoy his bewilderment, but his simplicity must not be exaggerated; after all, he could not be expected to see through, or even begin to imagine, so preposterous a trick of fate as the Phantom.

500. τὸ δεινὸν προσπόλου: Pearson has some good parallels for the generic force of the gen. προσπόλου without article, 'a servant's bogy-tales': *Bacch.* 29 τὴν ἁμαρτίαν λέχους, *El.* 368 αἱ φύσεις βροτῶν, S. *Ant.* 365 τὸ μηχανόεν τέχνας.

501. ὧδε . . . ὅς: like 'Breathes there the man with soul so dead, Who never to himself hath said . . . ?'

503 and 505. Two asyndeta.

506. ἔχει for παρέχει, subj. ἄναξ.

507. κρύψας ἐμαυτὸν: usually κρύπτειν δέμας or σῶμα, but the reflexive pronoun is surely reasonable. To take it as 'conceal my identity', as Italie, is unnatural. He plans to observe from concealment what the king looks like and how he behaves before approaching him or retreating to the wreck. The aor. indicates '*stay* in concealment', and he probably suits the action to the word here (perhaps by a pilaster of the tomb) since the Chorus and Helen do not at first see him. There is no point in κρύψων, since once he was seen it would be too late to conceal himself on the seashore.

508. ἐνδιδῷ τι μαλθακόν one would have expected to mean 'give way to compassion', but comparison with *Andr.* 225 indicates 'show signs of . . .' simply.   τὰ πρόσφορα: the adj. takes a dat., but here its substantival sense (cf. 429) predominates and so has the gen.

510. [δέ θ'] LP: the combination is epic, not tragic.   μὲν . . . ἀλλὰ is common.

513: 'not my saying, but a wise word' is perfectly appropriate, and λόγος and ἔπος are all but synonyms, though ἔπος is commoner for the epigrams of authority. Triclinius's σοφῶν, wherever it came from, is no improvement, and σοφῶν δέ του (Dobree) still less; Menelaus is not being so humble.

515–27.

ἤκουσα τᾶς θεσπιῳδοῦ κόρας,   s. i. trim.
ἃ χρῄζουσ' ἐφάνη τυράννοις
δόμοις, ὡς Μενέλαος οὔ-
-πω μελαμφαὲς οἴχεται
δι' ἔρεβος χθονὶ κρυφθείς,
520 ἀλλ' ἔτι κατ' οἶδμ' ἅλιον
τρυχόμενος οὔπω λιμένων
ψαύσειεν πατρίας γᾶς,
ἀλατείᾳ βιότου
ταλαίφρων, ἄφιλος φίλων,
525 παντοδαπᾶς ἐπὶ γᾶς   hemiepes
πόδα χριμπτόμενος εἰναλίῳ
κώπᾳ Τρῳάδος ἐκ γᾶς.

After the iambic introduction this is all, except for hemiepes 525, aeolo-choriambic in various lengths (resolution counting as one syllable), heptasyll., octasyll., and one enneasyll. 516 (hipponactean).

The Chorus re-enters first, briefly conveying to the audience the news of Theonoe's pronouncement. Menelaus in half-concealment has to be forgotten; at least he does not take in the mention of his name and his fortunes. Naturally this is no moment for a full-dress stasimon.

516. ἃ fem. sing. τυρ. δόμοις: local dat. of poetry; Triclinius's ἐφάνην should not be taken as indicating ἐφάνη 'ν (Herwerden), which would be hard to hear, but as due to a misunderstanding of χρῄζουσ', with ἃ as neut. plur. 'what I clearly desired'. χρῄζω = χράω, give an oracle, though a ἅπ. λεγ. here, is recognized by ancient grammarians. χρῄζουσ' ἐφάνη = φανερῶς ἔχρηζε, 'clearly announced', without oracular ambiguity, cf. S. *OT* 790 προυφάνη λέγων, often emended to προύφηνεν, but the two instances defend each other.

518. μελαμφαὲς: Wecklein well recalls the same oxymoron in Ar.'s skit on Euripidean monody *Ran.* 1331 νυκτὸς κελαινοφαὴς ὄρφνα. οἴχεται indic. combined with ψαύσειεν opt. 522.

523. ἀλατείᾳ βιότου: a wanderer's life.

525–6. The reading is uncertain. χρίμπτομαι is usually intrans. with dat. of the place skirted; so act. also A. *PV* 712 πόδας χρίμπτουσα ῥαχίαισιν, 'keeping close to the shore'. If he were walking, there would be nothing unusual in retaining πόδα with the intrans. form (see Denniston on *El.* 94), but he is sailing. The instrumental dat. κώπᾳ might cause a prepositional phrase for the locality, but the prep. ἐπί has to have a highly 'pregnant' sense—coming close *to* the shore to set foot *on* it. Wecklein's ποτιχριμπτόμενος would get rid of πόδα, but ἐπί would then be less appropriate, and Wecklein emends that line too. Nor has Euripidean lyric any attested compound of ποτί. On the whole the text is better left.

528-39: addressed, with very little pretence, to the audience. She remains, meanwhile, by the door.

530-1. The redundancy is a little feeble, but it is impossible to take ἐν φάει with φησὶ as 'says openly', which would need Jacobs's ἐμφανῶς. The phrases are so automatic for 'alive' that the different sound of φάει and φέγγος is enough to support repetition.

532-40. Interpretations are varied, but the lines make the best sense as they stand in LP, with comma deleted after πλάνοις and without δ' 534. She says that he is alive, 'and wanders hither and thither sailing countless straits [πορθμοὺς internal acc.], and will be coming all worn out [not untried, litotes] by his rovings, when he reaches the end of his troubles'. ἥξειν means come *here*, as 540 makes clear; hence her anxiety over what will happen when he reaches this place with its hostile king. She has refrained from putting this question, in her relief at hearing he was alive up to now—after all, it is the subject of the rest of the play! Thus πημάτων τέλος 534 is relative to his trials as a wanderer only.

At 540 she turns to go to the tomb, and Menelaus steps forward to intercept and speak to her. She tries to dodge him with little runs, till her accusation 550-2 makes him step back haughtily; then she skips round him and reaches her goal at 556. The juxtaposition of 540 and 541 makes a good dramatic moment.

541. κρυπτεύομαι pass.: 'I am being ambushed.'

544. συνάπτειν πόδα τινί as *Ion* 538 = link one's step to someone, hence 'meet', and by a further twist of artificiality link one's limb to a place = move over to it, reach it.

546. σὲ τὴν: exclamatory acc. of reference, cf. S. *Ant.* 441 σὲ δή, σὲ τὴν νεύουσαν.

547. For the appearance of the tomb see p. 69. ὀρθοστάται elsewhere in Eur. always means 'uprights', whether of masonry or wood, and it is a mere red-herring that Pollux and Porphyrius quote ὀρθοστάτης from the lexicographers as a 'sacrificial cake'. Since ἔμπυρα = burnt-offerings (though at S. *El.* 405 it seems to be 'offerings for the dead' in general), it was thought that ἐμπύρους ὀρθ. might be 'cakes for burnt offering', ranged on the tomb as on an altar. But for Menelaus to describe her as 'racing for the base and sacrificial cakes of the tomb' would be curious, whereas 'base and uprights' (= pilasters) gives the horizontal and the vertical aspects of the asylum where the suppliant sits and clasps. The exact meaning of ἐμπύρους is uncertain—'where burnt-offerings are made', or perhaps 'smoke-burnt'.

553. οὐχ: There is little doubt that οὐδ' (Dindorf) is required here. It is no use objecting that 'repeated οὐ is common'; it needs the excuse of lyric (*IT* 173-4), or of combination with οὐδέ or οὔτε (*Hec.* 1234), or of built-up accumulation (*Bacch.* 757) or of passion or pathos (*Phoen.* 919, a pure repetition, *Tro.* 403-4). The only possible parallel is *IT* 486, where also Hermann emends to οὐδ', since οὐχ or οὐκ and οὐδ' are liable to be confused, cf. app. crit. on 564 here.

554. στολήν γ': 'the clothes you wear are villainous enough' (Warner). She notices his clothes before him, which staves off a premature recognition.

555. φόβου: the only reason for gen. rather than as everywhere else acc. with act. μεθίημι would be the avoidance of momentary ambiguity in the construction.

556. τόπου: τάφου (Elmsley) would give better sense for a very slight change.

558. λόγος ἔχει με: the unusual inversion is protected by Ar. *Thesm.* 906, which also gives αὐτός for αὑτός.

560. All other cases of the apotheosis of abstracts in Eur. are at least substantives—αἰδώς, ἐλπίς, πλοῦτος, etc., and even in *Or.* 213 it is πότνια Λήθη τῶν κακῶν that is a εὐκταία θεός, not τὸ τῶν κακῶν ἐπιλανθάνεσθαι. This seems to be a whimsical by-product of the exclamation ὦ θεοί.

561. The missing line is conveniently supplied by Ar. *Thesm.* 907, and is a neat illustration of the havoc caused by a repetition of the same word at the beginning of consecutive lines. Neither scribe nor corrector noticed the obvious gap in the sense, since change of speaker was only indicated by the paragraphos.

567. ποίας: 'how do you mean, *wife?*' ποῖος with a noun in scornful questions is like τί or ποῦ with a verb, cf. τί ζῶσιν; *Alc.* 807, ποῦ δέ μοι πατὴρ σύ; *Ion* 528. But ποίων 572 is literal.

568. Cf. on 33.

569. φωσφόρ': 'torch-bearing', as Goddess of the Crossways, Ἐνοδία 570, attended by πρόπολοι, ghostly apparitions.

571. οὐ μὴν . . . γε of firm rejection, whatever else may or may not be possible.

572–3. The various complicated manœuvres for transferring these lines to follow 581, so as to make 581 the first statement of the dilemma, are not worth while; the sequence of thought is natural enough as it stands.

575. οὔ που (cf. 135) carries both μέν and δέ clauses; 'can it be that though I am in my right mind my eyes are at fault?'

577–8. Can 577 be given a meaning? And how should the unmetrical 578 σκέψαι· τί σου δεῖ; τίς ἔστι σου σοφώτερος; be emended?   **577:** 'You *look* like her, but what I *know* for certain deprives me of you'— 'privat me te uxore' Hermann. Or (feebly) 'but certainty fails me', which in any case would need F. W. Schmidt's γ' ἄπεστ' ἔτι. 'But you withhold certainty from me' (with ἀποστερεῖς)—Pearson. τὸ δ' ἀσαφές μ' ἀποστρέφει, 'the unclearness of it turns me away'— A. Y. Campbell. Little encouragement here.   **578:** Seidler's τί σοὐνδεῖ (= σοι ἐνδεῖ) 'Look at me: what more do you want?' makes

a splendid moment on an English or French stage, but would a Greek
have said it (and with that crasis)? And the follow-up, τίς δὲ σοῦ σοφ.
to be interpreted as 'who knows me better than you do?' savours of
editorial desperation. Nothing short of Badham's elegant rewriting
(v. app. crit.) will save the line, and if anyone could produce a
tolerable rendering or revision of 577 one might acquiesce in this.

But it is evident that the clumsy obscurity of expression, the
bungled metre, and the mingled redundancy and irrelevance of the
point have all the marks of the interpolator. (Perhaps the poor man
meant σκέψαι· τί σ' οὐ δεῖ; ἔστι σου σοφώτερος; 'Think it out; why
should you not? is there anyone better qualified?') 579 follows 576
without a ripple.

581. νοσοῦμεν: not as 575 but quite general: 'my trouble is that . . . .'

584. αἰθήρ, called οὐρανός 34, is the *material* of which phantoms are
made by a god (θεοπόνητα).

585. ἄελπτα: not here 'too good to be true' but simply 'beyond belief',
as in Archilochus on the eclipse χρημάτων ἄελπτον οὐδέν.

586. A terse construction.   **διάλλαγμ'**: 'as a changeling.'

587. There are two problems here: (1) is ἂν ἦσθα sensible? (2) how to
make up the missing syllable. (1) ἄν+past indic. must, as Pearson
says, imply a suppressed condition: 'how, if this were true, would
you have been in two places at once?' 'This is absurd': true, but
Menelaus is in a state of total bewilderment and might not have
thought it out. But the double ἅμα (v. app. crit.), as in S. *Ant.* 436, is
an easy enough emendation and usually adopted—'how did you
manage to be . . . .' (2) Barnes's τ' is rather awkwardly misplaced.
ἦσθας is a Menandrian form, not attested for the fifth century (Nauck
believed 587–8 to be a later interpolation). A. Y. Campbell πῶς οὖν;
ἅμ' ἐνθάδ' ἦσθ' ἄρ' is neat by itself, but the next line looks like an
answer to πῶς; and would really need a γάρ for his version. Mekler
ἐν 'Ιλίῳ for ἐν Τροίᾳ, Jackson ἅμ' ἐν Τροίᾳ τε κἀνθάδ' ἦσθ' ἅμα;—either
blameless, but less easy to account for.

591. καὶ χαῖρέ γ': I do leave you—with my blessing, for your likeness
to Helen. Menelaus has to reject her finally, in order to get the full
dramatic effect of the Old Servant's report the next minute.

593. ἐκεῖ: he knows his sufferings at Troy were concrete enough—as
though he felt the airiness of the Phantom would envelop all in a
mist of unreality.

597. The Old Servant intercepts him as he strides off. 'Messenger' is
not quite the appropriate title, since in tragedy ἄγγελος is a technical
term for a special kind of 'reporter' who receives the barest minimum
of characterization and leaves the scene after discharging his function
of reporting. Anonymous titles in general are often very loosely
assigned in the 'dramatis personae' of MSS. and papyri.

598. χθόνα: γῆ and χθών are words particularly susceptible of this 'acc.

of space travelled over'.   μαστεύων . . . πλανηθεὶς . . . πεμφθεὶς:
the pile-up of parts. is considerable, but in their different functions
quite clear.

601: 'A miracle, though miracle is too weak a word.'

602: 'Such emphasis declares your news strange indeed.'

604. παλαιά: Menelaus does not perceive the force of μάτην.

607. σεμνὸν: the epithet seems idle because unexplained, unless the
cave is meant to be self-evidently 'hallowed' ͵by having sheltered
the disappearing Phantom, or as being, like many caves, sacred
to the Nymphs.

609. πάντες τ' Ἀχαιοί = Panachaean host; Pearson compares χὠ
Πανελλήνων στρατός *IA* 350. ταλαίπωροι of course embraces them.

616. Helen must here move somehow into his line of vision. A very
neat confirmation of the total identity of appearance between real
and phantom Helen.

618. He is forced to regard the ascent into upper air as a delusion, since
she is clearly earth-bound now, though apparently 'winged' (sarcastic; he is annoyed).

619. οὐκ ἐῶ: he steps forward to grasp her by the arm. ἡμᾶς is object
of κερτομεῖν and τόδ' internal acc.: play this vanishing-trick on us,
'delude us like this'. Cf. *IA* 849 and κέρτομος χαρά 'delusive joy'
Alc. 1125. This sense of κερτομεῖν has eluded most editors, with
strange results. ὡς is not to be taken with τόδε (taunt us with this,
that . . .), but is simply 'since'.

622. τοῦτ' ἔστ' ἐκεῖνο: like τοῦτ' ἐκεῖνο, a colloquialism, as it were 'So
this is what that was; now I understand'.   ξυμβεβᾶσιν ἀληθεῖς:
prove to have been true, by cohering with some new piece of evidence.
This is implied by the compound, and there is no need for Herwerden's
τοῖς τῆσδ'.

624. ἢ σ': ὡς LP, ὥς σ' Hermann, ὡς εἰς ἐμάς σ' Pearson, defended by
the latter as = ὅτι οὕτως. But, as his examples show, such a ὡς
means either 'for the degree to which . . .' or 'for the manner in
which . . .', cf. on 862. Here one needs simply 'the day which', and
it is hardly conceivable that Eur. should have obscured the point.

Duo **625–97**.

625 Ελ. ὦ φίλτατ' ἀνδρῶν Μενέλεως, ὁ μὲν χρόνος
          παλαιός, ἡ δὲ τέρψις ἀρτίως πάρα.   ‖   2 trim.
              ἔλαβον ἀσμένα   πόσιν ἐμόν, φίλαι,
              περί τ' ἐπέτασα χέρα
              φίλιον ἐν μακρᾷ   φλογὶ φαεσφόρῳ.   5 doch.
630 Μεν. κἀγὼ σέ· πολλοὺς δ' ἐν μέσῳ λόγους ἔχων
          οὐκ οἶδ' ὁποίου πρῶτον ἄρξωμαι τανῦν.   2 trim.
     Ελ. γέγηθα, κρατὶ δ' ὀρθίους ἐθείρας
          ἀνεπτέρωσα καὶ δάκρυ στάλασσω,   2 trim. cat.
          περὶ δὲ γυῖα χέρας   ἔβαλον, ἡδονὰν

635 ὦ πόσις ὡς λάβω. ‖ 3 doch.

Μεν. ὦ φιλτάτη πρόσοψις, οὐκ ἐμέμφθην·

ἔχω τὰ τοῦ Διὸς ⟨τε⟩ λέκτρα Λήδας θ', 2 trim. cat.

Ελ. ἂν ὑπὸ λαμπάδων κόροι λεύκιπποι 2 doch.

640 ξυνομαίμονες ὤλβισαν ὤλβισαν— enop.

Μεν. τὸ πρόσθεν, ἐκ δόμων δ' ἐνόσφισαν θεοί. trim.

Ελ. πρὸς ἄλλαν γ' ἐλαύνει

θεὸς συμφορὰν τᾶσδε κρείσσω. 5 bacch.

τὸ κακὸν δ' ἀγαθὸν σέ τε κἀμὲ συνάγαγεν,

πόσι, enop.

645 χρόνιον, ἀλλ' ὅμως ὀναίμαν τύχας. 2 doch.

Μεν. ὄναιο δῆτα· ταῦτὰ δὲ ξυνεύχομαι·

δυοῖν γὰρ ὄντοιν οὐχ ὁ μὲν τλήμων, ὁ δ' οὔ. 2 trim.

Ελ. φίλαι φίλαι, iamb. met.

τὰ πάρος οὐκέτι στένομεν οὐδ' ἀλγῶ.

650 πόσιν ἐμὸν ⟨ἐμὸν⟩ ἔχο- μεν ἔχομεν ὃν ἔμενον

ἔμενον ἐκ Τροίας πολυετῆ μολεῖν. 6 doch.

Μεν. ἔχεις, ἐγώ τε σ'· ἡλίους δὲ μυρίους

μόλις διελθὼν ᾐσθόμην τὰ τῆς θεοῦ. 2 trim.

Ελ. ἐμὰ δὲ χαρμονᾷ δάκρυα πλέον ἔχει

655 χάριτος ἢ λυπᾶς. 3 doch.

Μεν. . . . . . lacunam Zuntz . . . .

Ελ. τί φῶ; τίς ἂν τάδ' ἤλπισεν βροτῶν ποτε; ‖ trim.

ἀδόκητον ἔχω σε πρὸς στέρνοις. enop.

Μεν. κἀγὼ σὲ τὴν δοκοῦσαν Ἰδαίαν πόλιν trim.

μολεῖν Ἰλίου τε μελέους πύργους. 2 doch.

660 πρὸς θεῶν, δόμων πῶς τῶν ἐμῶν ἀπεστά-

λης; trim.

Ελ. ἒ ἔ· πικρὰς ἐς ἀρχὰς βαίνεις, res. cret.+doch.

ἒ ἔ· πικρὰν δ' ἐρευνᾷς φάτιν. res. cret.+doch.

Μεν. λέγ'· ὡς ἀκουστὰ πάντα δῶρα δαιμόνων. trim.

Ελ. ἀπέπτυσα μὲν λόγον οἷον οἷον ἐσοίσομαι. paroem.+doch.

665 Μεν. ὅμως δὲ λέξον· ἡδύ τοι μόχθων κλύειν. trim.

Ελ. οὐκ ἐπὶ βαρβάρου λέκτρα νεανία

πετομένας κώπας

†πετομένου δ' ἔρωτος† ἀδίκων γάμων 5 doch.

Μεν. τίς ⟨γὰρ⟩ σε δαίμων ἢ πότμος συλᾷ πάτρας; trim.

670 Ελ. ὁ Διὸς ὁ Διὸς ὦ πόσι ∪ – ⌣ –

ἐπέλασεν Νείλῳ. 3 doch.

Μεν. θαυμαστά· τοῦ πέμψαντος; ὦ δεινοὶ λόγοι. trim.

Ελ. κατεδάκρυσα καὶ βλέφαρον ὑγραίνω

δάκρυσιν· ἁ Διός μ' ἄλοχος ὤλεσεν. ‖ 4 doch.

675 Μεν. Ἥρα; τί νῷν χρῄζουσα προσθεῖναι κακόν; trim.

Ελ. ὦ μοι ἐγὼ κείνων λουτρῶν καὶ κρηνῶν

ἵνα θεαὶ μορφὰν

ἐφαίδρυναν, ἔν- θεν ἔμολεν κρίσις.   5 doch.
Μεν. τί δὴ κρίσιν σοὶ τῶνδ᾽ ἔθηχ᾽ ῞Ηρα κακόν;   trim.
680 Ελ.   Πάριν ὡς ἀφέλοιτο Μεν. πῶς; αὔδα.
Ελ.   Κύπρις ᾧ μ᾽ ἐπένευσεν Μεν. ὦ τλήμων.   2 enop.
Ελ.   τλάμων τλάμων ὧδ᾽   ἐπέλασ᾽ Αἰγύπτῳ. || 2 doch.
Μεν. εἶτ᾽ ἀντέδωκ᾽ εἴδωλον, ὡς σέθεν κλύω.   trim.
Ελ.   τὰ δὲ ⟨σὰ⟩ κατὰ μέλαθρα
685   πάθεα πάθεα μᾶ- τερ, οἲ ᾽γώ. Μεν. τί φῄς;   3 doch.
Ελ.   οὐκ ἔστι μάτηρ· ἀγχόνιον δὲ βρόχον   iambel.
        δι᾽ ἐμὰν κατεδήσατο δυσγάμου αἰσχύναν.   enop.
Μεν. τίς μοι θυγατρὸς δ᾽ Ἑρμιόνης ἐστὶν βίος;   trim.
Ελ.   ἄγαμος ἄτεκνος ὦ   πόσι καταστένει
690   γάμον ἄγαμον ἐμόν. || 3 doch.
Μεν. ὦ πᾶν κατ᾽ ἄκρας δῶμ᾽ ἐμὸν πέρσας Πάρις,   trim.
        τάδε καὶ σὲ διώλεσε μυριάδας τε   enop.
        χαλκεόπλων Δαναῶν.   + hemiep.
Ελ.   ἐμὲ δὲ πατρίδος ἄπο   κακόποτμον ἀραίαν
695   ἔβαλε θεὸς ἀπό ⟨τε⟩   πόλεος ἀπό τε σέθεν,
        ὅτε μέλαθρα λέχεά τ᾽   ἔλιπον οὐ λιποῦσ᾽
        ἐπ᾽ αἰσχροῖς γάμοις.   7 doch.

625–97. This Recognition Duo, like those of *IT* 827–99, *Ion* 1437–1509, *Hyps.* fr. 64. 70–111 (incomplete), is astrophic (ἀπολελυμένα in Greek terminology), composed in a mixture of trimeters and 'associable' metres (cf. *Lyric Metres of Greek Drama*, p. 198) of the types which could easily pass into a half-spoken delivery: chiefly dochmiacs, bacchiacs, cretics, enoplians, hemiepe. Aeolo-choriambic and ionic are rigidly excluded, dactylo-epitrite restricted to an occasional iambelegos. In all these plays the male character performs wholly or mainly in trims., the more emotional female wholly or mainly in lyric. Menelaus (not elsewhere in the play a singing character) recites catalectic trims. 636–7, and syllables which could form segments of iambic 681–2 and 685. He also has two more ambitious lyrical sallies: one (659) to mark the end of the first part of the Duo, the Recognition proper, and a dicolon (692–3) to end his Interrogation.

Dochmiacs are of the usual type, the commonest being ∪∪∪–∪–. Several are dragged ∪∪∪–⏓– or ⏓––⏓–,[1] others have the first two, or the first and third, or all three longs resolved. 694 κακόποτμον ἀραίαν presents an awkward ambiguity: *either* it has a 'dragged' penult with preceding resolution instead of enclosed between longs

---

[1] I mark the first syllable of this form anceps, but not that of –∪∪–∪–, since the latter seems sometimes to behave as a full long, as in 664 οἷον ἐσοίσομαι, where it follows a short anceps at the end of the first member of the dicolon ∪–∪∪–∪∪–⏓ –∪∪–∪–. Anceps iuxta anceps is impossible.

(not securely attested elsewhere in any metre) *or* the -*αἰ*- is short as sometimes in δίκαιος, γεραιός, Πειραιᾶ, etc. Whether (apart from -οι-) the correption can occur in an accented syllable is uncertain; certainly it could not with a circumflex, but ὀρείαν is perhaps ∪ ∪ – in *Alc.* 446, and I prefer this explanation to the former alternative. Nearly all the dochmiacs are either separated by diaeresis or overlap by one short syllable, and are easy to read, an exception being perhaps 650 with Seidler's necessary emendation; Helen's emotion is here a rising flood. Enoplians vary in size from three to six longs, and open with single- (664) or double-short (692). These two end pendant, but the majority blunt, like the dochmiac itself. In most the movement changes from double-short to single-short at the end: ∪ ∪ – ∪ ∪ – ∪ –, ∪ ∪ – ∪ ∪ – ∪ ∪ – ∪ –, or the last *two* short elements may be single ∪ ∪ – ∪ ∪ – ∪ – ∪ –, but in this form the colon is in this passage always 'dragged': 657 ἀδόκητον ἔχω σε πρὸς στέρνοις ∪ ∪ – ∪ ∪ – ∪ – $\overline{\times}$ –, as again 680 and 681 (cf. *Ion.* 1494). 687 is a form with five longs and dragged close ∪ ∪ – ∪ ∪ – ∪ ∪ – ∪ ∪ – $\overline{\times}$ –, repeated *Ion* 1442. 644 with six longs ∪ ∪ – ∪ ∪ – ∪ ∪ – ∪ ∪ – ∪ – ∪ – is again an echo of *Ion* 1466, followed here by two dochmiacs.

The textual problems of this scene have become acute since the recovery of a papyrus fragment (P.Oxy. 2336, published 1954) dating from the first century B.C., with parts of lines 630–51 and a few letters from the beginnings of lines 663–74. A reconstruction of this with the help of LP's text was given by G. Zuntz in *Mnem.* 1961, now revised with full and careful discussion in chaps. 4 and 5 of his indispensable *Inquiry into the Transmission of the Plays of Euripides*, C.U.P., 1965. To repeat or analyse these results at length would be beyond the scope of this commentary; some more detailed discussion of the difficult middle part will be found in the Appendix.

 Attribution to the right speaker is of course crucial for a proper understanding of this duo. LP are quite inadequate in this respect, and editors vary considerably in their solutions. Unfortunately the first parts of the lines in Π (the papyrus) with the informative 'paragraphos' (the dash under the beginning of a line when change of speaker is to follow) are missing in all the doubtful part; 663–74 where the paragraphos duly appears present no problems. Internal evidence, of both form and content, has to be carefully considered.

625. The time [of waiting] *has been* long, but the joy *is* here and now. Greek (cf. Fr. *depuis longtemps*) uses present tenses with words like πάλαι, παλαιός, where English has the perfect.

628. Hermann's correction is universally accepted; the syllables must all be short.

629. ἐν for our 'after' is idiomatic in such phrases, cf. Jebb on S. *OC* 88 ἐν χρόνῳ μακρῷ. The sun's course is thought of as a continuum, hence the sing. φλογί, although φαεσφόρῳ implies the sequence of dawns which mark the passage of time.

630. Menelaus, who has a far more bewildering adjustment to make than Helen, feels there is still so much to be *said* between them before the situation can become real.

632–3. The shiver of joy as in S. *Aj.* 693 ἔφριξ' ἔρωτι. ἀνεπτέρωσα Π or -κα LP are equally possible.

634–6. A most uncomfortable crux, which Π does nothing to solve. LP has here περὶ δὲ γυῖα χεῖρας ἔβαλον | ἡδονὰν ὡς λάβω, | ὦ πόσις ὦ φιλτάτη πρόσοψις· | οὐκ ἐμέμφθην. This would scan after a fashion: troch. dim. | two cret. || − ∪ ∪ − − ∪ − ∪ − ∪ cf. *Supp.* 1131, iambo-chor. trim. cat.|| troch. metron. Menelaus then presumably takes over with οὐκ ἐμ. Elmsley's correction, however, making (with χέρας) two dochmiacs down to ἡδονὰν and a third by transferring ὦ πόσις before ὡς λάβω, seemed self-evidently right. Menelaus then picks up at ὦ φιλ., and (with Διός ⟨τε⟩ in the next line) has two trim. cat. to match Helen's 632 -3. But now Π shows the main trouble to be already there fourteen centuries before, and even adds to it by ending the second dochmaic in ἡδονη and starting the third with . . . . c ὡς λάβω. This was at first taken to confirm Elmsley, but Zuntz is quite clear that there is room only for three or at most four letters; moreover the next line has a gap of six letters followed by ὦ φιλτάτα πρόσοψις, which strongly suggests ὦ πόσις here as in LP. The isolated trochaic there follows in the next line here too.

For Zuntz's solution see the Appendix. I find myself unable, for reasons there given, to accept it, and feel compelled to start from the wholly appropriate two trim. cat. given to Menelaus in our old standard texts. This throws back ὦ πόσις to the end of Helen's words, and since she cannot be allowed the horrible dochmiac ὡς λάβω ὦ πόσις we return gratefully to Elmsley. I admit to being totally baffled by Π's ἡδονη . . . .c, and this must leave the whole passage shadowed by a doubt which hardly existed before. The vagueness and inconsistency throughout over the 'Doric α' in both texts is quite usual, and need not trouble us. (I have chosen to systematize by giving Helen α and Menelaus η, as indicating a slightly different style of delivery.)

636–7. 'O dearest vision,' cries Menelaus, 'I have no fault to find: I hold my wife, child of Zeus and Leda.' ἐμέμφθην in pres. sense, as often in these impulsive judgements, cf. 463. For the absolute sense of οὐκ ἐμέμφθην cf. A. *Supp.* 137 οὐδὲ μέμφομαι. The reference is forward, to the next line, as the asyndeton shows. Pearson's transla-tion 'my heart is full' goes too far, but is right in principle, nor does the litotes seem to me offensive, as Zuntz finds it; on the contrary, 'I am not blaming *you*' (for whatever it may be, v. App.) would be an insufferable remark.

637 has the same form ἔχω τὰ τοῦ Διὸς λέκτρα Λήδας τε in Π as in LP. Here Zuntz says we must accept τοῦ, and I agree, but not with his translation. He argues that λέκτρα = 'daughter', and defends it by *Med.* 594; the two together are to prove that λέκτρα can mean either 'marriage-bed' or 'fruit of marriage-bed', i.e. if personal either 'wife' or 'offspring'. This seems to me both *a priori* improbable and in fact a misinterpretation of both passages. It is hardly conceivable that in *Medea*, a play in which λέχος and λέκτρον are constantly recurring keywords, the latter could suddenly change its meaning to one never found in any extant play, common though the word is. 594 γῆμαί με λέκτρα βασιλέως ἃ νῦν ἔχω cannot mean 'marry the king's daughter whom I now possess' (for one thing, this should on the analogy of *Hel.* 573 and 639 be ἦν νῦν ἔχω. Elmsley's βασιλέων must be right, though not for his wrong reasons or in his wrong sense (as a masc. plur. used with fem. sing. reference), but simply = λέκτρα τυράννων 140, royal bride or royal marriage: the word fluctuates between the personal and the impersonal sense. 'Make this royal marriage (marry into the bed of kings) which is now within my grasp.' So here, Menelaus is saying in effect, not 'I hold the daughter of Zeus and Leda', as though pluming himself on his aristocratic connexions, but 'I hold my Zeus-and-Leda-born wife', my own wife, the real Helen. ἔχω τὰ λέκτρα really cannot be spoken by Menelaus at this supreme moment of realization in any other sense than 'my own wedded wife'. In terms of ordinary grammar ἔχω τὰ λέκτρα implies τἀμὰ λέκτρα, a phrase which Helen could use of herself (cf. *Phoen.* 14) or Menelaus could use of Helen (cf. 1634). In full the expression would be ἔχω τὰ ἐμὰ λέκτρα, τὴν τοῦ τε Διὸς καὶ τῆς Λήδας, but here τὰ ἐμὰ and τὴν have been telescoped into τὰ and the order artificially involved. Since ἔχω τὰ τοῦ Διὸς λέκτρα would be a highly misleading way to begin the sentence, as though = 'I hold Hera', Διός ⟨τε⟩ is needed, to keep both meaning and metre straight. ἔχω τὰ τῆς Διὸς λέκτρα with the double gen. would be of no help; Menelaus is not saying 'I am married to Helen', nor could one supply 'I hold my wife consisting of Helen'.

638 ff. The next passage holds both the worst discrepancy between Π and LP and a complicated problem of attribution. To begin with, Zuntz argues irrefutably that ἂν ὑπὸ λ. . . . must have been given to Helen in the Alexandrian edition because (p. 234) 'an elided syllable at the end of a verse-line is written in full if it is followed by a change of speaker, and only then; where there is no such change, the syllable is apostrophized and prefixed to the following verse'. Of this he gives ample demonstration, the practice having descended to our MSS., though we have adopted different conventions of print. Helen then picks up at 638 after an elision and on a relative pronoun = ἂν (for λέκτρα . . . ἂν Pearson compares 573), and changing to dochmiac utterance; this we must reckon with as acceptable duo-style. The next clear change of speaker is between 641, where the subject of ἐνόσφισαν is θεοί, and 642–3, where it becomes θεός. (Elmsley's emendations 641–2 followed by edd. are attempts at tidying up rather than probable conjecture.) Π's 'assenting' γ' 642 emphasizes the change. But the metre and the tone of hope in κρείσσω 643 and ἀγαθὸν 644 mark 642–5 as all Helen's, with Menelaus taking over in the two following trimeters (neither Helen, as LP, nor Chor., as Wilamowitz, has any probability). This means that somewhere between 638 and 642 Menelaus must have intervened, and it is here that the text is at its most problematical.

I have explained in the Appendix why I feel unable simply to discard the text of LP here and adopt Π as reconstituted by Zuntz. It is, I think, clear that there are two discrepant traditions in these lines; LP is too coherent, in sense and metre, to be the product simply of wild corruption which has somehow after all omissions and intrusions closed up and left (with the deletion of the last word) a satisfactory text. So we are left with two alternative versions, and I confess that of the two I find LP the easier to believe. Zuntz restores Π as ὤλβισαν: (Men.) ὤλβισαν ἐμὲ σέ τε μάταν | θεοὶ δόμων | δ' ἐνόσφισαν. (1) LP: 'whom . . . my brothers hailed as happy, happy—' ⟨Menelaus⟩ '—once, but the gods took [you] from home.' ἂν carries through from 639. (2) Π ap. Z: 'whom . . . my brothers hailed as happy.' Menelaus: 'They hailed as happy me and you— in vain, and the gods took [us] from home.' ὤλβισαν . . . μάταν as in Andr. 1218 μάτην δέ σ' ἐν γάμοισιν ὤλβισαν θεοί. For the strange repetition of ὤλβισαν by a different speaker, the order of words, and the formidable metrical problem, v. App.

642–5. 'Yes, god is driving us on to a different lot, better than this; it was a fortunate misfortune that brought you and me together, my husband—after a long time indeed, but still may I live to enjoy my lot.' ἐλαύνει: pres.; the process is still going on. συμφορὰν LP, giving an unbroken line of bacchiacs, cf. Ion. 1446, is clearly superior to τύχαν, which is all Π has room for. συνάγαγεν, πόσι: I take it that this is implied in the text of Π. Zuntz gives συνάγαγεν ῳ ποσ(ε)ι, but the ῳ is denied by other experts, and πόσει, as he says, is probably[1] the common misspelling of πόσι. The whole of 644–5 is thus metrically an exact echo of Ion 1466–7, down to Pause at the end of the penultimate line before the two-dochmiac clausula.

646–7. 'May you indeed; and I join you in the same prayer'—δέ as Π, rather than δὴ after δῆτα, since Menelaus means ὀναίμην καὶ ἐγώ— 'for of us two the one is not unhappy without the other'. The phrase

---

[1] It could also be dative, but the zeugma of 'joined you [to a wife] and me to a husband' seems an ineffective complication.

is normally used of a number of people, meaning 'all alike', with no exceptions; here it is more pointed.

648-51. Helen is resolved to repine no more over the past, though from 661 to the end of the duo her will fails her. Π anticipates LP in an unmetrical 650; the second ἐμὸν (restored by Seidler) has already dropped out. Possibly Hermann's πόσιν ἔχομεν ἔχομεν   ἐμὸν ἐμὸν ὅν ἔμενον should be adopted as more in tune with the other dochmiacs in this passage. The threefold repetition almost matches Aristophanes' parody *Ran.* 1351-5.

653. i.e. I now understand the part played by Hera (the Phantom).

654-5. LP divide ἐμὰ δὲ δάκρυα χαρμονὰ | πλέον ἔχει χ. ἢ λ., a colometry which is probably Alexandrian, carrying on to the first word-end that makes a familiar colon (lekythion). Elmsley's transposition gives three dochmiacs separated by diaeresis, and a better word order. With Murray's punctuation the text could then stand, but the causal dat. (Hermann) makes it less disjointed.   χάριτος: opposed to λύπας, χάρις being sometimes almost interchangeable with χαρά, cf. Bond on *Hyps.* 64. 61.

656. This trim. follows badly on the previous line, and Zuntz's calculation from the length of adjacent papyrus-columns that LP are two lines or so shorter in this part probably means as he suggests that an utterance of Menelaus has dropped out here.   τάδ': referring to the next line.

659. End of Recognition proper.

660. Menelaus here begins to ask the things he needs to know. Helen answers reluctantly and with distress. Twice she fails to bring herself to start, though gently encouraged, and the third time gives negative answer, before coming to the direct reply 670.

661. Of the alternatives given by LP the plural πικρὰς ἀρχὰς is stylistically preferable.

663. 'All that the gods give is fit to hear', or 'we must bear to hear'.

664. οἶον οἶον as *Ion* 1471 οἶον οἶον ἀνελέγχομαι, where the verb is passive. One might wonder whether the echo of this line in Eur.'s ear produced the middle voice here, since εἰσφέρω in this sense ('come out with') is elsewhere always active. Lenting ἐσοίσομεν, but there are so many verbs that sooner or later drop into a rare middle, especially in the future, cf. on 1061.

665. τοι: the phrase has a proverbial sound, and is rather elliptically phrased—past troubles, he means, told as a tale by the survivor.

666-8. A thoroughly unsatisfactory bit of lyric. λέκτρα for λέκτρου is essential, and the transposition of λέκτρα and βαρβάρου gives better dochmiacs than οὐκ ἐπὶ λέκτρα βαρ- βάρου νεανία, but what is the construction? The double gen. abs. has no *pied à terre*; Wecklein refers them back to ἀπεστάλης across all intervening obstacles; most take them as the beginning of the sentence 670-1, but Menelaus' trimeter, especially with ⟨γάρ⟩, has anything but the air of an interruption; moreover 670–1 are much more natural as a self-contained answer to 669. Nor is it easy to believe in two gen. abs. left *in vacuo*, to express Helen's agitation. The repetition πετομένας . . . πετομένου in different kinds and degrees of metaphor—on the wings of the oar and the wings of desire of sinful marriage—seems to me a strange conflation rather than 'elegant' (Pearson). Worst of all, although we are told (without parallels) that οὐκ 666 'carries through' to the end of the sentence, the easier sense of the Greek as it stands seems to be not 'not A *nor* B', but 'not A *but* B' (cf., e.g., S. *Phil.* 971), and it is difficult to resist Reiske's suggestion that πετομένου δ' ἔρωτος conceals the missing finite verb and οὐδέ. His κέλομεν οὐδ' ἐρῶντες is good save for the unsatisfactory main verb, for which it is difficult to find a substitute; possibly something like εἰπόμεθ'.

669. συλᾷ σε πάτρας: apparently 'bore you off as spoil *from* . . .'.

670. Π, which here vouchsafes a few line-openings, has ΟΔ . . . | Μ | Μ. Zuntz reasonably interprets this as ὁ Διὸς ὁ Διὸς ὦ πόσι | Μαίας τε παῖς | μ' ἐπέλασεν Νείλῳ. This was Elmsley's conjecture for the obviously defective LP (Hermes cannot be identified from 'the son of Zeus'), but he meant πόσι Μαίας τε παῖς μ' as a dochmiac, naturally. It would be interesting to know whether the original of Π's colometry did not recognize ∪∪−−∪− as a permissible dochmiac, or whether it was the supposed form πόσ(ε)ι (cf. on 644) which gave the scansion lekythion | iambic metron | dochmiac for 670–1. There must be three dochmiacs here, but the form of the middle one is very perplexing. ∪∪−−∪− is very poorly attested; see Barrett on *Hipp.* 670, p. 434. Hermann's πόσι με παῖς Μαιάς τ' would have been such a simple way to compose a regular dochmiac, but now it postulates a tangled little process of corruption.

673. κατεδάκρυσα: again the 'emotional' aor. 'I burst into tears and my eyelids are wet with tears': Eur. does at times compose lyric with this kind of indifference to redundancy.

675. τί νῷν: Hermann ingeniously supplies the essential dat. after προσθεῖναι.

676–7. LP's reading, though widely accepted, would be unintelligible in dochmiac utterance, and even with punctuation in print is pitiable Greek. As Wilamowitz says (*GV* 565), the sudden reference to 'baths and springs' would be easier if they were localized 'on Ida', but ὤμοι 'Ιδαίων with hiatus instead of correption is unpleasing, and τῶν "Ιδᾳ too far from the text. Perhaps ὤμοι ἐγὼ κείνων might serve the same kind of purpose. **ἵνα** = 'where'.

679. The sense needed is clear: why should the Judgement of the Goddesses have made Hera afflict you? Murray's attempt to keep the text as an unfinished sentence, sc. αἰτίαν, is unlike the style of Menelaus' trimeters. Wilamowitz: τάδ' εἰς κρίσιν σοι τήνδ' ἔθηχ'

Ἥρα κακά; but Helen answers the question 'Why?' not 'Did she?' and neither ἐς κρίσιν τήνδ' = 'with reference to this judgement' nor ἔθηκέ σοι κακά = 'caused you trouble' is quite idiomatic. The really clinching conjecture eludes us; perhaps Herwerden's, adopted here, is as good as any: 'Why did Helen make a calamity for *you* of their judgement (= the judgement on them)?' To Menelaus the Judgement of Paris is a familiar story; it is only the subsequent turn given to it by Hera's resentment that is new.

680–2. Helen's words are a continuous sentence with με the object of all three verbs: 'It was in order to withhold me from Paris, to whom Cypris had promised me, that she—cruel, cruel—brought me thus to Egypt.' Since τλάμων must mean 'cruel' in 682 it is better to take it the same way for Menelaus 681 ὦ τλήμων (as Hermann) apostrophizing Hera rather than pitying Helen. Πάριν . . . Κύπρις (Reiske) is essential for the sense. Kirchhoff's elaborate emendation of 682 (app. crit.), on the other hand, though surprisingly adopted by many, seems due to the idea that τλήμων must mean 'miserable', whereas it has the same range as the verb τλάω, cf., e.g., *Med.* 865 and my note on *Alc.* 1.

686–7. Many edd. make four dochmiacs of these lines: οὐκ ἔστιν μάτηρ | ἀγχόνιον βρόχον | δι' ἐμὲ κατεδήσατο | δύσγαμον αἰσχύνᾳ. LP end δύσγαμος αἰσχύναν, but δύσγαμος must be wrong, since it is Helen's adjective, not Leda's; αἰσχύναν is inconsistent with ἐμὲ, and one or the other must be emended. I have no doubt that Murray is right in choosing δι' ἐμὰν . . . αἰσχύναν, thus making the line a dragged enoplion, and preceding it by the iambelegos as given by LP, since exactly the same couplet is found *Ion* 1441–2. (Cf. supr. on 642–5.) Moreover the form of δι' ἐμὲ κατεδήσατο as a dochmiac ∪ ∪ ∪ ∪ ∪ ⲭ ∪ ∪, with 'drag' between two resolutions, is (even if possible) too outlandish for this conventional context. I would, however, read δυσγάμου αἰσχύναν.

689. There is no parallel for LP's unlikely way of saying 'Is our daughter Hermione alive?' and Badham's τίς μοι θυγατρὸς δ' is well calculated to receive Helen's answer (βίος = manner of life). For postponed δέ see Denn. *GP* 187–8.

690. Hermann's ἐμόν completes both sense and metre. αἰσχύνα LP is an intrusion from 687.

691 ff. Does Menelaus here break loose and follow his trimeter with lyric? Triclinius prefixed Ἐλ. to 694, P seems to have found it at 692. On general grounds one might have supposed that Helen would sing this more unorthodox rhythm, but καὶ σὲ, 'you *too*', would have no meaning, and διώλεσε is too strong a word. So as the final strand in the pattern Menelaus must speak and sing of the wreck of his house and the devastation of the war, and Helen adds in agitated dochmiacs, steadying at the close, a summary of her own misfortunes.

692–3. Wilamowitz proposes τάδε ⟨πόλιν τε σὰν⟩ καὶ σὲ διώλεσεν two dochmiacs, as a better balance of retribution than the single death against so many thousands of Greeks. That is undeniable, but Menelaus may have left his hearers to include Troy in the ruin that overwhelmed Paris. If the whole made four dochmiacs as Wilamowitz intended, it would be much more probable, but μυριάδας τε χαλ- κεόπλων Δαναῶν cannot be two dochmiacs, whether the syllable -οπ- be long or short. The anapaestic ∪∪−∪∪− is not a *form* of dochmiac; it can in certain circumstances be associated with dochmiacs, but only if self-contained. We should have to read (with διώλεσε) ∪∪∪−∪−|−∪∪−∪∪−∪∪−∪|−∪∪−∪∪−, which is inferior to the enopl. + hemiepes given by LP.

696. ἔλιπον οὐ λιποῦσ': as Pearson says, not to be separated, i.e. not 'when I left . . ., though not for a base love', but 'when I left-without-leaving my home and bed for a base love'. It was not true, but the consequences happened as if it had been. The fact that she really did go has been given by ἔβαλε.

698. εἰ καί: 'if indeed', if it should prove that . . . ; indicating 'cautious reserve rather than scepticism', Denn. *GP* 303.

699. They would be enough in relation to the past, 'they would make up for the past'.

700. πρόσδοτον is the simplest and best emendation of πρόσδοτε. The dual is a constant source of trouble. προσδίδωμι + gen. 'give a share of' is not unusual, cf. *Cyc.* 531, *Supp.* 351.

701: 'I see without properly understanding.'

702. The ἀλλά of compliance, falling in with a request.

703. βραβεύς: lit. 'arbitrator', a curious application of the word. (The meaning 'author' given for this one reference in LS would be quite disconnected from all other uses of the word.) The nearest approach to this passage seems to be *Or.* 1065, where Orestes asks Pylades to act as βραβεύς of his and Electra's self-slaughter, decreed by the Argives; is Pylades to be merely, as it were, presiding officer to see that both carry out the deed properly, 'overseer'? Conceivably some kind of rivalry in nobility (1064) could be the subject of a 'judgement between two parties' such as the word seems to require. Here, however, Helen would more naturally be the βράβευμα (Soph. fr. 317P), the judge's award to the winning side, and it is only by a kind of shorthand that she is herself seen as actually 'arbitrating', in default of any human judge. The word, masculine in form but used of a woman, is a nomen agentis of the same kind as φονεύς 280, διαφθορεύς *Hipp.* 682.

705–6. νεφέλης ἄγαλμ': the Phantom is again described as a 'cloud-image' 1219. λυγρόν was deleted by Badham to make room for τί φής; but ἀντιλαβή so late in the line would be as unusual as τί φής; extra metrum, and if a word had been inserted as a stop-gap one would

perhaps expect a perfunctory κακόν rather than the more exact
λυγρόν. There is no close parallel to τί φῄς; extra metrum in Eur.,
but it is in effect as exclamatory as ἔα (cf. τί φῶ; S. OC 315). The next
line is thus thrown into high relief, and its content is indeed the
central irony of the play, but the Servant, though apparently once
a fighting man (734–5), does not elaborate upon the theme as one
might expect.

To delete 705 and τί φῄς; with Kirchhoff and Wecklein, just to
preserve the short stichomythia, is impossible; the old man obviously picks up νεφέλης ἄγαλμα with νεφέλης ἄρ' ἄλλως, and would
not have made that step in the deduction unprompted.

708. The Judgement of Paris is assumed to be common knowledge,
though not of course Hera's reaction to it (cf. on 679). The expression is abbreviated: this is Hera's doing, *the outcome of* the
contest.

709–10. 'And your real wife is this woman here?'—'She and no other—
take my word for it.' The δ' is a typical unwanted intrusion.

711 ff. The Servant's first comments on this shattering revelation are
limited to the lessons he can draw from his own circle of relation-
ships—master, mistress, loyal servant. Menelaus suffered and toiled
for years and got nothing for it; now a curious turn of fortune throws
everything into his lap, so capricious is the power that controls our
destinies. Helen had suffered too, from scandal, but now he is
happy to find her innocent and can renew the sentiments of his
bridal song at her wedding. For though a slave he is capable of the
virtues of loyalty and sympathy with his masters.

The first part of this is cast in the common rhetorical form:
generalization, followed by its particular application in the present
case. The generalization (711–15) found its way into Stobaeus'
selection in a form beginning σκέψαι γὰρ ὁ θεὸς ὃς ἔχει τι ποικίλον, but
that is unlikely to be anything more than a little clipping and
grooming (plus a corruption ὅς for ὡς) for its place in an anthology.
After that, however, it continues as our text does, with a hardly
tolerable obscurity; perhaps it had already been garbled in an earlier
collection of gnomic excerpts. God (says the Servant piously, using
the sort of language more often applied to τύχη) is many-sided and
hard to interpret, εὖ δέ πως ἀναστρέφει | ἐκεῖσε κἀκεῖσ' ἀναφέρων.
ἀναστρέφει 'turns upside down' (cf. *Supp.* 331 ὁ γὰρ θεὸς πάντ' ἀναστρέφει πάλιν) and ἀναφέρων disposing? adjusting? without any object
are of a baffling vagueness. εὖ δέ πως, 'rather ingeniously', 'with a
curious sort of skill', is too idiomatic to lose (cf., e.g., *Phoen.* 1466,
I A 66), and Herwerden's πάντα στρέφει would supply an object for
both verbs; perhaps it is best left at that: he turns things this way
and that and changes all their dispositions. Now comes the generalization, expressed as an antithesis. There was an old Greek adage

which said (cf. Eur. frag. 701N² μοχθεῖν ἀνάγκη τοὺς θέλοντας εὐτυχεῖν) 'Success is the reward of effort'. One man makes the effort, another makes none. The consequences for the latter are put first (714–15): 'and then another day comes to a bad end, finding no stability in fortune as it stands at any given time.' We now expect to be told that the former gains the reward of his toils, but this is where the capriciousness of the gods comes in. The general point the Servant wants to make seems to be: He who does make the effort may even appear to fail and yet later win his desire, when he has ceased trying. But instead of completing the generalization the Servant hurries on to his particular instance: So you, Helen, [Helen, whose πόνοι were of the passive, not the active kind, is included for form's sake] and your husband had your share of trouble. He strove earnestly, and so long as he strove got nothing for it, but now winning the highest good fortune he finds blessings unsought.

Undoubtedly this would have been much clearer and more in line with Eur.'s normal patterns of rhetoric if the generalization had been completed first, and perhaps it is not fanciful to see in this utterance a degree of artlessness deliberately intended to characterize the speaker. Eur. is not in general much given to mixing what Aristotle would call his διάνοια with ἦθος, but it can perhaps be claimed that he has a way of letting his plebeian figures (the unnamed ones, excluding Messengers) dilate at some length on minor aspects of no great relevance to the immediate situation; cf. the Nurse in *Med.* 119–30. It is certainly curious that the speeches of this particular Old Servant should so persistently raise the question of how much awkwardness and doddering irrelevance we must accept. 726–7 just below, for instance, would make an acceptable couplet of gnomic self-satisfaction to close this speech, and to pursue the point for six lines more verges on the silly. 744–57 sets an even harder problem, v. infr.

724. ἵπποις: dat. after the παρά in the verb, not, as LS oddly suggests, with τροχάζων, of a charioteer. He ran on foot. The only other occurrence of τροχάζω in poetry is lyric, Eur. *Hyps.* 64. 59 ἐτρόχασεν, probably also to be taken, with Bond, as intrans. = τρέχω.

725. ἔλειπες: the correction is from the Aldine. The gaiety and ceremony of the wedding procession of Helen and Menelaus had been described by Stesichorus; Athenaeus gives us an extract 'from the *Helen*' (187PMG), and since here 720–5 also recalls the lyrics of the ἀναγνώρισις 639–41 the whole is quite likely to be a deliberate reminiscence of Stesichorus.

729. That a slave can be γενναῖος is a favourite oxymoron of Eur., cf. infr. 1641, and for similar sentiments *Ion* 854, frr. 495, 511, 831; frequent repetition does not make it less a personal conviction.

731–2. δυοῖν ... ἕν': 'a single person ... a double misfortune'; the

formal antithesis is a peculiarly Greek way of emphasizing the lack
of essential connexion between the two κακά.

733. ἀκούειν: 'obey' = ὑπακούειν in Eur. only here and infr. 1415.

734. ἄγ' with ἄγγειλον 737. πολλὰ μὲν ... καὶ νῦν: cf. S. *Aj.* 1-3 ἀεὶ
μὲν ... καὶ νῦν.

738. οἷ τ' ἐσμὲν τύχης: οἷ (ποῖ, ὅποι), and οὗ, ᾗ, etc., are easily mixed,
and it is often difficult to decide whether the 'directional' form can
stand. Where the verb itself implies previous motion, like καθέσταμεν
in *OC* 23, there need be no hesitation, but with εἰμί the problem is
harder. In the famous passage of Dem. on the Athenians' reactions
to Philip's tactics (4. 40) which Pearson quotes, κἂν ἑτέρωσε πατάξῃ τις,
ἐκεῖσε εἰσὶν αἱ χεῖρες, ἑτέρωσε prepares for ἐκεῖσε, and the whole point
lies in the immediacy of the picture. A complete parallel would be
Ar. *Av.* 9 ποῖ γῆς ἐσμὲν with good MS. authority, and these two
passages must stand or fall together. In both the sense of the context implies movement, there literal, here metaphorical—their fortunes have changed considerably since he last saw his companions.
Infr. 1607 is different again: in ὅποι νόσοιεν ... ταύτῃ προσῆγε χεῖρα
the ὅποι and the ταύτῃ seems as it were to have changed places and
produce a kind of balance which supports the traditional reading.

740. οἳ μένουσιν οὓς ἐλπίζομεν LP could only mean 'which await those
I am expecting them to await', and I cannot understand the Budé
translation 'en perspective des combats que j'appréhende'.

741-3. LP καὶ τήνδε πῶς δυναίμεθ' ἐκπλέξαι χθονός; where P's corrector
substitutes ἐκκλέψαι. It is usual to adopt this, with L. Dindorf's κεὶ
τήνδε πως and a comma either after χθονός or after φρουρεῖν. But
neither φρουρεῖν ὅπως ἂν + subj. nor φρουρεῖν εἰ + opt. is at all reassur-
ing, and εἰ δυναίμεθα followed within the same sentence by the correct
ἦν δυνώμεθα is strange and clumsy. Herwerden, with εἰ for καὶ 741,
deletes 742-3, but the notion of combining their own escape with
Helen's deliverance is surely essential. Jackson (p. 240) makes excellent sense by cutting out πῶς ... φρουρεῖν, leaving ἀγῶνας οἳ
μένουσί με ... καὶ τήνδ'. The intrusive words, meant to supply a verb
for καὶ τήνδε, are not more of a muddle than such interpolations tend
to be.

744-60. If Eur. had wanted to bring home to his hearers the futility
of war, or the frivolous cruelty and irresponsibility of the gods in
their dealings with men, here would have been the moment, but the
Old Servant would hardly be the person. Instead he manages to
retain his piety, and singles out human μαντική for his attack: why
had not the seers warned them that the sack of Troy was all for
nothing? The way to approach the gods is by sacrifice and prayer,
letting be divination. The Chorus applauds this: to have the gods as
your friends is the best home-mantic. How sacrifice and prayer would
have helped in this situation is not explained, and concentration

at such length on a minor side-issue is undoubtedly a typical reaction of the limited mind and outlook (as of the Servant); it is nevertheless not surprising that Eur. has often been credited here with a desire to lash out at contemporary divination and the recent part it had played before the Sicilian Expedition (cf. Thuc. viii. 1), but cf. *El.* 399–400, *IT* 570–1, *Phoen.* 954–9, *Bacch.* 255–7, *IA* 955–9, in all of which, whatever the prejudices of the speaker, the tone of hostility and contempt is unvarying.

For an assessment of this speech in comparison with others the reader may be referred to Holger Friis Johansen, *General Reflection in Tragic Rhesis* (Copenhagen, 1959), pp. 92–99, and particularly to his arguments for rejecting sections of the speech of Orestes *El.* 367 ff., which contrast with his more conservative attitude here. Some editors let the whole through as it stands, alia alii excidunt aut transponunt, and Hartung once threw out 744–60 at one sweep. Suspicion centres on 746–8, 752, and 755–7, which are discussed as they arise in the following.

745. ἐσεῖδον: 'I do now see', the aor. expressing the flash of realization just after it has occurred.

746–8. Mantic is subdivided into the observation of (*a*) sacrificial flames, (*b*) the cries of birds, with a further note that the mere idea of deriving help from birds is manifestly silly. There is nothing to object to here, but the connexion of the sentence and the grammar are doubtful. At 746 one would expect asyndeton, with either οὐκ ... οὐδὲ or οὔτ' ... οὔτε. φθέγματα 747 has no construction : the common colloquialism ὑγιὲς οὐδέν can be worked into the construction either as an acc. (οὐδὲν ὑγιὲς λέγων, etc.) or more elaborately with a (partitive) gen. dependent on οὐδέν, as 746 here, *Bacch.* 262, *Cyc.* 259. No plausible emendation has been suggested, and I am inclined to suspect an intrusion from another passage which had the connexion οὐδ' in 746 and in 747 a further sentence beginning οὐδὲ πτερωτῶν φθέγματα ... (lacuna of one line) εὔηθες δέ τοι κτλ., the lengthier second subdivision being followed by the contemptuous comment. **Κάλχας γὰρ** 749 fits on easily to 745 as its concrete illustration.

751. Porson's οὐδ' Ἕλενος ingeniously adds the most famous Trojan seer.

752. Most edd. delete, because of the awkward reference right back to οὐκ εἶπε and the late, untragic imperf. ἠβούλετο. Cobet conjectured, in deleting it, the handiwork of some pious defender of μαντική.

753. μαντευόμεθα is only found as a correction of LP μαντευόμεσθα in a late copy, and self-evident though this seems, it is worth noting that the word-rhythm – – ⌣ ⌣ is almost unexampled in tragedy, even in late Eur. The only parallels I have found are the extremely dubious εἱλισσόμεθα *Or.* 444, and Crates fr. 4N² ἐργαζόμενος. I am aware, however, that this will seem insufficient grounds for extending suspicion from the preceding lines.

755–7 have a degree of irrelevance to this context, and in particular to the rest of the speech, which few readers find themselves able to take, and the Chorus's agreement 758 is with the sentiments of 753–4, not at all with 755–7, for all the close echo in ἀρίστη μάντις ... ἀρίστην μαντικήν, an echo which is itself no doubt responsible for the intrusion of this 'associated parallel' here.

The whole speech, if reduced to the seven lines 744–5, 749–51, 753–4, acquires much greater clarity and ends in the approved manner with two gnomic lines. In this form it has just enough irrelevance to the main issue and relevance to the character of the Servant to be conceivable as a deliberate touch of Euripidean irony.

761. εἶεν: the formula for dismissing one subject or one aspect of a question and taking up another.   **δεῦρ' ἀεὶ** go together (δεῦρο in the sense of 'up to now'), a phrase found several times in Eur. but also in A. *Eum.* 596.

762 ff. Eur. neatly avoids holding up the action by unwanted narrative, while yet not leaving Helen indifferent to her husband's past troubles.

764. αἰσθέσθαι: apparently 'to hear of', 'be informed', for which Pearson quotes *Or.* 1550 as the nearest parallel, but it strikes strangely here as used of the sufferer's own narration of his story, especially with the word κακά: 'those who love long to be told of their loved ones' misfortunes'—one would at least rather expect τύχας. There is much to be said for Schenkl's deletion of 764 as one of those lines mistakenly added (perhaps suggested by ἡδύ τοι μόχθων κλύειν 665) to complete the sense of an elliptical phrase. The balance of κέρδος μὲν οὐδὲν—πόθος δέ τις makes it easy to sc. εἰδέναι with the second too.

765. ἐνὶ λόγῳ Pierson for ἐν ὀλίγῳ, which is always used in a spatial sense, 'in small compass', not metaphorically. **μιᾷ ὁδῷ** is a curious phrase, presumably a colloquialism (Pearson quotes Herondas 5. 66 μιῇ δεῖ σ' ὁδῷ γενέσθαι ποικίλον, of the effect of tattooing); and the jingly repetition is clearly deliberate—'in one word and at one go'.

766. φθοράς: 'shipwrecks' of his companions, cf. *IT* 276 ναυτίλους ἐφθαρμένους.

767: 'the Euboean beacons of Nauplius.' In 415 Eur. had made the treacherous murder of Palamedes the subject of a play which must have brought in in some form the misleading beacons lit in revenge on S. Euboea by his father Nauplius to lure the Greek ships to destruction. Cf. also Poseidon's prophecy *Tro.* 90–91. There is a further reference to this in the Chorus 1126 ff.

769. Hdt. ii. 15 places the 'look-out place of Perseus' at the western extremity of the Nile Delta; here Andromeda was chained to her rock, and the play *Andromeda* may have put the landmark into Eur.'s mind here.

769–71. Pearson's substitution of εἰ for οὐ (for the confusion he cites *Tro.* 356, *El.* 538) is much the most economical way of giving shape to this sentence; if οὐ is left, the string of four paratactic clauses ἐμπλήσαιμι ⟨ἄν⟩, ἀλγοίην ἄν, ἔκαμνον, λυπηθεῖμεν ἄν, connected by τε ... τε ... δὲ, quite obscures the close connexion of the two middle ones, λέγων τ᾽ ἂν ἀλγοίην, πάσχων τ᾽ ἔκαμνον, an idiomatic Greek way of saying paratactically 'I *should* suffer in the telling *as I did* in the actual experience'. εἰ γὰρ ἐμπλήσαιμί σε μύθων: 'if I were to give you your fill of words.' ἔτι: not 'once more', but 'I should *still* be feeling the pangs'. δὶς: cf. 143.

772. κάλλιον: adv., lit. 'you have spoken better than I asked', your answer is better than my question was.

775–6. Undoubtedly the simplest correction of ἐνιαύσιον is ἐνιαυσίων. The hyperbaton from here to the end of 776 is a long one, but the initial statement of the unit of calculation is well placed. There is, however, no instance of ἐνιαύσιον ἔτος, which is hardly saved by Ar. *Ran.* 347 χρονίους τ᾽ ἐτῶν παλαιῶν ἐνιαυτούς, and Mekler's κύκλων for ἐτῶν would be an improvement. Apelt's ἐν ναυσὶν ὢν is a slightly off-Greek phrase for ναυστολῶν or ναυσθλούμενος, and Jackson's ἐνταῦθ᾽ ἰών, 'on my way here', though palaeographically neat, seems a slightly improbable phrase for seven years of erratic drifting about the eastern Mediterranean.

780 = *Phoen.* 972, besides which, (1) it is a hysteron proteron with 781, which is the obvious answer to τί λέξεις; (2) 779 is the natural place for stichomythia to begin, (3) it anticipates 805. If it were not for these other objections the defence might be made that the verse is an ordinary one which could easily recur in the same words in a similar situation. But it is *no* answer to say that 'there seems no conceivable reason for interpolating it here'. These things happen, for whatever reason.

783. Badham is of course right (see app. crit.): 'your unexpected arrival' *is* the obstacle. τ᾽ is another unwanted connector as in 710.

784–5. As they stand, these lines would mean: 'Did someone conceive the desire to marry my wife?' 'Yes, and to offer me violence, which I had to endure in my person.' In such a context Menelaus could interpret this in only one way, and it is a mere evasion to say that some 'scene' is implied which forced Helen to take refuge at the tomb. F. W. Schmidt's suggestion (app. crit.) assuming ἐγώ to be a stop-gap added when εὐνὴν ἔτλη had coalesced, though in accordance with the best critical principles, is open to the same objection even more strongly with the word εὐνήν. ἐβουλήθη must at all costs be left in command of both lines. No satisfactory emendation is recorded for ἦν ἔτλην ἐγώ. εἰς ἐμὴν εὐνήν, πόσι would fill the gap harmlessly, as a gentle reminder that she too had regarded herself as the wife of Menelaus.

788. At 477 f.

789. Wecklein's βαρβάρων would be an improvement.

790. ἐξηλαυνόμην: not, as Pearson, 'I was like to be driven', but 'I was [at the time the hint was given] being chased away'.

791. Helen feels the social disgrace no less keenly than Menelaus 510 ff.

792. Eur. seems obsessed with the antithesis ἔργον/ὄνομα in this play. εἶχεν is smoother, but εἶχον gives good sense: 'that is what it came to, though I did not call myself such' (πτωχός, a mendicant).

793. ἔοικας: v. on 497.

794. τάδ': best taken not with λέκτρα, but as object of ἔχω, summing up the εἰ-clause. οὐκ ἔχω εἰ is difficult to parallel.

796: 'What assurance have I of this? It would be welcome news if true.'

798. Why τάλαινα when he has still to ask what it has to do with her? p's correction ταλαίνας is probably right: 'I see a miserable couch of leaves', though τάλας is not used so freely as ἄθλιος (797) in a depreciatory sense of inanimate objects. Cf., however, S. *Phil.* 1088 αὐλίον τάλαν.

799. ἱκετεύομεν imperf. The verb, normally used only with acc. of the person, takes here the construction of αἰτέω—supplicating an escape from this marriage.

802. ναυστολεῖν can be either trans. or intrans.; here the next line shows the addition of σε to be essential to the sense.

805. καταιδοῦ sc. φεύγειν ἐκ τ. χ.

808. ἄρ' (LP) would be meaningless here, whereas 'exclamatory' γε (Denn. *GP* 126) is exactly right.

810. Many commentators, from Cobet to Jackson, have rejected **οὕτω** here. Pearson says roundly 'οὕτω is indefensible', and Jackson agrees with Hermann on 'the irregularity and clumsiness of the verse'. The point is not really arguable; there is no exact parallel, and the only answer is a counter-assertion that as a variation on the more prosaic 'so vulnerable' this οὕτω with a neg. clause is blameless, and that the line read in its context is infinitely preferable to any proposed emendation.

811. εἴσῃ: 'you will know soon enough', cf. *IA* 675. The second-sight of his sister Theonoe would be sufficient guarantee of the king's personal safety (1044–6). It is not quite time to introduce her name.

812. σιγῇ: 'quietly', tamely.   **δῆτα** as so often the equivalent of οὖν in a question.   **παράσχω δῆσαι**: 'am I to hold out my hands for binding?'

813. ἄπορον: the point where there is no way out of the dilemma. **μηχανή**: *the* Euripidean formula according to the comic poets: now for some clever ruse.

816. Bribes, daring, eloquence—three ways of getting out of a predicament. The form of expression recalls *Cyc.* 358 (app. crit.)—boiled, roasted, or off the charcoal—and, with only two alternatives, *Hipp.* 514. In both of these the prep. is ἄπο, but the likeness is formal only and need not extend to the particular preposition. Pearson quotes *Andr.* 321 in defence of ὑπο.

818. ὅς as often for ὅστις. The reading and sense are uncertain here. As it stands the dubious points are μ', for 'who will tell him I have [arrived]?' and γ' where we seem to need γάρ, 'he won't know who I am [without being told]'. (It is hardly possible to interpret γνώσεται in some special sense such as 'know from looking at me'.) Italie would supply τίς as the subject of γνώσεται, but it is more natural in a quick reading or hearing to make 'he' = the king, and it is for this reason that Herwerden and Vitelli suggest ἐρεῖ δὲ τίς; τίς γνώσεται δ' ὅς εἰμ' ἐγώ; An alternative, perhaps better, would be Pearson's ἐρεῖ δὲ τίς; τοῦ γνώσεταί μ' ὅς εἰμ' ἐγώ; P's later corrector gives a version—perhaps only a conjecture but a reasonable one—ἐρεῖ δὲ τίς μ' ἢ γνώσεταί γ' ὅς εἰμ' ἐγώ; who will tell him, or even so much as know, who I am? which relieves the μ' and perhaps does not over-press the γ'.

820. A private oracle? φήμη is an inspired voice.

822: 'An oracular *name*; tell me what she *does*', cf. on 792.

824. θνῄσκοιμεν ἄν: v. on 91.

825. εἴ πως ἄν LP would need some rather forced grammatical acrobatics to carry on from 824 ('you can remain undiscovered if there is a chance to . . .'), and the construction with ἄν in the protasis is a prosaic one (see Goodwin, *MT* 506–7). But the independent potential clause given by Kirchhoff's ἴσως seems an over-simplification. Was νιν perhaps repeated with both verbs? εἴ πώς νιν ἀναπείσαιμεν ἱκετεύοντε νιν.

830. σὸν ἔργον: 'your job', in this brief form a colloquialism fairly common in Ar. πρόσφορον: something like 'woman to woman is a suitable line of approach'; the exact construction of πρόσφορον is elusive, and it remains so in Adesp. 364N² γέρων γέροντι γλῶσσαν ἡδίστην ἔχει | παῖς παιδί, καὶ γυναικὶ πρόσφορον γυνή. It is clearly an elliptical proverbial expression.

831. ὡς = 'be sure that', cf. 126; here with fut. as *Med.* 609. χερῶν gen. after α-privative. The devious expression has something of the oedema of tragic diction.

834: v. on 91. Not 'that would be to betray me', but 'False woman!' an explosion of jealousy.

835. κατώμοσα: impulsive aor., 'I swear', cf. 348.

836. ἀλλάξεις need not be changed to ἀλλάξειν even if κοὔποτ' is grammatically possible with the infin.

838. ἐπὶ τοῖσδε: the regular formula in ratification of a solemn pledge, cf. *Alc.* 375.

841. Their death must be a clear gesture of their noble resolve, so that the world may understand, and applaud. The form of the sentence may have encouraged the interpolation 298 ff.

842. νώτῳ: elsewhere, as Herwerden points out, the metaphorical sense always has plur. νῶτα, and probably we should emend here. Cf. 984.

844. 'Let any who will come near', a general warning challenge. (Not, as the Budé edition, 'Celui qui veut ravir ma femme, qu'il approche'!)

847–50. This is the usual idiom by which ὅστις introduces a clause which is both relative and explanatory (here of the ψόγον of 846). Cf. *IT* 381 ff., which also has a μὲν . . . δὲ subdivision, the point being the irrational combination of the two. Here, however, the sequence of thought is more elliptical: fully expressed it would be '. . . expose myself to reproach, as I *should do if* I, who caused the death of . . . , and saw . . . , were not now ready to die for my wife'. The δέ-clause (849) which answers is temporarily forestalled by an earlier one (848), and then breaks loose from ὅστις into an independent question; the sense, however, is perfectly clear.

848–9. 'Saw Telamonian Ajax's corpse and Nestor childless': the zeugma is slightly mitigated by the concrete sense of σφαγάς, for which cf. *El.* 1227. Lenting derived his correction of the senseless τὸν Θησέως τε παῖδα from the conjunction of names in *Od.* 3. 111. Antilochus' death in saving his father from Memnon, alluded to in *Od.* 4. 187, was an episode in the Cyclic *Aithiopis*, followed by Pindar, *Pyth.* 6. 28 ff. Evidently Thetis, Telamon, and Nestor (cf. S. *Phil.* 424–5) were the three great Sorrowers on the Greek side, in whose name the Greeks would have best right to reproach Menelaus for cowardly survival.

851–4. The contrast, adapted by Menelaus to his own circumstances, is between a hero's death facing his enemies (though πολεμίων ὕπο would be more appropriate for death in battle) and a coward's attempt to escape by sea. The former has a tomb, a covering of earth which lies lightly upon him (cf. *Alc.* 463), the latter is cast up unburied on a hard reef. There is a twofold verbal antithesis, between κούφῃ and στερεὸν and between καταμπίσχουσιν and ἐκβάλλουσι. The attempt to emend 854 to make it mean a heavy weight of solid earth on top of a coward is misguided.

857 ff. The Chorus's prayer is followed dramatically by a new peril. τῆς τύχης: the gen. with ἔχω like εὐμενείας 313. ὧδ': 'like that', referring to οἵ ἐγὼ τάλαινα.

858–61: an odd little hysteron proteron, but presumably no one else of importance is at home. The same kind of formula for an emerging actor, in the more natural order, occurs *Ion* 515–16 (δοῦπος), and again with κτυπέω *Or.* 1366–8, where the scholiast's athetesis is mistaken. It later became stereotyped in New Comedy round the words ψόφος, ψοφέω for the noise of unfastening bolts.

861. Theonoe's knowledge does not depend on her coming out and seeing Menelaus there.

862. δύστηνος of course fem., cf. the same phrase with exclamatory nom. *Andr.* 71. This is the ὡς that follows an exclamation, cf. *Alc.* 727, 1069, *Bacch.* 358, *Cyc.* 665, and is probably best taken as itself exclamatory.

863–4. A prep. with the second only of two nouns connected by καί or ἤ though in sense required with both is not uncommon in the tragedians, but here that construction would leave ἐλθών rather awkwardly stranded. It seems better to take Τροίας as gen. 'of separation' with σωθείς, cf. σωθῆναι κακῶν *Or.* 779, and then ἀπὸ β. χθ. ἐλθών.

865 ff. Enter Theonoe preceded by two handmaids, one of whom carries a θυμιατήριον (probably an open bowl in which the flame could be seen, set on a stem which made it portable), the other a torch. One is to purify the air Theonoe breathes, the other the ground she walks on; then they are both (κομίζετε 872) to take the flares back to the hearth-flame from which they were lit. Thus Theonoe's hearing of the supplication is unwitnessed and she can make her decision privately.

866. 'Bringing flame and sulphur from the inner chamber'—but an imperative telling her to burn it seems more wanted than a statement of where it came from, and μυχῶν as 'gen. of separation' is improbably isolated. The δέ of LP also points to a new clause, and Hermann's θείον, from θειόω 'fumigate', is an easy correction, to which αἰθέρος μυχόν (or better μυχούς Wecklein) provides an object; then σεμνόν for σεμνοῦ. Triclinius's note of explanation (v. app. crit.), 'sulphur = a *symbol of ether* because it is so inflammable', can only be a desperate attempt to make sense of θεῖον which he had before him. The difficulty of σεμνὸν θεσμὸν as a sort of internal accus. is small in comparison. 'And fumigate in holy ordinance the recesses of the air.' Plut. *Mor.* 383B speaks of Egyptian priests burning resin and myrrh to rarefy the air.

870. πυρός, especially at this distance from πεύκην, is pointless and awkward, and πάρος (Reiske, later accepted by Murray, cf. A. *Ag.* 1057 app. crit.) 'in front of me' seems likely. Unhallowed footprints are to be burnt off the ground, apparently by dashing the torch upon them, so that the priestess may tread her path safely through.

871. νόμον . . . ἀποδοῦσαι: apparently 'when you have paid to the gods my prescribed dues of service'.

872. ἐφέστιον: proleptic with κομίζετε.

873. Taken as a parenthetic question inside another question this is considerably harsher than the parallels usually cited, e.g. *Hipp.* 685, *Tro.* 299, *Bacch.* 649, and it has of course no connexion with the τίς πόθεν εἰς ἀνδρῶν; type with a double interrog. like 1543. 1579 is different again, since there each question is syntactically separate. The peculiarity of the present instance lies in the form of the outer question τί τἀμὰ θεσπ.; 'what of my oracles?' (probably a colloquialism). I believe Wecklein to be right in printing the line without marks of parenthesis, as it were 'What of how my oracles stand?', and in quoting as a near parallel Cic. *Off.* 2. 7. 25 'quid censemus . . . Dionysium quo cruciatu timoris angi solitum?' though there is still no equivalent of the τί; = what of?

875. Not a very accurate summary of the 'divinations' as quoted 531 ff., especially as the εἴδωλον–μίμημα was only removed subsequently, but Theonoe's knowledge extends to these later developments.

877. 'Know *of* your return home or *whether* you will stay here' (presumably a euphemism for death or dungeon) is a strange sentence, less for the change of construction than for the phrase οἶσθα νόστον in the sense of 'be sure of returning'. Pearson quotes *Hec.* 1266 πῶς οἶσθα μορφῆς τῆς ἐμῆς μετάστασιν of a future event; but to have foreknowledge of an apparently preposterous phenomenon is not the same as to feel sure of the fulfilment of an ordinary one. If the line is to stand I should prefer to take it as an omission of the first εἴτε of two (S. *OT* 517 λόγοισιν εἴτ' ἔργοισιν et al. saep.) and a zeugma in μενεῖς—whether you will [achieve] a home-coming or stay here. Herwerden's εἰ σ' αὐτοῦ μένει is tempting, in the 'I know thee who thou art' construction, with a deliberate suggestion of oxymoron in νόστον οἴκαδε and αὐτοῦ μένει. But the statement of two alternative possibilities is more closely in keeping with the sense of the following.

878–9. Theonoe's inside knowledge of the gods' counsels and motives is startling; here epic, of course, would transfer the scene to Olympus and describe the council, with the speeches of the two goddesses before the President.

885–6. With the MS. reading Ἑλένης οὕνεκ' is meaningless, and Cypris would be afraid of being found out purchasing the beauty-prize (τὸ κάλλος) by the bargain of a marriage—but of course what Helen's return from Egypt would expose was that the bargain had never been honoured. Pierson's ἀνονήτοις gives this sense: 'with a marriage that so far as Helen was concerned proved idle', though Ἑλένης οὕνεκ' is still a feeble phrase. Pearson, taking his cue from Herwerden, would read Ἑλένης οὐκ ἐπ' ὠνητοῖς γάμοις 'by Helen's hand which could not be bought' (was not available for bargain). Jackson, p. 208, proposes μηδὲ πριαμένη φάνῃ τὸ κάλλος Ἑλένης οὐκ ἐν ὠνητοῖς γάμος, 'lest it be seen that to her who purchased the prize of beauty the hand of Helen was one of things not to be bought'—ingenious but somewhat tortuous, especially in the divorce of πριαμένη from φάνῃ in the construction. No very satisfactory solution is available, and it may be best to acquiesce in the Oxford text as it stands.

887. τέλος δ' ἐφ' ἡμῖν: 'The decision rests with me whether to . . . speak out and destroy you or . . . save you by keeping silence.'

Perhaps, in English-style punctuation, better without a comma after ἡμῖν! See Introd., pp. xii–xiii.

890–1. κρύψασ' ὁμαίμον', sc. σ' ἐνθάδ' ὄντα from 888. προστάσσει pres. because she is under standing orders to tell him whenever it occurs. **τάδε** is defined by ὅταν κτλ. A short pause follows the sentence.

892–3. As her attendants (872) were dismissed and the order would be unintelligible to anyone inside the palace, she must be requesting (v. on 435) one of the Chorus, who are after all in the palace service (191), to act as messenger. It is natural therefore that no one is anxious to move, and with Helen's dramatic intervention the request lapses. Italie refers to *Ion* 1266 for an ignored command. There is no objective justification for Wilamowitz's rejection of these faultless lines (*Anal. Eur.*, p. 243, followed by Zuntz, *Fond. Hardt, Entretiens*, vol. vi, pp. 206 ff.) as an actor's interpolation aimed at titillating the spectators' emotions. Theonoe's first impulse is to think of the danger her silence would put her in (no idle fear, as the sequel shows), and these words add urgency to Helen's supplication. It is less likely that we should suppose her deliberately inviting by these words (never seriously meant) the pleading of the two whose lives depend upon her decision. In any case the dramatic impact is considerable, and if the lines were deleted something else would have to be put in their place; but it would be a dubious principle of textual criticism to make such a lacuna just in order to save our preconceived notion of Theonoe's psychology or Eur.'s way of registering moral seriousness. See Introd., pp. xiv–xv.

894 ff. We are now launched upon a scene which has the external form of an agon before a presiding arbiter, but actually presents two convergent pleas for the same decision, while the main interest lies in the decision itself and the arbiter's own analysis of her reasons.

897. ἐπ' ἀκμῆς + infin. = in acute danger of . . . , ἀκμή being, by the original metaphor ἐπὶ ξυροῦ ἀκμῆς *Il.* 10. 173, the edge on which such an issue is balanced, then the verge of castastrophe without mention of an alternative.

898: leg. μοι with Seidler, 'do not, I beg'; the gen. is hard to construe and the corruption easy.

901. προδῷς: 'sacrifice.'

902. χάριτας: 'tokens of gratitude' which he would pay for the favour of her information.

903–8. The question of how much to delete here is variously answered. Not, surely, the whole passage, because ἡμᾶς δὲ 909 follows the regular formula: general truth, particular application. But how much general truth? 905 must obviously go; apart from its form, it merely makes the argument unintelligible. 909 *could* follow directly on 904, but τἀλλότρια μὴ ᾽χειν (better than σχεῖν) is appropriate to the present situation—to 'hold on to what belongs to others' or try to take it from them by force. The deduction from a rather more grandiose general maxim than the situation seems to warrant is common form in these rhetorical displays.

904. ἐς ἁρπαγάς: adverbial, 'by way of unlawful seizure', cf. ἐς ἀμβολάς 1297.

909. μακαρίως seems an odd exaggeration: 'by blessed intervention'? Badham's καιρίως is often accepted.

914–15. ἤδη with imper. conveys 'wait no longer to . . .', sometimes with the implication 'it is time you did'. The practical application ends as often with a final twist towards generalization of the moral (τὰ τῶν πέλας 915).

917–18. δοκῶ μέν: assenting to the positive alternative. The formula is only used when the speaker is so certain of his case that he can afford to be ostentatiously fair-minded and throw in that provisional μέν. πλέον νέμειν: 'defer to' (Pearson); thus μᾶλλον is not redundant.

919. ἡγουμένη: 'believing in' (the gods) (s.v. LS III. 3), like νομίζω.

920–1. Reading uncertain. δώσεις δίκην LP, as corr. by Triclinius, means 'make amends', which will not do. σώσεις δίκην (which is what L originally wrote) contrasts with τὸ δίκαιον . . . διαφθερεῖς. Where διαφθείρειν is set against σῴζειν with such abstracts it is normally a question of 'losing' or 'keeping intact' one's *own* convictions or nature or qualities, cf. *Hipp.* 389, *Hec.* 598, A. *Ag.* 932, infr. 1004. Theonoe then might 'lose' her father's sense of justice as a precious inheritance, but she can only 'keep intact' her brother's δίκη by straining the analogy. Reiske's δώσεις χάριν, 'indulge', is suggested by 999–1001, where Theonoe is clearly recalling this plea.

922–3. Clark's emendation of **923** (cf. supr. 14) restores sense and shape to the line. μέν . . . δέ: 'while . . . yet not': it is the δέ-clause which is αἰσχρόν when considered in the light of the μέν.

924 ff. After all this we need a practical recapitulation: Then save my husband's life so that his wife can be restored to him (cf. 912–13), and incidentally bring to an end my troubles here.

924. The τ᾽ is altogether inadequate, after a full stop and in a changed construction, to bear the weight that Murray's interpretation (app. crit.) would put upon it. Nor can δ᾽ be substituted: 'non enim hic δέ, sed ἀλλά dicendum erat'—Hermann. His lacuna, in which Menelaus' safety and recovery of Helen are requested, is essential. οἷσιν ἔγκειμαι κακοῖς: best taken with ἀθλίαν, 'wretched, such miseries am I in'. The plain relative is here subordinate exclamatory, like ὅσος and οἷος, cf. on 74.

925. πάρεργον: so long as τῆς τύχης is taken as Helen's fortunes it is very difficult to give the word any appropriate meaning: 'granting this interlude in my sad lot'—Pearson; 'a trifling set-off to my fortunes'—LS. But the word always implies something incidental to the main issue—and the clue to the main issue, τῆς τύχης, here must lie in the lacuna before 924, the salvation of Menelaus and his recovery of Helen. In assuring this Theonoe would also be 'granting an extra grace of fortune' by delivering Helen from her present troubles, of undeserved odium and dependence on Egyptian charity (927-35).

930. κλύοντες εἰσιδόντες: the asyndeton requires the same tense in both parts., and this is one of several instances where κλύων and κλύειν have aor. force, cf. κλύειν, ἀκοῦσαι, A. *Cho.* 5.

931. φίλων: i.e. of my husband.

932. 'They will restore me to virtue' for the more obvious 'they will give me back my good name'.

933. ἐδνώσομαι Hermann, 'betroth', provide with ἕδνα in the post-Homeric sense, for ἐδώσομαι LP, corrected by the later hand in P to ἐκδώσομαι 'give in marriage'. Both words are normally used of the father.

934. ἀλητείαν: here as *Ion* 576 'beggary' in the sense of dependence on the charity of others, with no implication of 'wandering'.

935. ὄντων χρημάτων: the suggestion is of rich possessions stored on the spot, as in the Homeric great houses. In Hdt.'s version these treasures had been carried off by the eloping pair, and their safe custody (in Egypt) was an important part of the story.

936. κατεσφάγη, especially after θανών, cannot be right, but there is no need to assume grave corruption or a lacuna. ἀγαπάω and ἀγαπάζω are used by Eur. only in the sense of rendering service to a loved corpse, so that either κατεστάλη (Reiske), or better κατεστάθη (H. D. Broadhead) would be possible: 'dead and laid [out] upon the bier.' But either word is rather ordinary to have been replaced by κατεσφάγη, and Schenkl's κατεφθάρη, adopted by Italie, gives more point here. 'If, dead, he had been consumed upon the pyre [i.e. if he had died at Troy], I should have rendered the service of tears to one far away; shall I, now that he is alive and safely back, have him taken from me?' The antithesis is dead body reduced to ashes far away/living man whole-and-sound present.

941-2. κλέος κάλλιστον ὅστις: cf. on 267, 271. The παιδὶ of LP is due to a misunderstanding of this construction; Stobaeus preserves the correct generalizing plural.

943. τοὺς τρόπους acc. of respect need not be emended. The gen. (τρόπων or τρόπου) taken with ἐς ταὐτὸν as 'field of reference' would be an alternative construction, cf. *Tro.* 1036.

944-6. L. Dindorf's attribution of these words to the Chorus is one of those superficially 'obvious' corrections which prevent further consideration of the tradition. (Cf. A. *Ag.* 489 ff.) LP are perfectly right: only Theonoe can speak these words. Both her silence and the Chorus's speech (at least in these terms) would be impossibly bad-mannered. The formal resemblance of this to the conventional 'law-court scene' of tragedy, with the brief choral comment to round off each of the two speeches, has led all editors to overlook the special conditions here. In other Euripidean scenes where two characters plead their cause before an authoritative third, the presiding arbiter opens the case by an official invitation to both to speak, cf. *Hec.* 1129, *Tro.* 911, *Phoen.* 452. In *Hcld.* 132 ff. the situation is rather different: Demophon demands from the Herald an explanation of his violent conduct towards suppliants and the Herald after a blustering close is reminded by the Chorus that there are two sides to every dispute and only one has been heard, whereupon Iolaus claims the right to speak in his turn. But there the Chorus has been taking an active part, before Demophon's arrival, in restraining the Herald and protecting Iolaus, and even then it does not itself request the second speech. In the present scene of the *Helen* there has been no formal opening of the case; Helen flings herself in to prevent the threatened action of Theonoe, and for the august prophetess to stand silent at the end and leave the Chorus to comment with a judicious air: 'Very moving, Helen, but I want to hear how Menelaus will plead for his life' would make a scene whose absurdity would be at once apparent on the stage. It is a mistake to foist these rigid conformities upon the poets.

944. οἰκτρὸν: 'a pitiful thing.'   ἐν μέσῳ λόγοι is a phrase used in a variety of meanings, which should not be lumped together: *Med.* 819 'words that intervene before the deed', supr. 630 and S. *El.* 1364 'the story of the intervening time', and here 'words put forth for consideration', the dative counterpart of ἐς μέσον φέρειν.

947–8. τλαίην: 'bring myself to.'   δακρῦσαι: an unexpected use of the trans., for which Hermann suggests *Il.* 22. 491 δεδάκρυνταί τε παρειαί as the model. ἄν four times in three lines in the emphasis of his rejection.

950–1. Σ *Il.* 1. 349, quoting a proverb: ἀριδάκρυες ἄνερες ἐσθλοί.

953. εὐδαιμονίας LP, εὐψυχίας Tyrwhitt, assuming εὐτυχίας as a middle link in the process of corruption, εὐανδρίας p, read by Wecklein, Grégoire on the grounds that εὐτυχίας could not possibly require a 'gloss' εὐδ. That is probably true, but it is difficult to see how εὐδ. could displace a word with the required sense except through εὐτ. from εὐψ. Possibly it was a misguided attempt to make the line scan. εὐανδ. is likely to be itself a conjecture, especially since there seems too little distinction between πρὸς ἀνδρὸς εὐγενοῦς and εὐανδρίας.

957. οὐ νῦν ... πολλάκις: not for the first time by a long way, cf. *Med.* 292 with Page's note.

961. πόθῳ is as difficult to account for as to emend, and should perhaps be obelized. Both μνῆμα and πόθῳ require the definition σοῦ πατρός, but to take this ἀπὸ κοινοῦ ('at the tomb of your father, whom I miss

so much', or 'in default of your father, at his tomb') is awkward.
τόδ' ἀμ. μν. would remove this, but τάδ', referring both back to ἃ and
forward, 'as follows', is too idiomatic to sacrifice. A part. with ἀμφί
= 'at' is not, *pace* Pearson, essential grammatically; ἀμφὶ μνῆμα
λέξω is a variant on, e.g, ἀμφὶ βωμοὺς εὔχου *Ion* 422. πεσών, πίτνων
are inappropriate to the tone of the speech; τόδε (Dindorf) would be
better.

965–8 are an explanation of the sense in which the appeal ἀπόδος is
meant: it is his daughter who now 'has power to act' (κυρία).   **οὔποτε**
+ fut.: 'you never will' because it is an impossibility, cf. *Alc.* 300.

970–4. To kill Trojan warriors for Helen's sake was to enrich Hades
by the gift of young bodies before their time (cf. *Alc.* 55), so that as
an honest merchant Hades should either return the price (μισθὸν)
he had been paid in full (the warriors alive), or at least ensure that
Menelaus retained possession of Helen.

973–4: v. app. crit. The γε is really better placed as in LP than in the
next line, since one does not want it too far separated from ἤ, 'or
at least . . .'; one could read ἀνάγκασόν γε πατρὸς εὐσεβοῦς and then
τἄμ' ἐμοὶ δοῦναι Pflugk in 974 (which the Budé text leaves unmetrical). The sense of κρείσσω must be 'going one better than . . .',
'more effective', because Proteus had not after all been able to
restore Menelaus to Helen. Hermann proposes ἀνάγκασόν γε μὴ εὐσεβοῦς πατρὸς / ἥσσω, certainly a more usual form of exhortation
and an intelligible corruption, but the special twist given here by
κρείσσω should perhaps not be sacrificed.

975. συλήσετε: you and your brother.

977. κεκλήμεθα: 'I am held fast', for the more prosaic κατείλημμαι.

985. τάφου κατ.: 'drip down the tomb.'

991–2. Grammatically there are two ways of taking this, but only
one makes sense. δραστήριος, in spite of the absence of a part.,
must be opposed to δακρύοις . . . τρεπόμενος, not to ἐλεινός. 'What
talk is this? I should have won more pity by taking to tears like a
woman than by this forceful line.' τί ταῦτα; is not a request for information which is then given by himself in the next words ('Why
this stern resolve?'—Jerram); it implies 'This is useless'. Cf. *Phoen.*
382. And δραστ. cannot be contrasted with ἐλ. as 'effective' with
'pitiful'; to be pitiful in the circumstances *was* to be effective; in
any case this sense of δραστ. belongs to inanimate objects like
φάρμακον or μηχανή, something which *works*; with human beings
it is rather 'active', 'energetic'. ἦν before a vowel in Eur., especially
late Eur., is not enough to make a line suspect, though indeed it
can often be easily emended, cf. *Alc.* 655 n., *Ion* 280 (οὖσ' is neater
grammar), here ἦ τᾶν.

993. δυσκλεῶς LP would have to mean 'in a manner to bring dis-
honour upon *me*', which in strict grammar is not unparalleled

(v. Jebb on S. OC 586), but the ambiguity would not be very happy when δυσκλεᾶ could so easily have avoided it. δυσκλεῶς γὰρ οὖν (Reiske) however, referring in the normal manner to the subject, would make good sense and sum up the whole argument better.

These lines, 991-5, have often been suspected of interpolation, and sometimes all, sometimes 991-2, deleted. They seem to me necessary to keep the balance of the whole speech. In dividing the arguments between Helen and Menelaus so as to make them complementary and a contrast in style, Eur. has made Helen's an appeal, Menelaus' a demand, for justice. The effect is to give Menelaus' a somewhat unattractive truculence, which should not be held against his 'character'; it is masculine rather. But to end the speech at 990 would be altogether too harshly defiant, as he half admits himself. Nor incidentally do I believe an interpolator would have ventured on that final paeonic rhythm in τρεπόμενος 991, which Eur. first allows to become almost a habit in this play (eight instances). See Introd., p. xxvii.

996. βραβεύειν in the peculiar circumstances of this scene is not to give a decision between two opposing speeches but to resolve her own dilemma and so pass judgement on the rightness or wrongness of both speeches.

997. ἅπασιν: i.e. all of us present here.

998-1008. I see no reason to change the MS. reading, kept by Murray, anywhere in this passage with the exception of Κύπρις for Χάρις 1006; whatever view be taken of the problem of the wife of Hephaestus in *Il.* 18 and *Od.* 8, such a syncretism was not one ordinarily accepted in the fifth century. φανήσομαι and φανήσεται 1001 would merely be slightly different ways of developing the argument. σῴζειν Μενέλεων 1004 should not have found favour; that sense would require σῶσαι (cf. 954, in contrast to 964) and 1005 must be referred to Menelaus since he is the subject of ὀνειδίζεις 1009. Here σῴζειν as well as ἔχουσα goes with τοῦτο, cf. on 920-1. ξυμβέβηκε 1007 seems to mean has 'never come to terms with', 'never made close accord with' (the hint of aloof distaste is kept carefully clear of the sort of ὕβρις with which Hippolytus challenged the goddess), and is more effective fitting syntactically into ἡ Κύπρις δ' ἐμοί than with a change of subject ξυμβέβηκα. The sense in which Cypris can συμβαίνειν with a mortal is then made explicit by the following line, which has often been laughed out of the text. It is seldom an easy matter to mark the point beyond which simplicity turns to comic naïvety; one kind of audience, or one individual, will draw it differently from another. Probably the unfortunate πειράσομαι is meant as no more than a modestly expressed personal choice. Certainly the sense is much clearer if the line is kept.

1002. For the shrine of Justice in the heart edd. compare the famous frag. 170 from Eur. *Antigone* οὐκ ἔστι Πειθοῦς ἱερὸν ἄλλο πλὴν λόγος, | καὶ βωμὸς αὐτῆς ἔστ᾽ ἐν ἀνθρώπου φύσει. It was from Nereus that Theonoe inherited her gift of prophecy (15), though one might have expected her sense of justice to come from the father's side.

1009. ὀνειδίζεις πατρί: this is so strong a way of describing 965 ff. that Wecklein–Pearson would read πατρός (with τύμβῳ). But the text is probably right, cf. τίσις and τοῖς τε νερτέροις 1013.

1010. ὅδ᾽: the following words (ἀδικοίημεν ἂν κτλ.); hence the absence of connecting particle.

1011. βλέπων: 'if he had been alive.'

1013–16. τίσις: 'sanction', requital. τῶνδ᾽: moral obligations and the failure to discharge them. It applies to the dead no less than to the living because though there is no [individual?] survival the mind retains everlasting consciousness after death by merging with immortal ether. Dindorf's rejection of these lines has found some favour, but their connexion with the context (Proteus is affected as well as Theonoe) is not difficult to see; it is their internal coherence as a statement of philosophy that is inadequate: how does a τίσις apply to a piece of consciousness floating in the ether? This is not quite the ordinary cliché of fifth-century Athenian philosophy, cf. the famous Potidaea inscription *IG* I². 945. 6 αἰθὴρ μὲν ψυχὰς ὑπεδέξατο, σώματα δὲ χθών which is echoed *Supp.* 532–6 and fr. 839. Nor does it go far as an anticipation of the Platonic doctrine of rewards and punishments after death and of the immortality of the soul (cf. ζῇ μὲν οὔ). Grégoire's view of it as 'la pièce essentielle de la tragédie' is an extravagance. It is a piece of high-toned but vague mysticism appropriate to Theonoe, who reasonably excuses herself from further elaboration by ὡς οὖν παραινῶ μὴ μακράν (1017) 'to keep my lecture short'. παραινέω of a superior being giving guidance or admonishment (*Hipp.* 1435, *Andr.* 1234, *HF* 847, 854) is usually more precisely advisory in sense, often with an infin., but this is near enough to need no emendation to περαίνω.

1021. ἐκ δυσσεβείας ὅσιον. The normal idiom would be ἐκ δυσσεβοῦς ὅσιον, cf. τυφλὸς ἐκ δεδορκότος S. *OT* 454, and I can find no other instance of the abstract with ἐκ instead of the personal. It was unfamiliar enough to send someone groping after sense with εὐσεβείας LP.

1022. Clearly much the simplest correction of the faulty rhythm of LP τὴν ἔξοδόν γ᾽ εὑρίσκετε would be τιν᾽ for τὴν, accepted by several edd., and there seems no cogent objection to the order of words, the type of caesura, or the use of γε for emphasis. 'For a way of escape you must find something yourselves.'

1024. ἄρχεσθε: 'begin with the gods.' The gods still need propitiating; there is no question of Theonoe's decision's having pre-ordained the course of events. The gods determine, in harmony or in dissonance, and mortals make their choices by their own ethical standards but for the granting of their aims are still dependent upon the favour of heaven; if their course is just (τῷ δικαίῳ neut.) there is 'hope of salvation' 1031.

Theonoe withdraws into the palace, and the new scene is introduced by Helen in three lines before it settles down to a long distichomythia. Thus the effect is of Menelaus asking questions or making tentative suggestions while the decisive answers come from Helen.

1033. Jackson, p. 154, neatly suggests τοὐνθένδε δ' εἰς ἓν τοὺς λόγους φέροντε χρή, thus supplying a δέ for the μέν 1032 and making κοινὴν more clearly a 'joint plan' of escape. But Helen is yielding precedence to Menelaus, which he accepts in ἄκουε δή νυν 1035, and the following exchange down to 1049 shows her leaving him to flounder on with his own suggestions. As for the μέν, probably the whole sentence 1032–4 is a single complex, with μέν as if μὲν γάρ, cf. infr. on 1441–2. κοινὴν ξυνάπτειν could mean simply they will both have parts to play and both escape.

1036. συνέθραψαι: 'have grown familiar with.'

1038. ὡς δή with fut. part. is as Denniston says (*GP* 230) 'almost always ironical, sceptical, or indignant in tone'. Here if there is any scepticism it is politely held in check.

1039. οἵτινες ... ἀνάσσουσ' is substituted for τῶν ἀνασσόντων, cf. S. *Aj.* 1050 ὃς κραίνει for τῷ κραίνοντι. ἀνάσσω 'be in charge of' the four-horse teams, a slightly less metaphorical use than κώπης ἄναξ, πέλτης ἄναξ.

1042. πεδίων βαρβάρου τε χθονός: hendiadys for the Egyptian plains.

1043. ἀδύνατον εἶπας: given to Helen by LP, but it means 'put like that it is clearly impossible'.

1044: cf. on 811.

1045–6: to be construed as if οὐ σιγῶσ' ἂν ἀνάσχοιτό σε μέλλοντα . . . .

1046. κτανεῖν and κτενεῖν being metrically indifferent sometimes appear as MS. variants. It seems reasonable then to make *OT* 967 conform to the otherwise strict Sophoclean usage, but Eur. has so many undoubted cases of μέλλω + aor. infin., in all senses of μέλλω, that it is hardly worth while to emend a few easy ones.

1050 ff. λέγεσθαι λόγῳ θανεῖν is unattractive, and spoils the effect of λόγῳ θανεῖν just below as a more pointed summary of the proposal. Murray's idea of a slightly teasing echo in 1052, with four words, as it were, in inverted commas, hardly does justice to the seriousness of the dilemma. Cobet's τεθνηκέναι is exactly appropriate in 1050. λέγειν ἕτοιμός εἰμι 1051–2 is an impossible anticipation of Helen's idea soon to be disclosed. εἰ δὲ κερδανῶ λέγων (Barnes) could easily be taken in the sense 'if there is anything to gain by the story', as if λόγῳ or λεγόμενος.

The Greek reluctance to risk ill-omened words is similarly illustrated by the careful bravado of Orestes over the device of λόγῳ θανεῖν S. *El.* 56–64. He too justifies the risk by κέρδος 61. It seems scarcely possible that these two passages should be independent of each other, and if not, then a close time-sequence is required. (Cf. Bruhn's *Einleitung* to the *Electra*, 1912, and *J. für kl. Phil., Suppbd.* xv. 306 ff.) Comparison of the two shows unmistakably the priority of the *Electra*, which elaborates and illustrates the idea as something new and interesting, whereas the *Helen* picks it up fleetingly as one might a notion already familiar to the audience. Helen (1053) then adds the idea (καὶ μὴν) of a female lament to move the listener. Whether any recent play had used the motif of a *feigned* lament we do not know, but for us the obvious reference is to Electra's urn-speech. Menelaus' comment 1055–6 refers to the whole idea, λόγος and θρῆνος, and is less Menelaus than a rather mischievous interpolation of Eur.: 'The idea isn't a very original one.' Other evidence, mostly of a formal nature, shows that the *Electra* is to be grouped with Soph.'s late plays, and 413 (now that Zuntz, *Pol. Plays of Eur.*, 64 ff., has restored the Euripidean *Electra* to its proper place in the metrical chronology) is a quite possible date for it; it can scarcely be earlier.

1054. πρός: the laments would be directed 'at' him.

1059–60. καὶ δή: 'suppose he agrees', in Eur. a not uncommon form of graphic parataxis instead of an if-clause, often with a perf., cf. *Med.* 386 καὶ δὴ τεθνᾶσι. **κενοταφοῦντ'**: dual.

1061. καθήσομαι: the middle is unparalleled, cf. 1068, 1375, and Heath's καθήσομεν (in the sing. sense) would be an easy emendation. But since Helen is obviously going to 'have it done' rather than do it herself the middle is appropriate, and could easily be uncommon. Cf. on 664.

1064. οὐδὲν φέρει: 'brings no gain', as if οὐδὲν συμφέρει. This is probably the right reading at *Supp.* 596, and there is no need to interpret σ' after κελεύει as ἐς with prodelision.

1069. καί with δεῖ μάλιστα, adding emphasis to the whole.

1071–2: i.e. if you can arrange a ship at anchor I will embark my men in disciplined hoplite rows.

1074. καὶ νεὼς δρόμος seems to have no construction; one cannot satisfactorily supply either πόμπιμος γένοιτο or γένοιτο (may there be a running of the ship = may the ship run fast). κούριος (Prinz) would supply the missing predicate; χἴλεως (Maas) would be simple palaeographically but there is no parallel for ἵλεως = οὔριος, and νεώς could have arisen as an intrusive gloss to explain δρόμος.

1076. πεπυσμένη with τοῦ: 'from whom will you claim to have heard?', the perf. part. with a verb of saying as 537.

1077. σοῦ comes the answer in a flash; Helen enjoys her neat point.

1079. ναυτικῶν ἐρειπίων: the gen. is hard to place. Not with ῥάκη.

LINES 1054–1106 135

since τάδ' ἀμφίβληστρα σώματος ῥάκη is an indivisible phrase; Pearson
compares Telephus fr. 697 πτώχ' ἀμφίβληστρα σώματος ῥάκη. Nor is
ῥάκη ἐρειπίων a likely phrase; one can say 'tatters of reputation'
(met.), but not so well 'tatters of wreckage'. Pearson's συμμάρτυρές
σοι would pick up the gen. in more orthodox grammar, but the fut. is
better, and I suspect the phrase must be accepted as it stands—these
rags will be confirmatory witness of shipwreck—even if any such
explanation as 'sc. μαρτυρίαν' is slightly unreal.

1081. ἐς καιρὸν ἦλθε: met., as *Tro.* 744. ῥάκη is the subject of this and
of ἀπώλλυτο, though if he is wearing sailcloth (v. on 422) the sense
must be 'your clothes' rather than what he actually has on. The
impf. of 'past danger or likelihood' (Goodwin, *MT* 38) would then
refer more to the inopportuneness (ἄκαιρα adv.) of the loss rather
than its actual occurrence: 'at the time it seemed inopportune loss.'

1087–9. Shorn locks, to be laid on the corpse if available, and black
clothes are for male and female alike the prescribed ritual of mourning, cf. *Alc.* 215–17. Only women tore the cheeks, as the male cheek
would be a tougher proposition.   **χροός:** the only possible construction is gen. after φόνιον, making bloody the skin. *Andr.* 1194
has τοξοσύνα φονίῳ πατρός, 'the bowmanship that killed your father',
which is easier to relate to such phrases as ὀλέθριοι φίλων (A. *Ag.*
1156), cf. αἱματηρὰ δωμάτων infr. 1104. The text had better be left,
since emendation is unrewarding: χερός (with ὄνυχα) is a mere makeshift. *Bacch.* 768 has another slightly redundant χροός at the end of
a sentence, oddly enough again in conjunction with παρηίδων.

1090. μέγας γὰρ: for *Helen* so to deform herself a vitally important
issue is required. (In *Or.* 128–9 we are back with the old familiar
Helen of tragedy.) The effect would be correspondingly apt to produce belief in Theoclymenus.   **ῥοπάς:** possible ways the scale
could tip. Hence we get, in 1092 ff., a special prayer and reminder
to the gods—in accordance too with Theonoe's advice 1024—at this
decisive moment in the action, cf. infr. on 1446 ff.

1093. πίτνεις with ἐν as *Alc.* 1059, a 'pregnant' use of the prep., moving
on to the next stage beyond the action expressed by the verb.

1100. παρασχοῦσ': 'making available', as in παρέχειν ἑαυτόν.

1104: v. supr. on 1089.

1105. μετρία: cf. *Med.* 630 εἰ δ' ἅλις ἔλθοι Κύπρις, οὐκ ἄλλα θεὸς εὔχαρις
οὕτως.

1106. οὐκ ἄλλως λέγω: 'I don't deny it' (Denniston on *El.* 1035), cf.
Hec. 302, *Or.* 709.

Stasimon **1107–64,** the first proper stasimon of the play.

Eur. cannot here let the Chorus comment on the intrigue which is
just beginning to take shape, so, ignoring the more hopeful turn of
events on the stage, they summon the nightingale to help them sing
a threnody for the woes of Helen and the women of Troy, though

this is then deflected into the woes brought by the Phantom-Helen, first upon the Trojans and still more the Greeks, and then upon Helen herself in the execration she suffered from her countrymen. The first stanza ends with the picture of Paris sailing with (the supposed) Helen to Troy, the second with Menelaus sailing back with her and blown out of his course. The third reflects upon the unpredictability of mortal lot, but the illustration is not the ἀνέλπιστοι τύχαι of recent events but simply the strange eclipse of Helen's good name, daughter of Zeus as she was. The fourth assails the useless folly of using war to settle disputes when negotiation could have served, with the result that many are dead, Troy burnt, and Helen suffering.

(a) **1107–36.**

1107	σὲ τὰν ἐναύλοις ὑπὸ δενδροκόμοις	1. ⌣ – ⌣ – – ⌣ ⌣ – ⌣ ⌣ –
1122	πολλοὶ δ' Ἀχαιῶν δορὶ καὶ πετρίναις	
	μουσεῖα καὶ θάκους ἐνί-	x̄ – ⌣ – x̄ – ⌣ –
	ριπαῖσιν ἐκπνεύσαντες Ἅι-	
	-ζουσαν ἀναβοάσω,	– ⌣ ⌢ ⌣ – – ‖
	δαν μέλεον ἔχουσιν,	
	σὲ τὰν ἀοιδοτάταν	2. ⌣ – ⌣ – ⌣ ⌣ –
	ταλαιφρόνων ἀλόχων	
1110	ὄρνιθα μελῳδὸν ἀηδόνα δακρυόεσσαν	x̄ – ⌣ ⌣ – ⌣ ⌣ – ⌣ ⌣
		⌢ ⌣ – – ‖
1124	κείραντες ἔθειραν, ἄνυμφα δὲ μέλαθρα	
	κεῖται·	
	ἔλθ' ὦ διὰ ξουθᾶν γενύων ἐλελιζο-	
	μένα	3. x̄ – ⌣ – x̄ – ⌢ – ⌢ – ⌢ –
	πολλοὺς δὲ πυρσεύσας φλογερὸν σέλας	
	ἀμφιρύταν	
	θρήνων ἐμοὶ ξυνεργός,	x̄ – ⌣ – ⌣ – ⌣ ‖
	Εὔβοιαν εἷλ' Ἀχαιῶν	
	Ἑλένας μελέας πόνους	4. ⌣ ⌣ – ⌣ ⌣ – ⌣ –
	μονόκωπος ἀνήρ, πέτραις	
	τὸν Ἰλιάδων τ' ἀει-	⌣ – ⌣ ⌣ – ⌣ –
	Καφηρίσιν ἐμβαλὼν	
1115	-δούσᾳ δακρυόεντα πότμον	– x̄ – ⌣ ⌣ – ⌣ ⌢
1131	Αἰγαίαις τ' ἐνάλοις δόλιον	
	Ἀχαιῶν ὑπὸ λόγχαις,	⌣ – – ⌣ ⌣ – – ‖
	ἀκταῖς ἀστέρα λάμψας.	
	ὅτ' ἔδραμε ῥόθια πεδία βαρβάρῳ	
	πλάτᾳ,	5. ⌣ ⌢ ⌣ ⌢ ⌣ ⌢ ⌣ – ⌣ – ⌣ –
	ἀλίμενα δ' ὄρεα Μάλεα βαρβάρου	
	στολᾶς	

ὅτ᾽ ἔμολεν ἔμολε μέλεα Πριαμίδαις
ἄγων   ∪ ⌣ ∪ ⌣ ∪ ⌣ ∪ ⌣ ∪ – ∪ –
ὅτ᾽ ἔσυτο πατρίδος ἀποπρὸ χειμάτων
πνοᾷ

Λακεδαίμονος ἄπο λέχεα   6. ∪ ∪ – ∪ ∪ ⌣ ∪ –
γέρας οὐ γέρας ἀλλ᾽ ἔριν

1120 σέθεν ὦ Ἑλένα Πάρις αἰνόγαμος   ∪ ∪ – ∪ ∪ – ∪ ∪ – ∪ ∪ –
1136 Δαναῶν Μενέλας ἐπὶ ναυσὶν ἄγων

πομπαῖσιν Ἀφροδίτας.   🗙 – ∪ ⏖ ∪ – –
εἴδωλον ἱερὸν Ἥρας.

1107–36. The stanza is composed with much metrical art. Period-ends are not always certain; as given here 5 and 6 are unverifiable. The first three are in a kind of near-dactylo-epitrite:

1. iamb. + hemiepes **d d,** as it were iambelegus with link-anceps omitted. Sophocles uses the same opening for a dact.-epit. stanza *Tr.* 94 ὃν αἰόλα νὺξ ἐναριζομένα.

iamb. dim. + ithyphallic with resolved second long.

2. enoplian ∪ **s d,** link-anceps, praxillean (like ἀντιτύπᾳ δ᾽ ἐπὶ γᾷ πέσε τανταλωθείς) with the fourth long resolved so that the close echoes that of period 1. (On no account should this effect be lost by emending to ἄνυμφα μέλαθρα δέ to keep the rhythm dactylic.)

3. iamb., link-anceps, **d d d,** a prolongation of the iambelegus.

iamb. dim. cat., i.e. ithyph. preceded by link-anceps. The relation of period 3 to period 1 is obvious.

4. enoplian ∧ **d d s.**

telesillean + glyc. with resolved final long, pher.

5. two iamb. trims. much resolved.

6. enoplian ∧ **d d s** = opening of 4, resolved in the strophe only, enoplian in form of anap. dim.

iamb. dim. cat. = close of 3.

All periods take off in rising metre.

1108–10. μουσεῖα καὶ θάκους: hendiadys = halls of the muse where you sit, i.e. your sitting and singing there turns the leafy coverts into halls of song. We might have supposed Ar. in ἐπιφυλλίδες . . . χελιδόνων μουσεῖα *Ran.* 92–93 to be parodying this passage but for Σ's quotation from *Alcmene* (fr. 88 corr. Meineke) in which Eur. calls thick ivy ἀηδόνων μουσεῖα. The close similarity of phrasing in this half-stanza to *Av.* 210 ff., two years before, shows how much of a cliché this kind of description had become.

1111. ξουθᾶν: the strange ambiguity of this attribute between colour, sound, and movement haunts the word from its first appearance in Mycenaean as the name of one of a yoke of oxen on a tablet from Knossos (KN Ch 900). At first a brown ox might seem to us self-evident, contrasted with a κελαινός and an οἶνοψ, black and red,

until we also find an αἰόλος and a πόδαργος and wonder if it was
'nimble', since the same sort of ambiguity affects *all* these words
and cannot even be shown to determine itself chronologically (v.
Denniston–Page on A. *Ag.* 1142). We formulate our colour-percep-
tions as on a matt colour-card, whereas the Greeks 'saw' their
coloured world in terms of light-vibrations which could also pass
over into sound-vibrations and quick movement. When it is a question of translation, however, it must be said that whereas there is no
context which *demands* for ξουθός the sense of a colour-attribute,
the choice of objects to which it is applied—the nightingale, the
nightingale's throat, the bee, the wings of a bee, of an eagle, of the
Dioscuri, the winds—is almost unintelligible unless the common
attribute is felt primarily as the quick, throbbing vibrato of sound,
for which we have no single apposite word. So here : 'come trilling
through your vibrant throat to join with me in lament.'

1113 πόνους and **1115** πόνον both as objects of ἀειδούσᾳ make a scarcely
tolerable repetition, though it is uncertain which, if either, should
be emended. Badham's πότμον for πόνον is acceptable if scanned in
the same way, as a glyconic ending in resolution ; but it was intended,
and adopted, to make the line a hipponactean ending ⏑ – ⏕, with
antistrophe ἐνάλοισιν ἀκταῖς | δόλιον ἀστ. λαμ. As the pherecratean
1116 begins Ἀχαιῶν, this would give anceps iuxta anceps and therefore period-end between the two cola, with the pherecratean then
forming a single period by itself instead of a catalectic clausula in
the usual way. The arrangement given here (with πόνον or πότμον
and Hermann's adjustment of antistrophe) is much to be preferred.

1117–18. LP (v. app. crit.) wrote out these two trimeters in four lines,
with ὅς at the beginning of each pair. Since obviously Πρ. ἄγων
must lead into 1119, Triclinius transposed the second two before
the first two. But 'who came to the plains' unqualified is meaningless; also at least the first ὅς must be replaced by ὅτ' to give some
construction. Edd. have followed two main lines of restoration : (1)
adjustment of Triclinius's version by punctuation : ὅτ' ἔμολεν ἔμολε,
πέδια βαρβάρῳ πλάτᾳ ὃς ἔδραμε ῥόθια, μέλεα Πρ. ἄγων κτλ., 'when *he*
came, who sped over the surging plains, bringing . . .'. But doubts
arise over an involved piece of word-order which at two points
depends for its intelligibility somehow upon punctuation made
audible in *sung* verse full of rapid resolution. Herwerden's ΠΟΛΙΑ
for ΠΕΔΙΑ, leaving ῥόθια as the substantive ('grey surge' instead
of 'surging plains') would make things slightly easier. (2) The
Schultze–Murray version, later (*GV* 454) adopted by Wilamowitz too,
which assumes that only the first three words of each trimeter
needed transposing, this displacement having occurred earlier than
the splitting up into four cola ; ὅς then becomes ὅτε in both. The
second is much more likely, perhaps with a comma after πλάτᾳ

instead of after ἔμολε, so that the second ὅτε is simply anaphora rather than subordinate to the first. So: 'when there sped on barbarian oar over the surging plains, when there came, came bringing from Lacedaemon you, O Helen, as a bride baneful to the sons of Priam, Paris of fatal marriage, under Aphrodite's escort.'

1122 ff. After the Trojans, the Greeks: many perished at Troy, and many (1126) did Nauplius drown off Euboea. The second Ἀχαιῶν 1127 would be an otiose repetition if taken with πολλοὺς as edd. recommend. It must go with μονόκωπος ἀνήρ, a solitary rower, one of the Greeks themselves—it is this that adds bitterness to the tragedy.

1123. πετρίναις ῥιπαῖσιν: the occasional rock lofted by a Homeric hero is oddly generalized.

1124. The Dorian gen. plur. (so rare in drama) ταλαινᾶν might seem a temptingly easy escape from the unmetrical τάλαιναν but for the necessity it imposes of pronouncing ἀοιδοτάταν choriambic (ᾠδοτάταν) 1109. While the ᾠδή of ordinary Attic is used fairly freely by Soph. and Eur. alongside ἀοιδά, ᾠδός for ἀοιδός occurs only once in tragedy (*Hcld.* 488 in dialogue), and the form is very improbable in this highly poetic use of the superlative of ἀοιδός adjectival. Triclinius's τάλαιναν τῶν gives a rather improbable transferred epithet, and though metrically possible as an aeolochoriambic heptasyll. ∪ – ⏑ – ∪ ∪ – is an obvious makeshift fill-up. ⟨ὧν⟩ would import an extremely rare use of the possessive ὅς, ἑός referring to a plural subject, for which the grammarian Apollonius in the second century A.D. censured Hesiod (*Erg.* 58) and Callimachus (cf. fr. 471Pf.). ταλαντάτων (Wecklein) or ταλαιφρόνων would fill the gap.

1126. For the Nauplius episode see on 767. The later use of a lighthouse to *warn off* from a dangerous coast is liable to confuse our picture here; to a Greek such a shore-beacon meant a harbour. Apparently in this version Nauplius rowed out alone (the distances are formidable), and when he saw the Greek ships approaching lit his prepared beacon on a rocky headland of S. Euboea. The construction of πυρσεύσας with both an internal (φλόγ. σέλας) and a direct (ἀμφ. Εὔβ.) object recalls the troubles of 866. Italie compares *Ion* 495 χορούς στείβουσι στάδια. With the punctuation here given it is most natural to take Αἰγ. τ' ἐν. ἀκταῖς as well as πέτραις Καφηρίσιν as dat. after ἐμβαλών, 'dashing them on the Capherean rocks and the headlands of the Aegean sea by the light of his treacherous star'; if it is a local dat. with λάμψας as Pearson takes it the τ' would be better deleted (so Herwerden), 'making to shine over the headlands'. δόλιον ἀστέρα λάμψας = 'flashing his treacherous star' is again an unexpected acc. with a verb which is usually intrans.; Verrall's ἀνάψας, 'kindling his treacherous star', would be less repetitive of the earlier phrase.

1133–6 are unintelligible without a subject. Of the Greeks who did not die at Troy, some were drowned off Euboea, another group, the followers of Menelaus, were driven off course by a storm which swept them away from Greece and sent them wandering along harbourless coasts unable to land. With this group we return to the figure of Helen, whose phantom they carried. Wilamowitz's Μενέλας for νεφέλαν 1135 is the simplest solution, with commas deleted; the position of Μενέλας then balances the similar late-placed Πάρις of the strophe. Hermann's Μάλεα for the unsuitable μέλεα recalls the stormy cape of *Od.* 3. 287. **βαρβάρου στολᾶς** must be taken with γέρας, and the hyperbaton and involved order of the MSS. may be defended as part of the elaborate responsion of strophe and antistrophe (see the metrical scheme) with βαρβάρῳ πλάτᾳ / βαρβάρου στολᾶς, ὅτ᾽ ἔμολεν / ὅτ᾽ ἔσυτο, Ἑλένα / Μενέλας, Ἀφροδίτας / Ἥρας. 'And inhospitable were the cliffs of Malea when there ran before the storm-gusts away from his own country Menelaus carrying on his ships the prize of a barbarian's foray that was no prize but a quarrel with the Greeks, Hera's sacred Phantom.'

(*b*) **1137–64.**

1137	ὅ τι θεὸς ἢ μὴ θεὸς ἢ τὸ μέσον	1. ∪◡̆∪‒ ‒∪∪‒∪∪‒
1151	ἄφρονες ὅσοι τὰς ἀρετὰς πολέμῳ	
	τίς φησ᾽ ἐρευνήσας βροτῶν λόγχαισί τ᾽ ἀλκαίου δορὸς	⊼‒∪‒⊼‒∪‒
1140	μακρότατον πέρας εὑρεῖν ὃς τὰ θεῶν ἐσορᾷ	‒∪∪‒∪∪‒⊼‒∪∪‒∪∪‒
1154	κτᾶσθε, πόνους ἀμαθῶς θνατῶν καταπαυόμενοι·	
	δεῦρο καὶ αὖθις ἐκεῖσε καὶ πάλιν ἀντιλόγοις	‒∪∪‒∪∪‒∪‒∪∪‒∪∪
	εἰ γὰρ ἅμιλλα κρινεῖ νιν αἵματος, οὔποτ᾽ ἔρις	
	πηδῶντ᾽ ἀνελπίστοις τύχαις; λείψει κατ᾽ ἀνθρώπων πόλεις·	⊼‒∪‒⊼‒∪‒
	σὺ Διὸς ἔφυς, ὦ Ἑλένα, θυγάτηρ· ᾇ Πριαμίδος γᾶς ἔλαχον θαλάμους,	2. ⌣◡̆∪‒ ‒∪∪‒∪∪‒
1145 1159	πτανὸς γὰρ ἐν κόλποις σε Λή- ἐξὸν διορθῶσαι λόγοις	⊼‒∪‒⊼‒∪‒
	-δας ἐτέκνωσε πατήρ. σὰν ἔριν ὦ Ἑλένα.	‒∪∪‒∪∪‒
	κᾆτ᾽ ἰαχήθης καθ᾽ Ἑλλανίαν νῦν δ᾽ οἱ μὲν Ἅιδᾳ μέλονται κάτω,	3. ⊼‒∪‒‒∪‒‒∪‒
	ἄδικος ἄπιστος ἄθεος· οὐδ᾽ ἔχω μαθεῖν τείχεα δέ, φλογμὸς ὥστε Διός, ἐπέσυ- το φλόξ,	⌣◡̆∪‒∪◡̆∪⌣⌣∪⌣⌣∪‒

τί τὸ σαφές, ὅ τι ποτ' ἐν βροτοῖς   ∪ ⌣̄ ∪ ⌣̄ ∪ ⏞ ∪ –
ἐπὶ δὲ πάθεα πάθεσι φέρεις

1150 τῶν θεῶν ἔπος ἀλαθὲς ηὗρον.   – ∪ – ⌣̄ ∪ – ∪ – –
1164 ἀθλία συμφοραῖς ἐλειναῖς.

1137–64. Though without any verifiable period-close, this pair falls clearly into three major periods, of which the first two are dactylo-epitrite with units of **d d** (hemiepes) and iambic (epitrite) metra and dimeters, and the third pure iambic with more resolution and syncopation. Both 1 and 2 open with the same colon as the first pair (1107) but with resolved first long. 1140 and 1141 are both 'choerileans', dactylo-epitrite compounds **d d ◡ d d.**

1137 ff. 'As for what is god, or not god, or something in between, which of mortals after searching can claim to have found the distant end of this quest, when he sees the things of the gods leaping hither and thither and back again in contradictory unexpected turns of fortune?' The thought seems to be that in so vast and apparently chaotic a field as human fortunes one might have expected to find signs of divine ordering there, if anywhere, where the gods' own being was involved; but Helen, a daughter of Zeus, has been exe-crated throughout all Greece, and the Chorus has given up hope of determining [where certainty lies in these matters?]. Here text, sense required, and metre are all uncertain.

1137. This dubiety seems to me more limited to a particular issue than edd. would have it. The Chorus is not asking 'what god is or what he is not' (Pearson) with τὸ μέσον added to round off the concept ('everything about god'), which would be a large and singularly irrelevant question here. They are wondering about the distinction between divine, mortal, and mixed, θεόσυτος ἢ βρότειος ἢ κεκραμένη A. *PV* 116. Helen as the offspring of Zeus and Leda seems a dis-tinguished example of the third category but has been quite peculiarly subject to extreme vicissitudes.

1147–50: v. app. crit. Hermann's restoration of 1147 is deservedly accepted by most edd., 'and then you were cried out upon in Greek lands for a wicked woman . . . ', but after that I have no idea what Eur. really said here, and the text as given merely rejects what I feel to be two impossibilities: (1) the construction οὐδ' ἔχω τί τὸ σαφὲς ὅ τι ποτ' ἐν βροτοῖς (? 'I do not grasp what the truth [is], what-ever [it is] among mortals'); one can say οὐκ ἔχω λέγειν, or οὐκ ἔχω τί χρὴ λέγειν, or οὐκ ἔχω τί φῶ, but not, I should have thought, οὐκ ἔχω τί τὸ σαφές, even if the further ὅ τι ποτ' could be explained as in 74 supr., nor even with the mitigating ἔτι for ὅ τι. (2) τὸ τῶν θεῶν ἔπος as 'the word of the gods' or 'the Word of God'. If ἔπος simply means 'pronouncement', a sudden burst of confidence in, e.g., oracles as against mantic would still be surprising here. There seems in fact very little to encourage the ⟨δ'⟩ which isolates this line in contrast to the previous one.

The text here given is Herwerden's extraction from the tangle 1148 ἀδίκως προδότης ἄπιστος ἄδικος ἄθεος οὐδ' ἔχω, and then along Kirchhoff's lines for 1149–50, assuming (for want of better evidence) that the beginning of 1164 gives a true lead metrically. His ἀμφὶ θεῶν would certainly be easier, but possibly τῶν θεῶν might be kept as objective gen. 'pronouncement about the gods'. 'I cannot determine where certainty lies as to what word current among mortals about the gods I have ever found true.' But the whole of 1147–50 is locus difficillimus necdum expeditus.

1151–64. The text of this stanza is also full of uncertainties. The words of LP 1152–4 are very neatly transposed by Murray into the required iambic dimeter and choerilean, and the only trouble is to account for the strange behaviour of the tradition in rearranging this so drastically in what is still not an obvious prose-order. Of attempts to adjust the words by minor modifications, only Wilamowitz's (GV 456) need be considered (Wecklein, Pearson, and Italie all print unmetrical versions): κτᾶσθε δορὸς ἀλκαίου τε λόγχαις καταπαυόμενοι πόνους θνατῶν ἀμαθῶς – ⌣̆⌣ – – – – ⌣ – | – ⌣ ⌣ – ⌣ ⌣ – ⌣ – – – ⌣ ⌣ –. The division of λόγχαις between two cola and the contraction in θνα. are not serious objections. More troublesome is the sense: should ἀπαθῶς 'painlessly' be kept, or emended (very easily) to ἀμαθῶς 'ignorantly'? If the former, οὐ or μή must be fitted in somehow, 'instead of ending mortal troubles by painless means'; I can see no metrical solution to this. With ἀμαθῶς, καταπαυόμενοι must mean 'clumsily trying to end the troubles of men', and the preceding τε might be better removed (easily in Murray's version with λόγχαισιν) so that λόγχαις can be taken with καταπαυόμενοι instead of with κτᾶσθε.

1155. νιν: generally explained as 'them' = πόνους, but A. Y. Campbell gets a more natural phrase by making it anticipate ἔριν : 'if the contest of blood is to settle it, never will strife cease among the cities of men.'

1158: no further emendation is required, certainly not, as most edd., Πριαμίδαι, since the Greek dead are as much or more in mind here. The subject (men who so foolishly insist on fighting out their quarrels) is perfectly intelligible from the context. 'By strife they won as their lot chambers of Trojan earth' (probably a direct reminiscence of the unforgettable θήκας Ἰλιάδος γᾶς A. Ag. 453) 'when they might have settled by argument the strife over you, O Helen.'

1162. (app. crit.) φλογμὸς ὥστε Διός 'like the bolt of Zeus' is usually accepted here.

1163. φέρεις: 'the personal pronoun is often omitted in Greek, though emphasis appears to require it, cf. A. Eum. 84'—Pearson.

1164. Nauck's ἐλεινοῖς (better ἐλεωαῖς) gives metrical correspondence at the end of the clausula; the earlier dat. adjective then becomes hopelessly redundant.

For the sentiment of this stanza cf. *Supp.* 748–9. The date 412 must not be over-pressed, nor can the stanza be made into the moral of this play. See Introd. p. xii.

1165 ff. Enter from the left Theoclymenus and attendants carrying hunting-gear with hounds on the leash (cf. 153–4). This clutter is quickly got out of the way by sending them through the doors (1169–70). The king greets his father's tomb, explaining with slightly naïve effect why it is to be found so near the palace-front. It takes the place, for dramaturgical reasons, of the usual statues of the θεοὶ πατρῷοι which are often greeted by stage-characters.

1168. προσεννέπει: is this the only instance in drama of ὅδε in the nom. used of himself by the speaker with a third person of the verb? MSS. sometimes vacillate: v. *Phoen.* 1760 and *El.* 44, where the variant recorded in L ἥσχυν(α) ἐν εὐνῇ should probably be adopted. Pearson refers to S. *Aj.* 864, which is, however, different, since there is no ὅδε and all the pride of Ajax is concentrated in the line. Possibly Eur. intends Theoclymenus to be pompous here, but the remark is really no more than a device for introducing himself to the spectators, and Lenting may be right in demanding προσεννέπω—unless Nauck's ὧδε παῖς is adopted (cf. on 9), in which case the third person is appropriate.

1171–3. πόλλ' in effect = πολλάκις, contrasted with καὶ νῦν 1173. δή emphatic, at the end of the line, cf. 134, Denn. *GP* 227. Murray's question-mark 1172 would make this line a direct quotation from the λοιδορία he has addressed to himself. But a question hardly seems compatible with οὐ ... τι, a very strong form of neg.: 'we are utterly failing to punish wrongdoers with death.' The γάρ instead of the hypotactic ὡς adds a touch of staccato emphasis. φανερόν almost 'as large as life'.

1177. διαπεπραγμένα: *fait accompli*.

1180 ff. χαλᾶτε κλῆθρα: the king bangs imperiously on the door of the σκηνή, which flies open, and to the ὀπαδοί who appear he gives orders to open the stables (ἱππικὰς φάτνας) and bring out his chariot-team. The visible stage-doors are to be imagined as opening on to a palace-courtyard, somewhere within which (as in *Bacch.*) are the stables. As the servants disappear to do his bidding, Theoclymenus sees Helen (οὓς 1184 ceremonial plur.) coming to the doorway, and calls after them to cancel his order. Once the simplicity of the stage-setting is grasped, the need for emendation in 1180 disappears. (Cf. *Bacch.* 509 ἱππικαῖς φάτναις.) λύειν 'unfasten' is used for 'open' by an easy transference, cf. frag. 1003 λῦε πηκτὰ δωμάτων, with Pollux's comment τῷ ἀνοίγειν ταὐτὸν τὸ λύειν.

1182. πόνου γ᾽ ἔκατι: it will not be for want of effort on his part if she escapes.

1192. 'is your heart broken?', a middle use of the transitive ψυχὴν διέφθαρκε Med. 226. Helen has startlingly changed her mask and dress.

1193. Cf. *Andr.* 56 and 64. Ar.'s sharp ear caught the turn of speech as a tragic (probably Euripidean) cliché, cf. *Vesp.* 1297, *Thesm.* 582.

1195. συμφορᾶς: partitive after interrog. τῷ;

1196. πῶς φράσω; her feigned sorrow and her real reluctance to speak the ill-omened words coincide. This immensely long stichomythia gives the maximum opportunity for such double play, with the audience on the alert to pick up the points.

1197-8. Either of these lines separately is a possible response to 1196. Together they are less happy, and not much improved by the insertion of δ'. That 1197 is spoken aside, or even 'half aside' (Pearson), is excluded by σοῖς. It also spoils the reaction of surprise in πῶς οἶσθα; 1198 is essential for the sequel, but a lacuna before it could only be filled by a pointless repetition of the news in 1196. The break in stichomythia, added to the slightly uncomfortable shape of 1197 (either χαίρων or εὐτυχῶν, with τάδ᾽, would made it easier), suggests that Hartung's excision of this line is the best solution. If so, it must have been interpolated by someone (presumably an actor) anxious to work in an expression of ambivalent feeling.

1199. The lie direct is faintly shocking where it involves Theonoe, but in 1370-3 we find the priestess herself preferring it to mere prevarication.

1201. ἐς κόρακας—ἐς τὴν πατρίδα (Wecklein). Lenting's οἱ σφ' supplies the missing object. The γὰρ here is difficult to pin down—Denniston, *GP* 94-95, must be pondered, but I cannot agree with his conclusion that δ' ἄρ' (Dobree, Pearson) should be accepted here. This example comes nearest to supporting *Cyc.* 261 as a use of γάρ with opt. almost as = εἰ γάρ. Wecklein suggests that γὰρ 'explains' the tone of voice in ἥκει, but the tone ought to be ambiguous, and in any case whether a mere tone would be so treated, when the word itself was quite neutral, seems doubtful. Perhaps γὰρ mainly reinforces the assent given by ἥκει.

1203-4. The nadir of Menelaus' fortunes as a tragic hero!

1209: the normal Greek feeling about drowning at sea, which left the victim without a tomb for the receipt of honour.

1214. ποῦ λιπὼν: the participle is the focus of the question. 'Where did he leave the wreckage of his ship before coming here?'

1215. The curse is a convenient way of evading an answer. The subject of ὄλοιτο is 'the wreck', but since as it stands the phrase is ambiguous she exempts Menelaus as a precaution.

1216. 'Menelaus *has* perished!'—a mild rebuke for the inappropriate future bearing of ὄλοιτο.

1225. Many emendations have been proposed for this meaningless line. The neatest is perhaps A. Y. Campbell's φίλος γάρ ἐστ' ἔθ' ὅσπερ ἦν ποτ' ἐνθάδ' ὤν.

1226. This is generally punctuated as a question: 'I take it you are genuinely weeping for this calamity?' but ὀρθῶς varies in meaning according to its construction, and the sense 'really', 'sincerely' is confined to cases with adjectives or nouns (οἱ ὀρθῶς φίλοι, etc., or with a copula ὀρθῶς ἦσθα πατήρ Alc. 636). Used with a verb it means 'properly' (supr. 322), or 'rightly' (ὀρθῶς ἔλεξας, etc.), or 'naturally' (= εἰκότως), and it is this last sense it must have here: 'you are quite right to weep...', cf. IT 542 (the μὲν implies reservations about other points unspecified). The response of Helen is thus a complete misfit, and two lines must have fallen out here; 1226a could be many things—for instance something like 'with such feelings as I shall never forget'. 1227 answers—perhaps by way of another question—some more direct objection, on the lines of 'How am I to know that this man's tale is true?—It's so easy, isn't it, to fool your sister?—No indeed'. γοῦν is sarcastic: 'quasi facile sit', Hermann. λαθεῖν is a fairly certain emendation; it is impossible to imagine any form of 1226b which would have made sense of θανεῖν.

1228. πῶς οὖν: cf. 1266, passing on to a new point.

1229-30. After all the efforts of editors and translators to paper over the senselessness of these remarks, it took the keen eye of J. Jackson (pp. 25-27) to observe the simple truth that 1229 must be said by the king to Helen. 1230 was then originally her reply: πιστὴ γάρ εἰμι τῷ πόσει φεύγουσά σε, and when the two lines were transposed suffered 'correction' to πιστὴ γὰρ ἔσσι σῷ ... με. The whole exchange thus falls into place:

'Well, now—will you be continuing to make this tomb your home?'
'Ah, you see, in avoiding you I am being faithful to my husband.'
'Why do you tantalize me instead of letting the dead be?'
'I won't tantalize you any more. Begin the wedding arrangements.'

The use of 'detached' ἀλλ' οὐκέτ', with punctuation following, is found at El. 577, Or. 1109, and (again with κερτομεῖν, as Jackson observes) Cyc. 688. Each time it is a finite verb which is negatived, not—as might seem easier in English idiom—an adjective or participle. Mr. E. W. Handley points out to me that Ar. Ach. 471 ἀλλ' οὐκέτ', ἀλλ' ἄπειμι (i.e. οὐκέτ' ἀπολῶ σε) suggests that Dicaeopolis was echoing a favourite Euripidean turn.

1232. τάδε first subject of ἦλθεν, then object of αἰνῶ. The attempt to keep ἦλθες by emending χρόνια to χρονία, as Barnes, is misguided.

1233. The familiar idiom is turned off from second to first person plural.

1236. With μεθίημι Pearson compares IT 298, Hec. 338, IA 1101, Ar. Av. 946 codd. νεῖκος τὸ σόν: my quarrel with you.

1242. The particular expertise of the Pelopid house is left un-explained.

1246. πῶς δαί; 'Then how *do* you bury them?' The colloquial particle δαί, used after interrogatives, should not be banished from Eur., though it is often confused with δή and δ' αὖ.

1247. ἐξορμίζομεν: 'take out to sea.'

1249. ὅδ' for οὐκ is confirmed by the king's change of address in the next line.

1250. μὲν: so far so good.

1252. θανόντας ἐν πόντῳ together.

1253. ὡς ἂν ἔχῃ with a partitive gen. would be common enough; ὡς ἂν ᾖ is more surprising, especially with the part. παρούσης.

1254. ταύτης χάριν goes with an implied 'I do not grudge it'.

1259. γε μὲν δὴ: the particles, as Denniston says, grammatically pick up from 1257.

1260. τῶνδ' if right must mean 'such as you imply', such as are not δυσγενῆ. Bruhn's ὧδ' is tempting.

1264. τάδ' refers back to ὅπλα, not to be taken with ἃ as = 'what'.

1265. βλαστήματα: fruit and flowers.

1267. Oar-masters = 'rowers' simply, as again in 1413. Cf. on 1039.

1271. The only relevant sense for λύματ' would be the blood from the victim, and 'pollution' seems too strong a word for that. θύματ', 'the sacrifices' (Hermann), surely makes the logical sense required.

1272. γενήσεται: 'shall be provided', like ἔσται 1262.

1276. ὡς λέγεις: '*from* what you say.'

1277. ἐν εὐσεβεῖ = εὐσεβές, cf. 1227 ἐν εὐμαρεῖ.   **κλέπτειν:** 'to cheat the dead of their due.'

1278. ἴτω in a self-contained sentence always = 'be it so', 'very well, then'.   **πρὸς ἡμῶν** [ἐστίν].

1282. ἀχλαινίας: in effect = δυσχλαινίας (*Hec.* 240, cf. on 416 supr.) rather than 'nakedness'.

1286–7. Pearson suggests τρύχου (med.) τοσοῦτον, but the following δ' must then also be excised; it cannot be pushed through on the plea that δὲ = γάρ. It seems more probable that (as Badham) there is a lacuna from the caesura of one line to that of the next. Possibly 1286 ended in πόσιν and gave rise to the intolerably weak πόσις of 1287. πάλιν (Reiske) or ποτε (Dobree) would leave the required generalization.

1288. σὸν ἔργον: different from 830, since here the reference is to the words which follow, as the asyndeton shows. The commonest construction in such cases is to complete the sense with an infin., but cf. the independent sentence, *Bacch.* 849, Διόνυσε, νῦν σὸν ἔργον . . . τεισώμεθ' αὐτόν. 'Now you know your task, young lady: you must be content with the husband you have here . . .' (all the words are loaded with double meaning).

1297. οὐκ ἐς ἀμβολάς: v. on 904. 'I shall not keep you waiting for kindnesses.'

1300. οἵων: agreeing with ἡμῶν, not neuter. Exeunt all three.

1301–68. Second Stasimon.

After the long-drawn-out, dangerous, and successful setting of the trap, this pause in the action is dramatically appropriate before it is finally sprung in a triumphant demonstration of Greek wits and barbarian foolishness. Any lyrical comment by the Chorus on the situation would be an enfeebling anti-climax. Instead it launches upon a strange ode, perhaps reflecting something of the style of contemporary dithyramb, about Demeter sorrowing for her ravished daughter and making the earth, and thus men and gods, suffer for her loss. The last stanza is particularly corrupt, but there can be no doubt that it proposed a tenuous link between this story and Helen's (ὦ παῖ 1356), who is held to have incurred the wrath of the goddess by some offence no longer decipherable. Zeus had devised an appeasement by offering to the goddess the instruments of her cult, but Helen had ignored the power of this cult—and to this owed her sufferings? There is no room for more than a hint, and indeed more would only have emphasized the complete irrelevance of this motif to all the rest of the play, and more particularly to the impending triumph of Helen now. The ode is in fact introduced for its own sake.

This is the most explicit indication we have in literature of the process of syncretism at work in fifth-century Greece, but there is of course no reason to credit Eur. himself with any deliberate innovation other than of detail. (Cf. Nilsson, *Gesch. gr. Rel.* i. 687–8.) Demeter, the corn-goddess, the mother of life, and mother of Kore, is one form of the Mediterranean Mother-goddess who appears in more orgiastic cults as Cybele, as Rhea, as the Great Mother, the Mountain (or Idaean) Mother, the Mother of the Gods, or of all gods and all men (*Hom. Hymn* xiv). Here the wildness of the Phrygian cults and the din of their ecstatic dances is grafted on to the myth of the sorrowing Demeter; the different elements fuse perhaps less easily in poetry than in worship. P. Maas, *Epidaurische Hymnen* II, 3, draws attention to some similarities in subject and phrasing in the hymn to the Mother of the Gods inscribed (faultily) on stone *IG* iv. i². 131 and attributed by him to Telesilla, who lived in the first half of the fifth century. Page, however *PMG* 935), puts this 'not earlier than the fourth century' B.C., while Koster, *Ned. Ak. Letterkunde* 25. 4 (1962), has good arguments for the time of Hadrian; he assumes an older poem as the source for both Eur. and this later hymn.

1301–68.

1301   ὀρεία ποτὲ δρομάδι κώ-   ∪ − − ∪ ∪ ⌣̆ ∪ −

1319   δρομαίων δ' ὅτε πολυπλανή-

-λῳ μάτηρ θεῶν ἐσύθη $- \underline{\times} - \cup - \cup \cup - \|$
-των μάτηρ ἔπαυσε πόνων

ἀν' ὑλάεντα νάπη $\cup - - \cup \cup -$
ματεύουσ' ἀπόνους

ποτάμιόν τε χεῦμ' ὑδάτων $\widetilde{\cup} \cup - \cup - \cup \cup -$
θυγατρὸς ἁρπαγὰς δολίους,

1305 βαρύβρομόν τε κῦμ' ἅλιον $\widetilde{\cup} \cup - \cup - \cup \cup -$
1323 χιονοθρέμμον' ἄγ' ἐπέρασ'

πόθῳ τᾶς ἀποιχομένας $\underline{\cup} - - \underline{\cup} - \cup \cup -$
'Ιδαιᾶν Νυμφᾶν σκοπιάν·

ἀρρήτου κούρας. $\underline{\times} - \ddot{-} - - \|$
ῥίπτει δ' ἐν πένθει

κρόταλα δὲ βρόμια διαπρύσιον $\cup \cup \cup \cup \cup \cup \cup \cup \cup \cup$
πέτρινα κατὰ δρία πολυνιφέα·

ἱέντα κέλαδον ἀνεβόα, $\triangleleft(?) - \cup \cup \cup \widetilde{\cup} \cup -$
βροτοῖσι δ' ἄχλοα πεδία γᾶς

1310 θηρῶν ὅτε ζυγίους $\underline{\times} - \cup - \cup \cup -$
1327a ⟨ . . . . ⟩

ζεύξασα θεὰ σατίνας $\underline{\times} - \underline{\cup} - \cup \cup -$
οὐ καρπίζουσ' ἀρότοις,

τὰν ἁρπασθεῖσαν κυκλίων $- \underline{\times} - \underline{\times} - \cup \cup -$
λαῶν δὲ φθείρει γενεάν.

χορῶν ἔξω παρθενίων $\underline{\cup} - - \underline{\times} - \cup \cup -$
ποίμναις δ' οὐχ ἵει θαλερὰς

1313a ⟨ . . . . $- \underline{\times} - \underline{\times} - \cup \cup -$
1331 βοσκὰς εὐφύλλων ἑλίκων,

. . . . ⟩ ἀελλόποδες $\cup \cup - \cup \cup - \cup \widetilde{\cup}$
πόλεων δ' ἀπέλειπε βίος,

1315 ἁ μὲν τόξοις Ἄρτεμις, ἁ δ' $- \underline{\times} - \triangledown - \cup \cup -$
1333 οὐδ' ἦσαν θεῶν θυσίαι

ἔγχει Γοργῶπις πάνοπλος. $- \underline{\times} - \underline{\times} - \cup \cup \underset{\smile}{\smile} \|$
βωμοῖς τ' ἄφλεκτοι πέλανοι.

αὐγάζων δ' ἐξ οὐρανίων $- \underline{\times} - \underline{\times} - \cup \cup -$
πηγὰς δ' ἀμπαύει δροσερὰς

1317a ⟨Ζεὺς ὁ παντάρχας ἑδράνων⟩ $- \underline{\cup} - \underline{\times} - \cup \cup -$
1336 λευκῶν ἐκβάλλειν ὑδάτων

ἄλλαν μοῖραν ἔκραινε. $- \underline{\times} - \cup \cup - -$
πένθει παιδὸς ἀλάστῳ.

1337 ἐπεὶ δ' ἔπαυσ' εἰλαπίνας   ⏕ – ⏑ – – ⏑ ⏑ –
1353 ὧν οὐ θέμις ⟨σ'⟩ οὐδ' ὁσία

    θεοῖς βροτείῳ τε γένει,   ⏑ – ⏑ – – ⏑ ⏑ –
    . . . .

    Ζεὺς μειλίσσων στυγίους   × – × – ⏑ ⏑ –
    μῆνιν δ' εἶχες μεγάλας

1340 Ματρὸς ὀργὰς ἐνέπει·   – ⏑ – – ⏑ ⏑ –
1356 Ματρὸς ὦ παῖ θυσίας

    Βᾶτε σεμναὶ Χάριτες,   – ⏑ – – ⏑ ⏑ ⌣ ‖
    οὐ σεβίζουσα θεᾶς.

    ἴτε τὰν περὶ παρθένῳ   ⏑ ⏑ – ⏑ ⏑ – ⏑ –
    μέγα τοι δύναται νεβρῶν

    Δηὼ θυμωσαμέναν   × – ◡ – ⏑ ⏑ –
    παμποίκιλοι στολίδες

    λυπᾶν· · · · · · · · ἀλαλᾷ   – × – × – ⏑ ⏑ –
    κισσοῦ τε στεφθεῖσα χλόα

1345 Μοῦσαί θ' ὕμνοισι χορῶν.   × – ◡ – ⏑ ⏑ –
1361 νάρθηκας εἰς ἱερούς,

    χαλκοῦ δ' αὐδὰν χθονίαν   × – × – ⏑ ⏑ –
    ῥόμβου θ' εἱλισσομένα

    τύπανά τ' ἔλαβε βυρσοτενῆ   ⌒⌒ ⏑ ⌒⌒ ⏑ – ⏑ ⏑ –
    κύκλιος ἔνοσις αἰθεριά,

    καλλίστα τότε πρῶτα μακά-   – × – ⏑ ⏑ – ⏑ ⌒⌒
    βακχεύουσά τ' ἔθειρα Βρομί-

    -ρων Κύπρις· γέλασεν δὲ θεὰ̣   – ⏕ – ⏑ ⏑ – ⏑ – ‖
    -ῳ καὶ παννυχίδες θεᾶς.

1350 δέξατό τ' ἐς χέρας   – ⏑ ⏑ – ⏑ –
1366 . . . .

    βαρύβρομον αὐλὸν   ⏑ – ⏑ ⏑ – – ‖
    . . . .

    τερφθεῖσ' ἀλαλαγμῷ   × – ⏑ ⏑ – –
    μορφᾷ μόνον ηὔχεις.

The dominant rhythm in both pairs is the 'choriambic dimeter' (a loose name for an indivisible aeolic colon akin to the glyconic and like it an octasyllable, i.e. the equivalent of dimeter-length), of the form cultivated by Eur. above all. In this the choriamb ends the phrase, being preceded by four syllables of which two are long and two anceps, most commonly in the form – × – × – ⏑ ⏑ – (anceps is never iuxta anceps). Anceps is more often long than short. The first long (1304–5 = 1322–3) may be resolved, or both the first and the second, in which case anceps is normally also short, giving six short syllables as in 1347 = 1363. Sometimes there is an inversion of the first two syllables, × – instead of –×, as in 1313 χορῶν = 1330 ποίμναις. Much rarer is the double inversion found in 1337–8 = 1353 × – ∪ –, where the first four syllables are in fact treated as an iambic metron. (Mixed iambo-choriambic is familiar from Anacreon.) These choriambic dimeters are varied as usual by an occasional glyconic, as in 1348–9 = 1364–5, of which the first has the final resolution, in quick synaphea with the following colon, which is so often found in later Eur. I have shown the opening colon 1301 = 1319 as glyconic too, since Eur. is more apt to play with resolution of the frame of the choriamb in glyconics than in choriambic dimeters. In 1308–9 = 1326–7 I have deliberately left the resolutions ambiguous, since it is uncertain whether these two lines are iambic dimeters, as they are generally taken to be, or whether the aeolic rhythm continued throughout and they should be shown as resolved glyconics. (The manner of the dance-steps could quite well distinguish the two if required.) Similarly ἀρρήτου κούρας is often 'dochmiac', but × – – × – would be unrelated to anything in the context, while if the middle syllable were a contracted double-short we should have a reizianum like the final double clausula 1351–2 = 1368. Among the dimeters Eur. characteristically interspersed some shorter lengths, especially the heptasyllable × –× – ∪ ∪ –, a headless version of the commonest form of dimeter, and in 1340–1 = 1356–7 – ∪ – – ∪ ∪ – as a headless echo of the octasyllables at the opening of the stanza; there are also hexasyllables × – – ∪ ∪ – 1303 = 1320 and – ∪ ∪ – ∪ – 1350. Finally, there is the (nameless) colon ∪ ∪ – ∪ ∪ – ∪ – 1342, and, with final resolution, 1332. This is not a variant of the glyconic, for the Athenian poets never use the two short syllables in responsion with other forms of 'aeolic base', as the Lesbians do.

Periods are peculiarly difficult to determine in this type of metre, and I have merely indicated where pause, and where synaphea, is unmistakable.

For the text and interpretation of this ode I am deeply indebted to P. Maas, *Epidaurische Hymnen* II, 3 Anh. The sequence of thought—or of pictures—is unintelligible if we try to take it as a chronological sequence of events in a narrative. Lyric has its own way of decorating or interpreting a story, and always takes for granted that its hearers know the story already. Eur. is not here concerned with Persephone in the underworld, or with her seasonal release, but with the grief and wrath of Demeter and the potency of the rites (of the Great Mother) which could bring relief and distraction even in the frenzy of that search. At the beginning of the first stanza and the beginning of the second the goddess is running on

foot, but in between, at 1308 ff., she is carrying on the search from
her car drawn by lions, to the ear-splitting din of those noisy instruments which we find her accepting from Cypris and the Graces at
the end of the third stanza. As a further complication, the intervention of Artemis and Athena 1315-16 belongs to the time of the Rape
itself.

Maas's reconstruction of the text starts from the assumption that
ζεύξασα θεὰ of codd. 1311 is to be kept. The dative so frequently
accepted from Hermann has to wait for its verb for five lines and
then take it across densely packed constructions. Moreover, it is
clear from L's reading 1317 αὐγάζων δ' ἐξ οὐρανίων that the lacuna
should follow, not precede, that line. θεᾷ is then left stranded, unless
we emend the unmetrical μετὰ κούραν to a verb: Wilamowitz
μεταθῦσαν ('stormed after'), but the picture of Artemis and Athena
in full armour as outriders beside the Mother's chariot is unfamiliar
and unwelcome, and the whole construction with acc. σατίνας and
dat. θεᾷ is dubious. A quite different approach (Wecklein, Pearson)
is to create a verb in 1310, θηρῶντό τε, with subject ζεύξασαι θεαὶ (or
θεᾷ) κοῦραι ἀελλόποδες, leaving μέτα as a preposition in anastrophe or
adverbially in tmesis. But apart from the general awkwardness of
the maiden goddesses (superfluously ἀελλόποδες) in a car with the
mother goddess on foot, or else acting as harnessing attendants,
the word ζυγίους has after ζεύξασαι no meaning at all without θηρῶν.
We are left with ζεύξασα θεὰ, the Mother at the centre of the picture,
yoking lions to her car; and to supply her with a verb (sought? called
upon?) we need a further lacuna after 1313, at the end of which μετὰ
κούραν has survived as a corrupt backwash. This also leaves room
for explanation of the activities of Artemis and Athena (see below).
In the antistrophe the placing of the lacuna enables us to keep λαῶν
δὲ 1329 to stylistic advantage.

1301. ὀρεία μάτηρ θεῶν must be taken together, the 'Mountain Mother
of the Gods'. ὀρεία μάτηρ is far too common a title (cf. *Hipp.* 144)
to allow the adj. to be taken predicatively, as if 'over the mountains
the goddess rushed through the glens' could mean 'rushed over
hill and dale'.

1307. ἀρρήτου: Κούρα or Κόρη was her usual appellation, to avoid the
ill-omened name Φερσέφασσα—spoken by Helen 175!

1308. κρόταλα: the 'noisy cymbals' were of bronze, cf. *Cyc.* 205 κρόταλα
χαλκοῦ τυμπάνων τ' ἀράγματα. There can be no question of giving
κρόταλα precedence over the rest of the orchestra, as if the Mother
had been limited to this instrument at first and only acquired the
kettledrums and flute later. All belong together, as in *Hom. Hymn*
xiv. 3 ᾗ κροτάλων τυπάνων τ' ἰαχὴ σύν τε βρόμος αὐλῶν, and any hearer
accustomed to lyric technique would know that the mention of
one implied the rest; so in the third stanza Cypris takes the 'rumbling

voice of bronze [the κρόταλα] and the drums stretched with hide',
and the Mother laughs and receives in her hands 'the deep-sounding
flute, being delighted with the throbbing din'. In 1362 it is the
ῥόμβος, the bull-roarer, which is whirled aloft; each time a different
element in the whole is picked out.

1314–16. The stress laid upon the *weapons* of Artemis and Athena shows
that Eur. is alluding to a version of the Rape in which these two were
playing with Kore and the Oceanids (*Hom. Hymn Dem.* 424, even
if the line is spurious there) and at first rushed to the help of the
maiden, threatening her ravisher, but were prevented from fighting
by Zeus, who aimed a thunderbolt between the combatants. Such
a version appears in Claudian's *De Raptu Proserpinae* ii. 205 ff., and
only by assuming general knowledge of the story in the fifth century
can we make sense of the allusions here; for instance, the 'different'
outcome devised by Zeus would have no meaning if all the goddesses
were doing was to 'hunt' Kore or accompany the Mother. Whatever
preceded ἀελλόποδες must have developed from ἁρπασθεῖσαν in 1312,
perhaps by way of a relative ('whom they rushed to defend'?).

1317a. Wilamowitz *GV* 215, *exempli gratia*.

1319 ff. Variously emended. Maas points out that *Hom. Hymn Dem.*
351 uses παύω intransitively, and Allen–Halliday defend it by other
examples. ἀπόνους is an ingenious coinage of Verrall's, adapted
to the epithets (*amens*, etc.) of Latin versions of the story; Wecklein's
φίλας is innocuous if dull. γ' has no meaning; no one has done better
than Murray's suggestion in app. crit.

1325. ῥίπτει intrans. as *Alc.* 897, where this passage should have been
added to my note.

1327a–8. [she makes . . .]: the exact sense and the construction of
ἀρότοις cannot be determined.

1330 ff. 'For the flocks she made to grow no fresh green sustenance of
leafy tendrils, and cities were dying out; there were no sacrifices to
the gods nor burnt offerings at the altars.' πόλεων rather than πολέων
(Triclinius, possibly from a collated source). 'The life of many [sheep,
to be supplied out of ποίμναις] was failing' would be a curious phrase
to use of beasts, and 'many' is debilitating. The devastation of the
countryside has its effect on the towns, and on the gods. Maas
objects that cities were not yet founded, but such a thought would
have troubled Eur. no more than it did the author of the *Hymn to
Demeter* 93 ἐπ' ἀνθρώπων πόλιας καὶ πίονα ἔργα.

1336. ἐκβάλλειν intrans., with ἀμπαύει 'stops from flowing'.

1337. πένθει ἀλάστῳ (L. Dindorf). Even though ἀλάστωρ can be used
of a female, the Homeric expression (*Il.* 24. 105, *Od.* 1. 342) is much
more probable.

1341 ff. Aphrodite, the Graces, and the Muses are to be the first minis-
trants of the ἀλαλά or ἀλαλαγμός, the wild clamour of voice and

instrument which accompanied the progresses of the Phrygian goddess. The assertion is deliberate, as a part of the assimilation of the Mountain Mother to Demeter, and on no account to be weakened by emending ἀλαλᾷ 1344 to make room for ἐξαλλάξατ'. The line of emendation in 1342–4 is uncertain, though the τὰν of codd. is certainly neater than the double dat.; we then need an imper. – ᴗ –.

1353 ff. Helen's offence is lost beyond recovery. It appears in the first two lines to be a sin of commission over a sacrifice, then in the next three one of omission; probably the second of these—*neglect* of the Mother's ceremonies—is right. Then at the end, after two lines of gibberish, she 'gloried only in beauty'. (*Hipp.* 144–7, compared by edd., is simple both in itself and in its relevance to Phaedra's sick, unhappy state.) ἔχεις 1355 is in no need of correction metrically, but the tense of Musgrave's εἶχες would at least put the Mother's wrath into the past, with less apparent irrelevance to the present situation, and tally better than ἔσχες (a less easy corruption) with ηὔχεις 1368.

1358 ff. The cult as here described is indistinguishable from that of the βάκχαι: the same assimilation appears in *Bacch.* 78 ff.   1358 δύναται must be right for the unmetrical δύνανται. It is the simplest form of σχῆμα Πινδαρικόν, in which a singular verb (most often ἦν or γίγνεται) precedes a fem. plur. subject.

1369. Does Menelaus enter here with Helen? If not, he must appear with the δμῶες in the wake of the king 1390, introduced, by implication only, in ὁ ξένος. There is no clear indication either way, since of course the first person plurals in this speech prove nothing at all. Quite possibly the answer was given in the lacuna after 1373, where a ὅδε or ὡς ὁρᾶτε, or a 'you will see when he arrives' would be conclusive. It is a great pity that we cannot be certain, since the answer must affect our judgement of the degree of comic effect intended in this play. It is a poor start to the heroic phase of Menelaus' actions if he has to be dumbly present while Helen points out at some length his improved appearance, his clean clothes, his armour, and his high hopes.

1370 ff. συνεκκλέπτουσα: 'helping to conceal' my husband's presence by deceiving Theoclymenus, cf. *El.* 364 'helps to conceal the truth about' [your marriage], and ἐκκλέπτειν *Ion* 946, S. *Phil.* 55 with Jebb's note.   πόσιν παρόντα does duty twice over.   ἱστορουμένη passive: 'being questioned.'

1372. ἐν χθονὶ suspectum, as Murray says, and should perhaps be obelized. It cannot be taken with αὐγὰς εἰσορᾶν as if it were ἐπὶ χθονί, on the surface of the earth, but could only mean 'inside the earth', dead and ἐν Ἅιδου.

1374–5 The γάρ of 1375 obviously explains a preceding statement, but no emendation of 1374, with or without lacuna, has produced a satisfactory one. ἐν τύχῃ is meaningless and δῆτα quite out of line with its normal use (Denn. *GP* 279); ἀνήρπασε if literal implies an act of which the γάρ-sentence is a redundant repetition (still more so with τεύχη for τύχῃ), and if metaphorical (Wecklein κάλλιστα δ' ἐκ τοῦδ' ἥρπασεν τύχην) is dubious Greek, however natural 'snatched the chance' may sound in English or German. I suspect the truth is to be found in 'versum ut lacunae explendae causa fictum delet Dindorf': κάλλιστα (= fine things) δῆτ' ἀνήρπασεν ἐν τύχῃ πόσις, absence of caesura, intrusive double-short and all, is about the level of the average interpolator (cf. on 1512).

1375. ἔμελλεν: 'was supposed to' according to Theoclymenus' intentions. The 'arms' are dealt with in two stages: (1) those which he carries, shield and spear, on left arm and in right hand, (2) those which he wears as defensive armour (προύργου ἐς ἀλκὴν)—corselet, greaves, helmet. ὡς δή with pres. part. 1378 of the pretence, ὡς with fut. part. 1380–1 of his own confident intention.

1376. πόρπαξ, as Miss Lorimer explains *BSA* 42 (1947), 76 and 130, is *at this date* the same as ὄχανον or ὀχάνη, the band through which the arm was thrust to hold the shield. The sense here makes this quite clear.

1378. συνεκπονῶν: together with Helen, as in 1406.

1381. θήσων: στήσων would of course be more usual, but in view of A. *Sept.* 277 need not be substituted here.

1382 ff. In the MS. text (v. app. crit.) the part. ἀμείψας tails very awkwardly after the main sentence and requires δ'. Helen here turns to her own contribution.   χρόνια: so long waited for.

1387–8. προσποιούμεθα does not fit ideally with σε εὔνουν (claim you as a well-wisher?) and still less with the acc. and inf. connected by τε (and that you should keep a curb on your lips); the zeugma is hardly tolerable. Probably the termination of the next line has been contagious. Rauchenstein's προσπίτνω μένειν is a possibility.

This perfunctory appeal to the Chorus, with its mere hint of winning their goodwill by holding out the prospect of their own freedom, contrasts with the long development of the same theme in *IT* 1056–77. It is dropped completely in the sequel.

1390. Enter Theoclymenus with a row of slaves bearing gifts [and Menelaus in full panoply?]. The slaves 'file off' (ἐφεξῆς) stage to the right.

1394–5. τε . . . τε where we should use a disjunctive; Italie compares 321.

1397. χάρισιν ἐκπεπληγμένην: 'distraught by fond memories'— Pearson.

1398. οὐ παρόνθ': though he is missing. It has been objected that the dead are always 'absent', and οὐ παροῦσ' is proposed with reference to 1394. But it is of course the corpse that is missing; the assumption that its presence would have led to yet heavier lamentation would not seem strange to a Greek. In any case οὐ παρόνθ' is essential for the rather simple irony that the audience is meant to enjoy.

1400. πρῶτα carries through to νυμφικὰς ὁμιλίας 'my first marriage, when I was a maiden bride'.

1409. δή τιν' ἐς τύχην: all this is leading somewhere. τύχην, ostensibly non-committal, is meant to be understood by Theoclymenus politely, by the others exultingly, as 'good fortune'.

1412. σύ: to an attendant.

1416–17. The point of this precaution is seen in the Messenger's speech 1550 ff.

1418. 'Blessings on you—and on my plans!'   ὄναιο, 'may you profit', can be used either with a gen. (profit *from*) or absolutely, as an expression of gratitude. Here it is the second—and out of it sc. ὀναίμην in the first sense with τῶν ἐμῶν βουλευμάτων.

1419. χρόα: 'cheeks', as *Andr.* 111.

1421–2. It is difficult to get any double meaning out of 1422, or any meaning at all out of the last three words. No suggested emendation helps much, and 1420 connects perfectly with 1423. It looks as though an interpolator had decided that a conventional piece of impiety should be added, and countered, not very successfully.

1424. τῆς τύχης: all I need is for it to turn out well—for Helen 'my plan', for Theoclymenus 'this marriage'.

1426. 'To love my friends is not a thing I have waited till now to learn.'

1427. The last thing Helen wants! βούλη ἐκπέμψω: the parataxis is a slightly colloquial form of offer, to just about the same extent as 'would you like me to . . .?'.

1429. εἶα: the imperative required with this hortatory exclamation appears in ἴτω τις 1431, but because of the long parenthesis is given a new start with δέ.   ἐῶ: I need think no more about . . . .

1433–5. πᾶσαν δὲ κτλ.: superficially the sentence looks easier with βοᾶσθαι med. in act. sense, and ὑμέναιον its object. But the 'shouter' is not the 'land' as in *IA* 437 λωτὸς βοάσθω the lute, or in Ar. *Vesp.* 1228 βοώμενος Philocleon; the land has a passive role and must be made full of clamour, 'ring with the joyful songs' (μακ. ὑμν.) of the men in it. Pearson compares the passives in *IT* 367, *Hcld.* 401, *El.* 691, *Ion* 463, which, however, are all bolder and simpler, with no dat.; Pind. *Ol.* 10. 76, which he also quotes, ἀείδετο δὲ πᾶν τέμενος τερπναῖσι θαλίαις, sounds a nearer parallel, but the dat. sits looser to the verb, in a local sense. Here with ὑμνῳδίαις there is no room for ὑμέναιον as 'internal acc.', and if it is explained as 'appositional' to the whole sentence the final addition ὡς ζηλωτὸς ᾖ comes feebly. Paley's ὑμέναιος Ἑλένης κἀμὸς ὡς . . . , with the comma transferred to the end of the preceding line, restores shape and sense.

1440. Exit Theoclymenus into the palace.

1441. Cf. 1032–4, a similar compound sentence containing an asyndeton; γὰρ is an unnecessary correction. (See *IT* 65 with Platnauer's note.)

1442. μετάστησον κακῶν: 'grant us a change from troubles.'

1443: like a mule-team dragging a cart uphill (λέπας a beautiful emendation of Musgrave's).

1445. τύχης: partitive with ἵνα = 'where'.

1446 ff. The respectful appeal to Zeus changes to a more admonitory note for the gods in general: I have had, says Menelaus, an unbroken run of misfortune for too long, and a change is overdue: ὀρθῷ βῆναι ποδί instead of bent beneath a load of misery. 1447 is in need of no emendation, merely of the appropriate punctuation: κέκλησθέ μοι, θεοί, πολλὰ χρήστ᾽ ἐμοῦ κλύειν, καὶ λύπρ᾽· and πολλὰ is not adverbial (= πολλάκις) but (with χρηστά) predicative: you have been called by me many names good to hear from me—and many offensive. κέκλησθε like κλήζῃ above, not absolutely in the sense of 'appeal to'; ἐμοῦ is in this sense not redundant, but either 'from me, mortal as I am', or 'from me, Menelaus', while μοι is quite unemphatic. χρήστ᾽ ἐμοῦ κλύειν καὶ λυπρά cannot mean to hear about my good experiences and my bad, since he is just emphasizing that he has had nothing but bad. Nauck's ὁμοῦ would mean not 'both good and bad', but 'things at once good and bad'. 'Agreeable and disagreeable'—the gods cannot have liked the tone of some of his addresses, but have only themselves to thank, having persecuted him so unendingly.

This is in fact one of the 'nouthetetic' addresses to the gods such as Eur. likes to make the close of a scene before the speaker goes off for decisive action, like that spoken by Helen earlier to Cypris 1097–1106. For a fuller discussion see *Maia* N.S. 15. 3 (1963), 310 ff.

1451–1511. Third stasimon.

The thoughts of the Chorus follow Helen—and in the third stanza Menelaus—on the voyage to Greece. The first stanza apostrophizes the ship; the second, addressed to Helen, runs ahead as Helen's own thoughts might, to wonder what she will find on arrival, one of the loved familiar festivals, perhaps, and her own daughter now grown up. In the third the migrating cranes are bidden to give news as they land by Eurotas that Menelaus will be coming from the capture of Troy, and the fourth prays the immortalized Dioscuri to bring fine weather for the ship and clear the fair name of Helen. The Chorus do not intrude any nostalgia of their own, unless it may be a sigh in the passing wish to join the flight of the cranes. Perhaps *IT* 1089 ff. was too recently composed for a repetition of the theme here.

1451   Φοίνισσα Σιδωνιὰς ὦ   1. x̄ – ∪ – – ∪ ∪ –
1465   ἦ που κόρας ἂν ποταμοῦ

ταχεῖα κώπα, ῥοθίοισι Νήρεως   ⏑–⏑––⏑⏑–⏑–⊠
παρ' οἶδμα Λευκιππίδας ἢ πρὸ ναοῦ

εἰρεσία φίλα,   –⏑⏑–⏑–
Παλλάδος ἂν λάβοις

χοραγὲ τῶν καλλιχόρων   2. ⏑–⏑––⏑⏑–
χρόνῳ ξυνελθοῦσα χοροῖς

1455 δελφίνων ὅταν αὔραις   –⊠–⏑⏑––
1469 ἢ κώμοις Ὑακίνθου

πέλαγος εὐήνεμον ᾗ,   3. ⌣̅⌣̅⏑––⏑⏑–
νύχιον εἰς εὐφροσύναν

γλαυκὰ δὲ Πόντου θυγάτηρ   ▽–⏑––⏑⏑–
ὃν ἐξαμιλλησάμενος

Γαλάνεια τάδ' εἴπῃ·   ⏑––⏑⏑––‖
τροχῷ τέρμονα δίσκου

Κατὰ μὲν ἱστία πετάσατ' αὔ-   4. ⌣̅⌣̅⏑–⏑⏑⌣̅⌣̅⏑–
ἔκανε Φοῖβος, τᾷ δὲ Λακαί-   ⌣̅⌣̅⏑–⊠–⏑⏑–'

1460 -ραις λιπόντες εἰναλίαις   –⏑–⏑–⏑⏑–
1474 -νᾳ γᾷ βούθυτον ἀμέραν   –⊠–⏑⏑–⏑–

λάβετε δ' εἰλατίνας πλάτας,   ⌣̅⌣̅⏑–⏑⏑–⏑–
ὁ Διὸς εἶπε σέβειν γόνος·

ὦ ναῦται ναῦται,   ⊠–⋰––‖
μόσχον θ' ἂν οἴκοις

πέμποντες εὐλιμένους   5. ––⏑–⏑⏑–
⟨κατέλιπες Ἑρμιόναν,⟩   ⏓⌣̅⌣̅

Περσείων οἴκων Ἑλέναν ἐπ' ἀκτάς.   –⊠–⊠–⏑⏑–⏑––
ἃς οὔπω πεῦκαι πρὸ γάμων ἔλαμψαν.

1479 δι' ἀέρος εἴθε ποταναὶ   ⏑–⏑⏑–⏑⏑––‖
1495 μόλοιτέ ποθ' ἵππιον ἅρμα

γενοίμεσθ' ᾇ Λίβυες   ⏑–▱–⏑⏑⥽‖
δι' αἰθέρος ἱέμενοι

οἰωνοὶ στολάδες   –⋰–⏑⏑⥽‖
παῖδες Τυνδαρίδαι,

1482 ὄμβρον λιποῦσαι χειμέριον   ⊠–⏑–⊠–⏑⏑–
1498 λαμπρῶν ἄστρων ὑπ' ἀέλλαισιν   ⊠–⊠–⏑⏑–⊠⏑‖

νίσονται πρεσβυτάτᾳ   ⊠–▽–⏑⏑–
οἳ ναίετ' οὐράνιοι,

σύριγγι πειθόμεναι   ⊠–⥾–⏑⏑–
σωτῆρες τᾶς Ἑλένας

1485	ποιμένος ἄβροχά θ' ὃς	– ∪ ∪ – ∪ ∪ –
1501	γλαυκὸν ἐπ' οἶδμ' ἅλιον	
	πεδία καρποφόρα τε γᾶς	⌣ ∪ ⏖ ∪ ⌣ ∪ –
	κυανόχροά τε κυμάτων	
	ἐπιπετόμενος ἰαχεῖ.	∪ ⌣ ∪ ⌣ ∪ – – ‖
	ῥόθια πολιὰ θαλάσσας,	
1487	ὦ πταναὶ δολιχαύχενες,	– x̅ – ∪ ∪ – ∪ –
1504	ναύταις εὐαεῖς ἀνέμων	– x̅ – x̅ – ∪ ∪ –
	σύννομοι νεφέων δρόμου,	– ⌣ – ∪ ∪ – ∪ –
	πέμποντες Διόθεν πνοάς·	
	βᾶτε Πλειάδας ὑπὸ μέσας	– ⌣ – ∪ ∪ ⌣ ∪ –
	δύσκλειαν δ' ἀπὸ συγγόνου	
1490	Ὠρίωνά τ' ἐννύχιον,	⏗ ∪ – ∪ – ∪ ∪ –
1507	βάλετε βαρβάρων λεχέων	
	καρύξατ' ἀγγελίαν	x̅ – ⌣ – ∪ ∪ –
	ἂν Ἰδαίων ἐρίδων	
	Εὐρώταν ἐφεζόμεναι	– x̅ – ⌣ – ∪ ∪ –
	ποιναθεῖσ' ἐκτήσατο, γᾶν	
	Μενέλεως ὅτι Δαρδάνου	⌣ ⌣ – ∪ ∪ – ∪ –
	οὐκ ἐλθοῦσά περ Ἰλίου	
	πόλιν ἑλὼν δόμον ἥξει.	⌣ ⌣ – ∪ ∪ – –
	Φοιβείους ἐπὶ πύργους.	

The metre is again aeolo-choriambic, with ingredients similar to the preceding stasimon, but with some different variations. In the first pair a hendecasyllable (the length of a catalectic trim.) appears as the second colon, a prolongation of the preceding line by a bacchiac ∪ – –; this is echoed at the end of the stanza by a similar clausula. In 1459–60 = 1473–4 there is a shift of the choriamb in responsion, so that glyc. = chor. dim. as often, especially in later Eur., and it is characteristic to repeat the effect: here glyc. + chor. dim. is in responsion to chor. dim. + glyc. The pentamakron 1462 = 1476 is ambiguous; it might be a contracted and dragged form of the aeolic hexasyll. – ∪ ∪ – ∪ – 1453, or a contracted hemiepes anticipating the next strophe, but I have chosen to make it a contracted reizianum like ἀρρήτου κούρας 1307, a headless form of the pherecratean clausulae above 1455 and 1458.

Periodic structure is more elusive in the second pair of stanzas, which opens with a remarkable series of four single cola each followed by Pause (discernible by anceps/anceps or brevis in longo). The hemiepes (×) – ∪ ∪ – ∪ ∪ – (×) here mingles with aeolic (1481 = 1497 is actually ambiguous) and in 1485–6 = 1501–3 makes a group with

iamb. dim. + dim. cat. For the form of 1456 = 1470 see 1340–1;
again it comes in the proximity of several × – ∪ – – ∪ ∪ – of which
it is the headless modification. The biggest problem is 1482 = 1498.
These enneasyllables are explicable metrically as they stand: take
away initial anceps and we are left with chor. dim. in responsion to
glyc., like 1487 = 1504 below. But the penultimate long anceps in
1498, in this free responsion, is an unwelcome added complication.
Hermann simplifies the metrical problem by assuming a double displacement, in strophe and antistrophe:

ὄμβρον χειμέριον λιποῦ-	glyc.
-σαι νίσονται πρεσβυτάτᾳ	chor. dim.
λαμπρῶν οἵτ᾽ ἄστρων ὑπ᾽ ἀέλ-	chor. dim.
-λαισιν ναίετ᾽ οὐράνιοι	chor. dim.

in which some edd. follow him, perhaps rightly; but I feel reluctant
to smooth away the less orthodox enneasyllables, which are not
without elegance. (For the punctuation of the antistrophe, which
in Murray's text demands their retention, v. infr.)

1451–3. Text, punctuation, and interpretation are all problematical.
In 'ship swift upon the surges, dear mother of the oarbeat', the
Oxford text does seem to make unnecessary difficulties; to put the
comma after κώπα gives more sense to φίλα: 'dear to the surges as
mother of the oarbeat.' μάτηρ (nom. for voc.) requires Fritzsche's
gen. εἰρεσίας, a strange expression which Italie defends by *Tro.* 1222
where Hector's shield is called μυρίων μῆτερ τροπαίων, but that is
after all a clear metaphor; the trouble with μάτηρ εἰρεσίας is that it
is not metaphorical *enough*. Badham's ingenious Νηρέως—palaeographically not a far cry from abbreviated μήτηρ—was suggested by
IT 425 ἐπ᾽ Ἀμφιτρίτας ῥοθίῳ, and leaves εἰρεσία in apposition to
κώπα: 'swift oar, whose beat is dear to the surges of Nereus.'

1454–8. The 'floating apostrophe' (cf. *Alc.* 1, *Hipp.* 752 with Barrett's
note), lacking a second person verb of its own, normally diverts
the construction on to a rel. clause; here we have a temporal rel.
ὅταν: the oarbeat is 'dance-leader of the dolphins *when* the sea-winds
are set fair and the grey-green Calm-goddess speaks'. εὐήνεμον
(Musgrave) for the metrically impossible νήνεμον, since there was
not a dead calm, and with ἀνήνεμον one would expect αὐρῶν rather
than αὔραις. Galeneia (personified as here or not) is a form confined
to Eur., perhaps his invention.

1460. λιπόντες: the idiomatic aor. part., 'coincident' with the aor.
imper. πετάσατ᾽, is on no account to be emended as most edd. do;
see Barrett's note on *Hipp.* 289–90.

1464. Περσείων οἴκων: Perseus was founder of Mycenae; no more than
a general direction here.

1466. Λευκιππίδας: Leucippus' daughters, wives of the Dioscuri.

1467. ἂν λάβοις: the verb carries right through the stanza, with objects κόρας ... μόσχον τε (1476).

1469–75. The Spartan festival of the Hyacinthia was in memory of the youth 'whom Phoebus killed with the round discus, having challenged him to the farthest throw with it' (to see who could throw it farthest). τέρμονα internal acc. with ἐξαμ. Wilamowitz's transposal of δέ is the most likely adjustment in the next clause; it leaves two consecutive cola in the same kind of free responsion.

1476–7. Murray's treatment of these lines is surely right; λίποιτ' is to be deleted, not emended (as, variously, other scholars do). Evidently the following line was early lost; then, since obviously the sense required 'left' in some form and the governing verb ἂν λάβοις was a long way off, someone not very brightly tried ἂν λίποιτ' here (though the association of Menelaus is not very appropriate in the circumstances). Triclinius, finding this in a half-'corrected' form ἂν λίποιτ', inserted ἰὼ before the second ναῦται in 1462, which some edd. have taken seriously. But that musical pentasyllable must of course be left untouched. 1477 supplied *exempli gratia*.

1479 ff. 'Would that we might find ourselves winging through the air where the Libyan bird-squadrons go, they who left the storms of winter, obeying the piping of their eldest, the shepherd who shrills as he flies over rainless and fruitful plains of earth. O winging long-necks, partners of the racing clouds, pass beneath the Pleiads at the zenith and Orion in the night, deliver the news as you settle on the banks of Eurotas that Menelaus having taken Dardanus' city will be returning home.'

The migrating cranes (Λίβυες οἰωνοὶ here) and their cry were a favourite of the poets from Homer onwards, and ever since Homer they had fled from winter and its rainstorms (*Il.* 3. 3; Hes. *Op.* 448); so they do here too, to establish their habits and identity, flying in line over deserts and fertile plains, a flock obedient to the σύριγξ of their shepherding leader. The description is so far quite general; it seems mistaken to identify the land beneath as Egypt, 'rainless yet fertile'. But the second half of the stanza pictures their reverse flight from south to north in early spring (the time of the play's performance); since only so would they be in a position to tell the Spartans of Menelaus' approach. It is this flight that the Chorus long to join, though the Homeric echoes of the general description really belong to the north–south migration.

1479–87. The traditional text shows a gap, in metre and grammar, where a rel. of some kind is needed to get from the wish-optative γενοίμεθα 1480 to νίσονται 1483. Hence it bundled together εἰ ποτανοὶ οἰωνοὶ (masc.) as if in some sort of protasis, and presumably began the main clause with στολάδες or στοχάδες ('formations' or 'in formation' adjectival: the word is uncertain). Barnes restored metre and sense to 1479 with εἰ⟨θε⟩, and the rel. has been variously supplied: Wilamowitz for instance (GV 220) gives ποταναὶ | γενοίμεθ' ἄνω, Λιβύας | οἶον αἱ στολάδες (aeolic hexasyll.). The 'ranks of Libya', however, even though the context shows them to be winged, seems less likely¦ than Λίβυες οἰωνοὶ στολάδες (adj.), and though οἰωνός is not elsewhere fem. it is not the sort of word whose gender need be immutable; here Eur. chose to make them feminine behind their (masculine) leader. Musgrave's solution for the missing rel. is the neatest and most economical, and the gradual contraction of the hemiepes in the first three cola is quite pretty. ποτανοὶ 1479 is possible if the word is substantival, 'winged creatures', but as δι' ἀέρος has to be fitted to the verbal notion in it the adjectival sense is easier, and then ποταναὶ as Wilamowitz seems essential. πρεσβυτάτᾳ 1483 transferred epithet. ἀββοχά θ' ὃς is Murray's neat suggestion (app. crit. ad 1501) for adapting the strophe to the metre of the antistrophe (v. infr.).

1487 ff. The rest of the stanza is of course addressed by the Chorus on the ground to the flying cranes, not, as Wilamowitz oddly takes it (followed by Barrett on Hipp. 979), by the leader to his flock, as if ἰαχεῖ 1486 meant τάδε ἰαχεῖ. His ἰαχή is his σῦριγξ, the long call which sustains them on their flight. If he had felt so garrulous in mid-air, why should he say 'go and tell . . .' and not rather 'come let us tell . . .'? And why should he address them as πταναί?

1488. σύννομοι νεφέων δρόμου: double gen., lit. 'partners in the racing of the clouds'. Blomfield wanted to read δρόμῳ, but the implication is rather νέφεσιν out of νεφέων: 'consorting [with the clouds] in the cloud-race'; δρόμου gen. of the field of activity shared by the partners. In plain prose 'keeping up with the swift clouds'.

1495. ἵππιον οἶμα and ἵππιον ἅρμα were old variants here, and the choice is not easy. οἶμα is a rare epic word for a lion's spring or (in plur.) an eagle's swoop: οἶμα λέοντος ἔχων, αἰετοῦ οἴματ' ἔχων, of a quick-footed hero. Can one get from there to ἵππιον οἶμα ἱέμενοι (internal acc.), as it were 'making horse-swoop haste' = rushing on horseback? How should we judge? Triclinius' correction to οἶδμα is an effort to be rid somehow of an outlandish word. Murray's οἶμον would be a horse-track cut through the heavens by the hooves of the riders' mounts; ἅρμα, quoted by Triclinius, might be possible if ἅρμα can mean simply 'team' or 'pair', since ἵππιος = 'of horsemen' as well as 'of horses'; the phrase would then be appositional nominative. But it must be admitted that 'horseman-pair' is less immediately appealing than the more complete metaphor of τρίπωλον ἅρμα δαιμόνων . . . τὸ καλλίζυγές, the team of goddesses brought up by Hermes, Andr. 277.

1498. ἀέλλαισιν: under the whirling of the bright stars' (the revolution of the firmament in which the stars are fixed) must with Murray's punctuation further define the horsemen's course; usually it is taken with the following rel. clause 'who dwell in the heavens under . . .'. The second is preferable, since as an introductory apostrophe this rel., 'you who dwell . . .', is rather awkward, and it requires Wilamowitz's rewriting of 1501 as an iambic trim.[1] with the imperative ἔπιτε. But γλαυκὸν ἐπ' οἶδμ' ἅλιον, 'over the green salt swell' is a blameless phrase echoing the earlier rhythms, and it seems better to adapt the strophe to this. The long straggling construction, with μόλοιτε carrying through to πνοάς, is ordinary lyric form.

1509. ποιναθεῖσ': punished for the strife on Ida.

1512. It is hardly possible to devise a satisfactory emendation of this line by itself. Since the Messenger comes from the sea, the only thing he could have 'found in the house' would be the king; but such simple remedies as κάλλιστά σ' ὦναξ will not do: 'a very good thing I have found you at home, sir, since you are going to hear some startling news from me' is not a messengerly greeting. Pearson's more sophisticated ἐς καιρὸν ὦναξ ἐν δόμοις σ' εὕρ. would need a verb of arriving to pick up ἐς, and in any case there is no parallel for ἐν δόμοις = outside the house as distinct from ranging the countryside. But more serious is the unmotived and unmentioned emergence of the king. Dindorf's assumption of a stop-gap line invented to fill a lacuna seems unavoidable. Could we perhaps suppose the messenger banging on the door and shouting something like ὦ δέσποτ' οὐκέτ' ἐν δόμοις μέλλειν ἀκμή, ὡς καίν' . . . followed by the king's instantaneous appearance? It is all rather excessively abrupt, and the sheer idiocy of the stop-gap line is perhaps more than would be expected from unaided invention. Conceivably there has been some incorporation of a half-obliterated longer exchange, such as:

Αγ. ἆρ' ἐν δόμοισι δεσπότην εὑρήκαμεν,
　　γυναῖκες; or is he elsewhere?
Χο. Here he is, just coming out.
Αγ. ἄναξ, [you will scarcely believe your ears](?)
　　ὡς καίν' . . . .

1513. ὡς καίν': subordinate exclamatory, cf. on 74: 'such strange news are you to hear . . . .'

In this preliminary exchange the king's reaction is kept down to incredulity, with time even for a little irony (did she fly or did she walk?). His outburst of rage is reserved for the end, nearly 100 lines later.

---

[1] Miss L. P. E. Parker informs me that a split resolution following long anceps, ⫶ ∪ | ∪ as in γλαυκὸν ἐπ-, is found nowhere in Eur. or Aesch., and only once in Soph., *Phil.* 201, where it is softened by elision.

1521. 'has gone off with your sailors too' is enough information for the moment; the story of their fate comes later.

1524. ὑπερδραμεῖν: that a 'single hand' should 'outrun' so many is a measure of the deadness of the metaphor.

1528. ἀνέστενε impf.: 'most skilfully proceeded to raise a lament, stepping delicately to it, for the husband not dead but there by her side.' Helen provides a Greek processional performance.

1531. πρωτόπλουν: the penteconter is brand-new.

1534-6. Mast—oars—sails—rudder: the order of jobs (ἔργα) is clear, but the intractable 1535 can only be left obelized. καθίστατο is needed in 1534 to keep the row of imperfects; ἱστία and πηδάλια should be taken as nom., with παρακαθίετο pass. (not med. as LS), 'the rudders were lowered' by the stern by means of their ζεῦγλαι, the ropes which lashed them together and adjusted their position.

1537. ἄρα: as we later realized, cf. Denn. *GP* 36 (2). They had been instructed by the Old Servant, in a general way (739), to 'watch for this'.

1542. ἐς μέσον φέρων: 'producing for our benefit a display' of pity.

1543: a straightforward double question sharing the same verb (unlike 873), cf. *Hyps.* 64. ii. 83 with Bond's note, p. 130.

1545. G. Zuntz, *CQ* 1955, p. 70, objects to the question ἆρα συνθάπτετε as grammatically dubious for 'do you wish to bury?', and unsuitable to the context since Menelaus must not give the impression that they knew of the situation beforehand. He proposes ἀλλ' for ἄρ', thus making συνθ. imperative. For all its logic, I can only say obstinately that the imper. sounds to me off-key and the question exactly right, in its courtesy, its hint of invitation, and its faint suggestion of accepting that fate has brought them there at this sad and crucial moment; it is just the tone of our 'Are you joining with us in burying Menelaus?' There are admittedly no quotable parallels; the situation is unique. The whole of this Messenger-speech is a masterpiece of rapid, economical, idiomatic narrative.

1548. Μενέλεῳ with ποντίσματα.

1549. ἥδ' by attraction for τάδε.

1550. τῶν ἐπεσβατῶν: 'of these extra passengers.'

1555-8. κουφίζοντα: being manageably light. The intrans. use is rare: Hes. *Op.* 463 uses ἔτι κουφίζουσαν ἄρουραν of the soil before rain has made it heavy, S. *Phil.* 735 has κουφίζειν in a medical sense, 'to feel relief'.   ταύρειος πούς: the baulking, slithering hooves take the centre of the picture, out of which ταῦρος is supplied for the rest. κυρτῶν . . .: 'humping his shoulders and squinting along his horns.'

1561-2. Ἑλλήνων νόμῳ: a tall story, unless it was a very small beast, cf. Denniston on *El.* 813.

1563-8. φάσγανον . . . ὤσει is unintelligible, since there is no evidence of an intrans. ὠθέω: 'the drawn sword shall thrust', nor is the bull to be killed just then (ἅμα). Bothe's parenthesis (app. crit.) is no improvement, for ὠθεῖ cannot mean 'he draws'. Even with εἶχε or αἴρει, or Pearson's easier οἴσω, the gesture is absurdly premature (cf. 1581 when they are well out at sea). The sudden appearance of a superfluous horse (presumably from 1258), even if the dubious acc. μονάμπυκον can be emended to gen. μονάμπυκος, makes an unwelcome anticlimax, and the animal disappears for good. It looks as if this passage had suffered some 'writing up'.

1570–1. πίμπλημι or (ἐκ)πληρόω are used of covering a whole area piece by piece, and in this sense cannot take a genitive, 'filling with' something. Jackson, p. 239, is surely right in reading εὐσφύρῳ ποδί (cf. the dat. πλάτῃ *Or.* 54); Helen with dainty foot mounts each rung to the top.   ἐδωλίοις: apparently they sit on the edge of the stern quarter-deck, cf. 1582 and 1603; Jebb on S. *Aj.* 1277.

1573–4. The Greeks line up equally to right and left, sitting in close formation man by man. The alternative 'Greek marking Egyptian' is not likely, since the phrase is a regular military one familiar to all hoplites, cf. 1072 and Ar. *Vesp.* 1083.

1575–6: 'the surge was filled with our shouting as we took up the boatswain's cry.'

1579. See on 873.

1583: 'with no mention of anyone among the dead.'

1587. ἐκ γῆς for ἐκ γῆς τῆσδε, the immediate problem.

1588. οὔριοι: from οὖρος a favouring wind. Not a freely transferable metaphor, but in *Hcld.* 822 it appears again as 'favourable' of omens at the sacrifice of a victim; perhaps this is an unconscious reminiscence.

1590. δεξιὰν is the best suggestion for ἀξίαν here. Jackson objects that there is no evidence for δεξιάν = 'to the right' or ἀριστεράν (or λαιάν) 'to the left'; no, but why not sc. κώπην? If they are to put about (πάλιν) quickly, the rowers and the steersman must know whether to starboard or to port, and the speaker tries to save time by making the decision. Or possibly the starboard turn was regular in the open sea.

1591. ἐκ: 'after', leaving σταθεὶς by itself, 'from where he stood'.

1597. λοῖσθον δόρυ: LS quote, from a fourth-century inscription, a noun λοῖσθος = beam, and therefore give 'boom, gaff, spar' here, but this is not Greek for 'pick up a spar as weapon'. Failing a plausible emendation, λοῖσθον must be the adj., a rare variant of λοίσθιον, and must particularize δόρυ, to match 'seat' and 'oar'. An 'end timber' might as Italie suggests mean one of the two πηδάλια at the stern.

1602. ἐρρεῖτο: passive (cf. on 1434). In this unequal fight the barbarians have suitably primitive weapons.

1603–4. 'Where is your Trojan reputation? Show these barbarians' sounds natural enough in English, but Hartung (v. app. crit.) is probably right in recalling the idiomatic ποῦ δείξεις of *Hec.* 828 in a similar exhortation : 'When are you going to show these barbarians the meaning of your Trojan reputation?'

1605: 'men fell down or kept their feet'; the ellipse of οἱ μέν is of a common type.

1606. ἔχων ὅπλα: a full suit (1379).

1607. ὅποι: see on 738.

1608–9. As the text stands, the only source for a subject of ἐκκολυμβᾶν would be ξύμμαχοι, but rather than make room for one at the expense of the harmless bit of padding χειρὶ δεξιᾷ (e.g. προσῆγ' ἐχθροῖσι δεξιᾷ Pearson) we could put a comma instead of a colon after ναός to make an anticipatory zeugma : 'till your sailors dived off the ship and he cleared the benches of them.'

1610. ἐπ' οἰάκων ἄνακτα together = to the helmsman ; not a metaphor like κώπης ἄναξ, A. *Pers.* 378, E. *Cyc.* 86.

1612. ἱστὸν: mast and sails together, which strictly speaking would hardly have been required for the ship's ostensible purpose at 1534 ff. There should only be a comma at the end of the line : 'favouring breezes sprang up, and now they are clear away.'

1615. ὁρμιατόνων: 'fishermen', a ἅπ. λεγ.; hence presumably the variant recorded by Triclinius ὁρμιὰν τ(ε)ίνων μέ τις, but the angler's line would hardly have taken the strain of so big a fish.

1617. A brief tag of popular wisdom is the normal end of a long Messenger-speech. 'Keep sober and don't believe all you hear' was attributed to Epicharmus. Exit Messenger.

1619. Pearson in a long and carefully argued note gives reasons for taking ἂν λαθεῖν together, with ἄν as so often put as early as possible in the sentence, cf. *HF* 1355. The effect of that position, however, was to spread its meaning over the whole sentence ; *anglice* 'I would never have believed that he could have . . . as he did'.

The Chorus are naturally anxious not to be suspected of complicity, but the king is too angry to notice the disingenuous remark. This looks like a deliberate departure from the pattern of *IT* 1420, 1431.

1621–41. The short interlude of tetrameters marks the headlong violence of the onset of the king's anger, and gives the opportunity for one of those balancing interchanges (for which the trimeter had less room and less symmetry) as the struggle sways evenly backward and forward. Cf. *Ion* 530–62, *IT* 1203–20.

1625. ἥτις: the form of relative which gives a reason.

1627 ff. The only defensible reason for rejecting LP's attribution of these verses to the Chorus (the Coryphaeus) is δοῦλος ὤν 1630. ἡμῶν ἑκόντων 1640 is the normal masc. form for any woman speaking of herself in the first person plural (cf., e.g., *Alc.* 383), since when the Coryphaeus speaks for the whole Chorus it is always open to him or her to use the collective singular. It might perhaps be suggested that in δοῦλος ὤν the king is generalizing their status, so that the masc. has the same depersonalizing effect as the plur. δεσποτῶν (and δούλοις 1641). But the neatest solution is Wecklein's later suggestion (in his Addenda) that we should read δοῦλος· Xo. οὐ φρονῶ γὰρ εὖ· The generalizing δοῦλος without ὤν presents no difficulty.

In any case the strongest argument for leaving the Chorus in possession is the much greater improbability involved in allotting the scene to any other speaker. No attendant appearing (unheralded and unidentified) like a jack-in-the-box from within to bar the king's entry could possibly be so well up in all that had happened and was happening; and for one of a king's habitual silent escort suddenly to turn out to be one of the actors and assert a vigorous independent existence would be an outlandish incident. Nor can the Messenger stay on, after a speech of 100 lines, to carry on further dialogue; it is part of the Messenger-concept that after delivering his grand set piece he goes offstage. Besides, the Messenger's sentiments here, *after* his recent experiences, would in effect characterize him to a distracting and quite unparalleled extent.

1628. ἀφίστασ' is Porson's necessary correction for ἀφίστασθ', where the long syllable ending a word before the final cretic would violate 'Porson's Law', observed by the tetrameter just as much as the trimeter.

1630–1. εὖ φρονεῖν = be in one's right mind; εὖ φρονεῖν τινί = be well disposed to someone. The king switches over to the second meaning by adding οὐκ ἔμοιγε, all the more easily since the previous line ended with εὖ.

The whole of this exchange is a perfect study of Greek *point* and economy in repartee, through the telling use of particles or of asyndeton. Note that in 1631–4 the king's grammar is continuous, ignoring the interpolations of the Chorus.

1638. 'In fact we are subject, not ruler', cf. *Med.* 120 ὀλίγ' ἀρχόμενοι, πολλὰ κρατοῦντες. So used, the verbs are properly absolute, and the infin. δρᾶν is loosely attached to the sense: [yours is a power] 'to do good, not to do wrong'.

1642: epiphany of the Twins as at the end of *El.*, and for the same reason, brotherly interest in a female character in the play. The manner of their appearance is quite uncertain. They may have been swung in (on dummy horses, 1665?) from behind the σκηνή, but our knowledge of the μηχανή is pitifully inadequate. In *El.* the preceding anapaests 1233–7 give time for the device to get into position; here they intervene peremptorily. They *could* of course simply walk on to the roof of the σκηνή from the back, Castor the

speaker leading; but to an audience by now accustomed to theo-
phanies that would perhaps have looked too tame.

1643. See on 9.

1646. οὐ with πεπρωμένοισι.

1650: a longer form of δεῦρ' ἀεί (761), with elaborated word-order.

1653–5. It is difficult to determine the extent of corruption here, but
the Oxford text has surely been too conservative. If οὐκέτι (sc.
ἐχρῆν κτλ.) is the whole of the apodosis of 1652–3, what is the meaning
of καὶ τοῖς θεοῖς παρέσχε τοὔνομ'—'but when Troy was sacked and
she lent her name to the gods'? Her name had been 'made available'
(1100) ten years before that, and the sack of Troy was rather the
beginning of the end of that chapter, when her name *ceased* to be
available (the Dioscuri seem to pass over the seven years of Menelaus'
wanderings). LP do not punctuate after οὐκέτι, which would therefore go with ἐν τοῖσιν αὐτοῖς . . . γάμοις, ἐλθεῖν δ' κτλ. Since Helen
had not been married to anyone in Egypt, this is clearly nonsense,
and Nauck therefore, followed by several edd., deleted 1653 and
substituted αὐτῆς for αὐτοῖς in 1654, with Hermann's τ' for δ' in the
next line: 'but when Troy was sacked she must be coupled in her own
marriage and go home and live with her husband.' The expression is
so clumsy and unnatural, even supposing that the perf. infin. ἐζεῦχθαι
can be rendered '*stay* coupled', that it is difficult to credit Eur. with it,
and I would rather cut out both 1653–4 and let ἐλθεῖν (deleting δ') and
συνοικῆσαι be picked up by the now reasonably adjacent ἐχρῆν, 'she
was meant to . . .'. Failure to see this could have led to the interpolation.

1656. μέλαν whether literal or psychological is probably proleptic: 'do
not blacken your sword with a sister's blood.'

1660. ἧσσον': dual. Our texts of Eur. abound in these false so-called
'split anapaests' (ἥσσονές ἦμεν ∪ ∪ | –) which accumulated in periods
of rudimentary metrical knowledge and can be removed by the
simplest of corrections (cf. 77 app. crit.). The recent campaign to
retain them indiscriminately is a sad reflection on the present state
of metrical studies.

1663. πλεῖν could be retained as infin. for imper.

1664: 'your two Saviour brothers'—the title of the Dioscuri.

1666. κάμψῃς: the metaphor, originally of 'rounding' the post in a race
of more than one lap, has here as often shrunk to a mere 'reach the
end of the course'. Cf. *Hipp.* 87, *El.* 956.

1668. ξένια: the Xenia or ξενισμός was a cult-feast associated with
the worship of the Dioscuri. Pindar's third Olympian claims Τυν-
δαρίδαις τε φιλοξείνοις ἀδεῖν καλλιπλοκάμῳ θ' Ἑλένᾳ, probably in
oblique reference to this joint cult.

1670–1. Murray's text, following Wilamowitz, is much the most satisfactory solution of this passage. It would be idle to waste words here

on Hermes' 'leaving his abode in heaven' (ἀπάρας τῶν ... δόμων);
what is needed is a reference to Helen's air-journey in his escort.
δόμος and δρόμος are apt to be confused, and once δρόμον is fixed
the rest falls into place; δρόμον is the object of ὤρισεν: where Hermes
'first put a limit to that flight of yours (σοι) through the air'. ἀπάρας
could be either trans., 'lifting' [you], or intrans., 'taking off' from
Sparta. Madvig's ὤρμισέν σε (app. crit.), keeping up the nautical
metaphor of intrans. ἀπάρας, was a reasonable conjecture; what is
not reasonable is to keep the σε with ὤρισεν and say with Hermann,
as some edd. do, that ὁρίζειν = ἱδρύειν as in S. *Trach.* 237 and 754.
You can set up an altar by 'delimiting' the consecrated area; you
cannot set down (or establish?) a lady by the same process.

1673. The long low island guarding the coast of Acte (old form of Attica)
is Makronnisi, off Sunium. It brings Hermes widely off course for
Egypt, and Eur. has here deflected the more usual legend which
makes Helene a stage-post on the way to or from Troy. In fact the
piece of concluding cult-aetiology which in *IT* 1450 ff. forms an organic part of the story has shrunk here to a mere perfunctory insertion, and the philology, if indeed ἐλ- is to be connected with κλέψας,
κλοπάς, 'taking' by stealth, is more than usually far-fetched.

1675. κλοπὰς σὰς (Triclinius) as a sort of abstract for concrete recalls
τὰς ἐμὰς ἀναρπαγὰς 50, and does not need emendation.

1678-9. It would be an extraordinary reversal of the content and
spirit of the whole body of Greek legend if such a sentiment really
rounded off the speech of the god from the machine. The idea of edd.
that this is in character with the 'haughty Spartan aristocracy' of
the speaker is stranger still; why should he gratuitously add that
it is rather the anonymous proletariat who get the hardships?
And was not Heracles (also promoted at death after a life of πόνοι)
the epitome of Dorian aristocracy? The only explanation would
be that Eur. was aiming a sly kick at accepted standards of divine
reward, but it would be an unsuitable moment and a highly unsuitable speaker to choose for such a sudden manifesto. In any case,
the epithet 'Wanderer' here applied to Menelaus shows that it is
precisely for his long-endured πόνοι that he is to be compensated in
this ultimate destiny (like a minor Heracles). 'For it is not that the
gods hate the nobly-born, but these have more trials to undergo
than men of no account.'

Many of course have seen the required meaning, but the clinching
emendation has yet to be made. Madvig's εἰσιν ἐν πόνοις is easiest,
but a poor phrase, and neither ἔμπονοι (a prose word) nor ἐπίπονοι
(a poor rhythm at this point) gives quite the right meaning, 'af-
flicted by πόνοι'. ἀσκοῦσιν πόνοις? or with change of subject ἀντλοῦσιν
πόνους? The sentence as it stands has the air of a weak garble such as
collectors of γνῶμαι tend to come up with.

1680–4. His 'quarrels hitherto' (cf. 1236) have been over his right to marry Helen; the immediate situation arising from them is the threat to kill Theonoe and the escape of Helen, and his submission is divided between ἐγώ and κείνη. The tribute which follows is the second part of what he has to say to the Twins, so that the δέ of 1684 is strictly the answer to τὰ μὲν πάρος.

1685. The double gen., apparently γεγῶτ' ἀφ' αἵματος ὁμογενοῦς ἀδελφῆς, is clumsy and difficult to explain. Hermann takes ὁμογενοῦς as active—sprung from the 'same blood as begot' Helen (i.e. Zeus'), quoting ὁμογενής S. *OT* 1361 which he takes as 'begetting children from the same blood' as produced me (in effect = ὁμόσπορος τοῦ πατρός 460). Jebb declares this impossible (but did Soph. realize this?), and takes it as 'sharing a brood with' my own parents; here in *Hel.*, however, the active sense seems the only way of accommodating the further gen. ἀδελφῆς. Even so, 'sprung from the same blood as produced a sister' who is the best . . . is to say the least a circuitous way of saying 'blood-brothers of . . .'. The μονογενοῦς of codd. should surely mean 'only child', and must be wrong. I have no suggestion to make.

1686. χαίρεθ' οὕνεκ': 'go rejoicing in . . . .'

1687. ὃ: 'a thing which'; Pearson compares S. *OT* 542, τυραννίδα . . . ὅ.

1688–92: the anapaestic finale of *Alc.*, *Andr.*, and *Bacch.*, and, with a variation in the first line, *Med.* Closely considered, it is fully appropriate only to *Alc.* (though passable here), but it was obviously not closely considered in its later occurrences, which may not be due to Eur. at all. Cf. Barrett's note on the end of *Hipp.*

APPENDIX I

PAPYRUS AND MANUSCRIPTS

It has long been held that one of the chief arguments for the descent of all our medieval MSS. from an authoritative Alexandrian edition, the work of Aristophanes of Byzantium, is their general agreement in lyric colometry; in such a daunting complexity of material, the key to which was for so long completely lost, the influence of this first great systematic ordering must have been paramount. LP show little more divergence from Π in this respect than they do (when Triclinius's alterations are removed) from MABV in the Select Plays; that is to say, colometry is, on the whole, the same, with a few minor discrepancies. Since, then, Π and LP are in the same general tradition, and Π is fourteen centuries nearer the source, and clearly no slovenly copy, it might seem that all we had to do was to choose Π in preference to LP wherever they diverged. But the matter is not so simple. On this principle we can accept ἀνεπτέρωca 633 (as lectio difficilior), γ' for δ' 642, and δὲ for δὴ 646. χέραc 634 (LP χεῖραc) confirms the universally accepted correction and the dochmiac colometry that goes with it. Π has the same faults as LP in 637 (omitted τε), in 638–9 (wrong colometry: glyconics are utterly alien to the metrical style, and are betrayed by the ugly Pause at brevis in longo λεύκιπποι ξυνομαίμονε͂c || ὤλβιcαν), and in 650 (unmetrical by the omission of two short syllables). In 642a LP are the better, since Π has no room for the cυμφορὰν which keeps bacchiac metre, and τύχαν must be supplied, the colometry being altered to fit it (L kept the wrong colometry but was corrected by Triclinius, as Zuntz notes). This could be accounted for by the occurrence of τύχαν as a gloss or variant on cυμφορὰν at some stage previous to Π. In 670–1 LP are defective, but disappointingly the fragments of Π seem to indicate a metrically doubtful supplement.

With these rather modest gains in mind we come to the two worst problems in these lines, the text of 634–6 and 640–1. Zuntz has most usefully reconstructed the lines of Π with exact calculations of the number of letters which each gap will hold; in an uncial text without spaces between words or punctuation this can be done with a high degree of accuracy. So we get:

634 περι] δε γυια χεραc εβ[αλλον] ηδονη
635 3–4]c ωc λαβω
636 ω ποcιc] ω φιλτατα προcοψιc
636a ουκ εμε]μφθην

ἐβαλλον, for which there is space, *could* have been a slip (though I suspect it of being an attempt to keep trochaic metre!). As for ἡδονη —as a slip for the accus.? easier for the dat.—without the first word of 635 we cannot judge the phrase. Certainly those missing 3–4 letters at the beginning of 635 suggest nothing obvious. (Could the ϲ be for ϲ', ϲε? Only as a garble, probably, but how do we know this was not a garble?) The sense of LP is complete in itself: 'that I may feel the pleasure of it'; and the setting-out in a self-contained metre (v. p. 108) does not look like the careless omission of a word after ἡδονάν. In fact the possibility of a second version, mostly identical with *Π* but with one or two divergences, current at a time when scholars still had some conception of the habits of Euripidean lyric metre, should perhaps be borne in mind, especially in connexion with 640–1. Could one suppose a later Alexandrian scholar with a reasonably good text of his own for collation working over the Aristophanean edition?

The muddle over 636 and 636a is common to both versions. For muddle it seems to me indubitably to be. Zuntz, starting from the view that we must (for the most part) take what we are given in *Π*, finds virtue in it; for instance, that the tenderness in line 636 is suitable only for Helen. I do not think so ill of Menelaus; ὦ φιλτάτα πρόϲοψιϲ, especially to a radiant Helen, seems to me quite in place. And Zuntz himself cannot accept the strange, abrupt trochaic οὐκ ἐμέμφθην, but is constrained to fill it out with ⨯ – ∪ – ∪ – ∪ οὐκ ἐμέμφθην, assuming that at some stage a phrase exactly equivalent metrically to ὦ φιλτάτα πρόϲοψιϲ had somehow disappeared. The required sense he supplies in 'e.g. τὸ ϲόν, γύναι, πρόθυμον οὐκ ἐμέμφθην' (no unmanly tenderness there!). I do not find the sequence of thought (with asyndeton) in 'I do not blame you for your display of feeling; I hold the daughter of Zeus and Leda' in any way persuasive. But the metre seems to me decisive. The triple dochmiac, ending blunt, for Helen after her two catalectic trimeters seems to my ear admirably in tune with the style of the whole piece, and the long trailing address after it, followed by two cat. trims. all ending in the same cadence, is lame; moreover— again a stylistic fault—the choriamb at the beginning of the syncopated trim. 636 is elsewhere only used by Eur. as a clausular motif (giving anaclasis) to iambic stanzas, never in these mixed duos. Since ὦ πόϲιϲ is not a likely marginal intrusion, it is driven back where Elmsley put it, and I prefer it to the unknown · · · ϲ of *Π*, since Helen has in this part of the duo no contribution of this length without a vocative address.

I am well aware that appeals to the ear and to metrical style will seem here arbitary and subjective, but in these matters what to one man has the categorical imperative of conviction is to another over-confident prejudice.

In 640–1 *Π* and LP look quite irreconcilable, and the possibility of two early discrepant versions should at least be considered. The appearance in Π of ἐμὲ cέ τε μάταν and two short lines following was not only disturbing for its implications of deep corruption in our existing text, but threw a spanner into the construction of the whole sentence from 639 onwards, which had seemed so straightforward. There were now two grammatical objects, ἄν and ἐμὲ cέ τε, both of which must go with ὤλβιcαν if the new phrase was to be related to *Andr.* 1218 μάτην δέ c' ἐν γάμοιcιν ὤλβιcαν θεοί which seemed its best justification. The only solution is to separate the two ὤλβιcαν and allot one to each object; thus ὤλβιcαν ὤλβιcαν are removed from the 'ecstatic' class of repetitions (cf. 649–51) and the second becomes a sad and reflective comment on the first. Zuntz, having demonstrated that Menelaus must take over somewhere between 638 and 642 (supr. p. 110), chooses this point for his intervention, and indeed the tone is quite inconsistent with Helen's all through this section of the duo. Since the unfortunate glyconics preceding made Π begin his colon with ὤλβ. ὤλβ. we should have to suppose his arrangement

ὤλβιcαν : ὤ]λβιcαν ἐμὲ cέ τε μάταν
8]ν
9]ν
Ελ. πρὸc ἄλλα]ν γ' ἐλαύνει θεὸc

the two dots (:) accompanied by paragraphos being the convention for change of speaker within a line. But what kind of line is it meant for? As it stands it would seem to be an 'alcaic decasyllable' with a monstrous resolution in the last long syllable before final anceps – ∪ ∪ – ∪ ∪ ∪͡∪ ∪ ∪͡∪ x̄. As no metre can have resolution in such a position we might assume the new phrase to be a slip for ἐμέ ⟨τε⟩ cέ τε μάταν (Kamerbeek) in dochmiac rhythm. (Is it perhaps a theory of the original metrician that a series of dochmiacs may each show Pause with brevis in longo at the end—ὤλβιcαν: ὤλβιc̄αν͡ || ἐμέ τε cέ τε μάταν, and would this account for 650 too : πόcιν ἐμὸν ἔχομε͡ν || ἔχομεν ὃν ἔμενο͡ν || ?) But whether we choose one or the other of these or restore the orthodox colometry from 639 onwards, giving ξυνομαίμονεc ὤλβιcαν : ὤλβιcαν ἐμὲ cέ τε μάταν, a long enop. with unparalleled resolutions at the end ∪ ∪ – ∪ ∪ – ∪ ∪ – ∪ ∪͡∪ ∪ ∪͡∪ –, it is equally difficult in all of them to imagine Menelaus picking up his cue between a double-short and the following long—or to imagine an Alexandrian original indicating by punctuation that he was expected to do so. Certainly nothing remotely like such ἀντιλαβή occurs elsewhere in Greek poetry. The only possibility I can see is

ξυνομαίμονεc ὤλβιcαν ∪ ∪ – ∪ ∪ – ∪ ‿ || enop.
Μεν. ὤλβιcαν ἐμὲ cέ τε μάταν – ∪ ∪͡∪ ∪ ∪͡∪ ∪ – lecyth.

but resolved iambo-trochaics do not belong to the 'associable metres' of the half-spoken type (supr. p. 106); only dochmiacs resolve like this.

Apart from the metrical question, what are we to make of the word ὤλβιcαν repeated (without any help from a particle) by a different speaker? None of Zuntz's parallels (p. 235) is in the least like this; they are question and answer, or different parts of speech, or assisted by γε, μάλιcτα, δῆτα, or the like, or part of an elaborate responding strophic pattern (S. *OC* 1677 = 1704) instead of an argumentative correction. I have absolutely no solution to offer to this puzzle, partly because I do not know what words followed in those two short lines each ending in ν, and without knowing I cannot judge this diagnosis of the situation.

Zuntz finds the answer by selecting from line 641 as given in LP τὸ πρόcθεν, ἐκ δόμων δ' ἐνόcφιcαν θεοί c' ὁμοῦ the words most essential to the sense: 'and (but?) the gods parted us from home', and if this could have been δόμων δ' ἐνόcφιcαν θεοί, iamb. dim. or dim. cat., one might have acquiesced. But to fit the repeated -ν he has to make it θεοὶ δόμων | δ' ἐνόcφιcαν. I find it difficult to believe either that Eur. would have composed such an awkward little sentence to make this statement—especially as without a visible comma after μάταν it would be easier to take θεοί as the subject of ὤλβιcαν than of ἐνόcφιcαν—or that it would occur to an Alexandrian editor to arrange an iambic dimeter as two separate monometers. Zuntz explains LP's line as an evident case of copying out a verbose gloss amplifying the short statement of *Π*, and suggests this may have run: ⟨ὤλβιcαν μὲν⟩ τὸ πρόcθεν· ἐκ δόμων δ' ἐνόcφιcαν θεοί c' ὁμοῦ ⟨καὶ ἐμὲ ὕcτερον⟩. To me it seems simpler to assume a trimeter, spoken by Menelaus *intervening at this point*. (c' ὁμοῦ, perhaps originally c' ἐμοῦ, is intrusive, the result of a failure to realize that ἂν carries through as the object of ἐνόcφιcαν.) Zuntz's objection that τὸ πρόcθεν is prosaic would of course apply only to lyric. As for the two short lines in *Π*, we should at least note the point that if *Π* were for some reason defective here and its original (mutilated at some stage) had the same words in the same colometry as LP:

τὸ πρόcθεN ἐκ δόμων
δ' ἐνόcφιcαN θεοί c' ὁμοῦ

the two *N*'s would fall in the right place.

APPENDIX II

SUGGESTIONS FOR A REVISED TEXT OF THE DIALOGUE

84. Τε. εἰς ὢν Ἀχαιῶν, ὦ γύναι, τῶν ἀθλίων—
85. Ελ. οὐ τἄρα σ᾽ Ἑλένην εἰ στυγεῖς θαυμαστέον.
86. Τε. ....
[86–88]
95. βίον] βίου
[121–2]
131. Μενέλαν] Μενέλεων
257–9 non delenda
279. οὗτος τέθνηκεν, οὗτος] εἴπερ τέθνηκεν οὗτος,
282. ἐμοῦ] ἐμόν
[287–92]
[298–302]
[324–6]
388–9. εἴθ᾽ ὤφελες τότ᾽ εὐθέως λιπεῖν βίον, del. ἡνίκ᾽—ἐποίεις
404. Λιβύης τ᾽] Λιβύης δ᾽
[416]
417. τῆς τύχης] τὰς τύχας
422. ἐκβόλοις ἃ] ἔκβολ᾽ οἷς
433–4. βίον | οὐδ᾽ εἰ θέλοιεν ὠφελεῖν,
441. ὦ γραῖα, ταὐτὰ ταῦτ᾽ ἔπη κάλλως λέγειν
448. πικρῶς ἂν οἶμαι σούς γ᾽ ἐσαγγέλλειν λόγους.
488. δόμοις.] δόμοις,
533–4. πλάνοις, | ἥξειν ⟨δ᾽⟩] πλάνοις | ἥξειν
553. οὐχ] οὐδ᾽
[577–8]
705. λυγρόν non delendum
741–2. καὶ τήνδ᾽, ὅπως ἂν   del. πως—φρουρεῖν
[746–8]
[752]
[755–7]
[764]
769. οὐ γὰρ ἐμπλήσαιμί σ᾽⟨ἂν⟩] εἰ γὰρ ἐμπλήσαιμί σε
775. ἐν ναυσὶν ὢν] ἐνιαυσίων
776. ἐτῶν] κύκλων
[780]
785. †ἣν ἔτλην ἐγώ.†
789. βαρβάροις] βαρβάρων

818. ἐρεῖ δὲ τίς μ'; οὐ] ἐρεῖ δὲ τίς μ' ἦ
866. θείου δὲ σεμνὸν θεσμὸν αἰθέρος μυχούς,
870. πυρός] πάρος
898. μου] μοι
908. μὴ σχεῖν] μὴ "χειν
post 923 lacuna indicanda
936. κατεσφάγη] κατεφθάρη
944. Χο.] Θέ.
993. δυσκλεᾶς γὰρ οὐ] δυσκλεῶς γὰρ οὖν
1006. Χάρις] Κύπρις
1022. ὁδόν τιν' ἐξευρίσκετε] τιν' ἔξοδόν γ' εὑρίσκετε
1050. λόγῳ θανεῖν] τεθνηκέναι
1051. κερδανῶ, λέγειν] κερδανῶ λέγων,
1074. καὶ νεὼς] κοῦριος
1172. κολάζομεν;] κολάζομεν.
1180–1. ἱππικὰ | φάτνης] ἱππικὰς | φάτνας
[1197]
1198. ⟨δ'⟩ del.
1225. †φίλος—ὤν.†
1226. post hunc v. duorum v. lacuna indicanda
1229 and 1230 transponenda
 Ελ. πιστὴ γάρ εἰμι τῷ πόσει φεύγουσά σε.
 Θε. τί κερτομεῖς με, τὸν θανόντα δ' οὐκ ἐᾷς;
1271. λύματ'] θύματ'
[1374]
[1421–2]
1434–5. ὑμνῳδίαις | ὑμέναιον Ἑλένης κἀμόν,] ὑμνῳδίαις, | ὑμέναιος Ἑλένης
 κἀμὸς
1447. πολλά, χρήσθ' ὁμοῦ] πολλὰ χρήστ' ἐμοῦ
1534. καθίσατο] καθίστατο
†1535†
1570. εὐσφύρου ποδὸς] εὐσφύρῳ πυδὶ
1603–4. κλέος; | δείξατε π. α. βαρβάρους.] κλέος | δείξετε π. α. βαρβάρους;
1609. ναός·] ναός,
1627. ΘΕΡΑΠΩΝ] Χο. et sic usque ad 1639
1630. δοῦλος ὤν; Θερ. φρονῶ γὰρ εὖ.] δοῦλος; Χο. οὐ φρονῶ γὰρ εὖ;
1643. γαίας] γῆς
[1653–4]
1655. τ' del.
1675. κλοπαίαν σ'] κλοπὰς σὰς
1679. †εἰσιν οἱ πόνοι†.

INDEXES

(Roman figures refer to pages; italic figures to lines)

1. GENERAL

abstract for concrete 71, 80, 82, 132, 168

accusative, internal and external 104, 124, 139, 160
  of space travelled over 104

Anaxagoras 69

aorist in present sense 98 *463*, 108 *636*, 118 *745*, 122 *835*

apostrophe 159

augment, omission of 91

Callisto 92

colour-words 138

commentaries xxxiv

costume 95, 144, 153

debates 128 f.

Demeter 147

doors 123, 143

Euripides, chronology of *Electra* xvii, *HF* xxvii, *Ion* xxviii, *IT* xxviii
  Helen, tone of xi ff., 83, 143
  text, xxix ff., 170 ff.

genitive of exclamation 81
  of field of reference 87, 123, 128, 161
  generic 99 *500*
  of separation 124

Gorgias viii

Helen, legend, viii ff., xvii ff.
  in Euripides vii ff.

Hermione 85, 113, 156

Herodotus xvii ff.

imperfect of past danger 135

infinitive of wish 84

interpolation xxxi ff., 70, 72, 74, 83, 85 ff., 93 ff., 103, 117 ff., 120, 126, 131, 144, 154 ff., 164, 167

interrogative request 96, 126

masculine for woman 86

messenger 103

metamorphoses 92 f.

middle voice for active 111, 134

nomen agentis 114

nouthetetic prayer 136, 156

optative, exclamatory potential 73 *91*, 98 *467*, 122 *824 834*

papyrus 107 ff., 170 ff.

parodos 75

passive of intransitive verbs 155, 164

periphrasis 94, 98

Phantom xvii ff.

polar expression 82

pregnant preposition 135

present in perfect sense 74

prologue 69, 93

prophets 117 ff.

questions 124, 163 f.

requests to unspecified persons 96, 126

scenery and staging 69, 72, 93, 95, 101, 143, 153 f., 166

scepticism 70

slaves 116

Sophocles, *Electra* x, 133 f.
  Inachus 92 f.
  OT 133
  Tereus 93

Stesichorus xvii ff.

stichomythia 72, 133, 144

subordinate exclamatory 72 *74*, 127 *924*

Telesilla 147

Theonoe 124 ff.

2. METRE

aeolo-choriambic iv, 100, 149, 158 f.

bacchiac 106, 158

choerilean 141 f.
choriambic dimeter 149 ff., 158 f.
correption 107
cretic 106

dactylic 75, 88 f., 91 f., 100
dactylo-epitrite 137, 141
dochmiac 104 ff., 150

enoplian 106, 137

glyconic 137, 150, 158

hemiepes 100, 106, 137, 141, 158

hendecasyllable 158
hipponactean 100

iambelegus 106, 137
iambic trimeter xxiv f., 70 *9*, 74 *131*,
  84 *263 267*, 94 *390*, 98 *492*, 118,
  131, 143, 166 f.
iambo-trochaic 76, 79 f., 81 f., 87 f.,
  100, 104, 141, 159

notation vi

pentamakron 158
praxillean 137

telesillean 137
trochaic, syncopated 76 f., 79 f., 88
trochaic tetrameter xxvii f., 165

3. GREEK

ἄγαλμα 83
ἀγαπᾶν, ἀγαπάζειν 128
ἀλλ' οὐκέτι 145
ἄν 129
ἄναξ 165 *1610*, ἀνάσσω 133 *1039*

βοᾶσθαι 155
βραβεύς 114

γάρ 74, 97 ff., 144
γε 74, 121
γοῦν 145

δαί 146
διαφθείρειν 127

εἶέν 119
ἔξεστι 96
εὖ δέ πως 115
θεός apotheosis of abstract 102, 560

ἱκετεύειν 121

καὶ δή 134
καιρόν adverbial accusative 98
κερτομεῖν 104
κλύειν 128

κουφίζειν 163
κρείσσων 130

λαγχάνειν 81

μέλειν 80
μέλλειν 133
μέσῳ, ἐν 129
μουσεῖα 78, 137

ξουθός 137

ὅδε 74, 143
οἱ 117, 165
ὀρθοστάται 101
ὀρθῶς 145
ὁρίζειν 168
ὅστις 84, 122 f., 128, 141
οὐ γάρ τι 143
οὐ μήν . . . γε 102
οὐ μόλις 89
οὐ νῦν 129
οὔποτε 130

παραινεῖν 132
πάρεργον 127

πικρῶς 97
πόρπαξ 154

ῥίπτειν 152

σήραγξ 90
τί δῆτα 71

τί ταῦτα 130
τλήμων 113

φήμη 122

ὡς 74, 104, 124, 133, 154, 162

PRINTED IN GREAT BRITAIN
AT THE UNIVERSITY PRESS, OXFORD
BY VIVIAN RIDLER
PRINTER TO THE UNIVERSITY